THE FLEETWAY PICTURE LIBRARY INDEX VOLUME 2
THE THRILLER LIBRARIES

compiled by

David Ashford and Steve Holland

BOOK PALACE BOOKS

www.bookpalacebooks.com

Contents

The Fleetway Picture Libraries Index Volume 2

A Book Palace book

Published by
Book Palace Books, Jubilee House, Bedwardine Road
Crystal Palace, London SE19 3AP

email: books@bookpalacebooks.com

Tel: 020 8768 0022 (from overseas +44 20 8768 0022)

www.bookpalacebooks.com

ISBN: 978-1-907081-05-7

Designed and produced by Stuart Williams
Photography by Geoff West

TOLD IN PICTURES
The Story of Cowboy Comics, Thriller Comics and Super Detective Library

I: "64 Picture-Packed Pages"

When the first issues of *Cowboy Comics* were published in April 1950 there was no fanfare of trumpets. The Amalgamated Press had spent no money promoting the new title – the comics just appeared one Thursday morning in the newsagents.

Nothing like them had been seen before: a pocket-sized monthly picture strip comic at the unheard-of price of 7d. At the time, most weekly comics cost less than half that price: *Comic Cuts*, *Chips*, *The Dandy* and *The Beano* were all 2d and *The Knockout*, the spiritual father of the new title and its companions-to-follow, was only 3d. *The Eagle*, when it appeared eight days later, had the high price of fourpence-ha'penny for which readers received a broadsheet paper partly printed in photogravure colour.

Having paid their seven pence, readers of *Cowboy Comics* were offered four complete stories in each of the two issues that went on sale on April 6, 1950, and a grand total of "64 picture-packed pages"[1], twice that of the American reprints of the era which usually contained 32 pages for 6d. This emphasis on the title being "all pictures" must have been considered a selling point as, even when the title was changed to *Cowboy Picture Library* in 1957, it continued to run its "64 picture-packed pages" cover line for another year and, for a while, also ran a banner headline "All in Pictures".

This banner was to distinguish *Cowboy Comics* and its companions, *Thriller Comics* and *Super Detective Library* from the traditional pocket library titles that were all text.

The popularity of the pocket library format dates back to around the turn of the century; the slim, cheaply printed pocket book was an inexpensive way for publishers like the Amalgamated Press, George Newnes and C. Arthur Pearson to reprint stories by their most popular authors from their weekly magazines. The format was particularly popular for producing romances and adventure stories for boys and girls and, before long, stories were being written especially for the format. The Amalgamated Press launched *The Sexton Blake Library* in 1915, although it was only in 1947 that the title slimmed down to 64 pages[2], the price having jumped to 7d for 96 pages in 1942 when wartime paper shortages began to bite.

It was in this 64 page, 7d format that the A.P. launched their post-war romance libraries, *Miracle Library* and *Oracle Library*, establishing the format for all library titles from the publisher for the foreseeable future.

The story of *Cowboy Comics* began four years before the first titles were released in the UK. For many years, the Amalgamated Press had enjoyed strong sales around the Commonwealth, but suffered a huge blow during the Second World War. The domination of British papers in countries like Australia and New Zealand came to an end and, in the post-war recovery, Australian publishers looked to America and the newly popular superhero comics that had taken root since the arrival of Superman in 1938. Like Britain, Australia began import restrictions during the war that were to remain in place for many years, creating the opportunity for an enterprising publisher to produce Australian editions of American comics.

Sydney-based publisher K. G. Murray began successfully reprinting American comics when, in 1947, they included 'Zatara' in their *Climax All Color Comic*; this was quickly followed by reprints from Quality Comics and, in mid-1947, by *Superman All Color Comic*.

It was against these new reprint titles that the Amalgamated Press had to battle when they tried to resume their distribution of comics to Australia and New Zealand. With the American comic book format proving popular with readers, the A.P. decided to take the bull by the horns and produce their own American-style comic books for the Antipodean market.

These new titles were to be edited by Edward Holmes, the editor of *Knockout*. Holmes, born on January 29, 1916, had joined the Amalgamated Press in the 1930s, earning his first sub-editorial position on *Wild West Weekly* (later shortened to *Wild West*), an all-text story paper launched in March 1938. Edited by a genial and colourful Irishman, Hedley O'Mant, *Wild West* was printed by Sun Engraving Co. in an oversized ($9^3/_4$" x $12^3/_4$") format with full colour photogravure covers, the best superbly painted by D. C. Eyles and Eric Parker. Its expensive format worked against it and *Wild West* folded after only 50 issues.

Holmes, with an eye to the American comics that were beginning to arrive in the UK, hoped to interest the board in a straight adventure comic when they began looking for new titles to counter the arrival of a pair of newcomers from rival publisher D. C. Thomson. *The Dandy* and *The Beano* were launched in December 1937 and July 1938, a double-punch in the traditional comics market that the A.P. had dominated since their first launches in 1890. The Amalgamated Press had a title in mind, *The Knock-Out Comic*, and managing editor Stanley Gooch was tasked with bringing this new title to life. However, the appointment of Dennis Castle as editor caused the new paper to change focus as Castle used his contacts to turn his new paper into the wireless equivalent of the long-running and highly popular *Film Fun*. Retitled *Radio Fun*, the new comic came out in October 1938 alongside another newcomer, *Happy Days*.

Percy Montague "Monty" Haydon, whose fiefdom within Amalgamated Press included the Companion Papers (*Magnet*, *Gem*, *Modern Boy*) and the Sexton Blake titles, was handed the task of creating a third new comic title – the first from his group. Given control of *Knockout*, as the new paper was to be called, Edward Holmes was to bring far more adventure to the mix than any A.P. title had previously seen.[3]

Holmes had the advantage of being able to draw on two of the A.P.'s most popular characters, Sexton Blake and Billy Bunter, for his new comic. Launched in March 1939, *The Knock-Out Comic*[4] contained a mixture of adventure and humour picture strips and text stories but Holmes signalled his intentions from the start by introducing *Wild West* illustrators Derek Eyles, Eric Parker and Fred Bennett to comics. An A.P. newcomer, Hugh McNeill, was to create a new knockabout style that was to become the backbone of the humour strips that appeared in *Knock-Out*.

McNeill had been enticed to the paper from D. C. Thomson by *Knock-Out*'s sub-editor, Leonard Matthews, who was to become a major figure in the history of British comics. In 1938 he had left his job as editor of the in-house magazine for the William Whiteley department store in Bayswater, attracted to the A.P. by an advert in the *Daily Telegraph*. Between them, Holmes and Matthews were to reshape the Amalgamated Press juvenile division – although their chance to do so was delayed for almost a decade by the advent of the Second World War.

Holmes and Matthews both served with the R.A.F. during the conflict, although Matthews was employed with the Air Ministry and able to keep in touch with wartime *Knock-Out* editor, Percy Clark. The two brought in adaptations of classic novels to relieve some of the pressure for finding scripts while many of the comics' writers – more often than not the editorial staff themselves – were serving their country. Matthews, raised on adventure stories, had a fondness for classic children's novels and the wartime *Knock-Out* (subtitled "The Victory Comic" between 1941 and 1945) contained picture story versions of W. H. G. Kingston's *Peter the Whaler*, Captain Frederick Marryat's *Mr Midshipman Easy* and *Children of the New Forest*, as well as older classics like *Gulliver's Travels*.

Ted Holmes returned to the Amalgamated Press in 1946 and continued this innovation with adaptations of Robert Louis Stevenson's *Treasure Island* and *Kidnapped* and R. M. Ballantyne's *The Coral Island*. The first of these brought Mike Hubbard into the picture story fold, the first of a line of superb illustrators that were to debut in the comics produced by Holmes and Matthews over the next few years.

The Amalgamated Press had been forced to cancel many of its titles in 1940 due to paper shortages. Victory over the Axis forces did not ease the many problems the company faced. Paper rationing continued for some years after the release of soldiers from service and staff were

returning to the company only to find their old papers gone. A ban on the launch of new titles was still in place, a problem the A.P. solved in the UK by buying up titles from other publishers that already had a paper allocation.

The situation in Australia and New Zealand was not as restrictive and Ted Holmes was put in charge of creating a series of titles for this market. Advised of the popularity of the new American reprints, Holmes used them as a template. The new papers he created were unlike any that appeared in the UK. In Britain the anthology title had ruled for almost 60 years, but the new comics put together by Holmes each contained the adventures of a single character in a series of short (usually 8-page) stories with the occasional page or half-page humourous strip as a filler, mostly lifted from *Knockout*.

The idea for putting together a new comic was not a new one and a dummy for a new title had been prepared as early as 1946, although it appears to have faltered by the spring of 1947. Originally to be called *Action Comics*, it was to feature Sexton Blake, Billy Bunter, Stonehenge Kit and Phantom Sheriff and two new strips, "A Day with the Dobsons" and "Captain Conquest and the Men from Mars" were also prepared. *Action Comics* was dropped – perhaps because there was already a similarly-named American comic book – and a new title, *Thriller Comics*, instated; however, the new title never became a reality and various strips already drawn were used in *Knockout* and *Knockout Fun Book*.

By 1948, when Ted Holmes began once again to put together titles for the Australian market, the anthology format was dropped in favour of single character titles.

The most popular genre for children's adventure stories was the Western. Westerns still dominated the Saturday morning cinema and most British comics, when it came to adventure strips, headed out to the Wild West before long. Holmes was well versed in Westerns, having edited *Wild West*, where he had penned the adventures of 'The Phantom Sheriff'.

Holmes chose as his leads two well known Western icons: Kit Carson and Buck Jones. Christopher Houston "Kit" Carson was a real historical figure (1809-1868), famous as a trapper, scout and Indian fighter. Dubbed "The King of Scouts", he became the hero of cheap paperbacked novels as early as 1849, the stories spun around his exploits adding to his status. Carson himself, on seeing the cover of one such novel, is quoted as saying "Gentlemen, that thar may be true, but I hain't got no recollection of it."[5]

Holmes' second character was used to having stories woven around him. Charles Gebhart (1889-1942) was better known to the world as actor Buck Jones, star of over 160 movies in 26 years. Jones had already been a star of British comics in the pages of *Film Fun*, in both picture strips (1933-38) and text stories, but this was the first time he'd had a title dedicated to his adventures.

However, Holmes did not limit himself to Westerns and, a third title was intended to compete directly with the American reprints in Australia: *Thunderbolt Jaxon*. The character was wholly inspired by American comic book superheroes and featured a young orphan boy called Jack

Sep E. Scott's original cover painting for *Kenilworth* (*Thriller Comics* 51).

James E. McConnell's original cover for *Forward, The Musketeers!* (*Thriller Comics* 93).

Jaxon, unjustly accused of a crime that earns him a place at a harsh reform school. Jack discovers a belt of ancient and curious design – the magic belt of Thor, the thundergod of the ancient Norsemen – and, in a flash, skinny Jack Jaxon becomes Thunderbolt, a muscular adult endowed with the might and magic of Thor himself. Jack sets out to vindicate himself and bring his wicked uncle Jasper to justice before becoming a champion of justice for all.

The initial storyline was written by T. C. H. Penower, a popular crime novelist who had written for D. C. Thomson's boys' papers in the 1930s. Pendower also created the intial storylines for another character who was to feature in Holmes' new titles, *Battling Samson*, a rough, tough pilot described as the Daredevil of the Skyways, whose only UK appearance was a reprint of one of his stories in *Knockout Fun Book*. This latter title was almost certainly intended to contain a rolling cast of characters as *Battling Samson* lasted only a single issue, to be replaced the following month by *Captain Flame*, a pirate-hunter of the Spanish Main whose adventures had then recently began appearing in *Knockout*. Scripts for a series of stories featuring newspaper reporter Splash Page were also prepared but it would appear that the idea for a series of one-off characters was quickly dispensed with. Splash Page failed to appear, although he would later see the light of day in the pages of *Comet*.

This rolling series was replaced by a reprint of *Tim Holt*, whose adventures were licensed from the American comic book of the same name published by Magazine Enterprises. Tim Holt was, like Buck Rogers, a star of the movies. Born Charles John Holt III, he had first appeared in movies in various minor roles in the 1930s before coming to the public attention in *The Law West of Tombstone* (1938) and *Stagecoach* (1939). Perhaps his finest hour was in *Treasure of the Sierra Madre* (1948) but his career waned as the popularity of Westerns declined. Magazine Enterprises published a regular comic book featuring his adventures from 1948 until 1954.

In Australia, his adventures lasted only four issues. *Thunderbolt Jaxon* was also axed after six issues and the decision was made to concentrate solely on two monthly titles.

Publishing information on these titles was minimal. No mention was made that the titles were prepared for publication in England: the rear covers of early issues noted only that the comics were "wholly set up and printed in Australia by The Land Newspaper Ltd., 57-59 Regent Street, Sydney. Sole distributors for Australia and New Zealand, Messrs. Gordon & Gotch (A'lasia) Ltd."

Although little known even amongst the most ardent collectors, these Australian titles launched in 1949 were the launching pad for the *Cowboy Comics Library* and the whole British pocket picture library phenomenon, which was to see, in the 1960s, dozens of titles being published each month. The two people we have to thank for this are the editors, Edward Holmes and Leonard Matthews.

II: Galloping Hooves and Blazing Six-Guns

Trying to regain the ground they had lost due to the war, but still faced with paper shortages, the Amalgamated Press purchased two titles from J. B. Allen. Allen, based in Sale, Greater Manchester, had used a loophole in the law to revamp two earlier titles: two registration issues for the *Gosport Courier* and the *Stretford Courier* mysteriously merged to become *The Comet*, a comic launched in September 1946.[6] A second title, *Sun* was presented as a new series of the fitness magazine *Fitness and Sun* when it was launched the following November.[7] That they bore no resemblance to the papers they supposedly grew out of was, it seems, not a problem. Both were attractively produced in two-colour photogravure and they certainly attracted the attention of the Amalgamated Press as both papers already had a precious paper allotment. The A.P. bought both titles in May 1949 and split them between their two most adventurous editors, Edward Holmes and Leonard Matthews.

Holmes had departed from *Knockout Comic* in 1948 in order to launch his Australian titles and his former assistant, Matthews, had taken over as editor. Matthews and Holmes shared similar views on what comics should be – full of adventure strips!

"I wanted to break away from the old British comic tradition of *Chips* and *Comic Cuts*," Matthews was later to explain.[8] "I had always loved adventure stories – particularly Westerns and swashbuckling tales of Robin Hood and Dick Turpin and the like – and I sensed that everything that had been done in the past with the written word could now be done in pictures. So when I started editing *Knockout* in 1948, I concentrated on putting in adventure strips."

Matthews added *Sun* to his workload and quickly steered it in the direction he was already establishing in *Knock-Out*, to the point of reprinting 'The Queer Adventures of Patsy and Tim', which had run in *Knock-Out* only a few years earlier, whilst seeking out new artists for his new paper. Holmes, meanwhile, introduced three new strips in *Comet*, a newcomer, 'June', the epitome of the beautiful scientist's daughter, by Norman Pett (recently relieved of his long-running duties on 'Jane' of the *Daily Mirror*), plus two favourites – Buck Jones and Thunderbolt Jackson.

The board of the Amalgamated Press were still seeking new launches and were lining up a new weekly title for girls, *School Friend*, produced by Reg Eves' department. The upcoming relaxation of paper restrictions, due to be implemented in April 1950, meant further expansion was possible.

Edward Holmes realised that he already had a ready source of material that could be used in new titles in his Australian comics. Unfortunately, his suggestion that these be produced in British editions was almost stillborn, as Leonard Matthews later recalled:

"Ted Holmes came up with the idea that it would be a good notion to use these over in this country because, after all, as far as we were concerned, it was going to be a nil pay sheet because all of the production costs had been paid for by the Australian publication. So Ted rang up the printing works to find out what machines were vacant one morning. I was with him when this took place and I can remember him rather disconsolately putting the receiver down and saying to me that the only machine where there was printing time available was the machine that printed the Sexton Blake Library. Nothing else was available. So the idea was just left there."

The problem was the size: the Australian comics were printed 8$\frac{1}{4}$" by 11" and the Sexton Blake Library was 5$\frac{1}{4}$" x 7".

The disappointed Holmes was not to be beaten, as Matthews recalls: "The next morning, Ted came in and said, 'Do you know, I think one could re-fashion those comic books and print them on the Sexton Blake Library presses!' He cut up these things himself and fashioned I should think about eight or ten pages at library size and took them to Monty Haydon."

Haydon had some misgivings about the idea but, with almost zero costs and a printing press standing idle, grudgingly gave Holmes the go ahead.

The first two issues of *Cowboy Comics* were unlike any Western comics series published before. All four episodes of the first issue were drawn by Geoff Campion, whose artwork was dynamic, punchy and witty and captured perfectly the rough, genial good nature of the character depicted in the strips. Campion had also painted the cover, based on the cover to the first Australian Buck Jones comic painted by George Cattermole. Campion was still a relative novice, producing his first strip work in 1948 after answering an advert seeking new artists. After a brief period drawing humour strips to ease the workload of Hugh McNeill, Campion was summoned to Fleetway House where he was told by Leonard Matthews: "Westerns are the thing and you're going to do 'em."

"I could only reply that I'd never drawn a 'straight' horse in my life and wouldn't that be something of a drawback? He shook his head and said 'Bloody well learn!'" Campion later recalled.[9] "He was right, of course, and very slowly I began to find out where the legs fitted onto the bit with the saddle on it. I still have a copy of *Cowboy Comics* no. 1 – 'Buck Jones' – and the awfulness of its contents still gives me the shudders, even though my first colour job on it's cover ain't all *that* bad." The contents are particularly fascinating as two of the four strips are, indeed, fairly awful, while the other two are extremely good. It is obvious that half the contents were drawn at a later stage, by which time Campion had really learnt how to do it!

The second issue, published at the same time, featured Kit Carson and contained two superb strips by D. C. Eyles that are considered amongst his very best work. The two other strips were by Eric Parker and from William Bryce Hamilton, a rather offbeat contribution from an artist not much at home on the range.

Derek C. Eyles had long been admired by young readers for the many spot illustrations – mostly on Western themes – which he had drawn for *Knockout*, as well as the magnificent 'Dick Turpin's Ride to York' that had appeared two years earlier in the same paper. Eyles' work was well known to editor Holmes from his days on *Wild West* and he was considered quite rightly to be the finest Western artist working for the A.P. It therefore was not surprising that

Holmes had chosen him to illustrate the first issue of his Australian *Kit Carson* comic, from which was taken one of the stories reprinted in *Cowboy Comics* no. 2.

The two characters, Kit Carson and Buck Jones, had already been introduced to British readers in the pages of *Knockout* and *Comet*. Kit Carson was appearing in *Knockout* at the time *Cowboy Comics* was launched, drawn by legendary Sexton Blake artist Eric Parker. Meanwhile, Buck Jones (billed "The Fighting Sheriff of Alkali City") was a regular in *Comet* from August 1949, drawn in robust style by Reg Bunn. One of the two newcomers discovered by the A.P. from their advertising for artists in 1948, Bunn had drawn some of his earliest work for Ted Holmes' Australian cowboy comics.

Campion drew relatively few strips directly for *Cowboy Comics*, although he was a regular cover artist for the Australian cowboy comics and many of these were reused in the UK between the summers of 1951 and 1952, his strong, colourful designs making the title hard to ignore on the newsagents' shelves. *Kit Carson* issue 17 features a particularly striking Campion cover, depicting Kit Carson hurling himself at an Indian warrior – you can almost feel the impact![10]

Buck Jones and Kit Carson continued to be the main focus of *Cowboy Comics* almost to its demise, although the two of them did not appear every month. In the early issues, one of the characters would occasionally step down to allow cowboy film star Tim Holt to take the stage. This was bad news for aficionados, because the Tim Holt issues, with its resized artwork, originally drawn with the intention of being printed in colour, were much inferior to the strips originated in the UK.

This was not true of another reprint, 'The Cisco Kid', which was superbly drawn by the great Argentinian strip artist, José Luis Salinas. Unfortunately this issue (no. 55) proved to be a one-off. The Cisco Kid was also an American strip, published by King Features who began distributing a daily newspaper strip version in January 1951. Although based on a character created by O. Henry in his 1907 story 'The Caballero's Way', The Cisco Kid of the comic strip shared nothing more with O. Henry's story than the name. Unlike the O. Henry *caballero* (who "killed for the love of it – because he was quick-tempered – to avoid arrest – for his own amusement – any reason that came to his mind would suffice" and whose pastime was "to shoot Mexicans 'to see them kick'"), the strip was based on the Cisco Kid of the big screen and radio where he was depicted as a Mexican Robin Hood of the Old West and from the TV version where he was portrayed by Duncan Renaldo. It was on the latter version, in which Renaldo wore an ornately embroidered *caballero* outfit, that Salinas based his splendid Cisco Kid strip.

Peter Sutherland made his first appearance in *Cowboy Comics* no. 22, drawing a rip-roaring strip entitled 'Kit Carson's One-Man Battle'. Previously he had been a mainstay of D. C. Thomson's story papers, drawing spot illustrations for tales of the early American West and it was something of a culture shock to find him working for A.P. comics.

"Peter Sutherland was Ted's favourite artist," says

Sep E. Scott's original cover painting for *Dick Turpin and the Man in the Blue Mask* (*Thriller Picture Library* 177).

John Millar Watt's original cover painting for *Thriller Picture Library* 230.

former A.P. sub-editor Barry Coker[11] and, indeed, Sutherland was to become the most prolific of all Kit Carson artists (surprisingly, he never drew a Buck Jones strip). His style was extremely vigorous and 'cartoony' — worlds away from the work of Eyles or Campion but nevertheless most likable, effective and extremely powerful.

Part of the attraction of *Cowboy Comics* was the diversity of the artistic talent. Hugh McNeill, Cyril Holloway, John Woods, E. C. Julian, Roland Davies, Robert Macgillivray and Tom Thursby, all appeared drawing strips within the first six months of the library's debut. One artist with a remarkably individual style was Adam Horne, who had been providing illustrations for the classic boys' paper *Chums* as early as the 1920s. Horne's Kit Carson strips have the same dash and élan that is to be found in the early Western films of the silent era. The comparison with the cinema is apt for another reason: both relied heavily on melodrama for their effects. William S. Hart, the first of the great Western stars, was, to put it kindly, not one for underplaying a role, particularly in the action sequences. Likewise, Adam Horne's Kit Carson has a tendency to 'ham up' the action. Nevertheless, few people would argue that this old-fashioned style is very effective. It is often imbued with humour, particularly in the scenes featuring roguish patent medicine tricksters or itinerant actors and magicians. Horne was as much at home drawing Buck Jones as he was with Kit Carson and he showed a particular penchant for the light-hearted comedy adventures in which Buck got himself involved in the early issues of the library.

Artists apt to drawing this kind of humour included Tom Laidler and Robert Rodger, although as the library progressed, the quality of the artwork began to diminish as more new artists were introduced. Some were quickly to find their way into the weekly papers, contributing to *Cowboy Comics* only briefly – Patrick Nicolle, Robert Forrest, Graham Coton, to name a few examples – whilst some became regulars. Peter Sutherland was one of only a handful of artists to contribute over 50 stories to *Cowboy Comics*. Other stylish artists such as H. C. Milburn and D. Gale were able to continue the high standards of the early issues but too many of the stories were drawn by styleless copyists such as R. Charles Roylance. Although later to make his name as the main artist on Captain Hurricane in *Valiant*, Roylance's contributions – and there were many – to *Cowboy Comics* were filled with swipes. One of his first strips, 'Buck Jones and the Buckboard Bandits' (no. 93) lifted panels from earlier stories by D. C. Eyles, Colin Merrett and Bill Lacey. Roylance's work was to continue in the same vein with barely a strip published that did not contain swipes from the works of superior artists.

Another frustration was when strips were drawn by more than one artist, as with the story 'Buck Jones and the Vengeance of Fire-Eye!' (no.109). The first four pages of the strip were by Philip Mendoza, as is the bottom panel of page 7; the rest, however, is an unhappy mix of Mendoza and Roylance, with the latter regrettably taking the lion's share.

Other oddities included episodes where a second artist was drafted in to redraw faces of the main characters, as happened with 'Kit Carson's Rustler Trouble' (no. 40) where Adam Horne redrew some of the faces on a strip otherwise drawn by Stephen Chapman.

Despite the occasionally patchy artwork, *Cowboy Comics* was a roaring success – although only after a shaky start. "They weren't accompanied by any publicity or any gifts of any kind and, for about four months, six months, they were really in the doldrums," recalled Leonard Matthews. "Then, suddenly, they started to gain in popularity and the circulation commenced to go up by leaps and bounds."

One reason for this may be that stories being prepared for the Australian *Buck Jones* and *Kit Carson* titles were now being drawn with *Cowboy Comics* in mind. A large opening panel which could be used as a splash page in the UK began appearing from issue 10 of the Australian titles and the artwork was obviously being drawn with resizing in mind. These newly designed stories began to appear in *Cowboy Comics* from the titles fourth month on the stands and earlier stories from the Australian comics that needed more work to fit the UK format were only used infrequently.

The Australian titles would continue to appear until 1952. Quite why they came to an end is open to speculation. Both series continued to appear, individually numbered until issue 36 after which changes could be seen. Issue 37 of *Kit Carson* was accompanied on the newsstands by a new title, *Billy the Kid*, numbered 38 in what the cover described as a "New Series".[12]

Buck Jones returned with issue 39, accompanied by *Kit Carson* no. 40. This new sequence of numbering lasted only another couple of months and the two titles folded with issues 43 and 44, which offered readers the "Great News!" that, from the following month, both titles would be appearing "in a new pocket-size!", 64-page format.

In March 1952 the Australian government announced that, in an effort to reduce its adverse overseas trade balance, it was to drastically cut imports. Whether this affected the publication of the Australian cowboy comics is not known but it may have been a factor.

The simpler solution may be that the comics were steadily declining in sales. Soaring newsprint costs forced prices of all Australian comics to increase in March 1951, including the A.P. comics which jumped from 6d to 8d. Increasingly, the Australian market was being dominated by American reprints such as K. G. Murray's Superman titles which, from 1950, were also being exported to the UK where they were distributed by Atlas Publishing & Distributing Co.

It is also a possibility that exports of the new *Thriller Comics Library* to Australia had showed that the oversized format was not necessary and costs could be reduced by simply exporting the pocket-library size issues.

The demise of the Australian cowboy comics had little effect on the title in the UK. Westerns were still hugely popular at the Saturday morning cinema and the BBC, before the days of Independent Television, screened the movies of Hopalong Cassidy (played by William Boyd) and Tex Ritter. In fact, the Singing Cowboys, Roy Rogers and Tex Ritter, could also be seen live in the UK in the early 1950s along with other cowboys in touring rodeos.

For most of the 1950s, the Western was the most

popular genre in boys' comics, only slowly supplanted by Science Fiction and stories of Second World War. In 1950-51, *Cowboy Comics* had proved to be hugely successful and very soon acquired the first of its companion titles. The new style British pocket-sized comics was really beginning to take off.

III: Heroes of the Sword and Pistol

In the opinion of many collectors, the swashbuckling historical adventures that appeared in the long-running *Thriller Comics Library* are amongst the best drawn, best scripted and most thoroughly enjoyable adventure comics ever to appear.

From the offset *Thriller Comics* (*Thriller Comics Library* from issue 41) concentrated on historical adventures. The first two issues featured the Three Musketeers and Dick Turpin and the following two numbers were of Robin Hood and an adaptation of *Treasure Island*.

In much the same way that *Cowboy Comics* had relied on reprints for its early issues, in three of the four issues of *Thriller Comics* there was little that could be called new – but Edward Holmes had some fine work to draw upon when it came to swashbucklers, even if the choices seemed a little odd in places.

'The Three Musketeers and the Man in the Iron Mask' was a reprint from *Knockout* (1949) with many panels omitted as well as additional frames (drawn by the original artist, W. Bryce-Hamilton) inserted in order to change the ending. In the original *Knockout* version, based on the 1929 silent movie starring Douglas Fairbanks, all four of the Musketeers died, an event that would not have made an auspicious beginning for a library intending to portray many further adventures of Dumas' famous creations.

The second issue contained three stories of Dick Turpin, the first of which was a reprint of 'Dick Turpin's Ride to York', also from *Knockout* (1948). Although the strip had obviously been squeezed into the small format and had lost its epic sweep, it was still easy to appreciate the graceful artistry of Derek Eyles. This was one of the finest of his strips. According to its writer, Leonard Matthews, 'The Ride to York' was to have lasted a great deal longer but Eyles found the pressure of drawing two pages of strip a week too much and the project had to be cut short. It was another odd choice of strip with which to start a series of Dick Turpin adventures because the highwayman's horse, Black Bess – who was to appear in all subsequent issues – died after the exhausting ride.

Treasure Island (no. 4) was a reprint of a 1945 *Knockout* serial, drawn by Mike Hubbard and based on the 1934 film starring Wallace Beery and Jackie Coogan. Again, this did not fit too well into the small library format and Hubbard's artwork did not appear to its best advantage. Its saving grace was its delightful cover by Philip Mendoza.

More *Knockout* stories were to follow in early issues of the new library. 'Hunted on the Highway' (no. 9) was a reprint of H. M. Brock's superb serial, 'Breed of the Brudenels' (*Knockout*, 1949-50), and two Captain Flame issues appeared in fairly quick succession (no. 12 and no.

28). All three strips had been written by Leonard Matthews, the latter two drawn with great style by Sep. E. Scott and rated by many collectors as the finest pirate strip series ever to appear in a comic. Once more, the reprints were a pale shadow of the originals, the wide panels being cut short for the library, the longer panels elongated and with extra figures drawn in, in the first issue by Stephen Chapman and in the second by Reg Bunn.

A happier compromise was reached with some issues such is *The Children of the New Forest* (no. 38). Apart from having a fine Sep. E. Scott cover (based on one of the interior panels which was itself inspired by the famous painting 'When Did You Last See Your Father?' by William Frederick Yeames), the library issue had a number of new panels especially drawn by the original artist, Eric Parker. Despite this, the story does not achieve the poignancy and stature of the original strip as it appeared in Knockout (1945).

Another Eric Parker *Knockout* strip was completely ruined when it was adapted for the library. As it appeared in *Knockout*, 'The Secret of Monte Cristo' (1949) was arguably the finest of all Sexton Blake strips. It was written by Edward Holmes who had borrowed the picturesque setting of the lonely island castle owned by descendents of a famous French nobleman from his 1940 *Detective Weekly* serial, 'A Case for Sexton Blake'. This was Parker's only Blake strip and was a masterpiece of mood and mystery. For some reason Holmes decided to change the names of Blake and his assistant, Tinker, and engaged Reg Bunn to adapt the strip to the library format. Whether it was his brief or not, Bunn more or less re-drew the strip and made a thorough hash of it, destroying all the magic of the original.

By the fifth issue, *Thriller Comics* had begun publishing new stories especially drawn for the library format and resizing reprints was kept to a minimum. Although the reprint stories were well chosen, the resulting issues always suffered in comparison with their original appearances in the weekly comics.

Thriller Comics soon settled into a routine with regular appearances of The Three Musketeers, Dick Turpin and Robin Hood, these issues usually being made up of three or four stories. Intermixed among these regular characters were full-length adaptations of classics like *Gulliver's Travels*, 'Ali Baba and the Forty Thieves' and *The Black Arrow*. Westerns were kept to a minimum, presumably so as not to rival *Cowboy Comics*, but *Thriller Comics* made the best of its broader remit with excellent adaptations of three of Clarence E. Mulford's novels. 'The Outlaw Orphan' (adapting Mulford's *The Orphan*), featured some of Colin Merrett's best artwork while the other two Mulford adaptations were mostly interesting to young readers for featuring the writer's famous hero, Hopalong Cassidy, who was shown to be totally unlike his screen portrayal.

In the beginning, it had been intended that *Thriller Comics* would cover 'thrillers' in the usual sense of the word. Monty Haydon had been the controlling editor of *Union Jack* and the *Sexton Blake Library* from the mid-1920s and was editor of *The Thriller*, which had run from 1929 to 1940, publishing some of the finest crime writers of the era. In the first issue of *The Thriller*, Haydon had published a new J. G. Reeder novella written by Edgar

Above left
James McConnell's
original cover for
The Outlaw Orphan
(*Thriller Comics* 17).

Above right
Interior panels from
The Outlaw Orphan
by Colin Merrett.

Left
Sep. E. Scott's original
cover for *The Children of
the New Forest* (*Thriller
Comics* 38) was based on
one of its interior panels,
itself inspired by the famous
painting 'When Did You
Last See Your Father?' by
William Frederick Yeames.

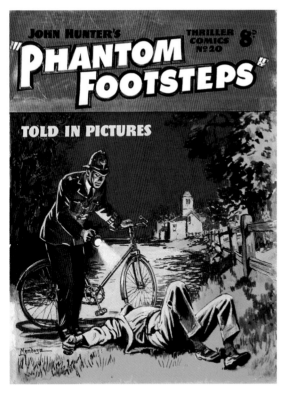

Below Sep E. Scott's original cover painting for *The Picture of Dorian Gray* (*Thriller Comics* 148).

Above top
Philip Mendoza's original cover painting for *Phantom Footsteps* (*Thriller Comics* 20).

Above bottom
A panel by H. M. Brock from *The Loring Mystery* (*Thriller Comics* 25).

Right
Sep E. Scott's dramatic linework for *Jane Eyre* (*Thriller Comics* 31).

Wallace and, within a few weeks, had helped launch the career of Simon Templar – The Saint – when he began featuring new long stories by Leslie Charteris.[13] Wallace and Charteris both featured in the pages of *Thriller Comics*, Wallace with adaptations of *The Green Archer* (no. 16) and *Again the Ringer* (no. 18) and Charteris with a reprint from The Saint's American syndicated newspaper strip (no. 23). John Hunter's 'Phantom Footsteps' (no. 20) was an adaptation of a 1934 *Thriller* story.

This mixture of Historical, Detective and Western lasted for only two dozen issues. The library format was proving so popular that Edward Holmes soon found himself working on the launch of a third title, which Haydon wanted to feature exclusively crime and detection: the *Super Detective Library*.

In order to launch this new project, Holmes was taken off *Thriller Comics* and the library was handed over to Leonard Matthews, whose remit for the title was to concentrate on historical stories. "Louis Hayward made a Dick Turpin film and also Captain Blood films and, of course, Errol Flynn's Robin Hood was still reappearing from time to time," he would later recall. "Then, later, Richard Greene's very popular Robin Hood character appeared on television. So we were receiving salvoes of these heroes from the film world, so why not introduce them into the comics? When I took over the *Thriller Comics Library*, I thought I could extend this interest in historical action strips, not only in the legendary swashbucklers and the out-of-copyright classics we had used in Knockout, but why not approach the agents or the authors of the popular Romantic books that were then commanding very high sales – Jeffrey Farnol, Rafael Sabatini – and turn those into picture strips? So we went over to buying in the rights to a lot of the well-known swashbuckling stories and adapted them into strips for use in the *Thriller Comics Library*. That started a new genre which I think proved very popular."

Matthews' influence can be seen taking hold with the appearance of Jeffrey Farnol's *The Loring Mystery*, drawn by H. M. Brock, an artist approaching the end of his life, who had long been associated with illustrated books as well as the boys' periodicals *Chums*, *Captain* and *The Boy's Own* of the 1920s and 1930s. Brock was not a complete stranger to comics, having contributed a picture strip ('The Mystery of Study 13') to *Sparkler* (1937) and spot illustrations to *Happy Days* (1938). His first true adventure strip, 'Breed of the Brudenels', which he had drawn for *Knockout* from a script by Matthews, had been one of the few successful reprints when it appeared in the library format. Adapted by Joan Whitford, *The Loring Mystery* is totally successful, full of the authentic Farnol atmosphere – robust, manly hero, delicate porcelain female, scheming aristocrat and an aura of mystery surrounding the entire proceedings.

Coincidentally, Brock had been introduced to Matthews by R. Ewart Oakshott, a director of A. E. Johnson, the artists' agency, who happened to be Jeffrey Farnol's nephew. C. E. Brock, had, many years earlier, illustrated three sumptuous gift volumes of Farnol's novels for Sampson, Low, Marston as well as dustjackets for ordinary

editions and, when his elder brother died, H. M. Brock was his natural successor. It is not surprising therefore that Brock should do such a superb job on the *Thriller Comic* version of Farnol's *The Loring Mystery*.

Matthews himself scripted the next full-length historical strip, 'The Strange Affair of the Lyons Mail', based on the real-life murder of a French courier on April 27, 1796. Robert Forrest, the strip's artist, had previously worked for the Inland Revenue Office processing the tax returns of many writers, artists and editors at nearby Amalgamated Press. Already in his forties, Forrest's first contributions were to Edward Holmes' *Cowboy Comics* and *Comet*, drawing Kit Carson. Lively though these are, it was for *Thriller Comics* that he was to produce some of his best work, developing a vigorous and atmospheric style in adaptations of *Bardely's the Magnificent* (no. 35), *Paul Clifford* (no. 46), *The Black Swan* (no. 61), *The Red Rapiers* (no. 78) and its sequel *The Black Dragoons* (no. 90) and *The Chronicles of Captain Blood* (no. 84).

Robert Forrest soon became one of the most popular and regular artists for the library. His finest work, however, came later in the library's run in his three frighteningly dark depictions of 19th Century England: *The Picture of Dorian Gray* (no. 148), 'The Mystery of the Red Barn' (no. 171) and 'Jack Thurtell, Gentleman Thief' (no. 197). The combination of Matthews' scripts and Forrest's artwork made these three issues classics of their kind. Murder prowls across desolate heaths and menacing lanes and through the ill-lit streets and filthy alleyways of the fog-shrouded capital. The contrast between the languid, aristocratic fops of Regency and Victorian London and the downtrodden working people of the slums has never been better portrayed in picture strip form. This is perhaps best exemplified in the adaptation of Oscar Wilde's *The Picture of Dorian Gray*, where the protagonist of the title becomes engulfed in a tide of corruption and vice and gradually sinks lower and lower into the moral abyss. Forrest's drawings not only capture the depravity of Dorian Gray's actions but manage to convey the turmoil going on inside his head. In Forrest's extraordinary drawings, the very buildings exude terror and decay.

Under Matthews, the majority of the library's covers were drawn by Sep. E. Scott. "He was very, very good indeed in the Romantic side of his drawings and it was for this reason that I switched him over from the black and white picture strips that we'd been using in *Knockout* to do coloured covers for *Thriller Comics*. Here he found, I think, his home. He drew literally dozens of first-class, beautiful covers for *Thriller Comics* that today would grace the walls of any stately home. His work was really beautiful; there was no doubt about that."

Scott was not limited to covers, however; he also drew five original full-length strips and two shorter stories. Never has *Jane Eyre* (no. 31) received a more sympathetic illustrator; the book comes alive with splendid pictures of which one feels Charlotte Brontë herself would have approved. The dark, brooding atmosphere of Thornfield Hall and the relations between Jane, the sweet-natured governess, and the mysterious, world-weary owner of the house, Mr. Rochester, are all movingly conveyed. *Pride of the Ring* (no. 53), based on a novel by Ben Bolt, brings the world of the Regency pugilists to life with stunning authenticity. 'The Man Who Stole the Crown Jewels' (no. 41) is a fictionalised account of Colonel Blood and his famous theft and it is interesting to compare the romanticised hero of this strip with Scott's more historically accurate portrayal of Blood in 'The Return of Captain Flame' (no. 28). Sep. Scott's other dashing Royalist adventure featured Rupert of the Rhine – 'The Cavalier and the Crown' (no. 116) – and was a reprint of a serial he drew for *Comet* (1951-52). Written by Leonard Matthews, he gave Prince Rupert a fighting girl comrade known as Black Velvet, who had much in common with Captain Flame's female companion, The Moth. This was something Matthews was particularly keen about, mainly because he wanted to keep his female readership happy: "Dick Turpin's comrade was Tom King but we equipped him with a lady companion, Moll Moonlight (for 'Highway Days' in *Sun*), and, of course, Robin Hood always had his Maid Marion."

After his adaptation of 'The Loring Mystery', H. M. Brock continued to contribute to the library, drawing picture versions of R. D. Blackmore's *Lorna Doone* (no. 47), D. H. Parry's 'To Victory With the Iron Duke' (no. 102) and a marvellous rendering of Charles Dickens' *A Christmas Carol* (no. 109). All three Brock brothers had illustrated Dickens' Christmas ghost story in various editions so H. M. Brock was quite at home with the story and the result is certainly the most satisfying adaptation of Dickens into picture strip form that has ever appeared.

Apart from 'Hunted on the Highway', H. M. Brock had contributed one other story featuring Dick Turpin for 'King of the Road' (no. 22) – drawn especially for the library – and, fittingly, his last work was also a highwayman yarn, 'Dick Turpin and the Followers of Fang' (no. 189). This strip plainly shows the difficulties he was encountering with the onset of old age and failing eyesight. For the first time, the grand old man's line was unsure; indeed, it was so bad that Patrick Nicolle was commissioned to "pull the drawings together".[14] Despite all the difficulty, however, the issue is a triumphant success, imbued with a rich, mysterious atmosphere and packed with exciting night-riding action.

Eric Parker, whose one Sexton Blake strip had been ruined in order to fit the format of the library, fared better with the rest of his work to appear in the series. Apart from *The Children of the New Forest* and *The Sea Lord* (no. 235), his biography of Lord Nelson, reprinted (and much abridged) from *Comet*, Parker's work for the library was original material. Titles such as Rafael Sabatini's *The Snare* (no. 43), set in the Peninsular War, D. L. Murray's 'Trumpeter Sound!' (no. 79), detailing the events leading up to the Charge of the Light Brigade in the Crimean War, and A. E. W. Mason's *The Four Feathers* (no. 67), in which the action takes place during the War in the Sudan, gave Parker full scope to use his immense knowledge of historical uniforms and artefacts. However sketchy Parker's drawings appeared – and he was notorious for refusing to give a 'finish' to his work – the reader feels assured that all the buttons on the tunics are in the right place. Of course, as in all Parker's work, his main aim was the portrayal of vivid action and movement in his inimitable, lively style.

This was the essence of Leonard Matthews' vision for *Thriller Comics*. "Until we started doing these adventure stories, the classics in pictures, etc., the artists who were being used were 'comic' in the true sense of the word, comic strip artists. Now, if we were going over to real-life heroes, we had got to find ourselves a new type of artist."

To find them, Matthews stepped back to the era of fine book illustrations and encouraged artists like Sep. E. Scott, H. M. Brock, Tom Peddie (who drew *Castle Dangerous*, no. 36, *Quentin Durwood*, no. 48, *Hereward the Wake*, no. 52, etc.) and T. Heath Robinson (*The Count of Monte Cristo*, no. 45, and *In the Reign of Terror*, no. 57). At the same time, he encouraged those artists already known for their illustrations for Amalgamated Press (D. C. Eyles, Stephen Chapman, Eric Parker, Colin Merrett) and newcomers (Geoff Campion, Pat Nicolle, Reg Bunn, Robert Forrest, etc.) to adopt a more vigorous, adventurous style, to match the excitement and mood of the stories that appeared in the *Thriller Comics Library*.

IV: Murder, Mystery and Mayhem

On leaving the library, the founding editor of *Thriller Comics*, Edward Holmes, had found that, apart from working on a new detective comic, he was expected to prepare another comic in the same library format. Largely forgotten now, Holmes launched, in September 1952, the *Love Story Library*. The Amalgamated Press was at the time one of the biggest publisher of women's papers – comics were a relatively small part of the operation in comparison – and there was potentially a huge market for a teenage girls' comic if the right format could be found. An earlier attempt, in 1950, at a romance title for young women entitled *Love Romance* had come to a swift end after only four issues. Holmes' *Love Story Library*, however, ran for nearly thirty years and a phenomenal 1,656 issues, folding in April 1980.

At the same time, Holmes was preparing a third title for boys. He would later recall: "The high-ups wanted me to start another title and Monty Haydon had his sights on a detective series. Now, I thought this would be a bad move. Crime fiction had had it's heyday in the '30s and '40s and we were already serving detective fans quite well with Sexton Blake, albeit in narrative form, so I didn't think we needed another crime series. I felt that, with the success of Dan Dare in *Eagle*, modern readers would want something with a more up-to-the-minute theme so I suggested one based on science fiction. But Monty didn't agree: 'Everyone knows you can't live on the Moon and there's no life on other planets,' he'd keep saying and he felt that stories of this type would be considered too ludicrous and unacceptable to the sort of readership we'd already built up on our existing libraries. I thought he was wrong and told him so, but my views were over-ruled and shortly after I received a directive to start this detective series."[15]

Crime had sat rather oddly amongst the swashbuckling stories of highwaymen and pirates in the *Thriller Comics Library*. One of the last titles shepherded through by Holmes had been a reprint of an American newspaper strip featuring Leslie Charteris' famous character, *The Saint in California* (no. 23), syndicated by the New York Herald Tribune.

Left
Sep E. Scott's original cover painting for *The Man Who Stole The Crown Jewels* (*Thriller Comics* 41).

Below
Two pages of original art by H. M. Brock from *A Christmas Carol* (*Thriller Comics* 109).

Above

Eric Parker's alternative version of the cover for *The Snare* (*Thriller Comics* 43) Sep E. Scott's version, the one used, can be seen on page 129.

Right top

Sep E. Scott's original cover painting for *The Four Feathers* (*Thriller Comics* 67).

Right bottom

The original artwork for the title page of *In the Reign of Terror* (*Thriller Comics* 57) drawn by T. Heath Robinson.

It was to this source that Holmes turned when he was planning *Super Detective Library*. The first two issues, released in April 1953, consisted of a Saint reprint, 'Meet the Saint in The Case of the Contraband People', and an all-new story, 'The Riddle of the Frensham Will'. David Ashford (co-compiler of this volume) recalls seeing these issues when they arrived in the newsagents: "Number one was a dull-looking reprint of a poorly-drawn US strip featuring Leslie Charteris' The Saint. I remember letting that one lie on the newsagent's counter. It's companion issue, however, was a different matter. Number two featured Ernest Dudley, the Armchair Detective, and was drawn by Reg Bunn whom I knew as a Buck Jones artist from *Comet* and the *Cowboy Comics Library*. Here was a full-length mystery, well scripted and illustrated, boding well for future issues.

'The following month, things were even better for both numbers contained excellent artwork and two great characters: Sapper's Bulldog Drummond and Graham Greene's Harry Lime, made famous by Orson Welles in the film *The Third Man*. It is unfortunate that no more Harry Lime adventures were to appear in the series and only one more Bulldog Drummond story."[16]

Holmes drew many of his stories from well known, classic mystery novelists – E. Phillips Oppenheim, Sax Rohmer, Edgar Wallace – for his early issues. Wallace was especially well represented. *The Fatal Feather* (no. 30) featured Wallace's popular characters the Three Just Men; *The Door With the 7 Locks* (no. 6) was an atmospheric adaptation drawn by Graham Coton; and Colin Merrett's art for *The Black Abbot* (no. 10) and Selby Donnisons' work on *The Treasure House of Martin Hews* (no. 7) rank amongst the best of their strip output.

Sax Rohmer's *The Island of Fu Manchu* (no. 9) was a particular effective issue, bringing out the best in its artist, Philip Mendoza. The atmosphere of malevolent evil, combined with the 1920s period 'feel', is tellingly captured in Mendoza's strip – as are the characterisations of the main protagonists, Fu Manchu and his adversary Nayland Smith.

Holmes had a sharp eye for the best of contemporary writers as well as for the classics of the genre. He notably adapted six novels, plus one collection of short stories, from the works of Victor Canning, who was then growing in popularity as a writer of suspense thrillers, his novels often serialised in *John Bull* and *Everybody's* before appearing in hardcovers. Five of these stand for all that is best in adventure strip art: top class 'readable' panels combined with a literate script. Ron Embleton drew *Panthers' Moon* (no. 58) and *The Golden Salamander* (no. 72); Bill Lacey drew *The House of the Seven Flies* (no. 60); C. E. Drury drew *The Jewel Smugglers* (no. 95, based on *The Man From the Turkish Slave*) and Ron Turner drew *The Oasis of Mystery* (no. 109, based on the story 'Oasis Nine'). All five are classics of the genre.

Super Detective Library featured a number of characters on a regular basis, chief amongst them – in the early issues at least – was The Saint. Most were reprints but occasionally an original strip appeared, the best of them, *The Saint Plays the Joker*, drawn (apart from Simon Templar's face) by Peter Sutherland.

Lesley Shane was the star of 22 issues of the library, first appearing in 'The Riddle of the Race Gang' (no. 16). Shane was the creation of Conrad Frost, a journalist and features editor with Kemsley Newspapers' Mercury Features, originally set up as a foreign news service by Ian Fleming in 1945. Frost, a prolific author of romance fiction before serving with the R.A.F. during the war, found himself in charge of syndicating feature material for Kemsley's newspaper empire which stretched from Cardiff to Aberdeen and included morning, evening, weekly and Sunday papers. As papers expanded in size after the war following the deregulation of paper controls, Mercury Features struck a deal with King Features Syndicate of New York to distribute comic strips, crosswords, columns, fashion and the INS news service. Frost dealt with 23 regional and 4 national newspapers and, before long, most of them were taking a full page of cartoon strips supplied from blocks made by Kemsley's Withy Grove presses in Manchester.

Knowing that King Features were likely to ask for higher rates in the future, Frost approached Fleming and suggested creating a Visual Features service, producing their own strips for syndication. Fleming took to the idea and, before long, Frost found himself writing not only for Kemsley but for the *Daily Express*, *Sunday Express*, *News of the World* and several magazines.

One of his first strip creations was female detective Lesley Shane, loosely based on Rip Kirby, the American newspaper strip syndicated by King Features. Whilst the scripts were excellent, artists Oliver Passingham and Basil Blackaller were no match for Kirby's Alex Raymond and perhaps it is no coincidence that the Lesley Shane stories were dropped shortly before Rip Kirby reprints were introduced to the *Super Detective Library* in later years.

Mercury Features may have also been behind the supply of the syndicated stories featuring racetrack reporter Vic Terry, whose adventures were mostly set around the world of horse racing. From the beginning ('Vic Terry and the Phantom Racehorse', no. 77), these were often rescripted by editor Holmes and others and Frank Lazenby's artwork was usually partly redrawn (by James Bleach and others). Seven Vic Terry stories appeared in *Super Detective Library*, some seemingly redrawn from stories featuring other sporting detective characters.

More successful were the stories based on already established characters. Inspector Chafik J. Chafik – an Iraqi policeman operating in Baghdad's Criminal Investigation Department – created by C. Vernon Frost[17] had appeared in a series of stories in *Collier's* under Frost's pseudonym, Charles B. Child. He featured four times in *Super Detective Library*, the first full-length story drawn by James Holdaway (*Baghdad Manhunt*, no. 47), who returned for a shorter story later. Holdaway also produced the first of three stories to feature John Hunter's seafaring adventurer Captain Dack (*Meet Captain Dack*, no. 43), a tough, devil-may-care character prone to sail close to the wind when engaged on some of his more dubious missions. Frank Crisp's Dirk Rogers, a salvage master and deep-sea diver, was to star in three adventures, John Creasey's The Toff (the Hon. Richard Rollinson, an upper-class righter of wrongs) featured in two adventures, as did T. C. H. Jacobs' private eye, Temple Fortune.

Perhaps the oddest inclusion was Ernest Dudley, the author and radio presenter, Dudley – actually Vivian Ernest Coltman-Allen – had been an actor in the 1920s before becoming a contract writer with the BBC in 1936. He had written the 'Mr Walker Wants to Know' series of stories featured in *Band Wagon* and created the acerbic and chauvinistic Dr Morelle for a series of plays in the *Monday Night at Eight* series during the war. In 1942, Dudley created *The Armchair Detective* radio show, in which he chatted about crime, discussed the latest novels and presented short, dramatic enactments from them. He even toured the music halls and starred as himself in the movie *The Armchair Detective* (1952). In his comic strip persona, Dudley was drawn by Reg Bunn and W. Bryce-Hamilton, and was depicted as an extremely dapper gent in suit and derby hat with a cigarette in a holder constantly at his lips. He often carried an umbrella ("My favourite umbrella – hadn't I told you about that?") that contained a slim rapier. Unlike his radio adventures which he simply narrated, Dudley became actively involved in his picture story mysteries and, in issue 46, introduced Captain Dack ("an old acquaintance of mine") a third of the way into the story.

The Armchair Detective was a useful device for telling original stories but attempts to create original characters seemed less successful: laboratory assistant Colin Benson starred in two issues (*The Rocket Racketeers* and *Diamonds to Burn*) and there were a number of one-off tales. But, with the exception of Lesley Shane, they were isolated amongst the adaptations and regular appearances of newspaper strip reprints, which not only included The Saint but others from the New York Herald-Tribune stable, including Jet Scott, Paul Darrow and Sir Arthur Conan Doyle's Sherlock Holmes.

Edward Holmes was still convinced that science fiction, rather than crime, was what people would want to read and, to that end, began writing scripts himself. "I wanted to prove my point that, handled correctly, these stories could be written and illustrated in an exciting fashion without appearing too ludicrous. So I wrote a story called *Men From the Stars* and had as my investigative hero Rod Collins, a test pilot for which I drew on my RAF experiences. The story took place on Earth and the mystery was as to why planes, trains, ships and buildings were disappearing."

The script was superbly drawn by Bill Lacey and was the launchpad for a series of other science fiction yarns written by Holmes and Conrad Frost, usually drawn by Lacey, Selby Donnison or Reg Bunn.

The storylines included some mystery element to justify their inclusion but, eventually, Holmes was caught out when Conrad Frost penned *Revolt on Venus*. "The story was pure science fiction! Straight out of Flash Gordon, in fact. No mystery whatsoever! It shouldn't have gone out, of course, but we were getting a little cocky by now, stretching the limit a little more with each successive story. Monty hit the roof when he found out and I got my knuckles rapped and told in no uncertain terms that these stories must not continue as they had no place within detective fiction. Fair enough, I suppose. But I reasoned that providing the emphasis was on crime and detection, the setting shouldn't matter one jot – and that's why Rick Random was created. His role as a space detective was purely a device to allow us to continue running SF stories."

Rick Random, chief trouble shooter of the Interplanetary Bureau of Investigation is, without a shadow of doubt, the most collected of the series characters in the *Super Detective Library*. He made the first of 27 appearances in *Crime Rides the Spaceways* (no. 37) and, as introductions go, it was reasonable, the story being a fairly straight-forward action-adventure with a space setting, entertainingly drawn by Bill Lacey. Holmes made sure that there was no mistaking the stories for anything but crime yarns via the titles: *Crime Rides the Spaceways*, *Kidnappers from Space* (no. 44), *The Riddle of the Vanishing Spacemen* (no. 48) and *The Case of the Man Who Owned the Moon* (no. 49).

It was with this latter title that Holmes' Rick Random stories really began to take off for a new artist had been introduced to the library. *The Case of the Man Who Owned the Moon* was drawn by Ron Turner who, by 1955, was recognised as one of Britain's finest Science Fiction artists. A technical illustrator with Odhams, where he had begun as a trainee at the age of 14, Turner had a passion for Science Fiction and had turned his talent and imagination to producing dozens of painted covers for paperback books, notably for Scion Ltd., and *Practical Mechanics* magazine. Turner combined the realism of Chesley Bonestell's space illustrations – often of planetscapes based on the then current scientific thinking – with the cinematic qualities of Alex Raymond's 'Flash Gordon'.

Unusually for the period, the editor of Scion's Science Fiction line, for which Turner was the main cover artist, began sending him manuscripts ahead of publication, resulting in a series of stunning, often symbolic covers based around elements of the stories rather than the generic cigar-shaped spacecraft favoured by his rivals. Shortly after the war, Turner had also begun drawing comic strips and, in 1953, began writing and drawing a Science Fiction comic book for C. Arthur Pearson – *Tit-Bits Science Fiction Comics* (a companion to the all-text *Tit-Bits Science Fiction Library* for which Turner was also producing full colour covers). Turner's confidence grew as a writer and, when the series came to an end after six issues, he became the writer/artist of 'Space Ace' in *Lone Star* magazine, published by Atlas. Turner was to continue to write and draw this character for over ten years, becoming so popular that, in 1960, Atlas gave him his own comic, *Space Ace*.

Turner developed rapidly as a picture story artist, developing an elegant chiaroscuro style, using shading to build up shape. With his eye-catching style, coupled with his impressive imagination when it came to futuristic townscapes, spaceships and other technology, Turner seemed the perfect choice to draw Rick Random in *Super Detective Library*. However, Turner was less successful when it came to human characters and this is why, in order to establish the kind of look he wanted, Edward Holmes turned to Bill Lacey to produce the first Rick Random adventure. Using Lacey's model for the characters, Turner's first Random adventure was highly successful and, with the occasional fill-in by other artists when he was busy elsewhere, he went on to produce 19 further episodes.[18]

As well as superb artwork, Rick Random also benefited from having stories written by authors with a sympathy for and knowledge of Science Fiction. Early episodes were in the main written or plotted by Conrad Frost but, from Rick Random's *Manhunt Through Space* (no. 90), the stories were written by Bob Kesten, a Canadian journalist and broadcaster who also penned a number of teleplays for *Hour of Mystery* and *Armchair Theatre* and the screenplays *The Day the Sky Fell In* (1959) and *K.I.L. 1* (1962).

Harry Harrison, a former comic strip artist and confessions writer who had established himself as a writer of Science Fiction in American pulp magazines, immigrated to England in 1957, arriving with other fans for the 1957 Worldcon, the first World Science Fiction Convention to be held outside the United States. Harrison and his family lived in England for a year but decided to move on. "These were the days of the killer smog – '57-'58 – and it was cold and miserable up in Camden Town. I got $500 doing one more confession and went off to Italy, to Capri."[19]

With almost no indigenous SF market, during his year in England, Harrison turned to comics and wrote four Rick Random adventures for *Super Detective Library*. The combination of Harrison and Kesten on scripts and Ron Turner on the artwork made Rick Random one of the finest Science Fiction strips to appear in any British comic.

V: The Go-Ahead Ed. Goes

It could be said of all three titles that they brought out something in the artists and writers who contributed the stories. Perhaps the fact that the stories were longer than episodes that would appear in the weekly papers (generally only one, two or three pages), allowing writers to develop more interesting plots that did not need to lurch from cliff-hanger to cliff-hanger; better and longer stories gave the artists something to get their teeth into and they generally answered the call with some of their best work.

Edward Holmes was especially keen to get the best out of his writers one way or another. A man of wide-ranging interests and skills,[21] he was, as one of his former sub-editors has said, quite a go-ahead character. It was Holmes, for instance, who first approached his directors with the idea of buying comic strip rights to modern thrillers, believing that a good plot was essential as the foundation of a good comic. "What we used to do – and it made life very easy, actually – was, Ted would buy in a story from some good writers and we would then break it down into scripts," recalls Barry Coker.[22] "I think Ted bought in material from quite good people. There was a good writer who did *Super Detective* textual stories and then we broke them down into picture stories for the libraries. It was an expensive way of doing it, actually, because you were paying twice for a script, but Ted felt you got better quality."

Jim Storrie, who had joined the Amalgamated Press after successfully submitting a story to *Western Library* in 1954, recalls[23]: "What they used to do was get somebody to do a synopsis of the story; they'd pass it on to someone else who would write a written story around the synopsis and then it was given to another person to write the actual picture script. Sometimes I used to get a synopsis of a storyline and had to write the story around it, or I was given the story, which somebody had written up from a synopsis and I had to do the picture script.

"We were paid pretty poorly in those days and Ted Holmes used to watch every penny. I think the written story was about 4,000 words and if you went to 4,500 he used to moan like mad because he had to pay an extra guinea or something like that. I'd argue my corner and say 'It needs it, Ted.'

"After a while they stopped that because it became a bit cumbersome and because the story writer would complain bitterly about not being given a full synopsis and the written stories might have gaps which, as the script writer, you had to fill-in for yourself. It led to a lot of bad feeling."

In the summer months of July and August, the three libraries published three rather than two issues and, in July 1954, *Cowboy Comics* published the first adventure of Billy the Kid alongside their regular twosome, Buck Jones and Kit Carson, although it was six years before Billy would reappear in new stories on a regular basis. In August, *Cowboy Comics* produced a rather bizarre story featuring 'Buffalo Bill' (no. 107). The bulk of the pages were from the American newspaper strip syndicated by United Features and drawn by Fred Meagher; however, Ron Embleton had been brought in to produce around 22 pages of new artwork dotted throughout the book.[24]

Another stranger who rode into the pages of the library stayed a little longer. His name was Lucky Lannagan and his usual home was A.P.'s *Western Library*, a popular all-text pocket library that boasted attractive full-colour covers (mostly by Derek Eyles and James McConnell). With artwork by Ron Embleton and Peter Sutherland, the Lucky Lannagan issues of *Cowboy Comics* are amongst the very best. At the time the library still published several short strips, usually three in each issue, but all six numbers featuring Lannagan contained single, full-length stories, based on stories by John Hunter. The three Embleton issues (no.115, 'Lucky Lannagan's Mystery Trail', no. 121, 'Lucky Lannagan Squares a Debt' and no.127, 'Lucky Lannagan's Treasure Hunt') contain some of his best work for comics.

The epitome of the easy-going, happy-go-lucky, drifting cowboy with a talent for finding trouble, Lucky Lannagan was an immediately likeable personality and it is a pity that his appearances were limited to just six issues. Ron Embleton did, in fact, draw one more Lannagan adventure but, for reasons known only to the editor, the strip was redrawn so as to feature Kit Carson when it eventually appeared in issue 137. Fortunately, Embleton did the changes himself, fitting the hero out with buckskins and long blonde hair. However, this still made a nonsense of the strip, with Kit Carson uncomfortably transformed into a gunfighter. In one panel he is shown lolling back in a chair and smoking a cheroot with an easy, devil-may-care attitude, completely out of character with Kit Carson's established persona.

To encompass Lucky Lannagan, *Cowboy Comics* had increased its schedule to three titles a month from November 1954, then, in June 1956, added a fourth monthly title. The new regular line-up featured Buck Jones, Kit Carson, Davy Crockett and the Kansas Kid.

David Crockett was a real-life frontiersman, Indian fighter and congressman, noted for his 'cracker barrel humour', who died in 1836 at the Battle of the Alamo at the age of 49. The character become immensely popular through the Walt Disney productions, *Davy Crockett, King of the Wild Frontier* (1955) and *Davy Crockett and the River Pirates* (1956). Released in the UK, these films spawned a huge merchandise boom amongst children, all keen to get a coonskin hat and sing along to the catchy theme tune, 'The Ballad of Davy Crockett', which told of how Davy was "born on a mountain top in Tennessee and killed him a b'ar when he was only three".

While Disney was able to exploit the popularity of the character in *Mickey Mouse Weekly* from August 1955, *Cowboy Comics* began featuring Davy from issue 165 (March 1956). His arrival was a welcome development for the series as the writers and artists of the strips in which he appeared made good use of the backwoods locations and the chance to deal with an earlier period in America's history (the 1820s and 1830s) and to bring a fresh approach to the stories.

Born and bred on the great cattle ranges, the fictional Kansas Kid was a more traditional Western hero: a lone, tough, cheery cowhand without much to distinguish him apart from the fact that he was constantly drifting into trouble. For some reason, the artwork for the most part was undistinguished, with R. Charles Roylance being for some time the main artist.

Davy Crockett, on the other hand, had some excellent artwork by such artists as C. E. Drury, D. C. Eyles, Reg Bunn and, above all, Stephen Chapman and Gerry Embleton. Chapman did some of his most interesting work in strips such as 'Davy Crockett Takes Command!' (no. 263) and his drawings of the buckskin-clad trapper roaming the vast forests are both attractive and true to the period. The most historically accurate artist ever to portray Crockett in comics, however, was Gerry Embleton, younger brother of Ron Embleton. He had begun helping his brother by inking in solid areas of black for his brother's strips at the age of nine and had his first illustration accepted when he was 14. He also took over Ron's 'Lore of the West' in Atlas' *Lone Star*, which involved researching all aspects of the history and lore of the American West and, as a result, his work was as authentic as it was vivid and gritty. All the characters – be they trappers, hunters, soldiers or Indians – are portrayed in rich period detail, set against majestic landscapes of mountains, forests and rivers.

Throughout the library's long run, the standard of scripting remained extraordinarily high. In the early years, the majority of the Kit Carson and Buck Jones stories were written by two men, Jimmy Higgins and 'Chick' Henderson. James Hart Higgins had been a sub-editor at Amalgamated Press before deciding to go freelance in 1937, writing, mostly anonymously, for boys' adventure and women's romance papers. After serving with the Army, he had

worked for R.K.O. Pictures and later rejoined the Amalgamated Press as sub-editor of *Knockout*. Alex Henderson, meanwhile, had been an animator and artist who enjoyed writing – scripting at least two plays for BBC Radio in the late 1940s.

A great many of the scripts were produced by the editorial staff working in and around the offices of the three libraries. The staff was housed in a group of rooms on the sixth floor of Fleetway House. In the early 1950s, one office contained Ted Holmes, who shared it with his secretary, Kay Ivens. Next door was Graeme Thomas, Steve Knight and, from October 1952, Angus Allan, who joined the staff as office boy. In another office, Leonard Matthews had taken over *Thriller Comics* (soon to be renamed *Thriller Comics Library*) and had installed Mike Butterworth as chief sub-editor with John Nicol and Trevor Chrismas as his assistants.

Steve Knight had something of a reputation of being dreamy. "He once went on holiday, having had the responsibility of sending the latest issue of *Cowboy Comics* to the works, and the boys of the Process Department there got in touch to say 'Where is it?'" recalled Angus Allan.[25] "A hunt traced the issue to the space between Steve's desk and the radiator. The pages were lettered but still pencil roughs!"

Knight was fired and replaced by Andy Vincent from the publicity department at Columbia Pictures. Vincent was put in charge of *Super Detective Library* under Edward Holmes but kept up a steady output of scripts for *Cowboy Comics*. Ralph Coveney was sub-editor of *Super Detective*, writing Dick Daring and Robin Hood scripts for *Thriller Comics Library* before joining the *Sexton Blake Library* under Howard Baker. Angus Allan, on his return from National Service in 1956, became editor on *Super Detective* with Margaret 'Marge' Conrick as art sub.

Other sub-editors working in the group included Frank Capern, who would later edit *Lone Rider Picture Library*, and, towards the end of its run, *Thriller Picture Library*; Richard (Dick) Wise, formerly with the RAF who worked as a sub-editor on *Cowboy Comics* and was a regular scriptwriter on *Super Detective Library*; Barry Coker, soon to leave to form the Bardon Art agency, which would supply many of the artists from Spain used by the Amalgamated Press; and Trevor Chrismas, the erratic but likeable sub-editor on *Thriller Comics Library*, who would later freelance many stories for *Express Weekly*.

In 1957, with *Cowboy Comics* now publishing four issues a month, Angus Allan moved back to edit two of them. The staff now consisted of Allan and art sub Graham Allen (later to find fame as the artist of 'Pub Dog' in the *Daily Express* and *Evening News*), handling Davy Crockett and Kansas Kid, while Alan Fennell (formerly on *Radio Fun* and *TV Fun*) and art sub Mike Jones produced Buck Jones and Kit Carson. Both Angus Allan and Alan Fennell became prolific scriptwriters for the series.

It was around this time that Edward Holmes, the founding editor of the three libraries, left to take over the editorial chair of *Everybody's*, a weekly magazine filled with news, features and photographs. *Everybody's* had once been the great rival to *Picture Post* but by the late 1950s

Above Davy Crockett (*Cowboy Picture Library* 283), an original painting by Giorgio de Gaspari.

Above Kit Carson (*Cowboy Picture Library* 289), an original painting by Jordi Penalva.

Above Buck Jones (*Cowboy Picture Library* 346), an original painting by Jordi Penalva.

Above Kansas Kid (*Cowboy Picture Library* 352), another original painting by Jordi Penalva.

Above Sep E. Scott's dashing portrait of Robin Hood from the cover of *Thriller Picture Library* 80.

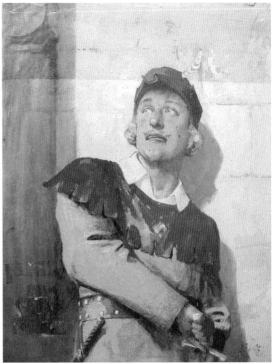

Above Another Scott original painting, this time for the cover of *Thriller Picture Library* 150.

Above Patrick Nicolle's original artwork for the title page for *Thriller Picture Library* 130.

Above John Millar Watt's beautifully detailed original artwork for *Thriller Picture Library* 255.

was in decline. It was still a great opportunity for Holmes to move into Fleet Street, and he jumped at it.

Leonard Matthews – now editorial director over all of the comics titles following Monty Hayden's appointment to the board of directors – handed the library titles over to Alf Wallace, a former sub-editor on *Radio Fun*, who, as managing editor, was soon to expand the libraries group in new directions. *Super Detective Library*, with its focus on crime, was, oddly enough, twinned with *Famous Romance Library*, which, for five and a half years, turned dozens of Mills & Boon romance novels into picture strips.

In 1959, the libraries were moved to the fifth floor of New Fleetway House (a neighbouring building to the 'Old' Fleetway House), located at the back of the building looking down into the well between the old and new buildings, which were connected by a bridge.

A snapshot of the staff on *Cowboy Comics* and *Thriller Comics* in around 1959-60 would include Mike Moorcock, still in his late teens but already a veteran with two years of solid editorial experience on *Tarzan Adventures* behind him; Brian Hind, who wasn't much older, around twenty, but who lasted only a few months on *Cowboy Comics*; at the other end of the scale was *Thriller Comics* sub-editor Bill Pike, who had joined the firm in 1915; Peter Stewart, another *Thriller Comics* sub, who was later to work on *Shoot!* and in Public Relations for West Ham United; Jim Storrie, an Australian whose successful attempts at scriptwriting had led to an invitation to join the staff, and who began working on *Thriller Comics* before switching to *Super Detective* and, later, *Cowboy Comics*. He replaced Alan Fennell, who moved first to *TV Comic* before launching the hugely successful *TV Century 21*.

Soon, Angus Allan was also to depart from *Cowboy Comics* for pastures new, working on *Marty*, a new girls' paper launched by Newnes. By then, 1960, all three libraries were very different from the titles they had been.

The turnaround of editorial staff at Amalgamated Press was not unique to the picture libraries – there were a great many changes across the whole comics division in the mid- to late-1950s as some of the long-serving staff retired or passed on and the ownership of the company changed hands – nor were the problems the staff faced. Having artwork slip down beside the radiator was only one way to lose it. In one memorable incident recalled by Ted Holmes, Philip Mendoza lost a whole book's worth: "We used to meet in a pub sometimes to discuss points of work and on this occasion Phil had a problem with the script and had brought the artwork along to show me. Anyhow, I soon put him right, we had a couple of drinks and he went on his way. The next morning I got this horrified call from Phil – he couldn't find the artwork! Apparently, when he left me he'd gone on to several other watering holes before going home. I had to go over and help him retrace his steps through the previous evening until we eventually found it, under a table at the back of a bar."[26]

Other problems could be caused by mis-translations of instructions to foreign artists – or, in one case, literal translations of instructions. Giorgio De Gaspari, one of the finest cover artists to work on the picture libraries, once produced a Kit Carson cover which caused problems: Alan Fennell had asked for an image of Kit Carson by a rock in the desert with a sandy background. De Gaspari had sent his wife by taxi from his studio in Milan to the coast to collect real sand, which he had glued to the artwork. This touch of genius was much admired in the subs office of *Cowboy Comics* but the sand had to be carefully peeled off and the background repainted because the scanning and printing process would never have been able to cope with loose grains falling into the machinery.

* * * * *

As previously mentioned, *Cowboy Comics* had increased its schedule to four titles a month in June 1956. *Thriller Comics Library* had also increased its schedule to three titles a month during the summer of 1954 and, in the summer of 1955, the increase became permanent; this increased again to four titles a month from November 1955.

The new schedule included a regular monthly title devoted to Robin Hood. Over the years, the 'Lord of Sherwood' had become more and more popular, boosted considerably by the appearance of Richard Greene in *The Adventures of Robin Hood*, which began airing on September 26, 1955 (the show ran for four seasons, a total of 143 episodes between 1955 and 1960). The Robin Hood character became so popular during this period that the Amalgamated Press produced four annuals between 1957 and 1960.[27]

Robin Hood had, of course, been a recurrent character in the library from the beginning, first appearing as early as issue 4. He had been drawn by such diverse talents as Geoff Campion, Philip Mendoza and Peter Sutherland, not all of them entirely suitable choices to portray the hero of Sherwood Forest. There was even a full-length Robin Hood adventure based on a story by Morton Pike (D. H. Parry), 'The Greenwood Outlaw' (no. 77), drawn for the library in a most unhappy manner by John McNamara. The best of the full-length Robin Hood issues were the two reprints from *Sun* drawn by Patrick Nicolle, 'Bold Robin Hood' (no. 74) and 'Robin Hood Rides Again' (no. 80). It was Nicolle who established the look of the library's Robin Hood: a slightly older and blonder version of Errol Flynn's definitive portrayal in the 1938 Hollywood film. Nicolle's work was meticulous and his historical research second to none and the result in these two issues was most successful. The majority of the later Robin Hood issues were by Reg Bunn – whose work, although lacking Nicolle's historical detail, managed to capture something of the atmosphere of the 'Merry Greenwood'.

The second most popular character to appear in the library was the highwayman Dick Turpin, who appeared frequently right from the second issue. As with the Robin Hood issues, at first the Dick Turpin numbers featured for the most part short adventures drawn by disparate artists, who were not particularly well suited to the task. Then, in 'Ho For the Highway' (no. 89), there appeared an advertisement describing the next Dick Turpin issue, which was to be 'Dick Turpin and the Lost Heir' (no. 92):

In this thrilling new full-length story, the King of the Highway and his old comrade Tom King are joined by a merry band of new friends – Jem Peters, a former

Bow Street Runner, Pat O'Flynn, a happy-go-lucky Irishman, Flick, a dashing young adventurer, and Beetles, a good-natured negro.

There then appeared a long series of full-length adventures based on stories originally written by Charlton Lea (A. M. Burrage) and Stephen Hamilton Agnew for the *Dick Turpin Library*, published by Aldine Publications between 1902-09. The paper ran for 183 issues before being relaunched as *New Black Bess Library* (18 issues, 1909-10). The rights to these stories were purchased by Newnes who produced in quick succession, between 1921 and 1923, no less then three Turpin series of their own: a thin, pocket-size *Black Bess Library* (18 issues); a larger format *Black Bess Library (New Series)*, which ran for 38 issues; and, in pocket book size, the *Dick Turpin Library* (138 issues). All three series reprinted, in slightly edited form, the blood and thunder stories from the Aldine publications.

Leonard Matthews had been a great admirer of these stories and, as Amalgamated Press had subsequently bought the rights to them, he decided the time was right to turn them into picture stories. These issues are amongst the best to be featured in the library's long run, thanks to the excellent plotting of the original stories and sympathetic scripting (mostly by Joan Whitford) and, above all, to the dashing, swashbuckling style of Cecil Langley Doughty, who brought tremendous panache to these tales of the High Toby.

The Three Musketeers, who had featured in the very first issue, were the next in line in the library's popularity stakes. As with Robin Hood and Dick Turpin, the early Musketeers issues contained short adventures drawn by somewhat unsuitable artists. These stories actually featured only three musketeers, poor Aramis being left out of the adventures until 'Aramis Rejoins the Musketeers' in issue 26. From then on, Captain D'Artagnan, together with his three comrades Porthos, Athos and Aramis, rode for the glory of France. Issue 70 adapted Alexandre Dumas' novel, *The Three Musketeers*, drawn by Robert Forrest and based on Leonard Matthews' 1946 script for *Knockout* (which had been drawn by Eric Parker). H. M. Brock's 1952 story from *Comet* was reprinted in issue 81, together with a short strip by Stephen Chapman. The latter artist had long been a mainstay of the library, drawing Robin Hood a d v e n t u r e s as well as full-length adaptations – *Tom Brown's Schooldays* (no. 33), *Kenilworth* (no. 51), *To Sweep the Spanish Main* (no. 56) and *St. George for England* (no. 63) – but it was as the main artist for the Three Musketeers that he is best remembered.

Stephen Chapman brought great style and feel for the period to his Musketeer drawings. Matthews had introduced him to the illustrations of Maurice Leloir, a French artist who had illustrated the 1894 edition of Dumas' *Les Trois Mousquetaires* and who had been invited, in 1928, to serve as artistic advisor by Douglas Fairbanks on his film version of Dumas' *The Man in the Iron Mask*. The result was an authentic look to Chapman's strips. Imaginative stories in the Dumas tradition by writers obviously well versed not only in Dumas' Musketeer novels but also in 17th Century France, both historically and

geographically, helped to make these strips some of the most enjoyable of all the swashbuckling issues of the *Thriller Comics Library*.[28]

Two other popular heroes of British folklore made appearances in the library: Claude Duval and Rob Roy. Both characters found their best delineator in Frederick Thomas Holmes. Claude Duval, the 17th century 'cavalier highwayman' had, like Dick Turpin, been the subject of a series of story papers published by Aldine at the turn of the century. Duval made his strip debut in *Comet*, written by Mike Butterworth and drawn by Fred Holmes, in 1953. Some of these serial strips were adapted into issues of *Thriller Comics Library* (nos. 99 and 144) and Holmes also drew another Duval adventure especially for the library (no. 181). The fourth issue was not drawn by Holmes but by Chapman and it was this number that contained the famous scene where, after holding up a coach, Duval dances with a female passenger on the heath.

The Rob Roy stories, all of which were scripted for the library by Mike Butterworth, are among the most entertaining issues in the library's canon, both in terms of artwork and scripting. The first Rob Roy issue (no. 86) was based on the novel by Sir Walter Scott and was drawn by Fred Holmes, as was the next (no. 113), which featured three new adventures of the 'Highland Rogue'. Subsequent issues by C. E. Drury and Robert Forrest continued the high standard, the last Rob Roy drawn by Forrest (no. 184) being a Gothic-style horror story set in a gloomy mansion on the lonely Scottish moors.

Westerns had not featured heavily in *Thriller* but, as *Cowboy Comics* concentrated on the adventures of only a small handful of characters, *Thriller* was able to plug the literary adaptation gap. The choice was on high quality Western novels, some classics, such as James Fenimore Cooper's *The Last of the Mohicans* (no. 15) and *The Prairie* (no. 60), but mostly from contemporary novelists whose work was appearing in the highly regarded American magazines, *Collier's* and *Saturday Evening Post*.

Novels based around the actions of the U.S. Cavalry were particularly popular, with sympathetic adaptations of some of the best work of Ernest Haycox and James Warner Bellah. These stories were mostly adapted by Barry Ford, the pen-name of Joan Whitford, who had spent some years living in America and was fascinated by the history of the American West. Recently divorced and with a young son to raise, Whitford was writing for *Woman* magazine when she met Leonard Matthews who suggested she try writing Western stories for him. From true life text features in *Sun* (as John Haslar) and text serials in both *Sun* and *Knockout* (starring variously Buffalo Bill, Wild Bill Hickok, Billy the Kid and Sitting Bull!), Whitford turned to scripting comic strips for the *Thriller Comics Library*.

Whitford adapted two of Ernest Haycox's novels, *The Border Trumpet* (no. 32), set in Arizona in the 1870s and noted for its geographical and historical accuracy, and *Bugles in the Afternoon* (no. 65), set against the Battle of Little Bighorn and a classic from the moment it began serialisation in *Saturday Evening Post* in 1943. Haycox's novel was made into a rather run-of-the-mill movie by Warner Bros in 1952 starring Ray Milland at a time when

Above Cecil Doughty's bright and dynamic original painting of Dick Turpin for the cover of *Thriller Picture Library* 223.

Above John Millar Watt's sombre and atmospheric original painting for the cover of *Thriller Picture Library* 231. This Turpin seems to be an ancestor of Gary Cooper!

Above and above right Some examples of Stephen Chapman's artwork for *Thriller Picture Library* 93.

Above left
D.C. Eyles' original cover painting for *The Border Trumpet* (*Thriller Comics* 32) complete with hand rendered lettering.

Above right
Sep E Scott's original cover painting for *Thriller Picture Library* 220, featuring Dick Daring.

Left
Giorgio De Gaspari's action-packed original cover painting for *Thriller Picture Library* 297, featuring Robert Hereward "Battler" Britton.

the Western movie was going through a tremendous revival. The pre-war Saturday morning serial type of Western exemplified by Buck Jones, Gene Autry and Roy Rogers was finding that its natural place was now television and cinemas had a new hero in the shape of John Wayne. Wayne had shot to fame in *Stagecoach* (1939), directed by John Ford, and it was the future collaborations between star and director that was to lift the Western movie out of the doldrums and give it a post-war resurgence as a genre that was something rather more than simply the domain of cattle rustlers, shoot-'em-up sheriffs and singing cowhands.

John Ford's series of Westerns included *My Darling Clementine* (1946), *Fort Apache* (1948), *She Wore A Yellow Ribbon* (1949), *Wagon Master* (1950), *Rio Grande* (1950), *The Searchers* (1956), *The Horse Soldiers* (1959), *Sergeant Rutledge* (1960), *Two Rode Together* (1961), *The Man Who Shot Liberty Valance* (1962) and *Cheyenne Autumn* (1964). Ford also shot some second unit footage for Wayne's *The Alamo* (1960) where he portrayed Davy Crockett, and the Civil War segment of *How the West Was Won* (1962). Many of these were adapted, in one way or another, in the pages of *Comet*, *Film Fun* and *Thriller Comics Library*.

Most of the best films featuring the U.S. Cavalry were based on stories written by James Warner Bellah, the same stories also forming the basis for some of the best Western strips in the *Thriller Comics Library*. Bellah's novel *The Apache* (1951) was adapted as *The Apache Curse* (no. 83); *The White Invader* (no. 88) took its title from the original serial, which was subsequently published in book form as *Rear Guard* (1951) and filmed by David Butler as *The Command* (1954); *Sabre and Tomahawk* (no. 95) and *War Party* (no. 103) were collections of short stories which included adaptations of 'Massacre' (the basis for *Fort Apache*), 'The Big Hunt' and 'War Party' (the basis for *She Wore a Yellow Ribbon*), 'Mission With No Record' (basis for *Rio Grande*) – John Ford's classic Cavalry trilogy. Two issues were derived from Bellah's 'The Valiant Virginians' – *Thunder in the South* (no. 195) and *Under the Stars and Bars* (no. 215).

VI: Years of Change

In 1955, Leonard Matthews struck a deal with the American publisher Fawcett Publications, who produced the hugely popular Gold Medal line of paperbacks.[29] The first title adapted for *Thriller Comics* was Bellah's *The Apache*, followed by novels by William Heuman, Dudley Dean, Logan Stewart, Mark Sabin, William F. Jenkins, Louis Lamour, Richard Jessup, Gordon D. Shirreffs, Joseph Chadwick, Lewis B. Patton and Richard Telfair, the last in 1960. The same publisher also supplied Western novels (by Ray Hogan, Richard Telfair and Frank Castle) for adaptation in the Cowboy Picture Library in 1960-62 as well as Crime novels to both *Super Detective Library* and *Sexton Blake Library*.

These adaptations were a reflection of an attempt to modernise the three libraries. After 1956, adaptations of classic novels in *Thriller Comics Library* became ever more rare. 1957 classic adaptations included *Moby Dick* (no. 157), *The Strong Room* (no. 163), *Captain Blood Sails Again* (no. 168), *Around the World in Eighty Days* (no. 180) and 1958 saw the last of the classics, *The Man They Called Bloodhound* (no. 208), based on Victor Hugo's *Les Misérables*.

Instead, *Thriller Comics Library* – shortly before changing its name to *Thriller Picture Library* with issue 163 (March 1957) – launched a new series of original stories featuring Second World War Ace, Battler Britton. Wing-Commander Robert Hereward Britton, to give Battler his full name – was the creation of Mike Butterworth, who had been Len Matthews' chief sub on *Thriller Comics* between 1952 and 1954.

Battler's first adventure in *Thriller Comics Library*, 'Battler Britton – War Ace', was drawn by Colin Merrett, the second – a collection of stories under the title 'Battler Britton Flies Again' (no. 179) – by regulars from the weekly strip, Geoff Campion, Guido Buzzelli and Eric Bradbury. The third issue, 'Battler Britton, Sky Commando' (no. 193) marked the arrival of various Italian artists to the pages of *Thriller Picture Library*, artists whose work was to dominate the picture libraries from then on.

European artists had begun to appear in British comics in 1954, attracted by the extensive market and relatively large pay rates. The pound, very strong in the 1950s and 1960s, had the equivalent spending power of four times its value in Spain and the Belgian agency A.L.I. (Agence Litteraire International) were able to introduce some of the best Spanish artists to the British market – Jesus Blasco, Julio Vivas, Sergio Tarquinio (an Italian), Angel Pardo, Francisco Hidalgo, E. T. Coelho, Romeu and Eugenio Giner all making their debut in the pages of *Sun*, *Comet* and *Thriller Comics Library* within a period of 14 months.

At the same time, an ex-partisan and sculptor, Enzo Plazzotta, had moved from Milan to London and, in around 1954, became the general director of Cosmopolitan Artists. Plazzotta and Giorgio Bellavitis (the first Italian known to have drawn for British comics when his 'Paul English' strip began appearing in *Swift* in March 1954), used their contacts in both Italy and London to place work by Italian artists in newspapers, magazines and comics.

One of the first artists they found work for was Rinaldo D'Ami, a 30-year-old Italian artist well known in his native country for Westerns like 'Mani in alto!' *[Hands Up!]* and 'I tre Bill' *[The Three Bills]* as well as adventures featuring the Rio Kid, Pecos Bill and – one of D'Ami's finest – Gordon Jim, a Scottish nobleman caught up in the American War of Independence.

As his workload increased following the creation of 'Il sergente York' *[Sergeant York]* in 1954, D'Ami was joined by Antonio Lupatelli, Carlo Porciani, Renzo Calegari and Giuseppe Montanari at his apartment in Milan. Cosmopolitan Artists made increasing use of D'Ami's studio, which began expanding rapidly.

The influx of European artists into the three libraries was gradual over a period of years. Spanish artist Ángel Pardo Ruiz had a fondness for Hal Foster's 'Tarzan' and 'Prince Valiant', which was visible in his historical strips. For four years from September 1955, when he drew for issue no. 98, he was a regular on *Thriller Comics Library*'s Robin Hood, a necessary and not unwelcome addition to the team of British artists who kept up a steady output of adventures for the outlaw of Sherwood Forest. Vitor Peon, a Portuguese artist, joined him in February 1956 but was to find regular work with D. C. Thomson after 1958.

New Spanish artists supplied by A.L.I. and Italian artists from Cosmopolitan trickled onto the library, some only appearing briefly, others staying longer. Vitor Peon produced the first full-length, European-drawn adventure for *Thriller Comics Library* in March 1956, 'Buffalo Bill and the Spectre of the Plains' (no. 119), followed by Sergio Tarquinio's 'Crazy Horse, Warlord of the Sioux' (no. 123) and Guido Buzzelli's 'The Three Bravos' (no. 124). A great many of the literary adaptations (now mostly Westerns, as mentioned above) were given over to artists such as Mario Cubbino, Enver Bongrani, Jesus Blasco, Guido Buzzelli and Ruggero Giovannini.

Surprisingly, *Cowboy Comics* (retitled *Cowboy Picture Library* from issue 205) was slower to take up this new influx of talent. Although Armando Bonato, born in Switzerland but resident in Milan, became a semi-regular on Kit Carson stories, following his debut in June 1956 (*Cowboy Comics* no. 169), only a handful of other European artists – Alfredo Marculeta, Franco Bignotti and Jorge Macabich – contributed in the first twelve months of the 'invasion'. Of these, Macabich was probably the best, becoming a regular on Kit Carson. Initially Macabich contributed through A.L.I. before moving to England for six months. In 1957, he teamed up with former *Cowboy Comics* sub-editor and scriptwriter Barry Coker to set up the Bardon Art artists' agency and, as an agent, went on to supply many Spanish artists to British comics.

In late 1956 cracks appeared in the relationship between Rinaldo D'Ami and Cosmopolitan Artists and D'Ami, along with his brother, Piero, set up their own agency, Creazioni D'Ami to supply artwork to the UK market and elsewhere. With some of the finest Italian talent on their books, it is not surprising that, when *Thriller Comics Library* launched Battler Britton, they turned to the D'Ami brothers to supply much of the artwork.

Battler Britton was a considerable success in the pages of *Thriller Picture Library*, bringing Second World War action to the title on a monthly basis from December 1957. The appearances of Dick Turpin and The Three Musketeers became less and less frequent.

With Robin Hood issues also appearing each month, there was less opportunity for one-off titles. Space for adaptations became even more of a premium with the arrival of another character who was to become a regular: Dick Daring of the Mounties.

The North-West Canadian Mounted Police had been a popular staple of story papers in the 1920s and 1930s, since Canada was still a frontier country as far as many a British lad was concerned. Heroes were made of everyone from trappers to lumberjacks, which not only made for exciting adventures but boosted sales in Canada. The Mounties had been given a considerable boost in popularity by the 20th Century Fox movie *Pony Soldier* (1952; released in the UK as *MacDonald of the Canadian Mounties* in 1953) starring Tyrone Power (adapted by Pat Nicolle in the pages of *Sun*) but Sergeant Dick Daring was

still something of a lone red coat in British comics. Based at the Mounties barracks at Moosejaw, Daring and his magnificent stallion, Pal, rode into the pages of *Thriller Picture Library* no. 217 and, from the start, was almost wholly produced by Creazioni D'Ami. The main artist was Italian Sergio Tarquinio, a superb draughtsman who captured the rugged essence of the Canadian landscapes and backwoods. At the same time he was also producing stories for *Cowboy Picture Library* featuring Kansas Kid, Davy Crockett and Billy the Kid, proving to be as adept at drawing the Wild West as he was the North-West.

D'Ami's studio made full use of its talent, with often more than one artist working on a story, making identification of individual artists somewhat difficult; sometimes three or four artists would be involved in the pencilling or inking of even a short tale. D'Ami himself penned at least one Dick Daring yarn.

The adventures of Dick Daring were to find an even bigger audience when the Canadian Broadcasting Corporation, in collaboration with the B.B.C. and others, produced the TV show *R.C.M.P.* in 1959 starring French-Canadian actor Gilles Pelletier as Corporal Jacques Gagnier and British actor Don Francks as his sidekick, Constable Bill Mitchell.

* * * * *

The appearance of more regular characters could also be seen in the *Super Detective Library*. Strangely, the editors chose not to include Sexton Blake, the famous detective whose adventures were published every month alongside *Super Detective*. Blake was often described as 'the other Baker Street detective', linking his name with Sherlock Holmes. The latter appeared in three adventures in the pages of *Super Detective Library*: no. 65 ('Sherlock Holmes Solves The Mystery of the Red-headed League and The Case of the Greek Interpreter'), no. 74 ('Sherlock Holmes in The Mystery of the Thames Afire and A Scandal in Bohemia') and no. 78 ('Sherlock Holmes Meets The Hound of the Baskervilles and The Missing Heiress'), each featuring two adapted reprints from the New York Herald-Tribune syndicated strip drawn by Frank Giacoia. Sexton Blake, on the other hand, featured in only one issue: 'Sexton Blake's Diamond Hunt' (no. 68), a rather dull and uninteresting tale drawn by Oliver Passingham. With so many superb Blake stories ready to adapt, one cannot help but question why such a rich resource was never used. The answer is rather simple: Sexton Blake had his own (text) library, with two new titles released monthly, and was also appearing in the pages of *Knockout* in a series of complete 2-page adventures each week. With this in mind, Edward Holmes decided against using Blake to avoid competing with titles from his own stable.

Instead, Holmes introduced the adventures of Blackshirt whose 15 adventures, based on the novels and stories of Roderic Graeme[30], ranked him the third most regular character behind Rick Random and Lesley Shane. Blackshirt was, in reality, Richard Verrell, best-selling mystery novelist by day and gentleman cracksman in a black hood by night. However, unlike his predecessor, Raffles, Verrell was using his skills at opening safes for the side of law and order – a motive somewhat foreign to

Hornung's famous creation. Bill Lacey made the character of Blackshirt his own and drew some of his very best work for these stories. The first adaptation was illustrated by Lacey's studio partner Selby Donnison and the second by Peter Sutherland but, with the third story, 'Wanted – Blackshirt!' (no. 103), Bill Lacey became the regular artist. They rank among the most readable of all the mystery series in the library.

Following Holmes' departure, Andy Vincent took over the library for a short time before handing over to Val Holding and Sydney Rossiter. It was under the latter that the character of Lesley Shane was dropped and *Super Detective Library* gained itself a true comic strip classic in the shape of Alex Raymond's Rip Kirby. First published in 1946, Raymond's strip – Raymond had already made a name for himself as the artist of Flash Gordon, which he had been drawing since 1934 – was an immediate success in American newspapers. Private eye Remington 'Rip' Kirby was bespectacled, smoked a pipe and played his hunches – in *The World Encyclopedia of Comics*, Maurice Horn describes him as a combination of Philo Vance and Philip Marlowe. Before long, the strip began appearing in the *Daily Mail* and proved so popular that Associated Newspapers reprinted the strip in five oblong books between 1948 and 1956.

Alex Raymond was hugely influential on young British artists learning their craft in the late 1940s; he possessed a clean, clear, fluid line, was the master craftsman when it came to the use of solid black and shading techniques and capped it all with a dynamic use of cinematic angles. His beautiful, glamorous women with such seductive names— Honey Dorian, Kismet Kildare, Pagan Lee—and his marvellously menacing hoods and trigger men such as Kirby's arch foe, the Mangler, were truly memorable. Sadly, Raymond was already deceased by the time Rip Kirby began appearing in *Super Detective Library* in January 1958 – killed in a car accident in September 1956.

Kirby soon had a British rival in *Super Detective*. Buck Ryan had been running in the *Daily Mirror* since March 1937 drawn by Jack Monk, a Lancastrian cartoonist working on the local *Bolton Evening News* who had moved to London to produce an adaptation of Edgar Wallace's *Terror Keep* for the *Daily Mirro r*. Although the rights had been cleared with Wallace's estate, a copyright dispute with an American syndication company led to the story being wound up quickly. The *Mirror*'s editor – and a champion of the daily comic strip – Guy Bartholemew, liked Monk's style and asked him to create an original detective strip. The result was 'Buck Ryan' which was to run in the paper for 25 years.

For some reason, the British 'tec caused more problems than the American Rip Kirby when it came to transferring him to pocket library size. In at least one of the issues, Alfred Taylor was given the thankless task of extending some of Jack Monk's frames in order to fit the new format. Nevertheless, the reprints worked well for the most part and were a good read. Again, it was the femmes fatales with their evocative names – 'Cuddles' Curvate, Twilight and Ryan's blonde assistant, Zola – who remain in the memory as well as the grotesques such as Madame Nogard ("dragon" in reverse), the fairground proprietor,

and Ma-the-Cache, the double-dealing fence. The latter characters were doubtlessly inspired by the great American strip artist, Will Eisner, creator of The Spirit.

However, resizing reprint material must have been a relatively easy task compared to some others the libraries faced. It is not uncommon to find issues of *Cowboy Comics* where the bulk of the artwork is by one artist while another has redrawn the faces of the main characters to make them recognisable to the readers. Occasionally, a problem would result in a script being re-worked, changing the hero featured; such was the case of *Cowboy Comics* no. 253 which featured Kit Carson but was almost certainly originally a Buffalo Bill script as it co-starred Calamity Jane.

From 1958 on, adapted reprints began appearing more regularly. This was most common in the Buck Jones issues where Lucky Logan, whose adventures had run in *Knockout* in 1953-54, was adapted to become Buck Jones; once suitable Lucky Logan stories ran out, old Billy the Kid (from *Sun*) stories became 'new' Buck Jones yarns. Wild Bill Hickok became Kit Carson on a couple of occasions, as did Buffalo Bill on another; Buffalo Bill stories were more often resized or redrawn from their original appearances in *Comet*, the work often being given to two artists fairly new to the comics, Brian Lewis and David Slinn.

Recycling comic strips was by now a tradition with Amalgamated Press – shortly to be renamed Fleetway Publications from the summer of 1959 and later to evolve into IPC Magazines – and stories from the *Thriller*, *Cowboy* and *Super Detective Libraries* would reappear in other comics many times over the coming years. Many tales of Robin Hood and Rick Random appeared in the *Buster Adventure Library* in the 1960s as relatively straightforward reprints bar a change in the story title. Rick Random was still appearing in the early 1980s in the annual *Space Picture Library Holiday Special* where, in an attempt to make the strips appear new, he was often given a new name—Dair Avalon or Rod Rogan. These seemingly pointless attempts to disguise the original character may have worked for some readers but, for the long-time fans of the three libraries, there was no disguising the fact that they were beginning to run out of steam and that their future seemed very much in doubt.

VII: The Picture Library Goes to War

In September 1958, Amalgamated Press launched the first of a new line of titles under the editorship of Alf Wallace (who had taken over the *Cowboy Comics Library* following the departure of Ted Holmes), which were eventually to supersede the original trio of pocket libraries. *War Picture Library* initially covered all aspects of the Second World War – on the ground, in the air and at sea – and proved so successful that *Air Ace Picture Library* and *Battle Picture Library* were launched in January 1960 and January 1961 respectively.

The success of these new titles reflected a steady change in what children wanted to read. At the beginning of the 1950s, when *Cowboy Comics* and *Thriller Comics* were launched, the most popular genres were Westerns and Historical Swashbucklers. However, unlike their parents, the children born after the War were growing up in the Jet Age and this too was being reflected in children's comics where Dan Dare and Captain Condor were to be found on the front pages of *Eagle* and *Lion*. Edward Holmes could see the potential in these new Science Fiction stories as he began work on *Super Detective Library* but had to sneak these stories in under the guise of crime stories with a space setting. Not that 'Monty' Haydon, the group's director, was oblivious to the attraction of Science Fiction to young readers: each group would regularly put together dummies of potential new comics and, in 1954, Mike Butterworth created Jet-Ace Logan for just one such dummy under Haydon's control. In the event, the new title did not see publication and Jet-Ace had to wait a couple of years before making his debut in *Comet* in 1956.

War stories were also becoming increasingly popular in the weekly comics; air aces had always been popular heroes for story papers, especially in the 1920s and 1930s when writers like Captain W. E. Johns and George E. Rochester were producing dozens of stories for magazines and books. In *The Champion*, Rockfist Rogan, the "boxing airman", would run for years, as would bomber pilot Braddock in *Rover*. By the mid-1950s, many papers had a picture strip featuring one or other aspect of wartime heroics. Battler Britton began appearing in *Sun* in January 1956 – a year before his first appearance in *Thriller Picture Library* – and was the cover star from June 1958. Biographies in book form and epic movies on the cinema screens led to an upsurge in interest in the War amongst youngsters born in the post-War baby boom, who were now old enough to read comics.

Thriller Picture Library added another war hero to its list of regular characters in Spy 13, a British agent, real name David Doughty, whose running battle with the Nazis would eventually run to 44 issues. The first issue (no. 242) had been drawn by two of Creazioni D'Ami's best war artists, Annibale Cassabianca and Ferdinando Tacconi, but with the *War Picture Library* being launched at the same time, many of D'Ami's best artists were moved to the new title. Spy 13 underwent a metamorphosis as the next few stories reprinted the adventures of *Knockout*'s wartime spy, Captain Phantom, drawn by Graham Coton with additional drawings by Reg Bunn. By mid-1959, Bunn was producing new Spy 13 stories with occasional contributions by others, most notably Alberto Breccia.

Breccia was one of the first South American artists who found work in the UK and was part of a wave of new talent working for the British market. With the addition of *War Picture Library*, it became increasingly necessary to attract new artists and the Amalgamated Press threw their net wide. From France came Guy Moumineux and from Milan, Italy, three artists (Giovanni Sinchetto, Dario Guzzon and Pietro Sartoris) known as Studio SGS, debuting in March 1959 in *Thriller* and *Cowboy Picture Libraries* respectively; April saw the debut of Ivo Pavone, an Italian who had worked in South America; and, in September, Hugo Pratt made his debut in *War Picture Library*, followed soon after with a contribution to the Battler Britton canon in *Thriller Picture Library*.

Pratt was an Italian who, in 1945, became part of what

was known as the Venice Group and co-created *Asso di Picche*, an almost legendary Italian comic that brought together the talents of Pratt, Dino Battaglia, Alberto Ongaro, Giorgio Bellavitis, Ivo Pavone and others. Many of these creators were invited to South America by Argentinean publisher Cesar Civita, a call answered by Pratt, Ongaro and Mario Faustinelli in 1950. In South America Pratt created some of his most important strips, including Sergeant Kirk, Ernie Pike and Anna della Jungla. However, an argument with writer and publisher Hector Oesterheld led to his departure in 1959.

Pratt moved to London where he found work producing illustrations for the *Sunday Pictorial* and with Fleetway, having submitted his first work whilst still living in Argentina. Pratt introduced other Argentinean artists to the British market, including Francisco Solano Lopez, whose first contribution – commissioned as a *War Picture Library* – became the first issue of *Air Ace Picture Library*. Alberto Breccia made his debut in April 1960 with *Passport to Peril* in *Super Detective Library* (no. 172) and before long was appearing regularly in both *Cowboy* and *Thriller*. His work on Spy 13, whilst deceptively 'rough', had a tremendous feel for dynamic angles and Breccia could build a sense of furious tension in the sea battles he was often called to depict.

Pratt returned to South America (via Ireland) in the summer of 1960, but continued to contribute strips until 1963; Breccia's last strip appeared in early 1962. Although both already had a substantial body of work behind them, they were both to find even greater fame – Pratt with Corto Maltese and Breccia with Mort Cinder and *El Vida del Che* (a biography of Che Guevara) – and their work in the UK has become something of a footnote.

A year after the appearance of Spy 13, *Super Detective Library* added its own wartime spy in the shape of Captain John Steel of British Military Intelligence. Steel was sent behind enemy lines in fifteen tightly plotted Second World War stories, drawn at first by Bill Lacey, now free of his work on Blackshirt, but including episodes by Ron Turner and various Italian artists.

Not to be outdone when it came to creating new characters, in March 1960 Dogfight Dixon of the Royal Flying Corps was introduced to the pages of the *Thriller Picture Library*. These tales featured Lieutenant Don Dixon, the crack-pilot of no.13 Fighter Squadron of the Royal Flying Corps, the action taking place in the skies over Europe during the Great War. Dogfight Dixon was the archetypal fighter-ace, the only difference between him and *Thriller*'s other ace, Battler Britton, being the planes – Sopwith Camels rather than Spitfires.

The writer responsible for some of the early stories was Mike Moorcock, then working for Fleetway Publications on the *Cowboy Picture Library* and *Thriller Picture Library* and shortly to move to the *Sexton Blake Library*. Moorcock – who admits that "Dogfight Dixon remains dear to my heart"[31] – was interested in the history of flight. Whilst editing *Tarzan Adventures* he had written features on World War Two fighters and a series on early flight under the title 'Canvas and Wire'. Moorcock was as much at home writing about dog-fights between Camels and Fokkers –

Left
Giorgio De Gaspari's original painting for the cover
of *Thriller Picture Library* 270.

Below left
Pino Dell'orco's cover painting originally used for *Thriller
Picture Library* 374, featuring Dogfight Dixon.

Below right
Allesandro Biffignandi's expolsive cover for *Thriller Picture
Library* 398, again featuring Dogfight Dixon.

and Zeppelins, his favourite theme – as he was writing gun-fights for Kit Carson, Buck Jones or Dick Daring. One full-length Dick Daring story was written overnight. "Started Tuesday evening, delivered Wednesday morning, because Wednesday was pay-sheet day. That would have earned me about a hundred quid, which in 1959 was good money for one night's work," he recalls.

The Dogfight Dixon stories were drawn by a mixed group of English, Italian, Spanish, Maltese and German artists,[32] although this constantly shifting artistic line-up soon settled down to two main artists, Kurt Caesar and Aldoma Puig. Caesar, born in Montigny, Lorraine, whilst it was still part of the German Empire (Montigny-lès-Metz is now part of France), had begun his working career as a journalist in Germany but settled in Italy where he became a noted illustrator and comic strip artist, creating 'Romano il Legionario', about an Italian pilot in the Spanish Civil War. He found a ready home for war in the air stories in both *Thriller* and *Air Ace Picture Libraries*. Artur Aldoma Puig was a young Spanish artist who would work in the UK for over 25 years. Another Spaniard, Amador Garcia, was a later regular after Caesar and Puig had moved on to other work.

With the arrival of Dogfight Dixon, *Thriller Picture Library* had a cast of four regular characters and the move from historical strips to more modern fare was complete. Robin Hood's last adventure appeared in issue 303, and the four monthly titles now featured Battler Britton, Spy 13, Dick Daring and the aforementioned Dogfight Dixon. The odd western scripted by Barry Ford (Joan Whitford) occasionally disturbed the schedule but, on the whole, it was a conveyer-belt period for the library, stories (up to three in each issue) written by competent writers and farmed out to competent artists, but with none of the literary derivation of the old days of *Thriller Comics* which had helped keep the series varied and the readers on their toes.

Fleetway Publications was undergoing a great many changes. In 1959 they folded two of their long-running comics, *Comet* and *Sun*, merged into *Tiger* and *Lion* respectively. Both *Comet* and *Sun* had been in the doldrums for a while, ever since the change from colour photogravure printing to letterpress, relying on reprints as part of their weekly menu – many of them from the pages of *Thriller Comics*. In 1959, both *Comet* and *Sun* reprinted Robert Forrest issues: 'The Strange Affair of the Lyons Mail' and 'The Red Rapiers' in the latter and 'Paul Clifford' in the former. It seems somewhat strange that these papers were using stories taken from the *Thriller Picture Library* in order to bolster falling sales while, at the same time, the library was moving away from them, switching instead to war stories, which were already catered for in *War Picture Library*, *Air Ace Picture Library* and *Battle Picture Library*.

The latter title, launched in January 1961, replaced *Super Detective Library*, which came to a close in December 1960 after 188 issues. Blackshirt, Rick Random and Rip Kirby had all disappeared from the library in 1959 and John Steel shared the final year with Buck Ryan, alternating each month, apart from April and December of its last year, 1960. Writing in 1992, David Ashford noted: "*The Super Detective Library* had a run of almost eight years and, during that time, presented readers with a range

of quality adventure strips. They were aimed at the older reader and there was no attempt to write down to a younger audience. Reading them in maturity, one realises that those issues that were adapted from thriller novels retained the essence of those stories with no watering down of the plot and those written especially for the library – particularly the Rick Random stories – are in no way juvenile. This is perhaps why they were so popular in their day with young readers."[33]

VIII: Endings and Beginnings

The new decade was proving one of great change. The arrival of new characters was also to be found in *Cowboy Picture Library* where Billy the Kid was added to the roster from June 1960. The heroic Billy of British comics was nothing like his namesake, the frontier outlaw born Henry McCarty but better known as William Bonney. Billy the Kid is reputed to have killed 21 men in his 21 years before he was shot by Sheriff Pat Garrett in 1881. In the pages of *Sun* he became a Lone Ranger-style figure, a masked fighter for justice.

Billy the Kid began appearing regularly in *Sun* in 1952 and, in 1956, earned himself the accolade of becoming the paper's cover strip. These stories, complete and much longer than the usual one or two pages dedicated to a weekly strip, proved so popular that *Sun* was renamed *Cowboy Sun Weekly* and, later, *The Cowboy Sun* for some months in 1957.

Billy had his first issue dedicated to his exploits in *Cowboy Comics* in 1954 (no. 105) but did not reappear as a regular character until 1960 (bar some reprints which, as mentioned previously, were redrawn to turn Billy into Kansas Kid and Buck Jones). After the first story by F. Alan Philpott, Billy's adventures were drawn by Sergio Tarquinio, R. Charles Roylance and others (including a single episode by Don Lawrence).

The character seemed not to take hold and his regular appearances lasted for only ten months until April 1961.[34]

In July, Fleetway Publications tried an even bigger experiment, launching *Lone Rider Picture Library* with impressive covers and excellent artwork by the likes of Arturo Del Castillo, Renato Polese, Luis Dominguez, Carlos V. Roume and Sergio Tarquinio. One suspects that it was launched to try and lure back readers who had grown somewhat tired of the regular foursome who were appearing in *Cowboy Picture Library* but the decline in the Western market – which was also biting into sales of rival titles like Pearson's *Western Picture Library* – and the success of the War libraries meant that *Lone Rider* folded after only 16 issues.

Cowboy Picture Library had itself become more of a young adult title as the 1960s progressed. The emphasis on innocent and joyful adventurers was beginning to give way to a more miscellaneous cast of darker characters. One welcome addition from *Lone Rider Picture Library* was Larrigan, a wanderer who encountered trouble wherever he roamed; the stories were satisfying enough but the artwork by Arturo Del Castillo (and a second artist who made a pretty good job of looking like Del Castillo) was exceptional.

Jordi Penalva's original cover painting for *Cowboy Picture Library* 281.

Jordi Penalva's original cover painting for *Cowboy Picture Library* 319.

Buck Jones, Kansas Kid and Kit Carson still made regular appearances, although the covers were redesigned with issue 401 to give the library a fresher look. Internally, the artwork could boast some of the top Italian, Spanish and Argentinean artists: Jesus Blasco, Ruggero Giovannini, Alberto Breccia, Carlos V. Roume, Sergio Tarquinio and Alberto Salinas to name a few. There was still room for some fine work by British artists, notably Robert Forrest, who drew the splendidly atmospheric 'Iron Cage' (no. 448) and Gerry Embleton who contributed a most authentic Civil War story entitled 'The Fighting Blues and Greys' (no. 456).

The plots had become more complex and involving and this, coupled with the always outstanding draughtsmanship of the artists, meant that the final eighteen months of the *Cowboy Picture Library* included some of the best work to appear in its 12-year history. Nevertheless, good scripting and fine artwork could not save the *Cowboy Picture Library* and the end came in September 1962 with issue 468. Young people's tastes had changed and its demise had already seemed inevitable when, the previous February, Fleetway had launched its fourth War title, *War at Sea Picture Library*.

* * * * *

With the demise of *Cowboy Picture Library*, the original trio of titles was down to one. *Thriller Picture Library* had taken on board *Super Detective*'s one surviving original regular character, John Steel. The first Steel story appeared in *Thriller Picture Library* in the same month that *Super Detective* ended (December 1960), replacing Dick Daring and making *Thriller* in essence another War library as its monthly line-up was now John Steel, Spy 13, Battler Britton and Dogfight Dixon.

John Steel's adventures as a spy in war-torn Europe lasted only a few months – not surprising as *Thriller* already had its own regular World War II agent in Spy 13. Thus, at the end of 'Meet Me In Lisbon' (no. 355), in which he tracked down three Nazis who had escaped from Berlin in the last days of the war, it was revealed that this was to be his final wartime adventure.

The next John Steel tale was, in fact, a reprinting of 'The Door With the Seven Locks' from *Super Detective Library* (based on an Edgar Wallace story but with the hero's name—Dick Martin—changed to John Steel). Steel was no longer a spy and, with the following story, 'Blues for Danger' (no. 363), the character became a private detective for hire, taking residence above a café, a hang-out for the trendy where live music is provided by young musicians. The new stories showed that the scriptwriters were trying something completely new for *Thriller Picture Library*: a picture strip series set in modern-day London. The scriptwriters peppered the stories with beat slang and references to jazz and the blues and its tone was unique, downbeat and often ending on a mournful note.

The new series found its perfect artist in Luis Bermejo, a Spaniard who had already drawn three of John Steel's World War II adventures. The change of setting suited him perfectly; his artwork was filled with moody blacks and shadows and details that made the settings wholly

convincing, whether it was the inside of a jazz dive or a London street. Bermejo is probably now best remembered for the adventures of Pike Mason in *Boys' World* and as the artist who alternated with Frank Bellamy on Heros the Spartan in *Eagle* – by which time he had developed a studio set-up and had a number of artists working with him on each strip. However, the John Steel stories prove how good Bermejo was as a solo artist.

The last of the great characters to appear in *Thriller Picture Library* was futuristic adventurer, Jet-Ace Logan whose adventures had begun in *Comet* in 1956 and was, at the time of his *Thriller* debut, a popular character in the pages of *Tiger* where his adventures were drawn with considerable skill by John Gillatt and Brian Lewis. Billed as the "Dare-Devil Ace of the RAF Space Command", there can be little doubt that the editors were trying not to alienate air-war fans too much as they were to lose the Sopwith Camels of Dogfight Dixon in favour of the spaceships of Jet-Ace Logan.

Once again, the series was fortunate to find a good artist in Kurt Caesar, who had already proved himself an excellent delineator of aircraft and aerial warfare in the War libraries. Jet-Ace and his tubby companion, Plum Duff (Digby to Jet-Ace's Dan Dare), were whisked through the void with considerable panache by Caesar and his scriptwriters; the series could also boast two issues drawn by Ron Turner, who had lost none of the skill he had shown on Rick Random

The *Thriller Picture Library* entered 1963 with a seemingly solid line-up, consisting of Battler Britton, Spy 13, John Steel and Jet-Ace Logan but all was not well. Fleetway had experimented with three titles launched in the summer of 1961.Two of them were unsuccessful: the aforementioned short-lived *Lone Rider Picture Library* and the even shorter lived *Tiger Sports Library*, which could muster only twelve issues. The only new title with any measure of success was the *Princess Picture Library*, which was to run for five years.

The cracks in the *Thriller Picture Library* were on display in February 1963 when two of the issues replaced the regular characters with titles that were, for the library, completely out of character. 'Penalty of Fear' (no. 444) was a story of football and racketeering; the team at the centre of the story, Barford, was clearly a renamed Carford, one of the two sporting sides whose adventures had been told in *Tiger Sports Library*. Issue 445 was a Western, 'Return of the Renegade' and a second Western would appear the following month – remnants from the *Cowboy Picture Library*.

Using up leftovers from now departed pocket libraries were indicative that the end had arrived. March 1963 was to see the last four titles, *Thriller Picture Library* closing its doors with issue 450, as downbeat and mournful an ending as any of the John Steel stories that had been recently published.

* * * * *

The three original pocket libraries – if we ignore *Love Story Library*, which was aimed at a completely different, late teen/adult market – may have lost the fight for space in the newsagents' racks but their legacy lived on. The 1106 issues were a useful source of stories for other publications; *Comet* and *Sun* were both reprinting stories, with 'Paul Clifford' (*Thriller* no. 46), 'Island of Peril' (*Super Detective* no. 55), 'The Secret of Paul Barron' (*Super Detective* no. 22), 'The Strange Affair of the Lyons Mail' (*Thriller* no. 30), 'No Dust on My Saddle' (*Thriller* no. 71) and 'The Red Rapiers' (*Thriller* no. 78) all appearing in 1959. That same year, *Film Fun* reprinted 'Last of the Mohicans' (*Thriller* no 15), 'Rob Roy' (*Thriller*, various issues), 'The Planet of Peril' (*Super Detective* no. 29), 'Invaders From Space' (*Super Detective* no. 14), 'Kidnappers From Mars' (*Super Detective* no. 23) and 'Destination Venus' (*Super Detective* no. 35) In 1960 'The Gay Corinthian' (*Thriller* no. 39) was reprinted in *Top Spot*.

Eagle reprinted 'Stonewall Jackson' (*Thriller* no. 147) and, given the new title of 'The Sword of Fate', a newly coloured version of 'The Strong Room' (*Thriller* no. 163)[35]; *Swift* also had newly coloured episodes of Robin Hood as well as reprints of 'Captain Blood' (*Thriller* no. 50) and 'Rob Roy' (*Thriller* no. 86).

Over the years other weekly papers drew on the *Thriller Picture Library* for stories: *Hurricane* adapted Robin Hood, *Valiant* adapted Battler Britton and *Ranger* adapted 'Around the World in Eighty Days' (*Thriller* no. 180).

However, the successors of the three libraries made best use of the material as they were able to reprint without resizing: a few months after *Thriller Picture Library* ended, *Valiant Picture Library* was launched with a variety of former *Thriller* and *Cowboy Picture Library* reprints as part of the line-up. As was becoming increasingly common, characters' names were changed in some cases to make the stories appear new. Thus Spy 13 became Mike Stone adding to the confusion of later bibliographers as one episode had itself been adapted from a serial featuring *Knockout*'s Captain Phantom. *Lion Picture Library* turned *Thriller*'s Spy 13 into a new character named Nick Douglas and Dogfight Dixon into Daredevil Dawson.

Wild West Picture Library, launched in May 1966, was wholly derived from issues of *Cowboy Picture Library* and *Lone Rider Picture Library* and *Buster Adventure Library*, launched two months later, reprinted John Steel and Robin Hood stories from *Thriller* and Rick Random adventures from *Super Detective*. *Giant War Picture Library* reprinted Spy 13, Battler Britton and John Steel stories and *Air Ace Picture Library* reprinted Dogfight Dixon. Holiday Specials regularly reprinted stories from *Cowboy*, *Thriller* and *Super Detective* libraries. *Spy 13 Library Holiday Special* (1966), *Secret Agent Picture Library* (1967-70), *Super Picture Special* (1969), the first issue of *Top Secret Picture Library Holiday Special* (1976) and *Space Picture Library Holiday Special* (1977-81) all kept the reprints rolling out into the 1980s. *Wild West Picture Library Holiday Special* (1977-88), although deemed to be reprinting from the *Wild West Picture Library*, was, in fact, filled with ex-*Cowboy* and *Lone Rider Picture Library* stories.

Of all the original characters to appear in the adventure libraries, only two have seen any recent revivals. Rick Random, one of the stars of the *Space Picture Library Holiday Special*, was briefly revived in *2000AD* in 1979 after popular appearances in the *2000AD Sci-Fi Special* in 1978 and *Dan Dare Annual 1979*; and Battler Britton (already a star of *Sun* before he appeared in *Thriller Picture Library*), who starred in a new four issue adventure published by WildStorm in the USA in 2006.

It seems appropriate – since their origin began in an exported comic – to note that the stories featured in *Cowboy*, *Thriller* and *Super Detective Libraries* were widely translated in Europe, Scandinavia, South America and elsewhere abroad. For a brief period, some issues of *Thriller Comics* were reprinted in Canada.

Beyond this catalogue of reprinting, the chief legacy of the three titles that launched the pocket library boom is the picture stories themselves, still collected and read by comic fans around the world. The first-rate story-telling of the writers and the quality of the artwork made these titles amongst the best comic strips produced in the United Kingdom, if not the world, and a fitting testament to the editorial skills of Edward Holmes and Leonard Matthews who guided the titles for so many years.

Steve Holland
Colchester
February 2010

Notes

1 The cover line "64 picture-packed pages" first appeared on *Cowboy Comics* no.3, a banner being used from no.5.

2 *The Schoolgirls' Own Library* similarly slimmed down in 1947.

3 The Amalgamated Press had tried one earlier adventure comic, *Film Picture Stories*, in 1934, which adapted current movies into comics, but it ran for only 30 issues before being incorporated into *Film Fun*.

4 The cover title for the new paper changed over the years: *The Knock-Out Comic* (1939-40), *Knock-Out Comic* (1940-46), *Knockout Comic* (1946-48), *Knockout* (1948-61, 1962-63), *Billy Bunter's Knockout* (1961-62).

5 Quoted by J. Randolph Cox, *The Dime Novel Companion*, p.49, from *The Old Santa Fe Trail* by Col. Henry Inman (1897).

6 Even more mysteriously, the registration issues of *Gosport Courier* and *Stretford Courier* were not registered until March 1947.

7 Although labelled 'New Series' for the first few issues, no previous magazine of that title has been traced.

8 Quotes from Leonard Matthews used throughout are derived from an interview with Matthews by David Ashford, March 20, 1975.

9 Geoff Campion, private communication, November 10, 1990.

10 The cover was reused on *Cowboy Comics* 30 and later redrawn by Campion as the opening panel of a 'Billy the Kid' story for an issue of *Sun* in 1952; the panel was reused on the Australian *Billy the Kid* issue 38.

11 Barry Coker, interview, February 2, 1999.

12 An advert on the back cover of *Kit Carson* no.37 erroneously pictured the *Billy the Kid* title with the number 37.

13 Simon Templar had previously appeared in Charteris' novel *Meet the Tiger* (1928) but it was the stories in *The Thriller* that helped seal his position as one of the most enduring fictional characters ever.

14 Nicolle had been asked to work on Brock's drawings before. For *Lorna Doone* he was asked to draw in the faces of the hero and heroine, a task he hated.

15 Quotes from Edward Holmes used throughout are derived from a previously unpublished interview with Holmes by John Lawrence conducted in c.1998.

16 David Ashford, introduction to *Super Detective Library*, Colne, Lancashire, Byron Whitworth, 1992, p.4

17 Claude Vernon Frost was unrelated to Conrad Frost, although both Claude and his brother, Kelman Frost, were prolific writers of stories for D. C. Thomson.

18 Turner was also involved in a 20th episode – issue 91 – which he began but was unable to continue. The first page is by Turner and some subsequent panels on the next few pages are by him but the remainder of the issue is drawn by Terry Patrick.

19 Harry Harrison, 'The Beginning of the Affair', in *Hell's Cartographers*, London, Weidenfeld & Nicolson, 1975.

20 Rick Random later reappeared in *2000AD* (1979) with Ron Turner again on artwork (bar a final episode by Carlos Ezquerra). A failed experiment, it was inspired by one of the original stories, 'Rick Random and the S.O.S. from Space', being reprinted in the *2000AD Sci-Fi Special* for 1978. The story was wrongly credited to Harry Harrison; it was, in fact, written by Bob Kesten.

21 As well as being an editor and writer, Holmes was an expert on armour (carrying out repairs for the Tower of London), photography (he later became a photographer for Sotheby's) and horses and riding.

22 Barry Coker, interview, August 20, 2007.

23 James A. Storrie, interview, October 5, 2007.

24 Embleton drew pages 1-4, 28-43 and 64 plus a title page and the bottom panels of pages 7 and 63.

25 Angus Allan, private communication, February 6, 1999.

26 The artwork in question was probably for *The Island of Fu Manchu* (*Super Detective Library* no. 9).

27 In addition, Pearsons published an *Adventures of Robin Hood* pocket library as part of their *TV Picture Stories* series in 1959; Adprint produced three volumes of *The Adventures of Robin Annual* in 1956-58; Len Miller published a *Robin Hood* monthly in 1957-59, some issues reprinting American stories; and World Distributors and Streamline also published various issues of monthly titles reprinting American comics.

28 Many of the strips were scripted by Colin Thomas from plotlines devised by Mike Butterworth.

29 The Gold Medal line was reprinted in the UK by Frederick Muller Ltd.

30 Roderic Graeme was the pen-name of Roderick Jeffries, son of Graham Montague Jeffries, the creator of Blackshirt.

31 Mike Moorcock, private communication, March 15, 2004.

32 The Maltese artist was Henricus 'Harry' Farrugia, although he was living in Kensington, London, at the time.

33 David Ashford, *Super Detective Library*, Colne, Lancashire, Bryon Whitworth, 1992.

34 One further issue appeared in February 1962.

35 A coloured version of 'Under the Golden Dragon' also appeaed in *Eagle* but this was the full strip from *Comet* rather than the abridged version that appeared in *Thriller* no. 132.

Reused artwork

Artwork, especially covers, from the *Thriller Picture Library* was reused many times over the years. Occasionally the reprints differed from the originals, as in the examples here: Robin Hood has been stripped of his beard and other background adjustments have been made for this reprint of *Thriller Picture Library* 206; a reprint of *Thriller Picture Library* 183 in *Look and Learn* was doctored to add the queenly figure and a fourth musketeer.

High Toby

Dick Turpin and the Phantom of the Highway (*Thriller Picture Library* 117) was based on an H. M. Brock image originally published in 1906, carefully redrawn by Brock, as can be seen in the original artwork. The printed version had an additional insert of Turpin drawn by D. C. Eyles.

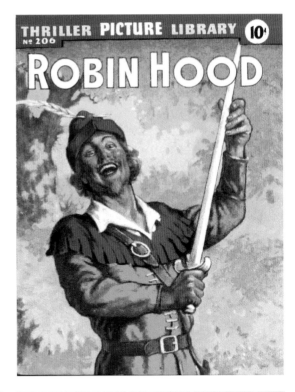

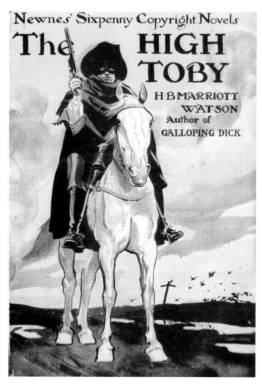

Acknowledgments

The following lists were originally pieced together in the late 1980s and the collated information published in three volumes of *Thriller Picture Library: An Illustrated Guide* published by Bryon Whitworth in 1991-92, soon superseded by a single volume edition; volumes covering *Super Detective Library* and *Cowboy Comics Library* followed in 1992 and 1993 respectively and a second edition of the *Super Detective Library* appeared in 1998.

The current volume thoroughly overhauls those lists with a great deal of new information, corrections to the original listings and coverage of a number of titles not included elsewhere.

We would like to acknowledge the tireless assistance of the many people who helped in the preparation of this volume with information and memories about their contributions to the various libraries, details culled from their collections and – something we're especially pleased to present with this volume – scans of original art boards which have, for the most part, not been seen since their original appearance fifty or so years ago.

Our thanks therefore go to Angus Allan, John Allan-Clark, John Barber, Roger Berry, Keith Chapman, Marc-André Dumonteil, Graeme Cliffe, Américo Fernandes Coelho, Barry Coker, Gerry Embleton, Duncan Goodyear, Ivan Harris, Ian Kellie, Albert King, Roy McAdorey, Jorge Magalhães, Leonard Matthews, Mike Moorcock, Peter O'Donnell, Gil Page, Kevin Patrick, Dominique Petitfaux, Peter Richardson, Colin Rudge, Jose Manuel Ruiz, François San Milan, David Slinn, Jim Storrie, Chris Street, Gerard Thomassian, Ron Tiner, Sergio Tuis, Joan Whitford, Bryon Whitworth, Geoff West and Norman Wright.

We would like to give a special thanks to John Lawrence for permission to quote from his previously unpublished interview with Edward Holmes; to David Roach and Alberto Becattini for rooting out the names of many European artists; and to Mick Harvey for giving us access to his collection of Australian AP titles.

Permissions and copyright clearance would have been a minefield had it not been for the help of David Abbott of IPC Media and Sandy Resnick of Time-Warner.

If we have inadvertently left your name off the list, please accept our apologies.

BATTLING SAMSON COMICS

DARE-DEVIL OF THE SKYWAYS

AUSTRALIAN A.P. COMICS

6D

Nº 1

The following checklist indexes the Amalgamated Press's Australian comic books for the very first time. Undated and with no internal clues as to when they were published, the dates given here are approximate, although thought to be reasonably accurate.

The early issues had a staggered release, although why this should be is unknown. The dates suggested are based on when contributors were paid, with particular note to the final stages of issue preparation, especially the colour mark-up for the covers, which usually occurred six to eight weeks before publication. Records show that regular payments were made until towards the end of 1949 when a gap of around four months occurred. It is thought that the fifth batch of titles (*Kit Carson* 5, *Buck Jones* 5, *Thunderbolt Jaxon* 5, *Tim Holt* 3) may have been delayed a month and the sixth batch, although prepared in 1949, not released until four months later in April 1950. This latter switch in schedule is based on records of when payments were made to Magazine Enterprises for reprinting strips from their *Tim Holt* comic book. It was during this latter break that the decision seems to have been made to drop *Thunderbolt Jaxon* and *Tim Holt* from the line-up. However, the precise release dates of titles around this time may be a month or two out.

Soaring printing costs caused a general price increase for all Australian comic reprints in March 1951 – an increase reflected in the A.P. comics with *Kit Carson* 16 and *Buck Jones* 16 when the price rose from 6d. to 8d. – and dates from this period onwards are throught to be correct.

From around August 1950, all the artwork was drawn in the UK *Cowboy Comics* format and was resized for the Australian comic book. Some strips were unique to the Australian comic book; other stories were subsequently reprinted in various places (mostly *Cowboy Comics*) and this is indicated in brackets after the title of each story.

  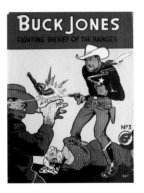 

BATTLING SAMSON

Battling Samson Comics no.1 (Jul 1949)
Cover: Geoff Campion (not reprinted)
**(a) Battling Samson and Jerry in
The Pirates of Bias Bay** (not reprinted)
Art: Geoff Campion
Script: T. C. H. Jacobs
(b) Battling Samson in The Case of the £5 Cigars!
(Knockout Fun Book 1956)
Art: Geoff Campion
Script: T. C. H. Jacobs

BILLY THE KID

Billy the Kid no.38 (Dec 1952)
Cover: Geoff Campion; reprinted from *Sun* 190 (27/09/52)
(a) Billy the Kid – Indian Fighter; reprinted from *Sun* 190,
185, 188, 186, 189 (23/08 – 27/09/52)
Art: Geoff Campion

BUCK JONES

Buck Jones no.1 (Jul 1949)
Cover: Film still
(a) Buck Jones in The Diamond Clue (*CC* 3)
Art: Geoff Campion
(b) Buck Jones & "The Joker" (*CC* 17)
Art: Geoff Campion
(c) Buck Jones & the Framed Foreman (not reprinted)
Art: Hugh McNeill

Buck Jones no.2 (Aug 1949)
Cover: Geoff Campion (not reprinted)
(a) Buck Jones—Framed! (*CC* 1)
Art: Geoff Campion
(b) Buck Jones in Golden Justice (*CC* 7, retitled)
Art: Geoff Campion
(c) Buck Jones in "Buck's Lucky Day" (*CC* 7)
Art: Geoff Campion

Buck Jones no.3 (Sep 1949)
Cover: Geoff Campion (not reprinted)
(a) Buck Jones in The War of the Fences (*CC* 5)
Art: Geoff Campion
Script: Percy Clarke
(b) Buck Jones & the Phantom Chief (*CC* 29)
Art: C. E. Montford
(c) Buck Jones in The Railroad Raid (*CC* 3)
Art: Geoff Campion
Script: Percy Clarke

Buck Jones no.4 (Oct 1949)
Cover: Geoff Campion (not reprinted)
(a) Buck Jones in The Golden Locket (*CC* 1, retitled)
Art: Geoff Campion
Script: Percy Clarke
(b) Buck Jones & the "Magpie of Marble Creek" (*CC* 3)
Art: Hugh McNeill
(c) Buck Jones in "The Deserted Town" (*CC* 17)
Art: Geoff Campion

 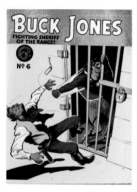  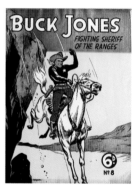

Buck Jones no.5 (Dec 1949)
Cover: Geoff Campion (not reprinted)
(a) Buck Jones in "Sterling Silver" (*CC* 21)
Art: Geoff Campion
Script: Percy Clarke
(b) Buck Jones in Rustlers' Round-Up (*CC* 41)
Art: C. E. Montford
(c) Buck Jones in "Outlaw Brand" (*CC* 5)
Art: Geoff Campion
Script: J. H. Higgins

Buck Jones no.6 (Apr 1950)
Cover: Geoff Campion (not reprinted)
(a) Buck Jones "on the Trail of the Ryders" (*CC* 1)
Art: Geoff Campion
(b) Buck Jones Outlaw! (not reprinted)
Art: Reg Bunn
(c) Buck Jones in The Hot Spot (*CC* 1, retitled)
Art: Geoff Campion

Buck Jones no.7 (May 1950)
Cover: Geoff Campion (not reprinted)
(a) Buck Jones – Rustler! (*CC* 5)
Art: Geoff Campion
(b) Buck Jones & the Wreckers of Gunsmoke Gulch
(*CC* 3)
Art: Reg Bunn
Script: J. Hunt
(c) Buck Jones & the Last of the Little Indians (*CC* 5)
Art: Reg Bunn
Script: R. V. Pothecary

Buck Jones no.8 (Jun 1950)
Cover: Geoff Campion (not reprinted)
(a) Buck Jones & the Skeleton Pass Hold-Up (*CC* 13)
Art: Robert Macgillivray
Script: J. H. Higgins
(b) Buck Jones & the Claim Jumpers (*CC* 7)
Art: Adam Horne
(c) Buck Jones Gets His Man (*CC* 29)
Art: C. E. Montford

Buck Jones no.9 (Jul 1950)
Cover: Geoff Campion (not reprinted)
(a) Buck Jones Wanted (not reprinted)
Art: Frank Bolle; redrawn (by Alf Saporito with BJ by Geoff
Campion) story from *Tim Holt Magazine* 4 (Magazine
Enterprises), Jan/Feb 1949
(b) Badge of the Lawman
Text story (Flip Carson); reprinted from *Tim Holt Magazine* 5
(Magazine Enterprises), Mar/Apr 1949
(c) Buck Jones & the Stranger (*CC* 59)
Art: Eric Parker
Script: R. V. Pothecary

Buck Jones no.10 (Aug 1950)
Cover: Geoff Campion (not reprinted)
(a) Buck Jones & the Ghost Miner
Art: Reg Bunn; reprint from *Cowboy Comics* 7
(b) Buck Jones in The Flying Spur Mystery (*CC* 13)
Art: Adam Horne
Script: R. V. Pothecary
(c) Buck Jones: The Telegrapher at Trotter's Creek
(not reprinted)
Art: Frank Bolle; redrawn (by Alf Saporito) from *Tim Holt
Magazine* 4 (Magazine Enterprises), Jan/Feb1949

Buck Jones no.11 (Sep 1950)
Cover: Geoff Campion (not reprinted)
(a) Buck Jones Meets Elmer (*CC* 11)
Art: Geoff Campion
Script: R. V. Pothecary
(b) Buck Jones & the Mystery Stampede (*CC* 35)
Art: Adam Horne
Script: J. H. Higgins
(c) Buck Jones & the Fighting Editor (*CC* 11)
Art: Reg Bunn
Script: J. H. Higgins

Buck Jones no.12 (Oct 1950)
Cover: Geoff Campion (not reprinted)
(a) Buck Jones & the "Bronco-Bus" (*CC* 17)
Art: Geoff Campion
Script: R. V. Pothecary
(b) Buck Jones & the Train Gang
Art: Robert Macgillivray; reprint from *Cowboy Comics* 11
Script: A. W. Henderson
(c) Buck Jones & the Golden Hide-Out (*CC* 13)
Art: Tom Thursby
Script: J. Hunt

Buck Jones no.13 (Nov 1950)
Cover: Geoff Campion (not reprinted)
(a) Buck Jones & the Rain-Maker
Art: Adam Horne; reprint from *Cowboy Comics* 13
Script: R. V. Pothecary
(b) Buck Jones in Tomb-stone (*CC* 19)
Art: Reg Bunn
Script: A. W. Henderson
(c) Marshal of Death Town
Text story (Flip Carson); from *Tim Holt Magazine* 6
(Magazine Enterprises), May 1949
(d) Buck Jones & the Greybeard Gang (*CC* 17)
Art: Adam Horne
Script: R. V. Pothecary

Buck Jones no.14 (Dec 1950)
Cover: Geoff Campion (not reprinted)
(a) Buck Jones & the Deadwood Dude (not reprinted)
Art: Adam Horne
(b) Buck Jones in The Battle of Ghost Town (*CC* 19)
Art: Graham Coton
(c) Buck Jones in The Mystery of Lone Valley (*CC* 31)
Art: C. E. Montford

Buck Jones no.15 (Feb 1951)
Cover: Geoff Campion (not reprinted)
(a) Buck Jones Meets the Kerrys & the Coys
Art: Geoff Campion; reprint from *Cowboy Comics* 19
Script: R. V. Pothecary
(b) Buck Jones & the Runaway Train (not reprinted)
Art: Cyril Holloway
Script: J. H. Higgins
(c) Buck Jones & the Petticoat Sheriff (*CC* 63)
Art: Tom Laidler
Script: A. W. Henderson

Buck Jones no.16 (Mar 1951)
Cover: Geoff Campion (not reprinted)
(a) Buck Jones & the Donovan Dude Ranch (*CC* 35)
Art: Robert Macgillivray
(b) Buck Jones & the Big Squirt
Art: Adam Horne; reprint from *Cowboy Comics* 21
(c) Buck Jones & the Kid Brother (not reprinted)
Art: Tom Laidler
Script: A. W. Henderson

Buck Jones no.17 (Apr 1951)
Cover: Geoff Campion (*CC* 33)
(a) Buck Jones Meets Dilly (*CC* 33)
Art: Robert Macgillivray
Script: A. W. Henderson
(b) Buck Jones Tells the Strange Story of Coy Hill
    (not reprinted)
Art: Ron Smith
Script: R. V. Pothecary
(c) Buck Jones & the Gay Caballero (*CC* 33)
Art: Robert Macgillivray
Script: A. W. Henderson

Buck Jones no.18 (May 1951)
Cover: Geoff Campion (not reprinted)
(a) Buck Jones & the Horse Thief
Art: H. C. Milburn; reprint from *Cowboy Comics* 21
(b) Buck Jones & the Great Oil Swindle
Art: Tom Laidler; reprint from *Cowboy Comics* 25
(c) Buck Jones & the Stolen Piebalds!
Art: H. C. Milburn; reprint from *Cowboy Comics* 25
(d) Buck Jones & the Killer Cougar
Art: C. E. Montford; reprint from *Cowboy Comics* 25

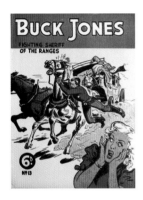   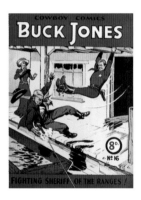

Buck Jones no.19 (Jun 1951)
Cover: Geoff Campion (*CC* 39)
(a) Buck Jones Meets the Gallant Gunman
Art: Colin Merrett; reprint from *Cowboy Comics* 27
(b) Buck Jones Battles with The Brain
Art: Robert Macgillivray; reprint from *Cowboy Comics* 27
(c) Buck Jones & the Circus Crooks (*CC* 49)
Art: H. C. Milburn
Script: A. W. Henderson

Buck Jones no.20 (Jul 1951)
Cover: Geoff Campion; also in *Cowboy Comics* 31
(a) Buck Jones & the Border Express
Art: Reg Bunn; reprint from *Cowboy Comics* 29
(b) Buck Jones & the Pistol-Packing Prince
Art: Tom Laidler; reprint from *Cowboy Comics* 27
(c) Buck Jones in the Cave of Terror
Art: Robert Macgillivray; reprint from *Cowboy Comics* 29

Buck Jones no.21 (Aug 1951)
Cover: Geoff Campion (*CC* 35)
(a) Elmer Twittley Rides Again!
Art: Geoff Campion; reprint from *Cowboy Comics* 31
(b) Buck Jones in Secret Canyon
Art: Tom Thursby; reprint from *Cowboy Comics* 21
(c) Buck Jones Meets Scarface the Scoundrel (*CC* 41)
Art: C. E. Montford

Buck Jones no.22 (Sep 1951)
Cover: Geoff Campion (*CC* 37)
(a) Buck Jones & the Mountain of Fire
Art: Colin Merrett; reprint from *Cowboy Comics* 31
(b) Buck Jones – Coward!
Art: Robert Macgillivray; reprint from *Cowboy Comics* 27
(c) Buck Jones and Bambino the Bandit! (*CC* 49)
Art: Adam Horne
Script: A. W. Henderson

Buck Jones no.23 (Oct 1951)
Cover: Geoff Campion (not reprinted)
(a) Buck Jones & the Cyclone Kid
Art: Colin Merrett; reprint from *Cowboy Comics* 35
(b) Buck Jones & the Valley of Vanishing Men (*CC* 37)
Art: Reg Bunn
(c) Buck Jones & the Boy Crook (*CC* 37)
Art: Adam Horne

Buck Jones no.24 (Nov 1951)
Cover: Geoff Campion (*CC* 41)
(a) Buck Jones & the Chinese Cook (*CC* 39)
Art: Reg Bunn
(b) Buck Jones & the Kidnapping of Dilly
Art: Tom Laidler; reprint from *Cowboy Comics* 33
(c) Buck Jones & the Cowboy Derby
Art: Unknown; reprint from *Cowboy Comics* 37
Script: J. Hunt

Buck Jones no.25 (Dec 1951)
Cover: Geoff Campion (*CC* 43)
(a) Buck Jones & the War on the Range! (*CC* 41)
Art: Geoff Campion
(b) Buck Jones & the Rancher's Money Belt
Art: Reg Bunn; reprint from *Cowboy Comics* 33
(c) Buck Jones & the Mystery Gang (not reprinted)
Art: C. E. Montford

Buck Jones no.26 (Jan 1952)
Cover: Geoff Campion (*CC* 45)
(a) Buck Jones & the 'Black Cat' Oil Gang
Art: Reg Bunn; reprint from *Cowboy Comics* 41
Script: A. W. Henderson
(b) Buck Jones & the Leaping Marshal!
Art: Tom Laidler; reprint from *Cowboy Comics* 33
(c) Buck Jones & the Dude Ranchers (*CC* 43)
Art: Reg Bunn

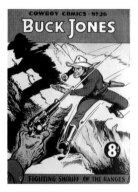

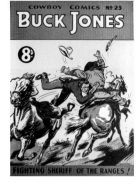

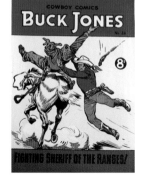

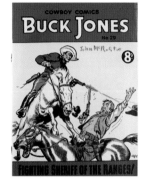
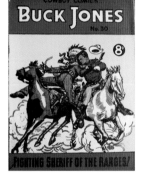

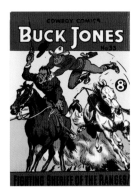 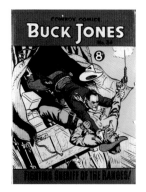  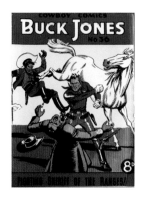

Buck Jones no.27 (Feb 1952)
Cover: Geoff Campion (*CC* 47)
(a) The Cyclone Kid Rides Again
Art: Colin Merrett; reprint from *Cowboy Comics* 43
(b) Buck Jones and Desperate Dilly (*CC* 83)
Art: Tom Laidler
(c) Buck Jones & the Chinese Trouble-Chaser (*CC* 45)
Art: Reg Bunn
Script: A. W. Henderson

Buck Jones no.28 (Mar 1952)
Cover: Geoff Campion (not reprinted)
(a) Buck Jones & the Rio Bandits!
Art: Colin Merrett; reprint from *Cowboy Comics* 45
Script: A. W. Henderson
(b) Buck Jones Meets Kid Dynamite (*CC* 53)
Art: C. E. Montford
Script: A. W. Henderson
(c) Buck Jones & the Battling Bronco
Art: Geoff Campion; reprint from *Cowboy Comics* 43

Buck Jones no.29 (Apr 1952)
Cover: Geoff Campion; also in *Cowboy Comics* 49
(a) Buck Jones in Gunman's Round-Up
Art: F. A. Philpott; reprint from *Cowboy Comics* 45
(b) Buck Jones' Rescue Ride
Art: Reg Bunn; reprints "Buck Jones' Rescue Mission" from *Cowboy Comics* 39
(c) Buck Jones Meets The Fighting Shepherd
Art: Cyril Holloway; reprint from *Cowboy Comics* 45
Script: A. W. Henderson

Buck Jones no.30 (May 1952)
Cover: Robert Forrest (not reprinted)
(a) Buck Jones & the Train Battle!
Art: Colin Merrett; reprint from *Cowboy Comics* 45
Script: J. Hunt
(b) Buck Jones & the Red Raiders (*CC* 53)
Art: Reg Bunn
Script: A. W. Henderson
(c) Buck Jones' Battle-on-Wheels! (*CC* 61)
Art: Reg Bunn

Buck Jones no.31 (Jun 1952)
Cover: Geoff Campion; also in *Cowboy Comics* 53
(a) Buck Jones & the Barn Dance Bandits
Art: Tom Laidler; reprint from *Cowboy Comics* 45
Script: A. W. Henderson
(b) Buck Jones & the Payroll Robbery
Art: H. C. Milburn; reprint from *Cowboy Comics* 45
Script: A. W. Henderson
(c) Buck Jones & the Millionaire Cowboy
Art: Reg Bunn; reprint from *Cowboy Comics* 51
Script: J. H. Higgins

Buck Jones no.32 (Jul 1952)
Cover: Geoff Campion (*CC* 61)
(a) Buck Jones & the Ghost Train
Art: H. C. Milburn; reprint from *Cowboy Comics* 51
Script: A. W. Henderson
(b) Buck Jones & the Spanish Treasure! (*CC* 57)
Art: Vic Anderson
Script: A. W. Henderson
(c) Buck Jones & the Kid Lawman
Art: Stephen Chapman; reprint from *Cowboy Comics* 45
Script: J. H. Higgins

Buck Jones no.33 (Aug 1952)
Cover: H. C. Milburn; also in *Cowboy Comics* 57
(a) Buck Jones & the Mail Thieves
Art: H. C. Milburn; reprint from *Cowboy Comics* 53
Script: R. V. Pothecary
(b) Buck Jones on the Vengeance Trail
Art: Colin Merrett; reprint from *Cowboy Comics* 45
(c) Buck Jones versus the Rough Rider Gang
Art: Robert Macgillivray; reprint from *Cowboy Comics* 37
(d) Buck Jones and El Toro
Art: Reg Bunn; reprint from *Cowboy Comics* 43
Script: J. Hunt

 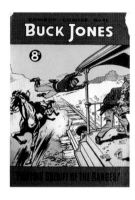  

Buck Jones no.34 (Sep 1952)
Cover: H. C. Milburn; also in *Cowboy Comics* 59
(a) Buck Jones & the Danger Trail
Art: C. E. Montford; reprint from *Cowboy Comics* 57
Script: A. W. Henderson
(b) Buck Jones & the Return of the Cyclone Kid
   (not reprinted)
Art: Tom Laidler
Script: A. W. Henderson
(c) Buck Jones in Skull City (not reprinted)
Art: Reg Bunn
Script: A. W. Henderson

Buck Jones no.35 (Oct 1952)
Cover: H. C. Milburn (not reprinted)
(a) Buck Jones & the Man Tamer
Art: H. C. Milburn; reprint from *Cowboy Comics* 57
Script: A. W. Henderson
(b) Buck Jones & the Phantom Bandits
Art: C. E. Montford; reprint from *Cowboy Comics* 51
Script: A. W. Henderson
(c) Buck Jones & the Rookie Ranger
Art: Tom Laidler; reprint from *Cowboy Comics* 59
Script: A. W. Henderson

Buck Jones no.36 (Nov 1952)
Cover: Graham Coton (*CC* 67)
(a) Buck Jones Meets Double Trouble (*CC* 67)
Art: H. C. Milburn
Script: J. H. Higgins
(b) The Six-Gun Justice of Buck Jones
Art: Vic Anderson, with additional art by Geoff Campion;
reprint from *Cowboy Comics* 61
Script: A. W. Henderson
(c) Buck Jones & the Gold Grab! (not reprinted)
Art: Reg Bunn

Buck Jones no.39 (New Series) (Jan 1953)
Cover: Graham Coton; reprint from *Cowboy Comics* 65
(a) Buck Jones & the King of the Rio!
Art: C. E. Montford; reprint from *Cowboy Comics* 59
Script: J. H. Higgins
(b) Buck Jones & the Lost Valley
Art: H. C. Milburn; reprint from *Cowboy Comics* 63
Script: A. W. Henderson

Buck Jones no.41 (New Series) (Feb 1953)
Cover: Geoff Campion, adapted from a Billy the Kid cover
from *Sun* 198 (22/11/52) with BJ by another artist
(a) Buck Jones & the Aztec God!
Art: Bill Lacey; reprint from *Cowboy Comics* 65
Script: A. W. Henderson
(b) Buck Jones & the Stagecoach Snatch
Art: Selby Donnison; reprint from *Cowboy Comics* 65
Script: J. H. Higgins
(c) Buck Jones & the Million Dollar Bandits
Art: C. E. Montford; reprint from *Cowboy Comics* 63
Script: A. W. Henderson

Buck Jones no.43 (New Series) (Mar 1953)
Cover: D. C. Eyles, adapted from a Billy the Kid cover from
Sun 208 (31/01/53) with BJ by another artist
(a) Buck Jones & the Pageant Pirates
Art: Bill Lacey; reprint from *Cowboy Comics* 65
Script: A. W. Henderson
(b) Buck Jones in the City of Gold!
Art: Colin Merrett; reprint from *Cowboy Comics* 67

CAPTAIN FLAME

Captain Flame no.1 (Aug 1949)
Cover: W. Bryce-Hamilton (not reprinted)
(a) Captain Flame (not reprinted)
Art: Eric Parker
Script: Leonard Matthews
(b) Captain Flame Joins The Navy (not reprinted)
Art: Eric Parker
Script: Percy Clarke
(c) Captain Flame & the Lady from the Sea
   (not reprinted)
Art: Eric Parker
Script: Percy Clarke

KIT CARSON

Kit Carson no.1 (Jul 1949)
Cover: Film still
(a) Kit Carson – King of the West! (*CC* 6)
Art: D. C. Eyles
(b) Kit Carson & the Dillon Killers (*Comet* 141-143)
Art: D. C. Eyles
(c) Kit Carson in Old Wyoming (*CC* 2)
Art: D. C. Eyles

Note: scripts by Leonard Matthews, Ron Clark

Kit Carson no.2 (Aug 1949)
Cover: D. C. Eyles (not reprinted)
(a) Kit Carson & the Black Hoods (*CC* 2)
Art: W. Bryce-Hamilton
Script: Edward Holmes
(b) Kit Carson & the Worthless Gold Mine
  (not reprinted)
Art: D. C. Eyles; reprint (with KC by E. C. Julian) from
'The Phantom Sheriff', *Knockout Fun Book* 1949
(c) Kit Carson Fights the Crooked Sheriff (*CC* 4)
Art: E. C. Julian

Kit Carson no.3 (Sep 1949)
Cover: D. C. Eyles (*CC* 48)
(a) Kit Carson Rides The Covered Waggon Trail
  (*CC* 64)
Art: E. C. Julian
(b) Kit Carson & the Tough Tenderfoot (*CC* 2)
Art: Eric Parker
(c) Kit Carson and Running Dog's Man Trap (*CC* 18)
Art: E. C. Julian

Kit Carson no.4 (Oct 1949)
Cover: D. C. Eyles (not reprinted)
(a) Kit Carson & the Haunted Cavern (not reprinted)
Art: E. C. Julian
(b) Kit Carson Gets His Man (not reprinted)
Art: E. C. Julian
(c) Kit Carson & the "Pay or Die" Gang (*CC* 14)
Art: Adam Horne

Kit Carson no.5 (Dec 1949)
Cover: D. C. Eyles (not reprinted)
(a) Kit Carson Rides the Pony Mail
  (*CC* 2/*Comet* 238-242)
Art: D. C. Eyles
(b) Kit Carson & the Stage Coach Killers (*CC* 6)
Art: Reg Bunn
(c) Kit Carson & the Boss of Thunder River (*CC* 4)
Art: John Woods

Kit Carson no.6 (Apr 1950)
Cover: D. C. Eyles (not reprinted)
(a) Kit Carson & the Salt-Water Waggoner (*CC* 4)
Art: D. C. Eyles
Script: Edward Holmes
(b) Inside the Rodeo
Text feature (Billy Jackson)
(c) Kit Carson Rides the Trail of Fire (*CC* 4)
Art: Cyril Holloway
Script: Edward Holmes
(d) Kit Carson and Killers' Justice (not reprinted)
Art: Reg Bunn
Script: J. H. Higgins

Kit Carson no.7 (May 1950)
Cover: D. C. Eyles (not reprinted)
(a) Kit Carson South of the Border (*CC* 6)
Art: E. C. Julian
(b) Kit Carson & the Border Bandits (*CC* 6)
Art: Cyril Holloway
Script: J. H. Higgins
(c) Kit Carson & the Hooded Avengers (*CC* 8)
Art: Adam Horne

Kit Carson no.8 (Jun 1950)
Cover: Geoff Campion (not reprinted)
(a) Kit Carson & the Battle of Death Valley (*CC* 10)
Art: C. E. Montford
Script: J. H. Higgins
(b) Kit Carson & the Safe Snatchers (*CC* 18)
Art: Adam Horne
Script: J. H. Higgins
(c) Kit Carson & the Gun-Runners (*CC* 10)
Art: E. C. Julian
Script: E. H. Hamil

Kit Carson no.9 (Jul 1950)
Cover: Geoff Campion (not reprinted)
(a) Kit Carson & the Rodeo Raiders (CC 8)
Art: Geoff Campion
Script: Edward Holmes
(b) Kit Carson & the Pretty Pioneer (CC 28)
Art: Cyril Holloway
(c) Kit Carson in the Valley of Burning Stones (CC 8)
Art: Adam Horne
Script: Edward Holmes

Kit Carson no.10 (Aug 1950)
Cover: Geoff Campion (not reprinted)
(a) Kit Carson & the Outlaw Senorita (CC 10)
Art: Roland Davies
(b) Kit Carson and Bad Bill's Baby (CC 10)
Art: Adam Horne
Script: J. Hunt
(c) Kit Carson & the Stage Coach Kidnappers
Art: Adam Horne; reprint from Cowboy Comics 8

Kit Carson no.11 (Sep 1950)
Cover: Geoff Campion (CC 18)
(a) Kit Carson & the Redskin Rising! (CC 14)
Art: Geoff Campion
Script: A. W. Henderson
(b) Kit Carson in Bad Medicine (CC 14)
Art: Adam Horne
Script: R. V. Pothccary
(c) Kit Carson in Redskin Canyon (CC 16)
Art: Cyril Holloway

Kit Carson no.12 (Oct 1950)
Cover: Geoff Campion (CC 38)
(a) Kit Carson & the Terror of Coyote Creek (CC 16)
Art: Edgar Spenceley
(b) Kit Carson Fights the Fire God! (not reprinted)
Art: Graham Coton
Script: J. H. Higgin
(c) Kit Carson & the Old Magician (not reprinted)
Art: Adam Horne
Script: A. W. Henderson

Kit Carson no.13 (Nov 1950)
Cover: Geoff Campion (not reprinted)
(a) Kit Carson's Double Trouble (CC 16)
Art: Graham Coton
Script: A. W. Henderson
(b) Kit Carson's Running Battle
Art: Graham Coton; reprint from Cowboy Comics 14
Script: J. H. Higgins
(c) Kit Carson & the Trail of the Phantom Rider
(not reprinted)
Art: Tom Thursby

Kit Carson no.14 (Dec 1950)
Cover: Geoff Campion (not reprinted)
(a) Kit Carson & the Colonel's Daughter (CC 18)
Art: Graham Coton
Script: J. Hunt
(b) Kit Carson & the Gold Rush (CC 18)
Art: Robert Macgillivray
(c) Kit Carson Meets Lord Clarence (not reprinted)
Art: Artist [A]

Kit Carson no.15 (Feb 1951)
Cover: Geoff Campion (not reprinted)
(a) Kit Carson & the Race to the Red Hills (CC 28)
Art: Reg Bunn
Script: J. H. Higgins
(b) Kit Carson & the Stolen Ranch (CC 22)
Art: Artist [A]
Script: J. H. Higgins
(c) Kit Carson & the Renegade Raiders (CC 36)
Art: Reg Bunn
Script: Maurice Creswick

Kit Carson no.16 (Mar 1951)
Cover: Geoff Campion (CC 94)
(a) Kit Carson & the River Raid (CC 56)
Art: Graham Coton
(b) Kit Carson Meets the Peaceful Irishman
(not reprinted)
Art: Adam Horne
(c) Kit Carson & the Bullet-Proof Buckaroo
(not reprinted)
Art: Alfred Taylor, with alts by Graham Coton
Script: A. W. Henderson

Kit Carson no.17 (Apr 1951)
Cover: Geoff Campion (*CC* 30)
(a) Kit Carson's One Man Battle!
Art: Peter Sutherland; reprint from *Cowboy Comics* 22
Script: A. W. Henderson
(b) Kit Carson & the Runaway River
Art: Graham Coton; reprint from *Cowboy Comics* 22
Script: A. W. Henderson
(c) Kit Carson and Fools' Gold (not reprinted)
Art: Adam Horne
Script: A. W. Henderson

Kit Carson no.18 (May 1951)
Cover: Geoff Campion (*CC* 32)
(a) Kit Carson & the Train Raid
Art: Graham Coton; reprint from *Cowboy Comics* 24
(b) Kit Carson & the Trail of Terror
Art: Artist [A]; reprint from *Cowboy Comics* 24
(c) Kit Carson & the Secret of Fort Mustang (*CC* 28)
Art: Cyril Holloway

Kit Carson no.19 (Jun 1951)
Cover: Geoff Campion
        (adapted by another hand as *CC* 99)
(a) Kit Carson & the Relief of Fort Lonesome
Art: Robert Forrest; reprint from *Cowboy Comics* 26
(b) Kit Carson & the Mail Race
Art: Adam Horne; reprint from *Cowboy Comics* 26
(c) Kit Carson & the Wheel-Chair Sheriff
Art: Graham Coton; reprint from *Cowboy Comics* 24

Kit Carson no.20 (Jul 1951)
Cover: D. C. Eyles (not reprinted)
(a) Kit Carson's Peaceful War
Art: Robert Forrest; reprint from *Cowboy Comics* 30
Script: A. W. Henderson
(b) Kit Carson & the Sun Worshippers
Art: Cyril Holloway; reprint from *Cowboy Comics* 30
(c) Kit Carson & the Border Wreckers
Art: Graham Coton; reprint from *Cowboy Comics* 28

Kit Carson no.21 (Aug 1951)
Cover: Geoff Campion (*CC* 34)
(a) Kit Carson's Blood Brother
Art: F. A. Philpott; reprint from *Cowboy Comics* 32
(b) Kit Carson & the Mule Train Crooks
Art: Adam Horne; reprint from *Cowboy Comics* 32
(c) Kit Carson & the Wild Stallion (*CC* 34)
Art: F. A. Philpott
Script: J. Hunt

Kit Carson no.22 (Sep 1951)
Cover: Geoff Campion (*Kit Carson's Autograph Book of Cowboy Heroes*, 1951)
(a) Kit Carson's Fire Magic
Art: Robert Forrest; reprint from *Cowboy Comics* 32
(b) Kit Carson & the Prairie Wolves (*CC* 48)
Art: Graham Coton
Script: J. H. Higgins
(c) Kit Carson & the Scarlet Feather
Art: Cyril Holloway; reprint from *Cowboy Comics* 34

Kit Carson no.23 (Oct 1951)
Cover: Geoff Campion (*CC* 40)
(a) Kit Carson & the Peril of Thunder River (*CC* 38)
Art: Peter Sutherland
(b) Kit Carson & the Mactaw Treaty
Art: Adam Horne; reprint from *Cowboy Comics* 36
(c) Kit Carson – Renegade! (not reprinted)
Art: Reg Bunn

Kit Carson no.24 (Nov 1951)
Cover: Geoff Campion (*CC* 42)
(a) Kit Carson & the Windmill War (*CC* 40)
Art: Robert Forrest
(b) Kit Carson's Desert Danger
Art: Patrick Nicolle; reprint from *Cowboy Comics* 34
(c) Kit Carson & the Haunted Sheriff (not reprinted)
Art: Reg Bunn
Script: A. W. Henderson

Kit Carson no.25 (Dec 1951)
Cover: Geoff Campion (*CC* 44)
(a) Kit Carson to the Rescue (*CC* 42)
Art: Robert Forrest
Script: A. W. Henderson
(b) Kit Carson in Crossbones County
Art: Adam Horne; reprint from *Cowboy Comics* 38
Script: A. W. Henderson
(c) Kit Carson Meets Sitting Bull! (*CC* 44)
Art: Eric Parker
Script: A. W. Henderson

Kit Carson no.26 (Jan 1952)
Cover: Geoff Campion (*CC* 46)
(a) Kit Carson & the Blackfeet Rising!
Art: Peter Sutherland; reprint from *Cowboy Comics* 42
(b) Kit Carson Fights Lynch Law! (*CC* 46)
Art: Robert Forrest
Script: J. Hunt
(c) Kit Carson versus the Moran Gang (*CC* 54)
Art: Adam Horne
Script: A. W. Henderson

Kit Carson no.27 (Feb 1952)
Cover: Robert Forrest; adapted from *Cowboy Comics* 36
(a) Kit Carson & the Buffalo-Indians (*CC* 42)
Art: C. E. Drury; reprint from *Cowboy Comics* 42
(b) Kit Carson & the Water Battle!
Art: Robert Forrest; reprint from *Cowboy Comics* 44
Script: J. Hunt
(c) Kit Carson & the Dynamite War! (*CC* 48)
Art: Adam Horne
Script: A. W. Henderson

Kit Carson no.28 (Mar 1952)
Cover: Geoff Campion (not reprinted)
(a) Kit Carson & the Magic Eye (*CC* 48)
Art: Robert Forrest
Script: J. Hunt
(b) Kit Carson's Fire Battle (*CC* 50)
Art: Patrick Nicolle
Script: A. W. Henderson
(c) Kit Carson's Phantom Squadron
Art: F. A. Philpott; reprint from *Cowboy Comics* 40
Script: A. W. Henderson

Kit Carson no.29 (Apr 1952)
Cover: Geoff Campion; also in *Cowboy Comics* 50
(a) Kit Carson & the Terror of Thunder Pass
Art: Peter Sutherland; reprint from *Cowboy Comics* 46
(b) Kit Carson & the Dance of the Drums (*CC* 50)
Art: Graham Coton
Script: J. Hunt
(c) Kit Carson & the Big Clean-Up (not reprinted)
Art: Artist [A], with additional art by J. Compari

Kit Carson no.30 (May 1952)
Cover: Geoff Campion; also in *Cowboy Comics* 52
(a) Kit Carson Battles Through
Art: Peter Sutherland; reprint from *Cowboy Comics* 48
Script: A. W. Henderson
(b) Kit Carson & the Bullion Bandits (*CC* 68)
Art: Robert Forrest
Script: J. Hunt
(c) Kit Carson Rides the Trail of Wire
Art: Adam Horne; reprint from *Cowboy Comics* 44
Script: R. V. Pothecary

Kit Carson no.31 (Jun 1952)
Cover: Geoff Campion (not reprinted)
(a) Kit Carson and Peril on the Pony Express (*CC* 60)
Art: Eric Parker
Script: J. Hunt
(b) Kit Carson Meets the Giant of Timber Canyon
Art: Cyril Holloway; reprint from *Cowboy Comics* 42
(c) Kit Carson & the River Raiders (not reprinted)
Art: Adam Horne

Kit Carson no.32 (Jul 1952)
Cover: Geoff Campion; also in *Cowboy Comics* 56
(a) Kit Carson & the Red White Man
Art: Joe Colquhoun; reprint from *Cowboy Comics* 52
(b) Kit Carson Rides the Pony Express (not reprinted)
Art: Graham Coton
(c) Kit Carson & the Secret Orders
Art: Philip Mendoza; reprint from *Cowboy Comics* 50
Script: A. W. Henderson

Kit Carson no.33 (Aug 1952)
Cover: H. C. Milburn; also in *Cowboy Comics* 58
(a) Kit Carson's One Man Army (*Comet* 192-197)
Art: Peter Sutherland
(b) Kit Carson & the Terror of Cactus City
Art: Robert Forrest; reprint from *Cowboy Comics* 54
Script: A. W. Henderson

Kit Carson no.34 (Sep 1952)
Cover: H. C. Milburn; also in *Cowboy Comics* 60
(a) Kid Carson & the Redskin's Revenge
Art: Robert Forrest; reprint from *Cowboy Comics* 56
Script: A. W. Henderson
(b) Kit Carson and Dizzy Dixon's Danger Drive
(not reprinted)
Art: Adam Horne
(c) Kit Carson & the Outlaw Tribe
Art: Artist [A], with additional art by J. Compari;
reprint from *Cowboy Comics* 58
Script: A. W. Henderson

Kit Carson no.35 (Oct 1952)
Cover: H. C. Milburn; also in *Cowboy Comics* 62
(a) Kit Carson & the Secret of the Swamps
Art: Robert Forrest; reprint from *Cowboy Comics* 58
Script: A. W. Henderson
(b) Kit Carson Takes the War Path! (*Comet* 198-203)
Art: Cyril Holloway

Kit Carson no.36 (Nov 1952)
Cover: Eric Parker (not reprinted)
(a) Kit Carson & the Redskin Rising (*Comet* 208-210)
Art: D. C. Eyles
Note: A different story to that of the same title in issue 11
(b) Kit Carson & the Iron Horse (not reprinted)
Art: Adam Horne
(c) Kit Carson Breaks the Tyrant
Art: Artist [A], with additional art by J. Compari;
reprint from *Cowboy Comics* 62
Script: A. W. Henderson

Kit Carson no.37 (Dec 1952)
Cover: Graham Coton; reprint from *Cowboy Comics* 64
(a) Kit Carson Saves the Dying Fort
Art: Peter Sutherland; reprint from *Cowboy Comics* 64
Script: A. W. Henderson
(b) Kit Carson & the Thunder-God
Art: Graham Coton; reprint from *Cowboy Comics* 52
Script: A. W. Henderson
(c) Kit Carson & the Kidnapped General!
Art: Adam Horne; reprint from *Cowboy Comics* 64
Script: J. Hunt

Kit Carson no.40 (New Series) (Jan 1953)
Cover: Graham Coton; reprint from *Cowboy Comics* 66
(a) Kit Carson and Rogues Round-Up
Art: Peter Sutherland; reprint from *Cowboy Comics* 60
(b) Kit Carson & the Vanishing Forts
Art: Graham Coton; reprint from *Cowboy Comics* 58
Script: A. W. Henderson

Kit Carson no.42 (Feb 1953)
Cover: Terry Patrick (not reprinted)
(a) Kit Carson & the Pill Pedlar
Art: D. C. Eyles; reprint from *Cowboy Comics* 66
Script: J. Hunt
(b) Kit Carson Meets Reckless Ryan
Art: Robert Forrest; resized reprint from *Cowboy Comics* 52
Script: A. W. Henderson
(c) Kit Carson Meets Zarna the Wild-Man
Art: Cyril Holloway; reprint from *Cowboy Comics* 60
Script: A. W. Henderson

Kit Carson no.44 (Mar 1953)
Cover: Graham Coton; reprint from *Cowboy Comics* 68
(a) Kit Carson's Perilous Mission!
Art: Peter Sutherland; reprint from *Cowboy Comics* 68
(b) Kit Carson & the Battle of the Floating Store
Art: Graham Coton; reprint from *Cowboy Comics* 62

THUNDERBOLT JAXON

Thunderbolt Jaxon no.1 (Jul 1949)
Cover: Hugh McNeill (not reprinted)
(a) Here Comes Thunderbolt Jaxon (not reprinted)
Art: Hugh McNeill
Script: T. C. H. Jacobs (story)/Leonard Matthews (script)
(b) Thunderbolt Jaxon & the Train Robbers
(not reprinted)
Art: Hugh McNeill
Script: T. C. H. Jacobs (story)/Leonard Matthews (script)
(c) Thunderbolt Jaxon & the Man Who Lost His Memory (not reprinted)
Art: Hugh McNeill
Script: T. C. H. Jacobs (story)/Leonard Matthews (script)

Thunderbolt Jaxon no.2 (Aug 1949)
Cover: Hugh McNeill (not reprinted)
(a) Thunderbolt Jaxon & the Frightened Lion Tamer
(*Knockout Annual* 1958)
Art: Hugh McNeill
(b) Thunderbolt Jaxon & the Mystery of Cavern Island
(not reprinted)
Art: Hugh McNeill
(c) Thunderbolt Jaxon & the Honest Safe-Breaker
(not reprinted)
Art: Hugh McNeill

Thunderbolt Jaxon no.3 (Sep 1949)
Cover: Hugh McNeill (not reprinted)
(a) Thunderbolt Jaxon & the Kidnapped Princess
(not reprinted)
Art: Hugh McNeill
(b) Thunderbolt Jaxon & the Flying Wreckers
(*Knockout Annual* 1959)
Art: Hugh McNeill
(c) Thunderbolt Jaxon & the Kidnappers
(*Knockout Annual* 1959)
Art: Hugh McNeill

Thunderbolt Jaxon no.4 (Oct 1949)
Cover: Geoff Campion (not reprinted)
(a) Thunderbolt Jaxon & the Island Princess
(not reprinted)
Art: Unknown
(b) Thunderbolt Jaxon & the Queen of the Ice
(not reprinted)
Art: Hugh McNeill
(c) Thunderbolt Jaxon – Genie
(*Knockout Annual* 1958)
Art: Hugh McNeill

Thunderbolt Jaxon no.5 (Dec 1949)
Cover: Robert Rodger (not reprinted)
(a) Thunderbolt Jaxon & the Golden Princess
(*Knockout Annnual* 1960)
Art: Hugh McNeill
Script: J. H. Higgins
(b) Thunderbolt Jaxon & the Unknown Fair
(not reprinted)
Art: Unknown
Script: Edward Holmes
(c) Thunderbolt Jaxon & the Glamorous Cannon-Ball
(*Knockout Annnual* 1960)
Art: Unknown
Script: E. H. Hamil (story)/J. H. Higgins (script)

Thunderbolt Jaxon no.6 (Apr 1950)
Cover: Geoff Campion (from a sketch by Hugh McNeill)
(not reprinted)
(a) Thunderbolt Jaxon & the Mountain of Diamonds!
(not reprinted)
Art: Geoff Campion
Script: Edward Holmes
(b) Thunderbolt Jaxon & the Bride of Tapu-Tapu
(not reprinted)
Art: Unknown
Script: Edward Holmes
(c) Thunderbolt Jaxon & the Precious Tennis Balls
(not reprinted)
Art: Hugh McNeill
Script: J. H. Higgins

TIM HOLT

Tim Holt no.1 (Sep 1949)
Cover: Geoff Campion (not reprinted)
(a) Satan's Stagecoach
Art: Frank Bolle; reprint from *Tim Holt A1* 14
    (Magazine Enterprises), Jul/Aug 1948
(b) The Sheriff of Rail's End
Art: Frank Bolle; reprint from *Tim Holt A1* 14
    (Magazine Enterprises), Jul/Aug 1948

Tim Holt no.2 (Oct 1949)
Cover: Geoff Campion (not reprinted)
(a) Crime's Pony Express!
Art: Frank Bolle; reprint from *Tim Holt A1* 17
    (Magazine Enterprises), Sep/Oct 1948
(b) The Spur of the Conquistadore!
Art: Frank Bolle; reprint from *Tim Holt A1* 14
    (Magazine Enterprises), Jul/Aug 1948
(c) The Masks of Massacre Bend
Art: Frank Bolle; reprint from *Tim Holt A1* 17
    (Magazine Enterprises), Sep/Oct 1948

Tim Holt no.3 (Dec 1949)
Cover: Geoff Campion (not reprinted)
(a) The Railroad at Apache Arroyo
Art: Frank Bolle; reprint from *Tim Holt A1* 19 (Magazine
    Enterprises),Nov/Dec 1948
(b) Six Guns at Snake Cave
Text story (Flip Carson); reprint from *Tim Holt A1* 19
(Magazine Enterprises),Nov/Dec 1948
(c) The Blanket of the Navajos
Art: Frank Bolle; reprint from *Tim Holt A1* 17 (Magazine
    Enterprises), Sep/Oct 1948
d) Prairie Poison
Art: Frank Bolle; reprints "Ramrod of Rustler Range" from
    Tim Holt A1 19 (Magazine Enterprises),Nov/Dec 1948

Tim Holt no.4 (Apr 1950)
Cover: Geoff Campion (not reprinted)
(a) Tim Holt's Last Ride!
Art: Frank Bolle; reprint from *Tim Holt A1* 19
    (Magazine Enterprises), Nov/Dec 1948
(b) Noose for a Killer
Text story (Flip Carson); reprint from *Tim Holt* 4
(Magazine Enterprises), Jan/Feb 1949
(c) The Ghost on Haunted Mountain!
Art: Frank Bolle; reprint from *Tim Holt* 4
    (Magazine Enterprises), Jan/Feb 1949

BUCK
JONES

HE
GHTING
HERIFF

COWBOY COMICS

COWBOY
COMICS
7.D
Nº 1

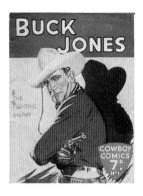  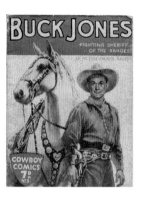 

01 (06/04/50)
Buck Jones – The Fighting Sheriff
Cover: Geoff Campion; based on the film still (used on
Buck Jones 1 (Australia)) of Buck Jones
(a) Buck Jones On the Trail of the Ryders
Art: Geoff Campion; also in Buck Jones 6 (Australia)
(b) Buck Jones & the Secret of the Locket
Art: Geoff Campion; reprints 'Buck Jones in The Golden
Locket' from *Buck Jones* 4 (Australia)
Script: Percy Clarke
(c) Buck Jones – Framed!
Art: Geoff Campion; reprint from *Buck Jones* 2 (Australia)
(d) Buck Jones & the Five Aces
Art: Geoff Campion; also as 'Buck Jones in The Hot Spot'
in *Buck Jones* 6 (Australia)

02 (06/04/50)
Kit Carson – King of the West
Cover: George Cattermole; based on a film still (used on
Kit Carson 1 (Australia)) of Jon Hall as Kit Carson
(a) Kit Carson & the Renegade Guns
Art: D. C. Eyles; reprints 'Kit Carson Rides the Pony Mail'
from *Kit Carson* 5 (Australia)
(b) Kit Carson & the Tough Tenderfoot
Art: Eric Parker; reprint from *Kit Carson* 3 (Australia)
(c) Kit Carson & the Black Hoods
Art: W. Bryce-Hamilton; reprint from *Kit Carson* 2 (Australia)
(d) Kit Carson in Old Wyoming
Art: D. C. Eyles; reprint from *Kit Carson* 1 (Australia)

03 (04/05/50)
Buck Jones – Fighting Sheriff of the Ranges
Cover: George Cattermole, based on a film still
(a) Buck Jones in The Diamond Clue
Art: Geoff Campion; reprint from *Buck Jones* 1 (Australia)
(b) Buck Jones & the Wreckers of Gunsmoke Gulch
Art: Reg Bunn; also in *Buck Jones* 7 (Australia)
Script: J. Hunt
(c) Buck Jones & the Magpie of Marble Creek
Art: Hugh McNeill; reprint from *Buck Jones* 4 (Australia)
(d) Buck Jones in The Railroad Raid
Art: Geoff Campion; reprint from *Buck Jones* 3 (Australia)
Script: Percy Clarke

04 (04/05/50)
Kit Carson – King of the West
Cover: George Cattermole, based on a film still of Jon Hall
as Kit Carson
(a) Kit Carson & the Salt Water Waggoner
Art: D. C. Eyles; reprint from *Kit Carson* 6 (Australia)
Script: Edward Holmes
(b) Kit Carson Rides the Trail of Fire
Art: Cyril Holloway; reprint from *Kit Carson* 6 (Australia)
Script: Edward Holmes
(c) Kit Carson & the Boss of Thunder River
Art: John Woods; reprint from *Kit Carson* 5 (Australia)
(d) Kit Carson Fights the Crooked Sheriff
Art: E. C. Julian; reprint from *Kit Carson* 2 (Australia)

05 (01/06/50)
Buck Jones – The Fighting Sheriff
Cover: George Cattermole
(a) Buck Jones—Rustler!
Art: Geoff Campion; reprint from *Buck Jones* 7 (Australia)
(b) Buck Jones in The War of the Fences
Art: Geoff Campion & another; reprint from *Buck Jones* 3
(Australia)
Script: Percy Clarke
(c) Buck Jones in Outlaw Brand
Art: Geoff Campion; reprint from *Buck Jones* 5 (Australia)
Script: J. H. Higgins
(d) Buck Jones & the Last of the Little Indians
Art: Reg Bunn; reprint from *Buck Jones* 7 (Australia)
Script: R. V. Pothecary

06 (01/06/50)
Kit Carson – King of the West
Cover: George Cattermole, based on a still of George
Montgomery from the film *Davy Crockett, Indian Scout*
(1950, released in the UK as Indian Scout)
(a) Kit Carson – King of the West
Art: D. C. Eyles; reprint from *Kit Carson* 1 (Australia)
(b) Kit Carson – South of the Border
Art: E. C. Julian; reprint from *Kit Carson* 7 (Australia)
(c) Kit Carson & the Border Bandits
Art: Cyril Holloway; reprint from *Kit Carson* 7 (Australia)
Script: J. H. Higgins
(d) Kit Carson & the Stagecoach Killers
Art: Reg Bunn; reprint from *Kit Carson* 5 (Australia)

07 (06/07/50)
Buck Jones – Fighting Sheriff of the Ranges
Cover: Adam Horne
(a) Buck Jones & the Ghost Miner
Art: Reg Bunn
(b) Buck Jones Meets Gentleman Joe
Art: Geoff Campion; reprints 'Buck Jones in Golden
Justice' from *Buck Jones* 2 (Australia)
(c) Buck's Lucky Day
Art: Geoff Campion; reprint from *Buck Jones* 2 (Australia)
(d) Buck Jones & the Claim Jumpers
Art: Adam Horne; reprint from *Buck Jones* 8 (Australia)

08 (06/07/50)
Kit Carson – King of the West
Cover: Adam Horne
(a) Kit Carson & the Rodeo Raiders
Art: Geoff Campion; also in *Kit Carson* 9 (Australia)
Script: Edward Holmes
(b) Kit Carson & the Stage Coach Kidnappers
Art: Adam Horne
(c) Kit Carson & the Valley of Burning Stones
Art: Adam Horne; also in *Kit Carson* 9 (Australia)
Script: Edward Holmes
(d) Kit Carson & the Hooded Avengers
Art: Adam Horne; reprint from *Kit Carson* 7 (Australia)

09 (03/08/50)
Tim Holt
Cover: Unknown
(a) Wanted
Art: Frank Bolle; reprint from *Tim Holt* 4 (Magazine
Enterprises), Jan/Feb 1949
(b) The Blanket of the Navajos!
Art: Frank Bolle; reprint from *Tim Holt* A1 17 (Magazine
Enterprises), Sep/Oct 1948
(c) The Ghost of Haunted Mountain!
Art: Frank Bolle; reprint from *Tim Holt* 4 (Magazine
Enterprises), Jan/Feb 1949

10 (03/08/50)
Kit Carson—King of the West
Cover: Adam Horne
(a) Kit Carson & the Outlaw Senorita
Art: Roland Davies; also in *Kit Carson* 10 (Australia)
(b) Kit Carson & the Gun-Runners
Art: E. C. Julian; reprint from *Kit Carson* 8 (Australia)
Script: E. H. Hamil
(c) Kit Carson & Bad Bill's Baby
Art: Adam Horne; also in *Kit Carson* 10 (Australia)
Script: J. Hunt
(d) Kit Carson & the Battle of Death Valley
Art: C. E. Montford; reprint from *Kit Carson* 8 (Australia)
Script: J. H. Higgins

11 (07/09/50)
Buck Jones
Cover: George Cattermole, based on a film still of Buck
Jones
(a) Buck Jones Meets Elmer
Art: Geoff Campion; also in *Buck Jones* 11 (Australia)
Script: R. V. Pothecary
(b) Buck Jones & the Train Gang
Art: Robert Macgillivray
Script: A. W. Henderson
(c) Buck Jones & the Fighting Editor
Art: Reg Bunn; also in *Buck Jones* 11 (Australia)
Script: J. H. Higgins

12 (07/09/50)
Tim Holt
Cover: George Cattermole, based on a film still of Tim Holt
(a) The Man Who Knew
Art: Frank Bolle; reprint from *Tim Holt* 4 (Magazine
Enterprises), Jan/Feb 1949
(b) The Law Trail
Art: Frank Bolle; reprints 'The Sheriff at Rail's End' from
Tim Holt A1 14 (Magazine Enterprises), Jul/Aug 1948
(c) Satan's Stagecoach
Art: Frank Bolle; reprint from *Tim Holt A1* 14 (Magazine
Enterprises), Jul/Aug 1948

13 (05/10/50)
Buck Jones
Cover: Unknown
(a) Buck Jones & the Golden Hide Out
Art: Tom Thursby; also in *Buck Jones* 12 (Australia)
Script: J. Hunt
(b) Buck Jones in The Flying Spur Mystery
Art: Adam Horne & Geoff Campion (p.21 only); reprint from
Buck Jones 10 (Australia)
Script: R. V. Pothecary
(c) Buck Jones & the Skeleton Pass Hold Up
Art: Robert Macgillivray; reprint from *Buck Jones* 8
(Australia)
Script: J. H. Higgins
(d) Buck Jones & the Rain/Maker
Art: Adam Horne
Script: R. V. Pothecary

14 (05/10/50)
Kit Carson
Cover: George Cattermole, based on a film still
(a) Kit Carson & the Redskin Rising
Art: Geoff Campion; reprint from *Kit Carson* 11 (Australia)
Script: A. W. Henderson
(b) Kit Carson in Bad Medicine
Art: Adam Horne; reprint from *Kit Carson* 11 (Australia)
Script: R. V. Pothecary
(c) Kit Carson's Running Battle
Art: Graham Coton
Script: J. H. Higgins
(d) Kit Carson & the "Pay or Die" Gang
Art: Adam Horne; reprint *Kit Carson* 4 (Australia)

15 (02/11/50)
Tim Holt
Cover: Unknown
(a) The Masks of Massacre Bend
Art: Frank Bolle; reprint from *Tim Holt A1* 17 (Magazine
Enterprises), Sep/Oct 1948
(b) The Spur of the Conquistadore
Art: Frank Bolle; reprint from *Tim Holt A1* 14 (Magazine
Enterprises), Jul/Aug 1948
(c) Crime's Pony Express
Art: Frank Bolle; reprint from *Tim Holt A1* 17 (Magazine
Enterprises), Sep/Oct 1948

(d) Prairie Poison
Art: Frank Bolle; reprint from *Tim Holt A1* 19 (Magazine
Enterprises), Nov/Dec 1948

16 (02/11/50)
Kit Carson
Cover: Unknown
(a) Kit Carson & the Terror of Coyote Creek
Art: Edgar Spenceley; reprint from *Kit Carson* 12 (Australia)
(b) Kit Carson in Redskin Canyon
Art: Cyril Holloway; reprint from *Kit Carson* 11 (Australia)
(c) Kit Carson's Double Trouble
Art: Graham Coton; also in *Kit Carson* 13 (Australia)
Script: A. W. Henderson

17 (07/12/50)
Buck Jones
Cover: George Cattermole, based on a film still of Charles
Starrett as the Durango Kid
(a) Buck Jones & the Bronco Bus
Art: Geoff Campion; reprint from *Buck Jones* 12 (Australia)
Script: R. V. Pothecary
(b) Buck Jones & the Deserted Town
Art: Geoff Campion; reprint from *Buck Jones* 4 (Australia)
(c) Buck Jones & the Greybeard Gang
Art: Adam Horne; reprint from *Buck Jones* 13 (Australia)
Script: R. V. Pothecary
(d) Buck Jones & the Joker
Art: Geoff Campion; reprints "Buck Jones & the Joker"
from *Buck Jones* 1 (Australia)

18 (07/12/50)
Kit Carson
Cover: Geoff Campion; reprint from *Kit Carson* 11
(Australia)
(a) Kit Carson & the Gold Rush
Art: Robert Macgillivray; also in *Kit Carson* 14 (Australia)
(b) Kit Carson and Running Dog's Man Trap
Art: E. C. Julian; reprint from *Kit Carson* 3 (Australia)
(c) Kit Carson & the Colonel's Daughter
Art: Graham Coton; also in *Kit Carson* 14 (Australia)
Script: J. Hunt
(d) Kit Carson & the Safe Snatchers
Art: Adam Horne; reprint from *Kit Carson* 8 (Australia)
Script: J. H. Higgins

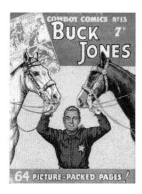

19 (04/01/51)
Buck Jones
Cover: George Cattermole, based on a film still
(a) Buck Jones Meets the Kerrys and the Coys
Art: Geoff Campion
Script: R. V. Pothecary
(b) Buck Jones in Tomb-stone
Art: Reg Bunn; reprint from *Buck Jones* 13 (Australia)
Script: A. W. Henderson
(c) Buck Jones in The Battle of Ghost Town
Art: Graham Coton; reprint from *Buck Jones* 14 (Australia)

20 (04/01/51)
Tim Holt
Cover: George Cattermole, based on a film still
(a) The Winter War
Art: Frank Bolle; reprint from *Tim Holt* 5 (Magazine Enterprises), Mar/Apr 1949
(b) Desperate Journey
Art: Frank Bolle; reprint from *Tim Holt* 5 (Magazine Enterprises), Mar/Apr 1949
(c) The Railroad of Apache Arroyo
Art: Frank Bolle; reprint from *Tim Holt A1* 19 (Magazine Enterprises), Nov/Dec 1948
(d) Along the War-Whoop Trail
Art: Frank Bolle; reprint from *Tim Holt* 5 (Magazine Enterprises), Mar/Apr 1949

21 (01/02/51)
Buck Jones
Cover: George Cattermole, based on a still from a *Hopalong Cassidy* film
(a) Buck Jones in Secret Canyon
Art: Tom Thursby
Script: J. Hunt
(b) Buck Jones & the Horse Thief
Art: H. C. Milburn
Script: A. W. Henderson
(c) Buck Jones & the Big Squirt
Art: Adam Horne
Script: R. V. Pothecary
(d) Buck Jones in Sterling Silver
Art: Geoff Campion; reprint from *Buck Jones* 5 (Australia)
Script: Percy Clarke

22 (01/02/51)
Kit Carson
Cover: George Cattermole, based on a film still
(a) Kit Carson's One Man Battle
Art: Peter Sutherland
Script: A. W. Henderson
(b) Kit Carson & the Runaway River
Art: Graham Coton
Script: A. W. Henderson
(c) Kit Carson & the Stolen Ranch
Art: Unknown Artist [A]; reprint from *Kit Carson* 15 (Australia)
Script: J. H. Higgins

23 (01/03/51)
Tim Holt
Cover: George Cattermole, based on a film still
(a) Gunman's Gamble
Art: Frank Bolle; reprint from *Tim Holt* 6 (Magazine Enterprises), May 1949
(b) The Stolen Town
Art: Frank Bolle; reprint from *Tim Holt* 6 (Magazine Enterprises), May 1949
(c) Tim Holt's Last Ride
Art: Frank Bolle; reprint from *Tim Holt A1* 19 (Magazine Enterprises), Nov/Dec 1948

24 (01/03/51)
Kit Carson
Cover: George Cattermole, based on a film still
(a) Kit Carson & the Train Raid
Art: Graham Coton
Script: J. H. Higgins
(b) Kit Carson & the Trail of Terror
Art: Unknown Artist [A]
Script: J. H. Higgins
(c) Kit Carson & the Wheel/Chair Sheriff
Art: Graham Coton
Script: A. W. Henderson

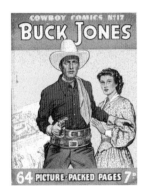

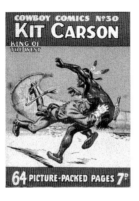
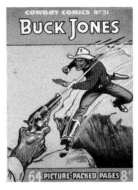

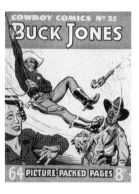

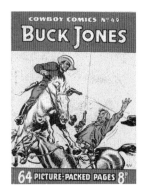  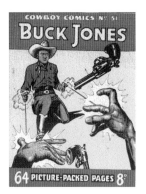 

25 (05/04/51)
Buck Jones
Cover: George Cattermole, based on a film still
(a) Buck Jones Meets Deadshot Dilly
Art: Robert Macgillivray; reprints 'Buck Jones Meets Dilly'
from *Buck Jones* 17 (Australia)
Script: A. W. Henderson
(b) Buck Jones & the Killer Cougar
Art: C. E. Montford
Script: A. W. Henderson
(c) Buck Jones & the Great Oil Swindle
Art: Tom Laidler
Script: A. W. Henderson
(d) Buck Jones & the Stolen Piebalds
Art: H. C. Milburn
Script: A. W. Henderson

26 (05/04/51)
Kit Carson
Cover: George Cattermole, based on a still of George
Montgomery from the film *Davy Crockett, Indian Scout*
(1950, released in the UK as *Indian Scout*)
(a) Kit Carson & the Relief of Fort Lonesome
Art: Robert Forrest;
Script: J. H. Higgins
(b) Kit Carson & the Mail Race
Art: Adam Horne
Script: A. W. Henderson
(c) Kit Carson Meets the Great White Wizard
Art: Robert Rodger
Script: R. V. Pothecary

27 (03/05/51)
Buck Jones
Cover: George Cattermole, based on a film still
(a) Buck Jones Meets the Gallant Gunman
Art: Colin Merrett
(b) Buck Jones Battles with the Brain
Art: Robert Macgillivray
Script: A. W. Henderson
(c) Buck Jones – Coward!
Art: Robert Macgillivray
Script: R. V. Pothecary

(d) Buck Jones Meets the Pistol-Packing Prince
Art: Tom Laidler
Script: J. Hunt

28 (03/05/51)
Kit Carson
Cover: George Cattermole, based on a film still
(a) Kit Carson & the Secret of Fort Mustang
Art: Cyril Holloway; also in *Kit Carson* 18 (Australia)
Script: J. Hunt
(b) Kit Carson & the Border Wreckers
Art: Graham Coton
(c) Kit Carson & the Pretty Pioneer
Art: Cyril Holloway; reprint from *Kit Carson* 9 (Australia)
(d) Kit Carson & the Race to the Red Hills
Art: Reg Bunn; reprint from *Kit Carson* 15 (Australia)
Script: J. H. Higgins

29 (07/06/51)
Buck Jones
Cover: George Cattermole, based on a film still
(a) Buck Jones in the Cave of Terror
Art: Robert Macgillivray
(b) Buck Jones & the Phantom Chief
Art: C. E. Montford; reprint from Buck Jones 3 (Australia)
(c) Buck Jones & the Border Express
Art: Reg Bunn
Script: J. H. Higgins
(d) Buck Jones Gets His Man
Title page: Adam Horne
Art: C. E. Montford

30 (07/06/51)
Kit Carson – King of the West
Cover: Geoff Campion; reprint from *Kit Carson* 17
(Australia)
(a) Kit Carson's Rescue Train
Art: Graham Coton
Script: A. W. Henderson
(b) Kit Carson's Peaceful War
Art: Robert Forrest
Script: A. W. Henderson
(c) Kit Carson & the Sun Worshippers
Art: Cyril Holloway
Script: A. W. Henderson

31 (05/07/51)
Buck Jones
Cover: Geoff Campion; also in *Buck Jones* 20 (Australia)
(a) Buck Jones & the Mountain of Fire
Art: Colin Merrett
Script: R. V. Pothecary
(b) The Mystery of Lone Valley
Art: C. E. Montford; reprint from *Buck Jones* 14 (Australia)
(c) Elmer Twittley Rides Again
Art: Geoff Campion
Script: R. V. Pothecary

32 (05/07/51)
Kit Carson – King of the West
Cover: Geoff Campion; reprint from *Kit Carson* 18
(Australia)
(a) Kit Carson's Fire Magic
Art: Robert Forrest
Script: R. V. Pothecary
(b) Kit Carson's Blood Brother
Art: F. A. Philpott
Script: A. W. Henderson
(c) Kit Carson & the Mule Train Crooks
Art: Adam Horne
Script: J. Hunt

33 (02/08/51)
Buck Jones
Cover: Geoff Campion; reprint from *Buck Jones* 17
(Australia)
(a) Buck Jones & the Rancher's Money Belt
Art: Reg Bunn
Script: A. W. Henderson
(b) Buck Jones & the Gay Caballero
Art: Robert Macgillivray; reprint from *Buck Jones* 17
(Australia)
Script: A. W. Henderson
(c) Buck Jones & the Kidnapping of Dilly
Art: Tom Laidler
Script: A. W. Henderson

34 (02/08/51)
Kit Carson – King of the West
Cover: Geoff Campion; also in *Kit Carson* 21 (Australia)
(a) Kit Carson's Desert Danger
Art: Patrick Nicolle
(b) Kit Carson & the Scarlet Feather
Art: Cyril Holloway
Script: A. W. Henderson
(c) Kit Carson & the Wild Stallion
Art: F. A. Philpott; also in *Kit Carson* 21 (Australia)
Script: J. Hunt

35 (06/09/51)
Buck Jones
Cover: Geoff Campion; reprint from *Buck Jones* 21
(Australia)
(a) Buck Jones & the Cyclone Kid
Art: Colin Merrett
Script: A. W. Henderson
(b) Buck Jones & the Donovan Dude Ranch
Art: Robert Macgillivray; reprint from *Buck Jones* 16
(Australia)
(c) Buck Jones & the Mystery Stampede
Art: Adam Horne; reprint from *Buck Jones* 11 (Australia)
Script: J. H. Higgins

36 (06/09/51)
Kit Carson
Cover: Robert Forrest
(a) Kit Carson & the Renegade Rodeo
Art: Reg Bunn; reprint from *Kit Carson* 15 (Australia)
Script: Maurice Creswick
(b) Kit Carson & the Pawnee Terror
Art: Graham Coton
Script: David Roberts
(c) Kit Carson & the Mactaw Treaty
Art: Adam Horne
Script: J. H. Higgins

37 (04/10/51)
Buck Jones
Cover: Geoff Campion; reprint from *Buck Jones* 22
(Australia)
(a) Buck Jones & the Boy Crook
Art: Adam Horne; also in *Buck Jones* 23 (Australia)
Script: A. W. Henderson
(b) Buck Jones & the Cowboy Derby
Art: Unknown
Script: J. Hunt
(c) Buck Jones versus the Rough Rider Gang
Art: Robert Macgillivray
Script: J. H. Higgins
(d) Buck Jones & the Valley of Vanishing Men
Art: Reg Bunn; also in *Buck Jones* 23 (Australia)
Script: J. Hunt

38 (04/10/51)
Kit Carson
Cover: Geoff Campion; reprint from *Kit Carson* 12
(Australia)
(a) Kit Carson & the Peril on Thunder River
Art: Peter Sutherland; also in *Kit Carson* 23 (Australia)
Script: J. H. Higgins
(b) Kit Carson – Duel With Danger
Art: Patrick Nicolle
Script: A. W. Henderson
(c) Kit Carson in Crossbones County
Art: Adam Horne
Script: A. W. Henderson

39 (01/11/51)
Buck Jones
Cover: Geoff Campion; reprint from *Buck Jones* 19
(Australia)
(a) Buck Jones & the Chinese Cook
Art: Reg Bunn; also in *Buck Jones* 24 (Australia)
Script: A. W. Henderson
(b) Buck Jones & the Leaping Marshall
Art: Tom Laidler
Script: R. V. Pothecary
(c) Buck Jones's Rescue Mission
Art: Reg Bunn
Script: J. H. Higgins

40 (01/11/51)
Kit Carson
Cover: Geoff Campion; reprint from *Kit Carson* 23
(Australia)
(a) Kit Carson & the Windmill War
Art: Robert Forrest; also in *Kit Carson* 24 (Australia)
Script: J. Hunt
(b) Kit Carson's Phantom Squadron
Art: F. A. Philpott
Script: A. W. Henderson
(c) Kit Carson's Rustler Trouble
Art: Stephen Chapman with some faces by Adam Horne
Script: A. W. Henderson

41 (06/12/51)
Buck Jones
Cover: Geoff Campion; reprint from *Buck Jones* 24
(Australia)
(a) Buck Jones & the War on the Range
Art: Geoff Campion; also in *Buck Jones* 25 (Australia)
(b) Buck Jones & the 'Black Cat' Oil Gang
Art: Reg Bunn
Script: A. W. Henderson
(c) Buck Jones Meets Scarface the Scoundrel
Art: C. E. Montford; reprint from *Buck Jones* 21 (Australia)
Script: A. W. Henderson
(d) Rustlers' Round/Up
Art: C. E. Montford; reprint from *Buck Jones* 5 (Australia)

42 (06/12/51)
Kit Carson
Cover: Geoff Campion; reprint from *Kit Carson* 24
(Australia)
(a) Kit Carson & the Blackfeet Rising
Art: Peter Sutherland
Script: A. W. Henderson
(b) Kit Carson to the Rescue
Art: Robert Forrest; also in *Kit Carson* 25 (Australia)
Script: A. W. Henderson
(c) Kit Carson & the Buffalo-Indians
Art: C. E. Drury
Script: J. Hunt

43 (03/01/52)
Buck Jones
Cover: Geoff Campion; reprint from *Buck Jones* 25
(Australia)
(a) The Cyclone Kid Rides Again
Art: Colin Merrett
Script: A. W. Henderson
(b) Buck Jones & El Toro
Art: Reg Bunn
Script: J. Hunt
(c) Buck Jones & the Battling Bronco
Art: Geoff Campion
Script: J. Hunt
(d) Buck Jones & the Dude Ranchers
Art: Reg Bunn; also in *Buck Jones* 26 (Australia)
Script: A. W. Henderson

44 (03/01/52)
Kit Carson
Cover: Geoff Campion; reprint from *Kit Carson* 25
(Australia)
(a) Kit Carson & the Water Battle!
Art: Robert Forrest
Script: J. Hunt
(b) Kit Carson & the Giant of Timber Canyon
Art: Cyril Holloway
(c) Kit Carson Meets Sitting Bull
Art: Eric Parker; reprint from *Kit Carson* 25 (Australia)
Script: A. W. Henderson

45 (07/02/52)
Buck Jones
Cover: Geoff Campion; reprint from *Buck Jones* 26
(Australia)
(a) Buck Jones & the Rio Bandits
Art: Colin Merrett
Script: A. W. Henderson
(b) Buck Jones & the Chinese Trouble-Chaser
Art: Reg Bunn; also in *Buck Jones* 27 (Australia)
Script: A. W. Henderson
(c) Buck Jones Meets the Fighting Shepherd
Art: Cyril Holloway
Script: A. W. Henderson

46 (07/02/52)
Kit Carson
Cover: Geoff Campion; reprint from *Kit Carson* 26
(Australia)
(a) Kit Carson & the Terror of Thunder Pass
Art: Peter Sutherland
(b) Kit Carson Rides the Trail of Wire
Art: Adam Horne
Script: R. V. Pothecary
(c) Kit Carson Fights Lynch Law!
Art: Robert Forrest; reprint from *Kit Carson* 26 (Australia)
Script: J. Hunt

47 (06/03/52)
Buck Jones
Cover: Geoff Campion; reprint from *Buck Jones* 27
(Australia)
(a) Buck Jones in Gunman's Round-Up
Art: F. A. Philpott
Script: R. V. Pothecary
(b) Buck Jones & the Barn Dance Bandits
Art: Tom Laidler
Script: A. W. Henderson
(c) Buck Jones on the Vengeance Trail
Art: Colin Merrett
Script: J. Hunt
(d) Buck Jones & the Payroll Robbery
Art: H. C. Milburn
Script: A. W. Henderson

48 (06/03/52)
Kit Carson
Cover: D. C. Eyles; reprint from *Kit Carson* 3 (Australia)
(a) Kit Carson Battles Through
Art: Peter Sutherland
Script: A. W. Henderson
(b) Kit Carson & the Magic Eye
Art: Robert Forrest; also in *Kit Carson* 28 (Australia)
Script: J. Hunt
(c) Kit Carson & the Dynamite War
Art: Adam Horne; reprint from *Kit Carson* 27 (Australia)
Script: A. W. Henderson
(d) Kit Carson & the Prairie Wolves
Art: Graham Coton; reprint from *Kit Carson* 22 (Australia)
Script: J. H. Higgins

49 (03/04/52)
Buck Jones
Cover: Geoff Campion; also in *Buck Jones* 29 (Australia)
(a) Buck Jones & the Train Battle
Art: Colin Merrett
Script: J. Hunt
(b) Buck Jones & the Bambino Bandit
Art: Adam Horne; reprint from *Buck Jones* 22 (Australia)
Script: A. W. Henderson
(c) Buck Jones & the Circus Crooks
Art: H. C. Milburn; reprint from *Buck Jones* 19 (Australia)
Script: A. W. Henderson
(d) Buck Jones & the Kid Lawman
Art: Stephen Chapman
Script: J. H. Higgins

50 (03/04/52)
Kit Carson
Cover: Geoff Campion; also in *Kit Carson* 29 (Australia)
(a) Kit Carson's Fire Battle
Art: Patrick Nicolle; reprint from *Kit Carson* 28 (Australia)
Script: A. W. Henderson
(b) Kit Carson & the Dance of the Drums
Art: Graham Coton; also in *Kit Carson* 29 (Australia)
Script: J. Hunt
(c) Kit Carson & the Secret Orders
Art: Philip Mendoza
Script: A. W. Henderson

51 (01/05/52)
Buck Jones
Cover: Geoff Campion
(a) Buck Jones & the Ghost Train
Art: H. C. Milburn
Script: A. W. Henderson
(b) Buck Jones & the Phantom Bandits
Art: C. E. Montford
Script: A. W. Henderson
(c) Buck Jones & the Millionaire Cowboy
Art: Reg Bunn
Script: J. H. Higgins

52 (01/05/52)
Kit Carson
Cover: Geoff Campion; also in *Kit Carson* 30 (Australia)
(a) Kit Carson & the Thunder-God
Art: Graham Coton
Script: A. W. Henderson
(b) Kit Carson Meets Reckless Ryan
Art: Robert Forrest
Script: A. W. Henderson
(c) Kit Carson & the Red White Man
Art: Joe Colquhoun

53 (05/06/52)
Buck Jones
Cover: Geoff Campion; also in *Buck Jones* 31 (Australia)
(a) Buck Jones & the Mail Thieves
Art: H. C. Milburn
Script: R. V. Pothecary
(b) Buck Jones Meets Kid Dynamite
Art: C. E. Montford; reprint from *Buck Jones* 28 (Australia)
Script: A. W. Henderson
(c) Buck Jones & the Red Raiders
Art: Reg Bunn; reprint from *Buck Jones* 30 (Australia)
Script: A. W. Henderson

54 (05/06/52)
Kit Carson
Cover: D. C. Eyles
(a) Kit Carson & the Redskin Army
Art: Cyril Holloway
Script: A. W. Henderson
(b) Kit Carson Versus the Moran Gang
Art: Adam Horne; reprint from *Kit Carson* 26 (Australia)
Script: A. W. Henderson
(c) Kit Carson & the Terror of Cactus City
Art: Robert Forrest
Script: A. W. Henderson

55 (03/07/52)
The Cisco Kid
Cover: José Luis Salinas
Art: José Luis Salinas, with some minor additional art by Graham Coton; reprint from US newspaper strip syndicated by King Features
Script: Rod Reed

56 (03/07/52)
Kit Carson
Cover: Geoff Campion; also in *Kit Carson* 32 (Australia)
(a) Kit Carson & the Redskin's Revenge
Art: Robert Forrest
Script: A. W. Henderson
(b) Kit Carson & the River Raid
Art: Graham Coton
(c) Kit Carson Plays A Lone Hand
Art: David Wright
Script: A. W. Henderson

57 (07/08/52)
Buck Jones
Cover: H. C. Milburn; also in *Buck Jones* 33 (Australia)
(a) Buck Jones & the Man Tamer
Art: H. C. Milburn
Script: A. W. Henderson
(b) Buck Jones & the Spanish Treasure
Art: Vic Anderson; reprint from *Buck Jones* 32 (Australia)
Script: A. W. Henderson
(c) Buck Jones & the Danger Trail
Art: C. E. Montford
Script: A. W. Henderson

58 (07/08/52)
Kit Carson
Cover: H. C. Milburn; also in *Kit Carson* 33 (Australia)
(a) Kit Carson & the Vanishing Forts
Art: Graham Coton
Script: A. W. Henderson
(b) Kit Carson & the Secret of the Swamps
Art: Robert Forrest
Script: A. W. Henderson
(c) Kit Carson & the Outlaw Tribe
Art: Unknown Artist [A], with additional art by J. Compari
Script: A. W. Henderson

59 (04/09/52)
Buck Jones
Cover: H. C. Milburn; also in *Buck Jones* 34 (Australia)
(a) Buck Jones & the King of the Rio!
Art: C. E. Montford
Script: J. H. Higgins
(b) Buck Jones & the Rookie Ranger

Art: Tom Laidler
Script: A. W. Henderson
(c) Buck Jones & the Stranger
Art: Eric Parker, with additional art by J. Compari; reprint
from *Buck Jones* 9 (Australia)
Script: R. V. Pothecary

60 (04/09/52)
Kit Carson
Cover: H. C. Milburn; also in *Kit Carson* 34 (Australia)
(a) Kit Carson & Rogues Round-Up
Art: Peter Sutherland
Script: H. H. C. Gibbons
(b) Kit Carson Meets Zarna the Wild Man
Art: Cyril Holloway
Script: A. W. Henderson
(c) Kit Carson & Peril on the Pony Express
Art: Eric Parker; reprint from *Kit Carson* 31 (Australia)
Script: J. Hunt

61 (02/10/52)
Buck Jones
Cover: Geoff Campion; reprint from *Buck Jones* 32
(Australia)
(a) The Six-Gun Justice of Buck Jones
Art: Vic Anderson, with additional art by Geoff Campion
Script: A. W. Henderson
(b) Buck Jones Rescues the Princess of the Sun
Art: Adam Hornc, with some additional art by J. Compari
Script: J. H. Higgins
(c) Buck Jones's Battle-on-Wheels!
Art: Reg Bunn; reprint from *Buck Jones* 30 (Australia)

62 (02/10/52)
Kit Carson
Cover: H. C. Milburn; also in *Kit Carson* 35 (Australia)
(a) Kit Carson & the Battle of the Floating Store
Art: Graham Coton
(b) Kit Carson's Secret Weapon
Art: Robert Forrest
Script: A. W. Henderson
(c) Kit Carson Breaks the Tyrant
Art: Unknown Artist [A], with additional art by J. Compari
Script: A. W. Henderson

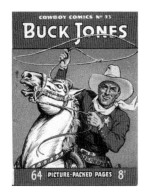

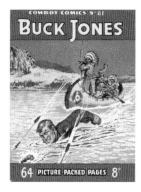

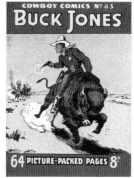

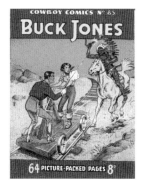

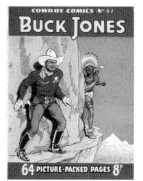

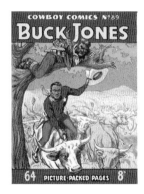

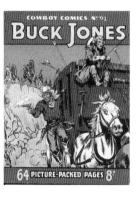

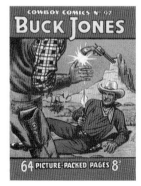

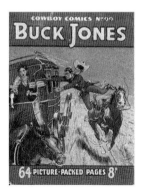

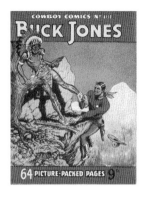

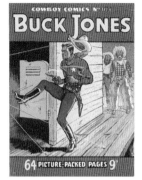

63 (06/11/52)
Buck Jones
Cover: Graham Coton
(a) Buck Jones & the Lost Valley
Art: H. C. Milburn
Script: A. W. Henderson
(b) Buck Jones & the Million Dollar Bandits
Art: C. E. Montford
Script: A. W. Henderson
(c) Buck Jones & the Petticoat Sheriff
Art: Tom Laidler; reprint from *Buck Jones* 15 (Australia)
Script: A. W. Henderson

64 (06/11/52)
Kit Carson
Cover: Graham Coton; reprint from *Kit Carson* 37 (Australia)
(a) Kit Carson Saves the Dying Fort
Art: Peter Sutherland
Script: A. W. Henderson
(b) Kit Carson & the Kidnapped General!
Art: Adam Horne
Script: J. Hunt
(c) Kit Carson Solves the Mystery of the Talking Totem!
Art: Joe Colquhoun
(d) Kit Carson Rides the Covered Wagon Trail
Art: E. C. Julian; reprint from *Kit Carson* 3 (Australia)

65 (04/12/52)
Buck Jones
Cover: Graham Coton
(a) Buck Jones & the Pageant Pirates
Art: Bill Lacey
Script: A. W. Henderson
(b) Buck Jones & the Stagecoach Snatch
Art: Selby Donnison
Script: J. H. Higgins
(c) Buck Jones & the Aztec God
Art: Bill Lacey
Script: A. W. Henderson

66 (04/12/52)
Kit Carson
Cover: Graham Coton; reprint from *Kit Carson* 40 (Australia)
(a) Kit Carson & the Pill Pedlar
Art: D. C. Eyles, with additional art by Colin Page
Script: J. Hunt
(b) Kit Carson Fights Mad Carew
Art: D. Gale
Script: A. W. Henderson
(c) Kit Carson Fights the Tonto Gang
Art: F. A. Philpott
Script: A. W. Henderson

67 (01/01/53)
Buck Jones
Cover: Graham Coton; reprint from *Buck Jones* 36 (Australia)
(a) Buck Jones in The City of Gold
Art: Colin Merrett
Script: A. W. Henderson
(b) Buck Jones Meets Double Trouble
Art: H. C. Milburn; reprint from *Buck Jones* 36 (Australia)
Script: J. H. Higgins
(c) Buck Jones Has A Cougar Round-Up
Art: C. E. Montford
Script: J. Hunt

68 (01/01/53)
Kit Carson
Cover: Graham Coton; reprint from *Kit Carson* 44 (Australia)
(a) Kit Carson's Perilous Mission
Art: Peter Sutherland
Script: A. W. Henderson
(b) Kit Carson & the Bullion Bandits
Art: Robert Forrest; reprint from *Kit Carson* 30 (Australia)
Script: J. Hunt
(c) Kit Carson Fights the Mexican Eagle
Art: Graham Coton
Script: J. Hunt

 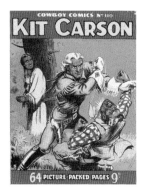  

69 (05/02/53)
Buck Jones
Cover: Robert Forrest
(a) Buck Jones & the Snake of Mexico
Art: C. E. Montford, with additional art by Colin Page
Script: C. A. Lewins
(b) Buck Jones & the Funfair War
Art: Eric Parker
Script: A. W. Henderson
(c) Buck Jones in Sleepy City
Art: R. Charles Roylance
Script: A. W. Henderson

70 (05/02/53)
Kit Carson
Cover: D. C. Eyles
(a) Kit Carson & the Swamp War
Art: H. C. Milburn
Script: A. W. Henderson
(b) Kit Carson Fights the Battle of the Bridge
Art: D. Gale
Script: C. Mattin
(c) Kit Carson & the Kidnap Killers
Art: Philip Mendoza
Script: A. W. Henderson

71 (05/03/53)
Buck Jones
Cover: Unknown
(a) Buck Jones & the Shadow Gang's Treasure
Art: A. W. Ende
Script: A. W. Henderson
(b) Buck Jones & the Bank Bandits
Art: Reg Bunn
Script: J. Hunt
(c) Buck Jones & the Railroad War
Art: A. W. Ende
Script: A. W. Henderson

72 (05/03/53)
Kit Carson
Cover: Unknown
(a) Kit Carson's Prairie Treasure Hunt
Art: Peter Sutherland

(b) Kit Carson & the Buffalo Bandits
Art: Graham Coton
Script: C. Mattin
(c) Kit Carson Solves the Mule Train Mystery
Art: Cyril Holloway
Script: A. W. Henderson

73 (02/04/53)
Buck Jones
Cover: Unknown
(a) Buck Jones – Texas Ranger
Art: Colin Merrett (p5-42) & another
Script: A. W. Henderson
(b) Buck Jones & the Underwater Tribe
Art: R. Charles Roylance
Script: A. W. Henderson

74 (02/04/53)
Kit Carson
Cover: Unknown
(a) Kit Carson & the War Mask
Art: D. Gale
Script: A. W. Henderson
(b) Kit Carson & the Black Hood Gang
Art: Eric Parker
Script: Maurice Creswick (story)/J. H. Higgins (script)
(c) Kit Carson & the Redskin's Revolt
Art: Adam Horne
Script: C. Lewins

75 (07/05/53)
Buck Jones
Cover: Unknown
(a) Buck Jones & the Vanishing Sea
Art: Bill Lacey
Script: A. W. Henderson
(b) Buck Jones & the Redskin Raiders
Art: D. Gale
Script: J. H. Higgins

 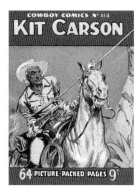  

76 (07/05/53)
Kit Carson
Cover: Robert Forrest
(a) Kit Carson & the White Wizard
Art: Peter Sutherland
Script: J. H. Higgins
(b) Kit Carson & the Pipe of Peace
Art: Selby Donnison
Script: J. H. Higgins
(c) Kit Carson On the Warpath
Art: Adam Horne
Script: A. W. Henderson

77 (04/06/53)
Buck Jones
Cover: D. C. Eyles
(a) The Great White Grizzly
Art: H. C. Milburn
Script: J. Hunt
(b) The Prairie Pirates
Art: Tom Laidler
Script: J. H. Higgins
(c) The Floating Battle
Art: Unknown
Script: A. W. Henderson

78 (04/06/53)
Kit Carson
Cover: Unknown
(a) Kit Carson & the Pawnee Trap
Art: R. Charles Roylance
Script: A. W. Henderson
(b) Kit Carson & Guns Across the Border
Art: Robert Forrest
Script: C. A. Lewins
(c) Kit Carson & the Federal Agent
Art: Adam Horne
Script: A. W. Henderson

79 (02/07/53)
Buck Jones
Cover: Adam Horne
(a) Buck Jones & the Great Redskin Rising
Art: H. C. Milburn
Script: A. W. Henderson

(b) Buck Jones & the Wonder Gold Finder
Art: Eric Parker
Script: J. Hunt
(c) Buck Jones & the Junior Lawman
Art: Reg Bunn
Script: A. W. Henderson
(d) Buck Jones & the Gold Snatchers
Art: Stephen Chapman

80 (02/07/53)
Kit Carson
Cover: Unknown
(a) Kit Carson's The Battle of the Forts
Art: R. Charles Roylance
Script: A. W. Henderson
(b) Kit Carson Meets the Terrible Twins
Art: H. C. Milburn
Script: J. H. Higgins
(c) Kit Carson – The Peacemaker
Art: Robert Forrest
Script: C. A. Lewins

81 (06/08/53)
Buck Jones
Cover: Geoff Campion
(a) The Canyon Battle
Art: D. Gale
Script: A. W. Henderson
(b) Buck Jones Fights the Battle of Mitchee River
Art: C. E. Montford
(c) Buck Jones Meets the Outlaw Hero
Art: Colin Merrett; reprints "Buck Jones Meets the Gallant Gunman" from *Cowboy Comics* 27 (05/51)

82 (06/08/53)
Kit Carson
Cover: Unknown
(a) Kit Carson Saves the Gold Wagons!
Art: R. Charles Roylance
Script: Mrs. J. Hopkinson
(b) Kit Carson's Redskin Pal
Art: Peter Sutherland; reprints "Kid Carson & the Blackfeet Rising" from *Cowboy Comics* 42 (12/51)
(c) Kit Carson's Riverboat Rescue
Art: J. R. Freeman
Script: A. W. Henderson

   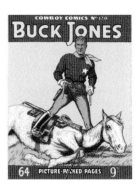

83 (03/09/53)
Buck Jones
Cover: Unknown
(a) Buck Jones & the Bandit's Brother
Art: H. C. Milburn
Script: J. H. Higgins
(b) Buck Jones & the Stolen Express
Art: Tony Weare
Script: A. W. Henderson
(c) Buck Jones & Desperate Dilly
Art: Tom Laidler; reprint from *Buck Jones* 27 (Australia)

84 (03/09/53)
Kit Carson
Cover: Unknown
(a) Kit Carson in Danger Valley
Art: R. Charles Roylance
Script: A. W. Henderson
(b) Kit Carson & the Devil's Highway
Art: Peter Sutherland
Script: B. Rowland
(c) Kit Carson & Flood Rescue
Art: Colin Page
Script: J. Hunt

85 (01/10/53)
Buck Jones
Cover: Unknown
(a) Buck Jones & the Buffalo Raiders
Art: Peter Sutherland
Script: J. Hunt
(b) Buck Jones & the Battle of the Railroad
Art: D. Gale
Script: A. W. Henderson

86 (01/10/53)
Kit Carson
Cover: Unknown
(a) Kit Carson & the City Kids
Art: R. Charles Roylance
Script: A. W. Henderson
(b) Captive of the Comanches
Art: Colin Page
Script: A. W. Henderson

(c) Kit Carson & the Chief's Daughter
Art: Unknown
Script: A. W. Henderson

87 (05/11/53)
Buck Jones
Cover: Unknown
(a) Buck Jones & the Circus Gun Runner
Art: H. C. Milburn
Script: A. W. Henderson
(b) Buck Jones & the Talking Totem
Art: Bill Lacey
Script: J. Hunt
(c) Buck Jones & the Pig Show Pirates
Art: George Parlett
Script: A. W. Henderson

88 (05/11/53)
Kit Carson
Cover: Unknown
(a) Kit Carson & the Roughneck Major
Art: Peter Sutherland
Script: A. W. Henderson
(b) Kit Carson & the River of Death
Art: Unknown
Script: C. Mattin
(c) Kit Carson & the Gold Race
Art: Patrick Nicolle
Script: A. W. Henderson

89 (03/12/53)
Buck Jones
Cover: Unknown
(a) Cattle Battle!
Art: D. Gale
Script: A. W. Henderson
(b) Buck Jones & the Stubborn Settlers
Art: R. Charles Roylance
Script: A. W. Henderson

90 (03/12/53)
Kit Carson
Cover: Geoff Campion
(a) Kit Carson on the Tomahawk Trail!
Art: Philip Mendoza
Script: F. R. Passmore
(b) Kit Carson Meets Walking Mountain
Art: Peter Sutherland
Script: Adrian Vincent
(c) Kit Carson at the Mercy of the Mohawks
Art: D. Gale
Script: B. Rowland

91 (07/01/54)
Buck Jones
Cover: Phillip Mendoza
(a) Buck Jones in The City of Terror
Art: H. C. Milburn
Script: A. W. Henderson
(b) Buck Jones & the Secret of the Tonto Moon
Art: D. Gale
Script: Percy Clarke

92 (07/01/54)
Kit Carson
Cover: Unknown
(a) Kit Carson & the Treasure of the Swamps
Art: Peter Sutherland
Script: J. H. Higgins
(b) Kit Carson & the War-Paint Bandits
Art: Unknown
Script: Angus Allan

93 (04/02/54)
Buck Jones
Cover: Unknown
(a) Buck Jones & the Buckboard Bandits
Art: R. Charles Roylance
Script: J. H. Higgins
(b) Buck Jones & the Rogue's Round-Up
Art: Adam Horne
(c) Buck Jones & the Witch Doctor's Plot
Art: Unknown

94 (04/02/54)
Kit Carson
Cover: Geoff Campion; reprint from *Kit Carson* 16
(Australia)
(a) Kit Carson & the Deep Sea Pioneer
Art: R. Charles Roylance
Script: A. W. Henderson
(b) Kit Carson & the Prairie Fire
Art: Adam Horne
Script: H. H. C. Gibbons

95 (04/03/54)
Buck Jones
Cover: Unknown
(a) Buck Jones & the Golden Hawk
Art: R. Charles Roylance
Script: Adrian Vincent
(b) Buck Jones & the Rancher's Treasure
Art: D. Gale
Script: A. W. Henderson
(c) Buck Jones & the Runaway Bus
Art: Tom Laidler
Script: Adrian Vincent

96 (04/03/54)
Kit Carson
Cover: Unknown
(a) Kit Carson & the Race to Silver Gulch!
Art: Peter Sutherland
(b) Kit Carson & the General's Son!
Art: Unknown
Script: J. H. Higgins

97 (01/04/54)
Buck Jones
Cover: Phillip Mendoza
(a) Buck Jones & the Battling Actors
Art: H. C. Milburn
Script: Adrian Vincent
(b) Buck Jones & the Thunder God
Art: R. Charles Roylance
(c) Buck Jones & Jed Crowley's Second Chance
Art: J. Stokes
Script: Adrian Vincent

98 (01/04/54)
Kit Carson
Cover: Unknown
(a) Kit Carson & the Battle of Dead End Canyon
Art: Unknown
(b) Kit Carson & the Singing Wire
Art: Peter Sutherland
(c) Kit Carson's Tenderfoot Trouble
Art: Colin Merrett
Script: A. W. Henderson

99 (06/05/54)
Buck Jones
Cover: Unknown; based on *Kit Carson* 19 (Australia)
(a) Buck Jones & the Dynamite Trail
Art: Unknown
Script: Eric Leyland
(b) Buck Jones & Kid Carr's Brother
Art: H. C. Milburn
Script: J. H. Higgins
(c) Buck Jones & Grandpop's Old Mine
Art: Harry Bishop
Script: J. H. Higgins

100 (06/05/54)
Kit Carson
Cover: Unknown
(a) Kit Carson & the Broken Treaty
Art: Peter Sutherland
Script: Adrian Vincent
(b) Kit Carson & the Mule Train Plot
Art: Peter Sutherland
Script: A. W. Henderson
(c) Kit Carson & the Railroad Rivals
Art: J. W. Butler

101 (03/06/54)
Buck Jones
Cover: Unknown
(a) Percy, the Two Gun Terror
Art: Reg Bunn
Script: Adrian Vincent
(b) The Redskin Plot
Art: D. Gale
Script: A. W. Henderson

(c) The Feudin' Fools
Art: George Parlett
Script: A. W. Henderson

102 (03/06/54)
Kit Carson
Cover: Unknown
(a) Kit Carson & the Pawnee Prisoners
Art: Peter Sutherland & another (woman & daughter)
Script: Graeme Thomas.
(b) Kit Carson's Mascot
Art: C. E. Montford, with some additional art by Don Lawrence
Script: J. Hunt
(c) Kit Carson & the Timber Wolves
Art: Adam Horne
Script: B. Rowland

103 (01/07/54)
Buck Jones
Cover: Unknown
(a) Buck Jones & the Return of Shircano
Art: H. C. Milburn
Script: Graeme Thomas
(b) Buck Jones & the Bad Man Who Made Good
Art: R. Charles Roylance
Script: A. W. Henderson
(c) Buck Jones & the Raiders of the Iron Road
Art: Reg Bunn
Script: Angus Allan

104 (01/07/54)
Kit Carson
Cover: Unknown
(a) Kit Carson & the Valley of Fear
Art: Peter Sutherland
Script: J. H. Higgins
(b) Kit Carson & the Triumph of Roaring Buffalo
Art: Ron Embleton
Script: Angus Allan

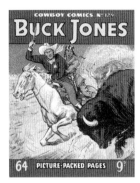

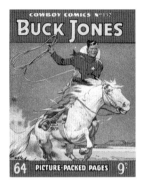

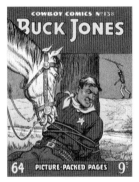

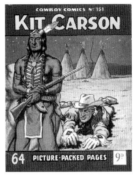
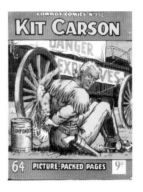

 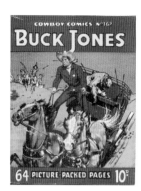  

105 (01/07/54)
Billy the Kid
Cover: Unknown
(a) Billy the Kid & the Gun Runners
Art: R. Charles Roylance
Script: A. W. Henderson
(b) Billy the Kid & the Pawnee Brothers
Art: Colin Merrett

106 (05/08/54)
Buck Jones
Cover: Unknown
(a) Buck Jones & the Iron Horse War
Art: Reg Bunn
(b) The Redskin Renegades
Art: Ron Embleton
(c) Buck Jones' Rustler-Trouble
Art: C. E. Montford

107 (05/08/54)
Buffalo Bill
Cover: Unknown
Art: Fred Meagher; reprints US newspaper strip syndicated
by United Features with linking art by Ron Embleton (22?
pages in all)
Note: Published in two chapters

108 (05/08/54)
Kit Carson
Cover: Unknown
(a) Kit Carson & the Cherokee Rising
Art: Peter Sutherland
(b) Kit Carson Fights the Trouble Mongers
Art: Unknown
(c) Kit Carson & the Buffalo Boy's Revenge
Art: Unknown

109 (02/09/54)
Buck Jones
Cover: Unknown
(a) The Vengeance of Fire Eye
Art: Philip Mendoza & R. Charles Roylance
(b) Buck Jones Rides the Arizona Trail
Art: Ron Embleton
Script: R. Phillips

110 (02/09/54)
Kit Carson
Cover: Unknown
(a) Kit Carson & the Death Valley Message!
Art: Peter Sutherland
(b) Kit Carson & the Race to Rattlesnake Rock
Art: Reg Bunn
(c) Kit Carson's River Rescue
Art: Adam Horne

111 (07/10/54)
Buck Jones
Cover: Unknown Artist [D]
(a) Buck Jones & the Double Trouble Totem
Art: R. Charles Roylance
(b) Buck Jones & the Braves of the Fire God
Art: H. C. Milburn
(c) Buck Jones in Ghost Town
Art: Reg Bunn
Script: C. A. Lewins

112 (07/10/54)
Kit Carson
Cover: Unknown
(a) Kit Carson & the Race to Fort Savage
Art: Peter Sutherland
(b) Kit Carson & the Legend of Eagle Mountain
Art: Reg Bunn
(c) Kit Carson & the Lost Cavalry
Art: C. E. Montford
Script: Graeme Thomas

113 (04/11/54)
Buck Jones
Cover: Unknown
(a) Buck Jones & the Riddle of the Shifting Sands!
Art: Reg Bunn
(b) Buck Jones to the Rescue
Art: Unknown
(c) Buck Jones & the Ghost Riders!
Art: Reg Bunn

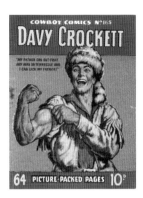   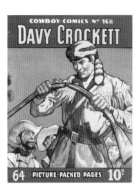

114 (04/11/54)
Kit Carson
Cover: Unknown
(a) Kit Carson & Red Cloud's Last Fight
Art: Peter Sutherland
(b) Kit leaves It To Annie
Art: Graham Coton
(c) The Men of the Mounties
Art: Unknown

115 (04/11/54)
Lucky Lannagan
Title: Lucky Lannagan's Mystery Trail
Cover: Unknown
Art: Ron Embleton
Script: John Hunter

116 (02/12/54)
Kit Carson
Cover: Unknown
(a) Kit Carson & the Fort of Lost Men
Art: C. E. Montford
(b) Kit Carson & Paleface Magic
Art: Peter Sutherland
(c) Kit Carson's Double Trouble
Art: H. C. Milburn

117 (02/12/54)
Buck Jones
Cover: Unknown
(a) Buck Jones & the Fighting M'Gees
Art: H. C. Milburn
(b) Buck Jones & the Easy Bank Robbery
Art: Reg Bunn

118 (02/12/54)
Lucky Lannagan
Title: Lucky Lannagan's Indian Trouble
Cover: Unknown
Art: Peter Sutherland

119 (06/01/55)
Kit Carson
Cover: Unknown
(a) Kit Carson & the Border Bandits
Art: Peter Sutherland
(b) Kit Carson & the Racing Redskins
Art: Reg Bunn

120 (06/01/55)
Buck Jones
Cover: Unknown
(a) Buck Jones & the Ghost Town Raiders
Art: Selby Donnison
(b) Buck Jones & the Gun Runners
Art: D. Gale

121 (06/01/55)
Lucky Lannagan
Title: Lucky Lannagan Squares a Debt
Cover: Unknown
Art: Ron Embleton
Script: John Hunter

122 (03/02/55)
Kit Carson
Cover: Unknown
(a) Kit Carson & Dangerous Dynamite
Art: Peter Sutherland
(b) Kit Carson's Hash Wagon Trouble
Art: Unknown with KC's face by Reg Bunn

123 (03/02/55)
Buck Jones
Cover: Unknown
(a) Buck Jones & the Justice of Black Arrow
Art: R. Charles Roylance
(b) Buck Jones Runs into Donkey Trouble
Art: Unknown
(c) Buck Jones & the Railroad Bandits
Art: F. A. Philpott

  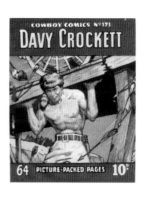 

124 (03/02/55)
Lucky Lannagan
Title: **Lannagan's Luck**
Cover: Unknown
Art: Selby Donnison
Script: John Hunter

125 (03/03/55)
Kit Carson
Cover: Unknown
(a) The Battling Peace Maker
Art: Peter Sutherland
(b) Kit Carson & the Buffalo Express
Art: Unknown
(c) Kit Carson Meets Old Man Morton
Art: Unknown with KC's face by Reg Bunn

126 (03/03/55)
Buck Jones
Cover: Unknown
(a) Buck Jones Has Totem Trouble
Art: R. Charles Roylance
(b) Buck Jones & the Gun Doctor
Art: F. A. Philpott
Script: Angus Allan

127 (03/03/55)
Lucky Lannagan
Title: **Lucky Lannagan's Treasure Hunt**
Cover: Unknown
Art: Ron Embleton
Script: John Hunter

128 (07/04/55)
Kit Carson
Cover: Unknown
(a) Kit Carson & the Vanishing Wagon Train
Art: Peter Sutherland
(b) Kit Carson & the Wind of Doom
Art: Reg Bunn
(c) Kit Carson & the Masked Riders
Art: Unknown

129 (07/04/55)
Buck Jones
Cover: Unknown
(a) Buck Jones & the Tomahawk Totem
Art: Tony Weare
(b) Buck Jones in War On the Range
Art: H. C. Milburn

130 (07/04/55)
Lucky Lannagan
Title: **Lucky Lannagan's River Boat Round-Up**
Cover: Unknown
Art: Peter Sutherland
Script: John Hunter

131 (05/05/55)
Kit Carson
Cover: Peter Sutherland
Title page: Selby Donnison
(a) Kit Carson & the Secret Tribe
Art: Peter Sutherland
(b) Kit Carson & the Golden Horses
Art: Peter Sutherland

132 (05/05/55)
Buck Jones
Cover: James E. McConnell
(a) Buck Jones & the Real Life Ghost!
Art: Selby Donnison
(b) Buck Jones & the Cannon Bandits!
Art: Selby Donnison

133 (05/05/55)
Kit Carson
Cover: Unknown
(a) Kit Carson & the Battle of Buffalo Creek
Art: D. Gale
(b) Kit Carson & the Mystery of Wolf Head Island
Art: Peter Sutherland

134 (02/06/55)
Kit Carson
Cover: Unknown
(a) Kit Carson & the Secret of the Temple
Art: Peter Sutherland

  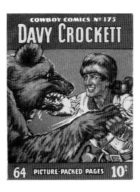 

(b) Kit Carson & the Yellow Totem
Art: Unknown
Script: Adrian Vincent.

135 (02/06/55)
Buck Jones
Title: **Buck Jones & the Redskin Treasure**
Cover: Unknown
Art: R. Charles Roylance

136 (02/06/55)
Kit Carson
Cover: Unknown
(a) Kit Carson & the Battle of Fort Stark!
Art: D. Gale
(b) Kit Carson & the Medicine Man!
Art: H. C. Milburn
Script: Eric Leyland
(c) Kit Carson & the Redskin Rising
Art: Unknown

137 (07/07/55)
Kit Carson
Title: **Kit Carson Fights the Bandit King!**
Cover: James E. McConnell
Title page: Selby Donnison
Art: Ron Embleton
Note: Features Lucky Lannagan redrawn as Kit Carson

138 (07/07/55)
Buck Jones
Cover: Unknown
(a) Buck Jones Has Pioneer Trouble
Art: R. Charles Roylance
(b) Buck Jones in The Battle of Beaver Creek
Art: Unknown
(c) Buck Jones & the Genuine Indian Cure!
Art: R. Charles Roylance

139 (07/07/55)
Kit Carson
Cover: Unknown
(a) Kit Carson & the Railroad Double-Cross
Art: Peter Sutherland

(b) Kit Carson's Buffalo Magic
Art: Reg Bunn
(c) Kit Carson & the Indian War
Art: Unknown

140 (04/08/55)
Kit Carson
Cover: Unknown
(a) Kit Carson & the Cherokee Mix-Up
Art: Peter Sutherland
(b) Kit Carson & White Man's Treachery
Art: D. Gale
(c) Kit Carson & the Gunman's Last Gamble
Art: Selby Donnison

141 (04/08/55)
Buck Jones
Cover: James E. McConnell
(a) Buck Jones & the Dude Double Crosser
Art: R. Charles Roylance
(b) Buck Jones & the Redskin Hostage
Art: Selby Donnison
(c) Buck Jones & the Bandit's Hoard
Art: Unknown

142 (04/08/55)
Kit Carson
Cover: Unknown
(a) Kit Carson & the Kidnapped Rancher
Art: Peter Sutherland
(b) Kit Carson & the Gunpowder Plot
Art: Unknown Artist [D]
(c) Kit Carson & the Fight at Fort Wayne
Art: Adam Horne

143 (01/09/55)
Kit Carson
Cover: Unknown
(a) Kit Carson & the War Drums of the Kiowas
Art: Unknown Artist [D]
(b) Kit Carson & the Fiery Horse
Art: Ron Embleton
(c) On The Vengeance Trail
Art: Unknown

  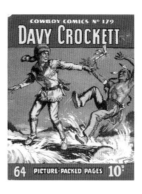 

144 (01/09/55)
Buck Jones
Cover: James E. McConnell
(a) Buck Jones & the Tall Man
Art: R. Charles Roylance
(b) Buck Jones & the Moving Statue
Art: Tony Weare

145 (01/09/55)
Kit Carson
Cover: Unknown
(a) Kit Carson & the Spaniard's Gold
Art: Peter Sutherland
(b) The Hate of Dark Eagle
Art: D. Gale

146 (06/10/55)
Kit Carson
Cover: Unknown
(a) Kit Carson & the Fighting Foyles!
Art: Peter Sutherland
(b) Kit Carson & the Riddle of the Broken Doll
Art: Unknown Artist [D]
(c) Kit Carson & the Cunning of Yellow Fox
Art: Unknown

147 (06/10/55)
Buck Jones
Cover: James E. McConnell
(a) Buck Jones & the Golden Snake
Art: R. Charles Roylance
(b) Buck Jones & the Clue of the Double Eagle
Art: Selby Donnison

148 (06/10/55)
Kit Carson
Cover: Unknown
(a) Kit Carson & the Pawnee Peace Belt
Art: Peter Sutherland
(b) Kit Carson & the Renegade Chief
Art: D. Gale

149 (03/11/55)
Kit Carson
Cover: Peter Sutherland
(a) Kit Carson & the Moon Goddess
Art: Unknown Artist [D]
(b) Kit Carson & the Vanishing Totem
Art: Unknown Artist [D]
(c) Kit Carson's Ransom Round-Up
Art: D. Gale

150 (03/11/55)
Buck Jones
Cover: James E. McConnell
(a) Buck Jones & the Thousand Horses
Art: R. Charles Roylance
(b) Buck Jones & the Secret of Hollow Mountain
Art: Ian Kennedy

151 (03/11/55)
Kit Carson
Cover: Unknown
(a) Kit Carson & the Railroad War
Art: Peter Sutherland
(b) Kit Carson & the Relief of Fort Henry
Art: Unknown Artist [D]

152 (01/12/55)
Kit Carson
Cover: Unknown
(a) Kit Carson & the Feathered Lance
Art: Peter Sutherland
(b) Kit Carson's Battle on Horseback
Art: D. Gale
(c) Kit Carson Rides the Robbers Road
Art: Unknown Artist [D]

153 (01/12/55)
Buck Jones
Cover: Unknown
(a) Buck Jones & the Honest Outlaw!
Art: Selby Donnison
(b) Buck Jones Has Twin Trouble!
Art: Unknown

  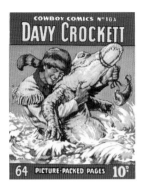 

154 (01/12/55)
Kit Carson
Cover: Unknown
(a) Kit Carson & the Magic Wagon!
Art: Peter Sutherland
(b) Kit Carson & the Ghost Dancers!
Art: Unknown

155 (05/01/56)
Kit Carson
Cover: Unknown
Title page: D. C. Eyles
(a) Kit Carson & the Thunder Wagon
Art: Peter Sutherland
(b) Kit Carson & the Traitor Scout
Art: Unknown Artist [D]
(c) Kit Carson & the Gun Runners
Art: D. C. Eyles; reprints "Kit Carson & the Dillon Gang" from *Comet* 141/143, 31/03-14/04/51 (itself possibly a reprint of "Kit Carson & the Dillon Killers" from *Kit Carson* 1 (Australia), 1948)

156 (05/01/56)
Buck Jones
Cover: James E. McConnell
(a) Buck Jones & the Wagon-Train Warriors
Art: R. Charles Roylance
(b) Buck Jones & the Fighting Forty-Niner
Art: Unknown Artist [D]
(c) Buck Jones & the Vanishing Stagecoach
Art: C. E. Montford

157 (05/01/56)
Kit Carson
Cover: Unknown
(a) Kit Carson & the Missing Patrol
Art: Unknown
(b) Kit Carson & Diablo, the Bandit
Art: Unknown Artist [D]

158 (02/02/56)
Kit Carson
Cover: Unknown
(a) Kit Carson & the Wolf River Battle
Art: Peter Sutherland

(b) Kit Carson & the Healing Poison
Art: Unknown Artist [D]

159 (02/02/56)
Buck Jones
Cover: James E. McConnell
(a) Buck Jones & the Red Tomahawk
Art: R. Charles Roylance
(b) Buck Jones & the Man From Nowhere
Art: Tom Laidler
(c) Buck Jones & the Vanishing Buffalo
Art: Unknown Artist [D]

160 (02/02/56)
Kit Carson
Cover: Unknown
(a) Kit Carson & the Floating Coach
Art: Unknown
(b) Kit Carson Meets Arikaras on the War-Path
Art: Peter Sutherland
(c) Kit Carson & the Outcast of Alder Creek
Art: Unknown Artist [D]

161 (01/03/56)
Kit Carson
Cover: Unknown
(a) Kit Carson & the Smoke Demon!
Art: Unknown
(b) Kit Carson & the Commanche Cannons!
Art: Peter Sutherland
(c) Kit Carson & the Ride to Fort Grant
Art: Peter Sutherland

162 (01/03/55)
Buck Jones
Cover: James E. McConnell
(a) Buck Jones & the Golden Lake
Art: R. Charles Roylance
(b) Buck Jones & the Ride to Yellow Sky
Art: Unknown

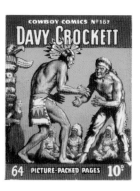

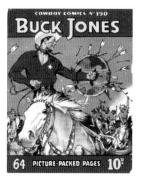
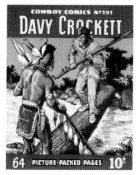

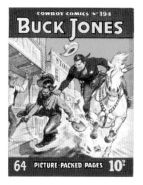
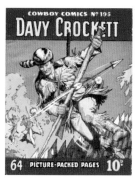

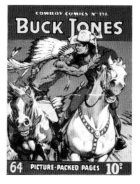
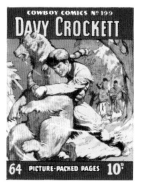

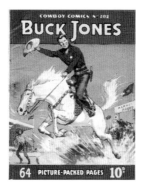
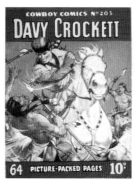

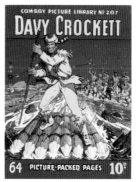

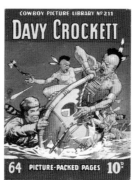

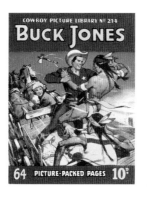

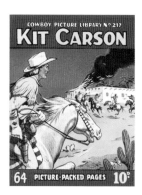  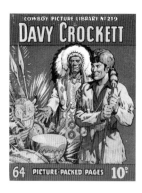 

163 (01/03/56)
Kit Carson
Cover: Unknown
(a) Kit Carson & the Telegraph Trouble!
Art: D. Gale
(b) Kit Carson & the Treachery of Red Elk
Art: Peter Sutherland
(c) Kit Carson & the Little White Chief
Art: Unknown Artist [D]

164 (29/03/56)
Buck Jones
Cover: James E. McConnell
(a) Buck Jones & the Secret Witness
Art: R. Charles Roylance
(b) Buck Jones & the Man on the Iron Horse
Art: Tom Laidler
(c) Buck Jones & the Renegades of Stormy Pass
Art: Unknown

165 (29/03/56)
Davy Crockett
Title: **Davy Crockett Takes the Trail**
Cover: Geoff Squire
Art: Unknown with Davy Crockett by Bill Lacey

166 (01/05/56)
Kit Carson
Cover: Unknown
(a) Kit Carson & the Redskin Fury
Art: Peter Sutherland
(b) Kit Carson & the Mountain Chase
Art: Unknown Artist [D]

167 (01/05/56)
Buck Jones
Cover: James E. McConnell
(a) Buck Jones & the White Man's Treachery
Art: R. Charles Roylance
(b) Buck Jones & the Peace of the Navajo
Art: Unknown Artist [D]
(c) Buck Jones & the Faces in the Night
Art: Unknown

168 (01/05/56)
Davy Crockett
Cover: James E. McConnell
(a) Davy Crockett & the Traitor Trappers
Art: Unknown
(b) Davy Crockett & the Ghost Horses
Art: Bill Lacey

169 (07/06/56)
Kit Carson
Cover: Unknown
(a) Kit Carson & the Trap at Thunder Pass
Art: Armando Bonato
(b) Kit Carson & the Pony Express
Art: Alfredo Marculeta

170 (07/06/56)
Buck Jones
Cover: James E. McConnell
(a) Buck Jones & the Crooked Mayor
Art: R. Charles Roylance
(b) Buck Jones – Badman's Pal!
Art: Tom Laidler

171 (07/06/56)
Davy Crockett
Title: **Davy Crockett – Mighty Trail Blazer!**
Cover: James E. McConnell
Art: Peter Sutherland

172 (07/06/56)
Kit Carson
Cover: James E. McConnell
(a) Kit Carson's Buffalo Trouble
Art: Peter Sutherland
(b) Kit Carson & the Golden Horse of Little Bear
Art: D. Gale

173 (05/07/56)
Kit Carson
Cover: Unknown Artist [D]
(a) Kit Carson & the Treaty Chief
Art: H. C. Milburn
(b) Kit Carson & the Outlaw Officer
Art: Unknown Artist [D]

  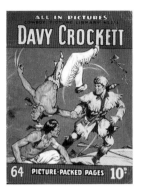 

174 (05/07/56)
Buck Jones
Cover: James E. McConnell
(a) Buck Jones & the Rock Fall
Art: R. Charles Roylance
(b) Buck Jones & the Apache Manhunt
Art: Ron Turner & another

175 (05/07/56)
Davy Crockett
Title: **Davy Crockett & the Man Who Vanished**
Cover: Geoff Squire
Art: Selby Donnison

176 (05/07/56)
Kansas Kid – King of the Cowboys
Cover: Unknown
(a) How the Kansas Kid Beat the Rodeo Raiders
Art: R. Charles Roylance
(b) How the Kansas Kid Met the Black Stallion Again
Art: Unknown Artist [D]
(c) How the Kansas Kid Helped the Masked Stranger
Art: Terry Patrick

177 (02/08/56)
Kit Carson
Cover: Unknown
(a) Kit Carson on Trouble Trail
Art: Armando Bonato
(b) Kit Carson & the Ghostly Coyotes
Art: Reg Bunn
(c) Kit Carson & the Horse Wrangler
Art: Unknown Artist [D]

178 (02/08/56)
Buck Jones
Cover: James E. McConnell
(a) Buck Jones & the Boy Gunman
Art: Unknown Artist [D]
(b) Buck Jones & Dad Macey's Guns
Art: Unknown
(c) Buck Jones & the Four Legged Deputy
Art: Unknown Artist [D]

179 (02/08/56)
Davy Crockett
Title: **Davy Crockett & the Captured Cannon**
Cover: Geoff Squire
Art: Peter Sutherland

180 (02/08/56)
Kansas Kid
Cover: James E. McConnell
(a) How the Kansas Kid Beat the Rustlers of the Ranges
Art: R. Charles Roylance
(b) How the Kansas Kid Became Trail Herd Boss
Art: Unknown Artist [D]

181 (06/09/56)
Kit Carson
Cover: James E. McConnell
(a) Kit Carson & the Legend of Grizzly Hollow
Art: Armando Bonato
(b) Kit Carson & the Race to Red Sand Gulch
Art: Unknown
(c) Kit Carson & the Mexican Double-Cross
Art: Unknown

182 (06/09/56)
Buck Jones
Cover: James E. McConnell
(a) Buck Jones & the Secret of the Totem
Art: D. Gale
(b) Buck Jones & the Gun-Slinger
Art: Unknown Artist [D]
(c) Buck Jones & the Branded Man
Art: Unknown

183 (06/09/56)
Davy Crockett
Cover: Geoff Squire
(a) Davy Crockett & the Treasure of the Tontos
Art: Terry Aspin
(b) Davy Crockett & the Riverboat Rogues
Art: Terry Aspin

184 (06/09/56)
Kansas Kid
Cover: Unknown
(a) How the Kansas Kid Beat the Redskin Horse-Thieves
Art: Bill Lacey
(b) How the Kansas Kid Foiled the Mexican Kidnappers
Art: Unknown

185 (04/10/56)
Kit Carson
Cover: James E. McConnell
(a) Kit Carson & the Thunder Bird's War Bonnet
Art: Peter Sutherland
(b) Kit Carson & the Pawnee Totem
Art: Terry Patrick

186 (04/10/56)
Buck Jones
Cover: James E. McConnell
(a) Buck Jones & the Outlaw Redskin
Art: R. Charles Roylance
(b) Buck Jones & the Redman's Gold
Art: Unknown Artist [D]

187 (04/10/56)
Davy Crockett
Title: **The Great Ghost Stallion**
Cover: Geoff Squire
Art: Peter Sutherland

188 (04/10/56)
Kansas Kid
Cover: James E. McConnell
(a) How the Kansas Kid Won the Great Chuck Wagon Race
Art: R. Charles Roylance
(b) How the Kansas Kid Met the Man in Silent Valley
Art: Terry Patrick
(c) How the Kansas Kid Took a Bus Ride to Adventure
Art: Terry Patrick

189 (06/11/56)
Kit Carson
Cover: James E. McConnell
(a) Kit Carson & the Buffalo Bandits
Art: Reg Bunn
(b) Kit Carson & the Golden Eagle
Art: Armando Bonato
(c) Kit Carson & the Missing Munition Wagon
Art: Terry Patrick

190 (06/11/56)
Buck Jones
Cover: James E. McConnell
(a) Buck Jones & the Outlaw's Reward
Art: Terry Patrick
(b) Buck Jones & the Terror Trail
Art: Franco Bignotti with faces by another artist
(c) Buck Jones & the Silver Wagon Trap
Art: Unknown Artist [D]

191 (06/11/56)
Davy Crockett
Title: **Davy Crockett – Florida Fighter**
Cover: Unknown
Art: Terry Aspin

192 (06/11/56)
Kansas Kid
Cover: James E. McConnell
(a) How the Kansas Kid Battled with the Bandits
Art: R. Charles Roylance
(b) How the Kansas Kid Solved the Mystery of the Vanishing Cattle
Art: Terry Patrick
(c) How the Kansas Kid Met the Outlaw Hero
Art: Unknown

193 (04/12/56)
Kit Carson
Cover: James E. McConnell
(a) Kit Carson & the Red Indian Rising
Art: Peter Sutherland
(b) Kit Carson & the Double Disguise
Art: Unknown

  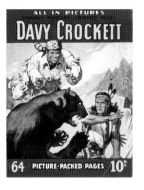 

194 (04/12/56)
Buck Jones
Cover: James E. McConnell
(a) Buck Jones Meets Crooked Eye, the Evil One
Art: D. Gale
(b) Buck Jones & the Gold Brigands
Art: Unknown Artist [D]

195 (04/12/56)
Davy Crockett
Title: **Davy Crockett & the Mask of Manitoba**
Cover: James E. McConnell
Art: Peter Sutherland

196 (04/12/56)
Kansas Kid
Cover: Unknown
(a) How the Kansas Kid Settled the Diaz Valley Feud
Art: R. Charles Roylance
(b) How the Kansas Kid Rescued the Kiowa Captive
Art: Terry Patrick
(c) How the Kansas Kid Met the Four-legged Stranger
Art: Unknown

197 (01/01/57)
Kit Carson
Cover: James E. McConnell
(a) Kit Carson & the Battle of Fort Strong
Art: Peter Sutherland
(b) Kit Carson & the Roaring River Race
Art: Terry Patrick
(c) Kit Carson & the Lawless Land Grabbers
Art: Unknown

198 (01/01/57)
Buck Jones
Cover: James E. McConnell
(a) Buck Jones & the Railroad Battlers
Art: R. Charles Roylance
(b) Buck Jones & the Redskins on the Warpath
Art: Unknown Artist [D]
(c) Buck Jones & the Domingos and the Doyles
Art: Unknown

199 (01/01/57)
Davy Crockett
Title: **Davy Crockett & the Tomahawk Totem**
Cover: James E. McConnell
Art: Terry Aspin

200 (01/01/57)
Kansas Kid
Cover: James E. McConnell
(a) How the Kansas Kid Beat the Redskin Raiders
Art: R. Charles Roylance
(b) How the Kansas Kid Rode to the Rescue
Art: C. E. Drury
(c) How the Kansas Kid Beat the Crooked Buyer
Art: Unknown Artist [D]

201 (05/02/57)
Kit Carson
Cover: James E. McConnell
(a) Kit Carson & the Flying Wagon Train
Art: Peter Sutherland
(b) Kit Carson & the Poisoned Pastures
Art: C. E. Montford

202 (05/02/57)
Buck Jones
Cover: James E. McConnell
(a) Buck Jones & the Fire God
Art: H. C. Milburn
(b) Buck Jones Wins Through
Art: Unknown Artist [D]
(c) Buck Jones & the Warning Bell
Art: Franco Bignotti

203 (05/02/57)
Davy Crockett
Title: **Davy Crockett & the Magic War Bonnet**
Cover: James E. McConnell
Art: D. Gale

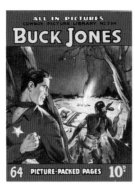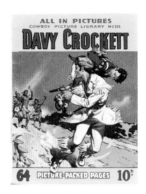

204 (05/02/57)
Kansas Kid
Cover: Unknown
(a) How the Kansas Kid Beat the Border Bandits
Art: Jorge Macabich
(b) How the Kansas Kid Foiled the Gunpowder Plot
Art: Terry Patrick

205 (05/03/57)
Kit Carson
Cover: James E. McConnell
(a) Kit Carson & the Prairie Racketeers
Art: Peter Sutherland
(b) Kit Carson & the Mask of Manitou
Art: Unknown

206 (05/03/57)
Buck Jones
Cover: Unknown
(a) Buck Jones & the Gunnar Gang
Art: R. Charles Roylance
(b) Buck Jones – Coward of Alkali City
Art: Unknown

207 (05/03/57)
Davy Crockett
Title: **Davy Crockett's Prairie Peril**
Cover: James E. McConnell
Art: Terry Aspin

208 (05/03/57)
Kansas Kid
Cover: James E. McConnell
(a) How the Kansas Kid Rode With the Indian Posse
Art: Jorge Macabich
(b) How the Kansas Kid Helped the Feudin' Families
Art: D. Gale
(c) How the Kansas Kid Saved the Too Trusting Senator
Art: Selby Donnison

209 (02/04/57)
Kit Carson
Cover: James E. McConnell
(a) Kit Carson & the Storm at Mustang Canyon
Art: Peter Sutherland
(b) Kit Carson & the Island of the Brave
Art: Armando Bonato & another

210 (02/04/57)
Buck Jones
Cover: James E. McConnell
(a) Buck Jones & the Pawnee Totem
Art: R. Charles Roylance
(b) Buck Jones Makes His Play
Art: Terry Patrick
(c) Buck Jones & the Mystery of Blue Springs Valley
Art: D. Gale

211 (02/04/57)
Davy Crockett
Title: **The Fight of the Fur Traders**
Cover: James E. McConnell
Art: Terry Aspin?

212 (02/04/57)
Kansas Kid
Cover: James E. McConnell
(a) How the Kansas Kid Beat the Riverboat Rustlers
Art: Jorge Macabich
(b) How the Kansas Kid Returned the Thunderbird Totem
Art: Unknown

213 (07/05/57)
Kit Carson
Cover: James E. McConnell
(a) Kit Carson Rides to the Rescue
Art: Peter Sutherland
(b) Kit Carson & the Chickasaw Wagon Trap
Art: Peter Sutherland & another

214 (07/05/57)
Buck Jones
Cover: James E. McConnell
(a) Buck Jones & the Battle at Badger's Creek
Art: R. Charles Roylance
(b) Buck Jones & the Stage Robbery Mystery
Art: H. C. Milburn

 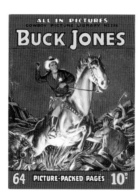 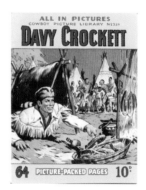 

215 (07/05/57)
Davy Crockett
Title: **Davy Crockett & the Shawnee War Plan**
Cover: James E. McConnell
Art: C. E. Drury and another (pp.1-3)

216 (07/05/57)
Kansas Kid
Cover: James E. McConnell
(a) How the Kansas Kid Beat the Hold-Up Plotters
Art: Bill Lacey
(b) How the Kansas Kid Won the Competition Colts
Art: Terry Patrick
(c) How the Kansas Kid Helped the Feuding Ranchers
Art: F. A. Philpott

217 (04/06/57)
Kit Carson
Cover: James E. McConnell
(a) Kit Carson & the Mexican's Cunning
Art: Peter Sutherland
(b) Kit Carson & the Captive Redskins
Art: Unknown

218 (04/06/57)
Buck Jones
Cover: James E. McConnell
(a) Buck Jones & the Million Dollar Map
Art: Unknown
(b) Buck Jones & the Dark Riders
Art: Unknown

219 (04/06/57)
Davy Crockett
Title: **Davy Crockett & the Great Pawnee Treasure**
Cover: James E. McConnell
Art: D. Gale

220 (04/06/57)
Kansas Kid
Cover: James E. McConnell
(a) How the Kansas Kid Beat the Bullying Bank Bandits
Art: Jorge Macabich

(b) How the Kansas Kid Foiled the Crooked Marshall
Art: Unknown Artist [D]

221 (02/07/57)
Kit Carson
Cover: James E. McConnell
(a) Kit Carson – Prairie Peacemaker
Art: Peter Sutherland
(b) Kit Carson & the River of Gold
Art: Unknown Artist [D]

222 (02/07/57)
Buck Jones
Cover: James E. McConnell
(a) Buck Jones Meets Lone Wolf the Redskin Robin Hood
Art: R. Charles Roylance
(b) Buck Jones & the Cow Girl
Art: Peter Sutherland & R. Charles Roylance

223 (02/07/57)
Davy Crockett
Title: **The Old-Timer's Secret**
Cover: James E. McConnell
Art: Terry Aspin

224 (02/07/57)
Kansas Kid
Cover: James E. McConnell
(a) How the Kansas Kid Foiled the Double-Crossing Cattlemen
Art: Unknown Artist [D]
(b) How the Kansas Kid Helped the Gun-Shy Rancher
Art: F. A. Philpott

225 (06/08/57)
Kit Carson
Cover: James E. McConnell
(a) Kit Carson's Commandos
Art: Peter Sutherland
(b) Kit Carson & the Lake of Fire
Art: Unknown

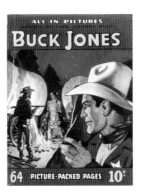
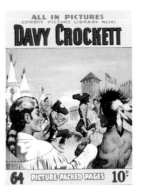

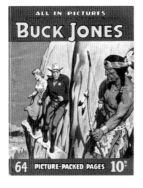

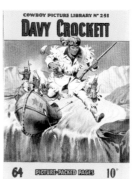

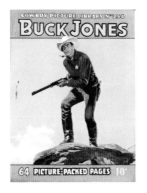
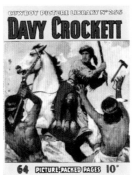

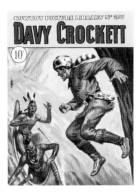

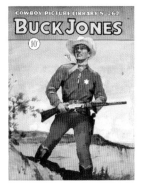

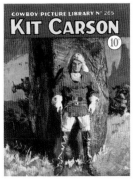

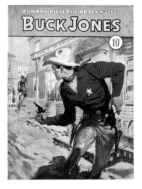

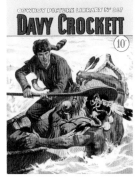

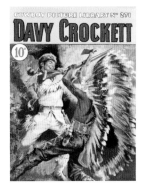

 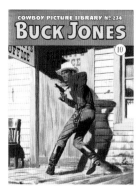 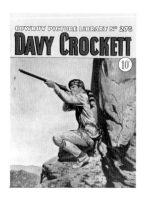 

226 (06/08/57)
Buck Jones
Cover: James E. McConnell
(a) Buck Jones & the "Never-Say-Die" Wilsons
Art: R. Charles Roylance
(b) Buck Jones & the Mexican Train Bandits
Art: Unknown

227 (06/08/57)
Davy Crockett
Title: **Davy Crockett & the Battling Briton**
Cover: Unknown
Art: Terry Aspin
Script: Joan Whitford

228 (06/08/57)
Kansas Kid
Cover: James E. McConnell
(a) How the Kansas Kid Met the Little Dogie
Art: Unknown Artist [D]
(b) How the Kansas Kid Saved the Golden Headress
Art: Unknown

229 (03/09/57)
Kit Carson
Cover: James E. McConnell
(a) Kit Carson & the Kiowa Captives
Art: Peter Sutherland
(b) Kit Carson in Seven Hours to Live
Art: Unknown

230 (03/09/57)
Buck Jones
Cover: James E. McConnell
(a) Buck Jones & the Starving Navahos
Art: R. Charles Roylance
(b) Buck Jones Meets the Boston Kid
Art: R. Charles Roylance

231 (03/09/57)
Davy Crockett
Title: **Davy Crockett & the White Indian**
Cover: James E. McConnell
Art: D. Gale
Script: Bob Kesten?

232 (03/09/57)
Kansas Kid
Cover: James E. McConnell
(a) How the Kansas Kid Won the Battle of Twin Rocks
Art: Jorge Macabich
(b) How the Kansas Kid Beat the Baloon Bandit
Art: Unknown
Note: Originally scripted as "Buck Jones' Air Fight"

233 (01/10/57)
Kit Carson
Title: **Kit Carson Deals with Texas Treachery**
Cover: James E. McConnell
Art: Peter Sutherland

234 (01/10/57)
Buck Jones
Cover: James E. McConnell
(a) Buck Jones Rides on the Trail of Trouble
Art: R. Charles Roylance
(b) Buck Jones & Frontier Justice
Art: Unknown
(c) Buck Jones & The Ghost of Hanging Valley
Art: Bill Lacey

235 (01/10/57)
Davy Crockett
Title: **Davy Crockett & the Phantom Redskin Army**
Cover: James E. McConnell
Art: Terry Aspin
Script: Conrad Frost

236 (01/10/57)
Kansas Kid
Cover: Unknown
(a) How the Kansas Kid Foiled the Crooked Deputy
Art: Selby Donnison
Script: Albert King
(b) How the Kansas Kid Won the Rodeo Prize
Art: Unknown Artist [D]

237 (05/11/57)
Kit Carson
Cover: James E. McConnell
(a) Kit Carson & the Angry Major
Art: Peter Sutherland
(b) Kit Carson & the Vanishing Raiders
Art: Armando Bonato

238 (05/11/57)
Buck Jones
Cover: Unknown
(a) Buck Jones & the Great Railroad Battle
Art: R. Charles Roylance
(b) Buck Jones & the Desert Secret
Art: Selby Donnison & another

239 (05/11/57)
Davy Crockett
Title: **Davy Crockett & the Lord of the Eagles**
Cover: James E. McConnell
Art: Terry Aspin
Script: Conrad Frost

240 (05/11/57)
Kansas Kid
Cover: Unknown
(a) How the Kansas Kid Caught the Circus Kidnappers
Art: Jorge Macabich
(b) How the Kansas Kid Broke Out of Jail
Art: Unknown

241 (03/12/57)
Kit Carson
Cover: James E. McConnell
(a) Kit Carson & the Magic War Robe
Art: Peter Sutherland
(b) Kit Carson & the Fighting Sioux
Art: Unknown
Script: Conrad Frost

242 (03/12/57)
Buck Jones
Cover: James E. McConnell
(a) Buck Jones & the Guns of Fort Camino
Art: R. Charles Roylance
(b) Buck Jones & the Spider Mine Mystery
Art: Unknown
(c) Buck Jones & the Gold Looters of Westwood
Art: Unknown Artist [D]

243 (03/12/57)
Davy Crockett
Title: **Davy Crockett & the Pawnee Trail Trouble**
Cover: James E. McConnell
Art: Unknown

244 (03/12/57)
Kansas Kid
Cover: Unknown
(a) How the Kansas Kid Tamed Young Elmer
Art: Unknown Artist [D]
(b) How the Kansas Kid Mastered the Mad Major
Art: Unknown

245 (07/01/58)
Kit Carson
Cover: James E. McConnell
(a) Kit Carson & the Cheyenne Cave Indians
Art: Peter Sutherland
(b) Kit Carson & the Peace Treaty Plot!
Art: Ron Embleton

246 (07/01/58)
Buck Jones
Cover: James E. McConnell
(a) Buck Jones & the Bad Medicine
Art: R. Charles Roylance
(b) Buck Jones & the Man Beyond the Law!
Art: C. E. Montford

247 (07/01/58)
Davy Crockett
Title: **Davy Crockett Meets the Other Davy Crockett**
Cover: James E. McConnell
Art: D. Gale

248 (07/01/58)
Kansas Kid
Cover: Unknown
(a) How the Kansas Kid Foiled the Jail-Breakers Plot
Art: Jorge Macabich
(b) How the Kansas Kid Beat the Barn Dance Bandits
Art: Unknown

249 (04/02/58)
Kit Carson
Cover: D. C. Eyles
Title page: D. C. Eyles
(a) The Guns of Kit Carson
Art: Peter Gallant
(b) Kit Carson Breaks the Blockade
Art: Peter Sutherland

250 (04/02/58)
Buck Jones
Cover: Unknown
(a) Buck Jones & the Battle of Black Rock Pass
Art: R. Charles Roylance
(b) Buck Jones & the Smartest Horse in the West
Art: R. Charles Roylance

251 (04/02/58)
Davy Crockett
Title: **Davy Crockett Picks a Chief**
Cover: James E. McConnell
Art: Terry Aspin

252 (04/02/58)
Kansas Kid
Cover: James E. McConnell
(a) Kansas Kid & the Fight at Fort Sabre
Art: Selby Donnison
(b) Buffalo Bill & the Lawless Land Grabber
Art: Geoff Campion; reprint from Comet
(c) Buffalo Bill & the War Drums of the Sioux
Art: Geoff Campion; reprint from Comet
(d) Buffalo Bill & the Cunning of Dull Knife
Art: Geoff Campion; reprint from *Comet* 491 (14/12/57)
(e) Buffalo Bill – Battling Peacemaker
Art: Geoff Campion; reprint from Comet

253 (04/03/58)
Kit Carson
Title: **Kit Carson & the Strange Adventure of Winged Ears**
Cover: Sep E. Scott
Art: Renato Polese
Note: Believed to have been scripted as a "Buffalo Bill" strip as it features Calamity Jane

254 (04/03/58)
Buck Jones
Cover: Jordi Penalva
(a) Buck Jones & the Silent Victims
Art: R. Charles Roylance
(b) Buck Jones & the Bullion Bandits
Art: Selby Donnison

255 (04/03/58)
Davy Crockett
Title: **Davy Crockett, Indian Fighter**
Cover: Sep E. Scott
Art: Terry Aspin
Script: Joan Whitford

256 (04/03/58)
Kansas Kid
Cover: James E. McConnell
(a) Kansas Kid & the Stableman's Secret
Art: Jorge Macabich
(b) Buffalo Bill
Art: Geoff Campion; reprint from Comet
(c) Kansas Kid & the Ambush at Rattlesnake Pass
Art: Unknown

257 (01/04/58)
Kit Carson
Cover: Unknown
(a) Kit Carson & the Payroll Bandits
Art: Peter Gallant
(b) Kit Carson & the Viking
Art: Peter Sutherland with faces by Reg Bunn

  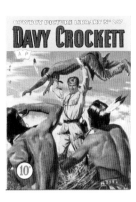 

258 (01/04/58)
Buck Jones
Cover: James E. McConnell
(a) Buck Jones & the Double Decoy
Art: R. Charles Roylance
(b) Buck Jones & the Bandit of Bear Creek
Art: Mike Western; adapts a "Lucky Logan" story from *Knockout*
(c) Buck Jones & the Runaway Rancher
Art: Mike Western; adapts a "Lucky Logan" story from *Knockout*
(d) Strongbow the Mohawk
Art: Unknown

259 (01/04/58)
Davy Crockett
Title: **Davy Crockett – Guardian of the Frontier!**
Cover: D. C. Eyles
Art: D. Gale

260 (01/04/58)
Kansas Kid
Title: **Kansas Kid & the Rio Grande Rustlers**
Cover: Rialdo Guizzardi
Art: Reg Bunn
Script: Kenneth Giggal (story)/J. H. Higgins (script)

261 (05/05/58)
Kit Carson
Cover: Jordi Penalva
(a) Kit Carson & the Four Legged Fury
Art: Unknown
(b) Kit Carson & the Disaster at Fort Rock
Art: Ian Kennedy
(c) Buffalo Bill & the Fighting Irishmen
Art: Geoff Campion; reprint from *Comet* 323 (25/09/54)
(d) Buffalo Bill Charges the Guns
Art: Geoff Campion; reprint from *Comet* 321 (11/09/54)
(e) Buffalo Bill & the Challenge of Fighting Hawk
Art: Geoff Campion; reprint from *Comet* 331 (20/11/54)
(f) Buffalo Bill Saves the Regiment
Art: Geoff Campion; reprint from *Comet* 319 (28/08/54)

262 (05/05/58)
Buck Jones
Cover: Sep E. Scott
(a) Buck Jones & the Trail of Treachery
Art: R. Charles Roylance
(b) Buck Jones & the Fake Medicine Man
Art: Mike Western; adapts a "Lucky Logan" story from *Knockout*
(c) Buck Jones & the Copper Creek Hold-Up
Art: Mike Western; adapts a "Lucky Logan" story from *Knockout*
(d) Buck Jones & the Fire Magic
Art: Dino Zuffi with faces by Reg Bunn

263 (05/05/58)
Davy Crockett
Title: **Davy Crockett Takes Command!**
Cover: Rialdo Guizzardi
Art: Stephen Chapman

264 (05/05/58)
Kansas Kid
Cover: James E. McConnell
(a) Kansas Kid & the Guns of Wyatt Earp
Art: Bill Lacey
(b) Buffalo Bill & the Hunt for Running Horse
Title page: D. C. Eyles
Art: Robert Forrest; reprint from *Comet* (297?, 27/03/53)
(c) Buffalo Bill & the Peril of Eagle Crag
Title page: D. C. Eyles
Art: Robert Forrest; reprint from *Comet* 324 (02/10/54)
(d) Buffalo Bill & the Mighty Crow Warrior
Title page: Geoff Campion
Art: D. C. Eyles; reprint from *Comet* 317 (14/08/54)

265 (02/06/58)
Kit Carson
Cover: Giorgio De Gaspari
(a) Kit Carson & the Tokens of Peace
Art: Jesus Blasco
(b) Kit Carson – Indian Fighter!
Art: Raffaele Paparella

  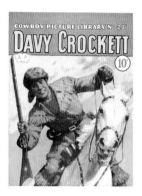 

266 (02/06/58)
Buck Jones
Cover: James E. McConnell
Title page: R. Charles Roylance
(a) Buck Jones & the Badman of Blue Heights
Art: Reg Bunn
(b) Buck Jones & the Deep River Bandits
Art: Mike Western; adapts a "Lucky Logan" story from
Knockout
(c) Buck Jones & the Bully of Buffalo Creek
Art: Mike Western; adapts a "Lucky Logan" story from
Knockout

267 (02/06/58)
Davy Crockett
Title: **Davy Crockett & the River of No Return!**
Cover: Mario Uggeri
Art: Terry Aspin

268 (02/06/58)
Kansas Kid
Cover: Jordi Penalva
(a) Kansas Kid & the Golden Map
Art: C. E. Montford
(b-f) Buffalo Bill (5 untitled stories)
Art: Geoff Campion, D. C. Eyles; reprints stories from
Comet

269 (07/07/58)
Kit Carson
Cover: James E. McConnell
(a) Kit Carson & the Boy Commander
Art: Gino D'Antonio
(b) Kit Carson & the Cheyenne Guns
Art: Mario Uggeri

270 (07/07/58)
Buck Jones
Cover: Giorgio De Gaspari
(a) Buck Jones & the Man From Wyoming
Art: R. Charles Roylance
(b) Buck Jones & the Crook of Trail's End
Art: Mike Western; adapts a "Lucky Logan" story from
Knockout

(c) Buck Jones & the Iron Horse Raiders
Art: Mike Western; adapts a "Lucky Logan" story from
Knockout

271 (07/07/58)
Davy Crockett
Title: **Davy Crockett & the Long Trek Against Time!**
Cover: Mario Uggeri
Art: D. Gale

272 (07/07/58)
Kansas Kid
Title: **Kansas Kid & the Trail of the Gunmen**
Cover: Mario Uggeri
Art: Jorge Macabich

273 (04/08/58)
Kit Carson
Cover: Giorgio De Gaspari
(a) Kit Carson & the Stolen Carbines
Art: Unknown, partly by Reg Bunn
(b) Buffalo Bill & the Treachery of Black Lance
Art: Robert Forrest; reprint from *Comet*
(c) Buffalo Bill & the Battle of Great Bear Pass
Art: Robert Forrest; reprint from *Comet*

274 (04/08/58)
Buck Jones
Cover: Jordi Penalva
(a) Buck Jones & the Stagecoach Race
Art: R. Charles Roylance
(b) Buck Jones & the Missing Prisoner
Art: Ian Kennedy
(c) Buck Jones & the Four-Legged Deputy
Art: R. Charles Roylance

275 (04/08/58)
Davy Crockett
Title: **Davy Crockett & the Trail to Fort Venture**
Cover: Jordi Penalva, based on a still of Burt Lancaster
from the film *The Kentuckian* (1955)
Art: H. C. Milburn with DC's face and last three pages by
Reg Bunn

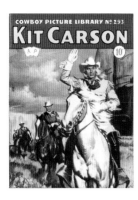  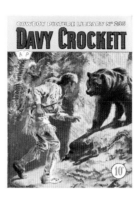 

276 (04/08/58)
Kansas Kid
Cover: Mario Uggeri
(a) Kansas Kid & Desert Gunsmoke
Art: Franco Bignotti
(b) Kansas Kid & the Trail Camp Raiders
Art: Jesus Blasco

277 (01/09/58)
Kit Carson
Cover: Giorgio De Gaspari
(a) Kit Carson & the Great Golden Stallion
Art: Reg Bunn
(b) Kit Carson & the Kidnapped Boy!
Art: Geoff Campion; adapts a "Buffalo Bill" story from
Comet
(c) Strongbow the Mohawk
Art: Virgilio Muzzi

278 (01/09/58)
Buck Jones
Cover: Jordi Penalva
(a) Buck Jones & the Trail to Twin Forks
Art: C. E. Montford
(b) Buck Jones & the Vanishing Bandit
Art: Ian Kennedy
(c) Buck Jones & the Boy Rancher
Art: Mike Western; adapts a "Lucky Logan" story from
Knockout
(d) Buck Jones & Mystery Canyon
Art: Mike Western; adapts a "Lucky Logan" story from
Knockout

279 (01/09/58)
Davy Crockett
Cover: Jordi Penalva
(a) Davy Crockett & the Traitor Trooper
Art: Reg Bunn
(b) Davy Crockett – Bear Slayer!
Art: D. Gale
(c) Davy Crockett Makes Big Medicine
Art: Terry Aspin

280 (01/09/58)
Kansas Kid
Cover: James E. McConnell
(a) Kansas Kid & the Railroad Wreckers
Art: C. E. Montford
(b) Kansas Kid & the Mystery of Bandit Peaks
Art: Jorge Macabich

281 (06/10/58)
Kit Carson
Cover: Jordi Penalva
Title page: D. C. Eyles
(a) Kit Carson & the Star Witness
Art: Stephen Chapman
(b) Kit Carson & the Tenderfoot
Art: Jose Bielsa
(c) Kit Carson & the Sacred Arrow
Art: Stephen Chapman

282 (06/10/58)
Buck Jones
Cover: Jordi Penalva
(a) Buck Jones & the Tarten Totem
Art: R. Charles Roylance
(b) Buck Jones & the Fancy Gun
Art: Franco Bignotti

283 (06/10/58)
Davy Crockett
Cover: Giorgio De Gaspari
Title page: adapted from drawing by Geoff Campion, with
DC drawn by Stephen Chapman
(a) Davy Crockett & the Longknife War God!
Art: Reg Bunn
(b) Davy Crockett Joins the Cavalry
Art: D. C. Eyles

284 (06/10/58)
Kansas Kid
Title: **Kansas Kid & the Chief With the False Face**
Cover: Giorgio De Gaspari
Art: Jorge Macabich

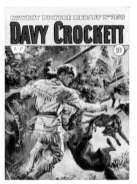

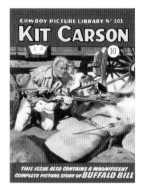
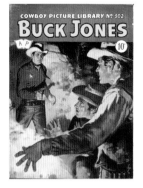

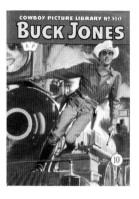

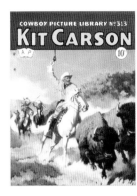
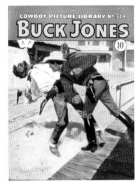

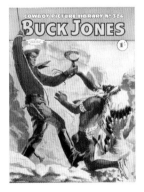
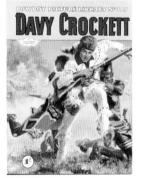

 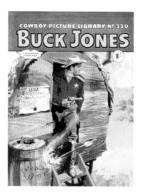  

285 (03/11/58)
Kit Carson
Cover: Jordi Penalva
(a) Kit Carson & the Crooked Tobacco Traders
Art: Peter Gallant
(b) Kit Carson & the Gambler
Art: H. C. Milburn

286 (03/11/58)
Buck Jones
Cover: Jordi Penalva
(a) Buck Jones & the Million Dollar Maverick
Art: Eric Parker
(b) Buck Jones & the Battle at Buffalo Wells
Art: Eric Parker

287 (03/11/58)
Davy Crockett
Cover: Jordi Penalva
(a) Davy Crockett & the River Renegades
Art: Terry Aspin
(b) Davy Crockett & the Quest of Eagle Mountain
Art: Stephen Chapman

288 (03/11/58)
Kansas Kid
Cover: Jordi Penalva
(a) Kansas Kid & the Six-Gun Politician
Art: Emilio Frejo
(b) Kansas Kid & the Carnival Crooks
Art: Reg Bunn

289 (01/12/58)
Kit Carson
Cover: Jordi Penalva
(a) Kit Carson & the River on Wheels
Art: Virgilio Muzzi
(b) Buffalo Bill – Town Tamer!
Art: D. C. Eyles; reprint from *Comet*
(c) Buffalo Bill & the Battle of River Bend
Art: Fred Holmes; reprint from *Comet*

290 (01/12/58)
Buck Jones
Cover: Jordi Penalva
Title page: D. C. Eyles
(a) Buck Jones & the Tower of Light
Art: Eric Parker
(b) Buck Jones & the Renegade Rancher
Art: G. Douglas
(c) Buck Jones & the Rodeo Show
Title page: Geoff Campion
Art: Mike Western and others; adapts a "Lucky Logan"
story from *Knockout*

291 (01/12/58)
Davy Crockett
Cover: Sep E. Scott
Title page: D. C. Eyles
(a) Davy Crockett & the Blackfoot Brigands!
Art: D. Gale with p.2 by Reg Bunn
(b) Davy Crockett's Secret Mission
Art: Stephen Chapman

292 (01/12/58)
Kansas Kid
Cover: Giorgio De Gaspari
Title page: D. C. Eyles
(a) Kansas Kid & the Barn Dance Kidnappers!
Art: Sergio Tarquinio
(b) Kansas Kid & the Unwelcome Guest
Art: Reg Bunn

293 (05/01/59)
Kit Carson
Cover: Jordi Penalva
(a) Kit Carson & the Sign of the Red Hand
Art: Jose Bielsa
(b) Kit Carson & the Indian Raiders
Art: Unknown

294 (05/01/59)
Buck Jones
Cover: Jordi Penalva
(a) Buck Jones & the Dash to Eagle Pass
Art: Franco Bignotti
(b) Buck Jones & the Left-Handed Gunman
Art: Virgilio Muzzi

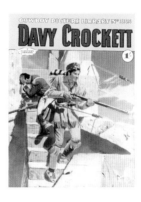

295 (05/01/59)
Davy Crockett
Cover: Giorgio De Gaspari
(a) Davy Crockett & the Curse of the Kutenai!
Art: Reg Bunn
(b) Davy Crockett & the Iron Man
Art: Renato Polese?

296 (05/01/59)
Kansas Kid
Title: **Kansas Kid & the Guns of the Rio Concho**
Cover: Giorgio De Gaspari
Art: R. Charles Roylance

297 (02/02/59)
Kit Carson
Cover: Giorgio De Gaspari
(a) The Lightning Guns of Kit Carson
Art: H. C. Milburn
(b) Kit Carson & the Renegade Chieftain
Art: Unknown
(c) Buffalo Bill & the Demoted Sergeant
Art: Fred Holmes; reprint from *Comet*

298 (02/02/59)
Buck Jones
Cover: Giorgio De Gaspari
Title page: D. C. Eyles
(a) Buck Jones & the Bird Man
Art: Eric Parker
(b) Buck Jones & the Broken Wheel Bandits
Art: Eric Parker
(c) Buck Jones & the Long Lost Treasure
Art: Eric Parker

299 (02/02/59)
Davy Crockett
Cover: Giorgio De Gaspari
Title page: D. C. Eyles
(a) Davy Crockett & the Mexican Masquerade
Art: Stephen Chapman
(b) Davy Crockett & the Master of Magic
Art: D. C. Eyles

300 (02/02/59)
Kansas Kid
Cover: Giorgio De Gaspari
Title page: D. C. Eyles
(a) Kansas Kid & the Kidnappers
Art: Jesus Blasco
(b) Kansas Kid Meets Fighting Joe Swain!
Art: Sergio Tarquinio

301 (02/03/59)
Kit Carson
Cover: Jordi Penalva
Title page: Gino D'Antonio
(a) Kit Carson & the Taming of Cunning Horse
Art: Unknown
(b) Kit Carson & the Captive Senator
Art: Franco Bignotti?
(c) Buffalo Bill & the Master of War Bonnett Pass
Art: R. Charles Roylance

302 (02/03/59)
Buck Jones
Cover: Jordi Penalva
Title page: Gino D'Antonio
(a) Buck Jones & the Dangerous Gold
Art: C. E. Montford
(b) Buck Jones & the Apache Duel
Art: Eric Bradbury; adapts a "Lucky Logan" story from *Knockout*
(c) Buck Jones & the Disappearing Men
Art: Eric Parker

303 (02/03/59)
Davy Crockett
Cover: Jordi Penalva.
(a) Davy Crockett & the Phantom Bugler!
Art: D. Gale
(b) Davy Crockett & the Frontier Outcast
Art: Studio SGS and another (faces)

304 (02/03/59)
Kansas Kid
Cover: Jordi Penalva
Title page: D. C. Eyles
(a) Kansas Kid & the Trail of the Silver Spur
Art: Jorge Macabich
(b) Kansas Kid & the House of Doom
Art: Fred Holmes

305 (06/04/59)
Kit Carson
Cover: Jordi Penalva
Title page: Gino D'Antonio
(a) Kit Carson & the Sergeant's Last Ride
Art: Jesus Blasco
(b) Kit Carson & the Evil Eye
Art: Antonio Correa

306 (06/04/59)
Buck Jones
Cover: Jordi Penalva, based on a still of James Stewart in
the film *Bend of the River* (1952, released in the UK as
Where the River Bends)
(a) Buck Jones & the Stunt Man
Art: D. C. Eyles
(b) Buck Jones & the Challenge
Art: C. E. Montford
(c) Buck Jones & Malone's Monster
Art: Eric Parker

307 (06/04/59)
Davy Crockett
Cover: Jordi Penalva
(a) Davy Crockett – One Man Peacemaker!
Art: Sergio Tarquinio
(b) Davy Crockett & the Calamity Kid
Art: Unknown
(c) Davy Crockett & the Mystery of Medicine River
Art: Ivo Pavone

308 (06/04/59)
Kansas Kid
Cover: Jordi Penalva
(a) Kansas Kid & the Golden Bear
Art: Franco Bignotti

(b) Kansas Kid & the White Chief of the Choctaws
Art: Geoff Campion; adapts a "Billy the Kid" story from *Sun*

309 (04/05/59)
Kit Carson
Cover: Giorgio De Gaspari
Title page: Gino D'Antonio
(a) Kit Carson & the Silver Dollar
Art: Jose Bielsa
(b) Kit Carson & the Bridge of Peril
Art: H. C. Milburn
(c) Buffalo Bill & the Outlaw Staghound
Art: Stephen Chapman; reprint from *Comet* 314 (24/07/54)

310 (04/05/59)
Buck Jones
Cover: Giorgio De Gaspari?
(a) Buck Jones & the War-Coach
Art: Eric Parker
(b) Buck Jones & the King of the Cattle Lands
Art: Eric Parker
(c) Buck Jones Battles Through!
Art: Fred Holmes and another; adapts a "Billy the Kid" story
from *Sun*

311 (04/05/59)
Davy Crockett
Cover: Jordi Penalva
Title page: D. C. Eyles
(a) Davy Crockett & the Georgia Gorilla
Art: Gerry Embleton
(b) Davy Crockett & the Treachery of the Dakotas
Art: Unknown
(c) Davy Crockett & the Gunpowder Pirates
Art: Reg Bunn

312 (04/05/59)
Kansas Kid
Cover: Jordi Penalva
Title page: D. C. Eyles
(a) Kansas Kid & the Ghost Rider of Thunder Gulch
Art: Reg Bunn
(b) Kansas Kid & the Two Gun Doctor
Art: Alfredo Marculeta
(c) Kansas Kid & the Gold Trail Gunman
Art: Sergio Tarquinio

313 (01/06/59)
Kit Carson
Title: **Kit Carson & the Pony Express Mystery**
Cover: Jordi Penalva
Art: Annibale Casabianca

314 (01/06/59)
Buck Jones
Cover: Jordi Penalva
(a) Buck Jones & the Siege of Sutler's Pass
Art: Eric Parker
(b) Buck Jones & the Ranch Robbers
Art: Colin Merrett with BJ's face mostly drawn by Reg Bunn

315 (01/06/59)
Davy Crockett
Cover: Giorgio De Gaspari
Title page: D. C. Eyles
(a) The Alligator Army
Art: Gerry Embleton
(b) The Pirate Stronghold
Art: Stephen Chapman

316 (01/06/59)
Kansas Kid
Cover: Jordi Penalva
Title page: D. C. Eyles
(a) Kansas Kid & the Fatal Shot!
Art: Franco Bignotti
(b) Kansas Kid & the Power of Red Fist!
Art: Jesus Blasco

317 (06/07/59)
Kit Carson
Title: **Kit Carson & the Secret Brotherhood**
Cover: Jordi Penalva
Art: Geoff Campion; abridged reprint of "The Quest of Wild Bill Hickok" from *Sun* (02/04 - 08/10/55)

318 (06/07/59)
Buck Jones
Cover: Jordi Penalva
Title page: Gino D'Antonio
(a) Buck Jones & the Assassin
Art: Eric Parker
(b) Buck Jones & the Rivals
Art: Jesus Blasco
(c) Buck Jones & the Kidnappers
Title page: D. C. Eyles
Art: Geoff Campion and another; adapts a "Billy the Kid" story from *Sun*

319 (06/07/59)
Davy Crockett
Cover: Jordi Penalva
Title page: Stephen Chapman, adapting a D. C. Eyles drawing
(a) Davy Crockett & the Phantom of the River
Art: Sergio Tarquinio
(b) Davy Crockett – Indian Bait!
Art: Stephen Chapman
(c) Davy Crockett's Redskin Army
Art: Gerry Embleton

320 (06/07/59)
Kansas Kid
Cover: Giorgio De Gaspari
(a) Kansas Kid—Jailbreaker
Art: Jorge Macabich
(b) Kansas Kid & the Thousand Dollar Man/Trap!
Art: Geoff Campion; adapts a "Billy the Kid" story from *Sun*

321 (09/59)
Kit Carson
Cover: Giorgio De Gaspari
Title page: Gino D'Antonio
(a) Kit Carson & the Great Darkness!
Art: Robert Forrest
(b) Kit Carson's Perilous Ride!
Art: Unknown
Script: Michael Moorcock
(c) Buffalo Bill & the Mighty Medicine Wizard!
Art: Stephen Chapman; reprint from *Comet* 316 (07/08/54)

 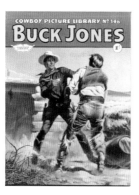  

322 (09/59)
Buck Jones
Cover: Mario Uggeri?
Title page: Gino D'Antonio
(a) Buck Jones & the Texas Tornado
Art: Franco Bignotti
(b) Buck Jones & the Finest Scalp in the West
Art: Colin Merrett; adapts a "Billy the Kid" story from *Sun*
with BJ drawn by Peter Gallant
(c) Buck Jones & the Indian Sheriff
Art: Eric Parker

323 (09/59)
Davy Crockett
Cover: Giorgio De Gaspari
Title page: adapts a drawing by Geoff Campion
(a) Davy Crockett & the Paddleboat Pirates!
Art: Gerry Embleton
(b) Davy Crockett & the Magpie of Medicine Falls
Art: Reg Bunn
(c) Davy Crockett & the SmArtest Horse in the West
Art: Gerry Embleton

324 (09/59)
Kansas Kid
Cover: Giorgio De Gaspari
Title page: Geoff Campion
(a) Kansas Kid & the Silent Spy
Art: Emilio Frejo
(b) Trigger Justice
Art: Renzo Calegari
(c) Kansas Kid & the Bandit Brothers
Art: Geoff Campion; adapts a "Billy the Kid" story from *Sun*

325 (10/59)
Kit Carson
Cover: Giorgio De Gaspari
(a) Kit Carson & the Siege of Lazoma
Art: Geoff Campion; adapts a "Wild Bill Hickok" serial from
Sun
(b) Kit Carson & the Snarling Puma
Art: D. Gale

326 (10/59)
Buck Jones
Title: **Two Gun Vengeance**
Cover: Giorgio De Gaspari
Title page: Reg Bunn
Art: Colin Merrett with BJ drawn by Reg Bunn

327 (10/59)
Davy Crockett
Cover: Giorgio De Gaspari
(a) Davy Crockett & the Valley of Fear
Art: D. Gale
(b) Davy Crockett & the Sea of Fire
Art: Ivo Pavone

328 (10/59)
Kansas Kid
Cover: Jordi Penalva
(a) Kansas Kid & the Cattle Ransom
Art: Jorge Macabich
(b) Kansas Kid & the Talking Totems
Art: Reg Bunn

329 (11/59)
Kit Carson
Cover: Jordi Penalva
Title page: Gino D'Antonio
(a) Kit Carson & the Cherokee Rebellion
Art: H. C. Milburn with pp. 35-42 by Reg Bunn
(b) Kit Carson's Nightmare Patrol!
Art: Jesus Blasco; adapts a "Buffalo Bill" story from *Comet*

330 (11/59)
Buck Jones
Cover: Giorgio De Gaspari
Title page: Gino D'Antonio
(a) Buck Jones & the Ships of the Desert
Art: C. E. Montford
(b) Buck Jones & the Fatal Inheritance!
Art: Fred Holmes with BJ drawn by Pat Nicolle
(c) Buck Jones & the Biggest Gun in the West!
Art: Geoff Campion; adapts a "Billy the Kid" story from *Sun*

  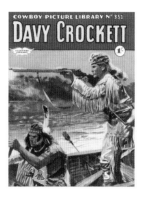 

331 (11/59)
Davy Crockett
Cover: Jordi Penalva
Title page: Gino D'Antonio
(a) Davy Crockett & the Duel With Danger
Art: Sergio Tarquinio
(b) Davy Crockett & the Secret of Sentinel Hill
Art: Raffaele Paparella

332 (11/59)
Kansas Kid
Cover: Jordi Penalva
(a) Kansas Kid & the Brand of the Double-D!
Art: Jorge Macabich
(b) Kansas Kid & the Disappearing Steers!
Art: Unknown
(c) Kansas Kid Plays a Lone Hand!
Art: Ian Kennedy

333 (12/59)
Kit Carson
Title: **Kit Carson & the Medicine Trail**
Cover: Jordi Penalva
Art: Jose Bielsa

334 (12/59)
Buck Jones
Cover: Jordi Penalva
(a) The Outlaw Deputy
Art: Robert Forrest
(b) The Sacrifice
Art: Reg Bunn

335 (12/59)
Davy Crockett
Title: **Davy Crockett's Private War**
Cover: Jordi Penalva
Art: Sergio Tarquinio

336 (12/59)
Kansas Kid
Cover: Jordi Penalva
Title page: Geoff Campion
(a) Kansas Kid & the War Sign of Thunder Wolf
Art: Jose Bielsa

(b) Kansas Kid & the Wild Men of the Mountain
Art: Colin Merrett

337 (01/60)
Kit Carson
Cover: Jordi Penalva
Title page: Gino D'Antonio
(a) Kit Carson & the Fighting Peacemaker
Art: Unknown
Script: Michael Moorcock?
(b) Kit Carson & the Treasure of Manitou
Art: D. C. Eyles
(c) Kit Carson & the Man from the Past
Art: Geoff Campion; adapts "Buffalo Bill & the Man from the Past" from *Comet* 338 (08/01/55)

338 (01/60)
Buck Jones
Cover: Unknown
(a) Buck Jones & the Trail of Treachery
Art: Franco Bignotti
(b) Buck Jones & the Hermit of the Hills
Art: Geoff Campion and George Parlett; adapts a "Billy the Kid" story from *Sun*

339 (01/60)
Davy Crockett
Cover: Jordi Penalva
Title page: Gino D'Antonio
(a) Davy Crockett – Ricaree!
Art: Gerry Embleton
(b) Gunpowder Justice!
Art: D. Gale
(c) Davy Crockett & the Dalesburg Dragon
Art: Sergio Tarquinio

340 (01/60)
Kansas Kid
Cover: Jordi Penalva, based on a still from the TV series *Bronco* with Ty Hardin's face redrawn as Kansas Kid
Title page: Gino D'Antonio
(a) Kansas Kid & the Railroad War!
Art: Reg Bunn
(b) Kansas Kid & the Forbidden Ranch-House!
Art: Unknown

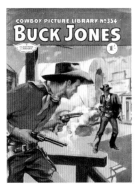
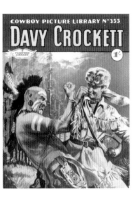

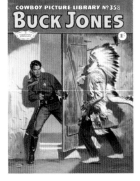
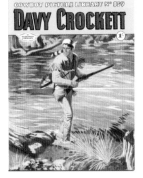
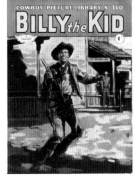

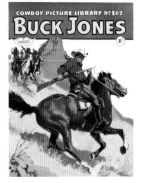
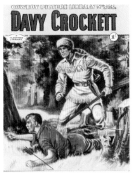

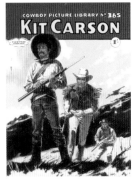
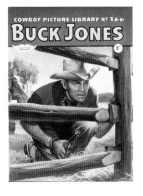

341 (02/60)
Kit Carson
Title: **The Wagons of Destruction**
Cover: Giorgio De Gaspari
Art: Jesus Blasco

342 (02/60)
Buck Jones
Cover: Jordi Penalva
Title page: Gino D'Antonio
(a) Shadow of the Noose
Art: Stephen Chapman
(b) Buck Jones & the Bandit Army
Art: Colin Merrett, adapted by Peter Gallant from a "Billy
the Kid" story from *Sun*

343 (02/60)
Davy Crockett
Cover: Jordi Penalva
Title page: Gino D'Antonio
(a) Davy Crockett & the Man Without a Name
Art: D. C. Eyles
(b) Davy Crockett & the Warrior Squaws
Title page: Unknown
Art: R. Charles Roylance
(c) Town to Ransom
Art: Stephen Chapman

344 (02/60)
Kansas Kid
Cover: Giorgio De Gaspari
Title page: Gino D'Antonio
(a) Kansas Kid & the Mystery Marksman
Art: R. Charles Roylance
(b) Kansas Kid & the Siege at Fort Lester
Art: Reg Bunn

345 (03/60)
Kit Carson
Cover: Jordi Penalva
Title page: Gino D'Antonio
(a) Kit Carson & the Three Desperate Men
Art: Raffaele Paparella
(b) Kit Carson & the War Totem
Art: Emilio Frejo

346 (03/60)
Buck Jones
Title: **Buck Jones & the Comancheros**
Cover: Jordi Penalva
Art: Sergio Tarquinio

347 (03/60)
Buffalo Bill
Cover: Giorgio De Gaspari
Title page: Gino D'Antonio
(a) Buffalo Bill & the Battle Wagon
Art: Emilio Frejo
(b) Buffalo Bill & the Treasure Raiders
Art: Pat Nicolle
(c) Buffalo Bill & the Bogus Trooper
Art: Mario Uggeri
(d) The Battle of the Plains
Art: Eric Bradbury

348 (03/60)
Kansas Kid
Cover: Giorgio De Gaspari
(a) Kansas Kid & the Gatling Gun
Art: Fred Holmes and another (faces)
(b) Kansas Kid & the Comanche War Trail
Art: Colin Merrett
(c) Kansas Kid & the Flying Bandits
Art: Unknown
(d) Kansas Kid & the Curse of the Mallingtons
Art: Fred Holmes

349 (04/60)
Kit Carson
Cover: Jordi Penalva
Title page: Gino D'Antonio
(a) Kit Carson & Ambush at Little Neck
Art: Unknown
(b) Kit Carson – Indian Tamer!
Art: Gerry Embleton
Script: Michael Moorcock?

350 (04/60)
Buck Jones
Cover: Jordi Penalva
Title page: Gino D'Antonio
(a) Buck Jones & the League of Outlaws
Art: C. E. Montford
(b) Buck Jones & the Winged Messengers
Art: C. E. Montford
(c) Buck Jones & the Arrows of Vengeance
Title page: Unknown
Art: Colin Merrett & another (top half p.49)

351 (04/60)
Davy Crockett
Title: **Davy Crockett & the White Indian**
Cover: Giorgio De Gaspari
Art: Stephen Chapman

352 (04/60)
Kansas Kid
Title: **Kansas Kid On the Vengeance Trail**
Cover: Jordi Penalva
Art: Emilio Frejo

353 (05/60)
Kit Carson
Title: **The Man Who Hated Redskins**
Cover: Nino Caroselli
Art: Jesus Blasco

354 (05/60)
Buck Jones
Cover: Nino Caroselli
(a) Buck Jones & the Spin Draw Outlaw
Art: Joao Mottini
(b) Buck Jones & the Stolen Safe
Art: Robert Forrest

355 (05/60)
Davy Crockett
Title: **Pirates of Cat Island**
Cover: Giorgio De Gaspari
Art: Unknown

356 (05/60)
Kansas Kid
Cover: Jordi Penalva
(a) Kansas Kid & the Trail-Drive
Art: Reg Bunn
(b) Kansas Kid – Rustler!
Art: R. Charles Roylance

357 (06/60)
Kit Carson
Cover: Jordi Penalva
Title page: Gino D'Antonio
(a) Prophecy of Doom
Art: Raffaele Paparella
(b) Kit Carson & the War Arrow
Art: Jesus Blasco

358 (06/60)
Buck Jones
Title: **Buck Jones & the Badge of Courage**
Cover: Jordi Penalva
Art: Carlos V. Roume

359 (06/60)
Davy Crockett
Title: **Davy Crocket & the Silver Trail**
Cover: Jordi Penalva
Art: Sergio Tarquinio

360 (06/60)
Billy the Kid
Title: **Billy the Kid & the Snakeband Stetson**
Cover: Leone Cimpellin?
Art: F. A. Philpott

361 (07/60)
Kit Carson
Title: **Kit Carson & the Commanche Prince**
Cover: Jordi Penalva
Art: Alberto Breccia

362 (07/60)
Buck Jones
Title: **The Ghost Town Mystery**
Cover: Nino Caroselli
Art: Robert Forrest

363 (07/60)
Davy Crockett
Title: **Davy Crockett & the Frontier War**
Cover: Unknown
Art: D. C. Eyles

364 (07/60)
Kansas Kid
Title: **Kansas Kid & the Trail of the Cougar**
Cover: Jordi Penalva
Art: Renato Polese

365 (08/60)
Kit Carson
Cover: Jordi Penalva
Title page: Gino D'Antonio
(a) **Kit Carson & the Courageous Coward**
Art: Unknown
(b) **Kit Carson & the Imposter**
Art: Stephen Chapman

366 (08/60)
Buck Jones
Cover: Henry Fox?
Title page: Gino D'Antonio
(a) **Buck Jones & the Debt to an Outlaw**
Art: Unknown
(b) **Buck Jones & the Vanished War Chief**
Art: Geoff Campion; a "Billy the Kid" story from *Sun*
adapted by Patrick Nicolle

367 (08/60)
Billy the Kid
Cover: Jordi Penalva
Title page: Geoff Campion
(a) **Billy the Kid & the Fortune Hunter**
Art: Sergio Tarquinio
(b) **Billy the Kid & the Trail of Justice**
Art: Sergio Tarquinio

368 (08/60)
Kansas Kid
Cover: Jordi Penalva
(a) **Kansas Kid & the Mountain of Flame**
Art: Colin Merrett
(b) **Kansas Kid & the Rustler's Frame-Up**
Art: C. E. Montford
(c) **Kansas Kid & the Bandit's Gift**
Art: Colin Merrett

369 (09/60)
Kit Carson
Cover: Jordi Penalva
Title page: Geoff Campion
(a) **Kit Carson & the Peril at Fort Kiowa**
Art: Leandro Sesarego
(b) **Buffalo Bill & the Two-Fisted Joker**
Art: Eric Bradbury, reprint from *Comet* 340 (22/01/55)

370 (09/60)
Buck Jones
Title: **The Wreckers at Comanche Canyon**
Cover: Jordi Penalva
Art: Franco Bignotti

371 (09/60)
Billy the Kid
Cover: Jordi Penalva
Title page: Geoff Campion
(a) **Billy the Kid & the Beardless Bandit**
Art: R. Charles Roylance
(b) **Billy the Kid & the Outlaw Traders**
Art: R. Charles Roylance

372 (09/60)
Kansas Kid
Title: **Kansas Kid & the Bull of Barajos**
Cover: Nino Caroselli?
Art: Peter Gallant

373 (10/60)
Kit Carson
Title: **Kit Carson & the Army Outlaws**
Cover: Jordi Penalva
Art: Jorge Macabich

 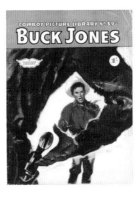  

374 (10/60)
Buck Jones
Cover: Jordi Penalva
(a) Buck Jones & the Double Showdown
Art: D. Gale
(b) Buck Jones & the Guns of Destiny
Art: Stephen Chapman

375 (10/60)
Billy the Kid
Cover: Jordi Penalva
Title page: Geoff Campion
(a) Billy the Kid & the Ranch Robbers
Art: Don Lawrence
(b) Billy the Kid & the Runaway Prisoners
Art: Jorge Moliterni

376 (10/60)
Kansas Kid
Title: **Kansas Kid & the Dangerous Land**
Cover: Jordi Penalva
Art: R. Charles Roylance

377 (11/60)
Kit Carson
Title: **Kit Carson & the Lawless Town**
Cover: Jordi Penalva
Art: Jose Bielsa
Script: Barry Ford (Joan Whitford), based on the novel
Marshal Without A Badge (Greenwich, CT, Fawcett
Publications, 1959) by Ray Hogan

378 (11/60)
Buck Jones
Title: **Buck Jones & the Wells Fargo Gold**
Cover: Jordi Penalva
Art: Carlos V. Roume

379 (11/60)
Billy the Kid
Title: **Billy the Kid & the Kidnap Gang**
Cover: Jordi Penalva
Art: Joao Mottini

380 (11/60)
Kansas Kid
Title: **Kansas Kid & the Renegade**
Cover: Jordi Penalva
Art: Leandro Sesarego

381 (12/60)
Kit Carson
Title: **Kit Carson & the Mutiny at Fort Blaine**
Cover: Jordi Penalva
Art: Emilio Frejo

382 (12/60)
Buck Jones
Title: **Buck Jones & the Gunsmoke Ghost Town**
Cover: Nino Caroselli
Art: Reg Bunn

383 (12/60)
Billy the Kid
Cover: Jordi Penalva
(a) Billy the Kid & the Outlaw's Map
Art: Sergio Tarquinio
(b) Billy the Kid & the Honour of Colonel Blade
Art: Geoff Campion

384 (12/60)
Kansas Kid
Title: **Kansas Kid & the Masked Sheriff**
Cover: Jordi Penalva
Art: Jorge Moliterni

385 (01/61)
Kit Carson
Title: **The Phantom Stage**
Cover: Jordi Penalva
Art: Virgilio Muzzi?

386 (01/61)
Buck Jones
Title: **Buck Jones & the Man From Montana**
Cover: Jordi Penalva
Art: Jesus Blasco

387 (01/61)
Billy the Kid
Title: **Billy the Kid & the Saddle Tramp**
Cover: Jordi Penalva
Art: Jorge Macabich?

388 (01/61)
Kansas Kid
Cover: Jordi Penalva
Title page: Gino D'Antonio
(a) Kansas Kid & the Treacherous Troopers
Art: Carlos V. Roume
(b) Kansas Kid & the Lawless McCardles
Art: Eric Parker

389 (02/61)
Kit Carson
Title: **Kit Carson & the Cheyenne War**
Cover: Jordi Penalva
Art: Jesus Blasco

390 (02/61)
Buck Jones
Title: **Buck Jones & the Young Rebel**
Cover: Jordi Penalva
Art: Joao Mottini

391 (02/61)
Billy the Kid
Cover: Jordi Penalva
Title page: Geoff Campion
(a) Billy the Kid & the Cautious Gunmen
Art: Sergio Tarquinio
(b) Billy the Kid & the Troubled Settlers
Art: Carlos V. Roume

392 (02/61)
Kansas Kid
Title: **Kansas Kid & the Gun-Shy Marshal**
Cover: Jordi Penalva
Art: Sergio Tarquinio

393 (03/61)
Kit Carson
Cover: Jordi Penalva
(a) Kit Carson & the Cunning of Black Wolf
Art: H. C. Milburn
(b) Kit Carson & the Dynamite Danger
Art: C. E. Montford

394 (03/61)
Buck Jones
Title: **The Man Condemned**
Cover: Nino Caroselli
Art: Martin Salvador

395 (03/61)
Billy the Kid
Cover: Allessandro Biffignandi
(a) The Outlaw's Vengeance
Art: Alberto Breccia
(b) The Gunsight Champion
Art: Jorge Moliterni

396 (03/61)
Kansas Kid
Title: **Kansas Kid & the 'Frisco Racketeers**
Cover: Jordi Penalva
Art: Gerry Embleton

397 (04/61)
Kit Carson
Cover: Jordi Penalva
(a) Kit Carson & the Mystery at Fort Wild
Art: Eric Parker
(b) Kit Carson & the Captured Wagon Train
Art: Unknown

398 (04/61)
Buck Jones
Title: **Buck Jones & the Death of an Outlaw**
Cover: Jordi Penalva
Art: Carlos V. Roume

 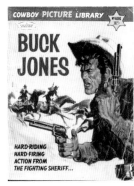  

399 (04/61)
Billy the Kid
Cover: Jordi Penalva
(a) Billy the Kid & the Town of Terror
Art: R. Charles Roylance
(b) Billy the Kid & the Bushwhacked Bull
Art: Sergio Tarquinio

400 (04/61)
Kansas Kid
Cover: Jordi Penalva
(a) Kansas Kid & the Mystery of Poisoned Creek
Art: R. Charles Roylance
(b) Kansas Kid & the Waiting Guns
Art: Sergio Tarquinio

401 (05/61)
Kit Carson
Title: The Trail of Treachery
Cover: Jordi Penalva
Art: Jesus Blasco

402 (05/61)
Apache Manhunt (Buck Jones)
Cover: Jordi Penalva
Art: Alberto Breccia

403 (05/61)
The Fugitive (Kansas Kid)
Cover: Jordi Penalva
Art: Ruggero Giovannini

404 (05/61)
The Gun-Tamers (Gun Tamers)
Cover: Jordi Penalva
Art: Carlos V. Roume

405 (06/61)
Kit Carson
Title: The Agency Outlaws
Cover: Jordi Penalva
Art: Carlos V. Roume

406 (06/61)
Buck Jones
Cover: Jordi Penalva
(a) Buck Jones & the Death Trap
Art: Unknown
(b) Masked Raiders
Art: Antonio Canale

407 (06/61)
Fast Company (Kansas Kid)
Cover: Jordi Penalva
Art: Sergio Tarquinio

408 (06/61)
Flame Over Missouri
Cover: Nino Caroselli?
Title page: Gerry Embleton
Art: Joao Mottini
Script: J. A. Stockbridge

409 (07/61)
Kit Carson
Cover: Jordi Penalva
(a) Border Raiders
Art: Jose Bielsa
(b) Buffalo Bill & A Life in Danger
Art: Antonio Canale

410 (07/61)
The Hunter (Buck Jones)
Cover: Jordi Penalva
Art: Alberto Breccia

411 (07/61)
The Kansas Kid
Cover: Jordi Penalva
(a) Desert Showdown
Art: Sergio Tarquinio
(b) Renegade Warpath
Art: Joao Mottini

412 (07/61)
The Rebel (Gun Tamers)
Cover: Jordi Penalva
Art: Carlos V. Roume

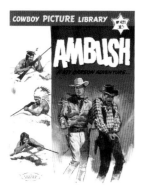

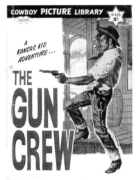

413 (08/61)
Kit Carson
Title: **Frontier of Fear**
Cover: Jordi Penalva
Art: Jesus Blasco

414 (08/61)
Buck Jones
Title: **The Lawbreakers**
Cover: Jordi Penalva
Art: Renato Polese

415 (08/61)
The Kansas Kid
Title: **Town That Was Afraid**
Cover: Jordi Penalva
Art: R. Charles Roylance

416 (08/61)
Fighting Patrol
Cover: Jordi Penalva
Art: Virgilio Muzzi/Mario Uggeri

417 (09/61)
Devil's Fort (Kit Carson)
Cover: Jordi Penalva
Art: Sergio Tarquinio

418 (09/61)
Buck Jones/Lawman
Cover: Jordi Penalva
(a) Valley of Spirits
Art: Eric Parker
(b) Blacked Gloved Bandit
Art: Colin Merrett; reprints a "Billy the Kid" story from
Sun with additions by Peter Gallant
(c) The Deserter
Art: Eric Parker

419 (09/61)
The Wild Ones (Kansas Kid)
Cover: Jordi Penalva
Art: R. Charles Roylance

420 (09/61)
Gun Hand
Cover: Nino Caroselli
Art: Unknown
Script: Barry Ford (Joan Whitford), based on the novel
Wyoming Jones For Hire (Greenwich, CT, Fawcett
Publications, 1959) by Richard Telfair

421 (10/61)
Ambush (Kit Carson)
Cover: Jordi Penalva
Art: Unknown

422 (10/61)
Outlaw Brand (Buck Jones)
Cover: Jordi Penalva
Art: Joao Mottini

423 (10/61)
Aim to Kill (Kansas Kid)
Cover: Jordi Penalva
Art: Franco Paludetti/Mario Uggeri

424 (10/61)
Way of the Outlaw (Gun Tamers)
Cover: Jordi Penalva
Art: Carlos V. Roume

425 (11/61)
Kit Carson
Title: **Gun Trail**
Cover: Jordi Penalva
Art: Luis Dominguez

426 (11/61)
Blood Money (Kansas Kid)
Cover: Jordi Penalva
Art: R. Charles Roylance

427 (11/61)
Fast Gun (Buck Jones)
Cover: Jordi Penalva
Art: Robert Forrest

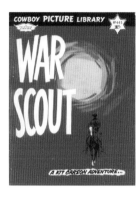   

428 (11/61)
Dead Or Alive
Cover: Jordi Penalva
Art: Alberto Salinas

429 (12/61)
Kit Carson
Title: **Apache Gold**
Cover: Jordi Penalva
Art: Jesus Blasco

430 (12/61)
Gun Play (Buck Jones)
Cover: Jordi Penalva
Art: Jose Bielsa

431 (12/61)
Running Wild (Kansas Kid)
Cover: Jordi Penalva
Art: Leandro Sesarego

432 (12/61)
The Defenders (Gun Tamers)
Cover: Jordi Penalva
Art: Carlos V. Roume

433 (01/62)
Kit Carson
Title: **The Devil's General**
Cover: Jordi Penalva
Art: Alberto Salinas

434 (01/62)
Beyond the Law (Buck Jones)
Cover: Jordi Penalva
Art: Carlos V. Roume

435 (01/62)
The Young Mavericks (Kansas Kid)
Cover: Jordi Penalva
Art: R. Charles Roylance

436 (01/62)
Fighting Cheyenne
Cover: Jordi Penalva
Art: Virgilio Muzzi/Mario Uggeri

437 (02/62)
Fighting Scout (Kit Carson)
Cover: Jordi Penalva
Art: Dino Zuffi

438 (02/62)
Billy the Kid
Cover: Allessandro Biffignandi
Title page: Geoff Campion
(a) The Marked Man
Art: Sergio Tarquinio
(b) The Last of the James Boys
Art: Sergio Tarquinio

439 (02/62)
The Gun Crew (Kansas Kid)
Cover: Jordi Penalva
Art: Alberto Breccia

440 (02/62)
Raw Deal
Cover: Nino Caroselli
Art: Renato Polese

441 (03/62)
Hunter's Moon (Kit Carson)
Cover: Jordi Penalva
Art: Julio Vivas

442 (03/62)
Firebrand Marshall (Buck Jones)
Cover: Jordi Penalva
Art: Unknown

443 (03/62)
The Last Gun (Kansas Kid)
Cover: Jordi Penalva
Art: R. Charles Roylance

444 (03/62)
One Man's War
Cover: Jordi Penalva
Art: Leandro Sesarego

445 (04/62)
War Scout (Kit Carson)
Cover: Jordi Penalva
Art: Franco Paludetti/Mario Uggeri

446 (04/62)
Gang Buster (Buck Jones)
Cover: Jordi Penalva
Art: Jesus Blasco

447 (04/62)
Danger Money
Cover: Allessandro Biffignandi
Art: Alberto Breccia

448 (04/62)
The Iron Cage
Cover: Jordi Penalva
Art: Robert Forrest
Script: Barry Ford (Joan Whitford), based on the novel *Gun Talk At Yuma* (Greenwich, CT, Fawcett Publications, 1957) by Frank Castle

449 (05/62)
War Fever (Kit Carson)
Cover: Jordi Penalva
Art: Alberto Salinas

450 (05/62)
Trigger Man (Buck Jones)
Cover: Jordi Penalva
Art: Alberto Breccia

451 (05/62)
Hell on Wheels
Cover: Jordi Penalva
Art: Carlos V. Roume

452 (05/62)
Ride With the Devil
Cover: Jordi Penalva
Art: Unknown

453 (06/62)
Gun Rule (Kit Carson)
Cover: Nino Caroselli
Art: Geoff Campion (1-18) & Gino D'Antonio

454 (06/62)
Trouble Shooter (Kansas Kid, but looks like Buck Jones throughout**)**
Cover: Jordi Penalva
Art: Jose Bielsa

455 (06/62)
Hate Town (Larrigan)
Cover: Jordi Penalva
Art: Unknown Artist [B]

456 (06/62)
The Fighting Blues and Greys
Cover: McEvoy?
Art: Gerry Embleton

457 (07/62)
Frontier Fury (Kit Carson)
Cover: Jordi Penalva
Art: Jesus Blasco

458 (07/62)
Kansas Gets Mad (Kansas Kid)
Cover: Jordi Penalva
Art: Sergio Tarquinio

459 (07/62)
Devil's Posse (Larrigan)
Cover: Jordi Penalva
Art: Carlos V. Roume

460 (07/62)
Gun Breed
Cover: Jordi Penalva?
Art: Joao Mottini

  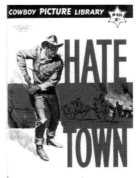 

461 (08/62)
Buffalo Bill
Title: **War in the Black Hills**
Cover: Toldo; reprint from *Comet*
Title page: Geoff Campion
Art: Raffaelle Paparella

462 (08/62)
Colt Law (Kansas Kid)
Cover: Allessandro Biffignandi
Art: Franco Paludetti/Mario Uggeri

463 (08/62)
Mark of a Gunman (Larrigan)
Cover: Jordi Penalva
Art: Arturo Del Castillo

464 (08/62)
Ride For the Rio!
Cover: Nino Caroselli
Art: Leandro Sesarego

465 (09/62)
Hunt the Man Down (Kit Carson)
Cover: Jordi Penalva
Art: R. Charles Roylance

466 (09/62)
Death and Glory
Cover: Jordi Penalva
Art: Carlos V. Roume

467 (09/62)
Ghost Town (Larrigan)
Cover: Jordi Penalva
Art: Unknown Artist [B]

468 (09/62)
A Man With A Gun
Cover: Jordi Penalva
Art: Leo Duranona

Sep E. Scott's original cover painting for *Cowboy Picture Library* 253.

Giorgio De Gaspari's original cover painting for *Cowboy Picture Library* 270.

The original cover painting for *Cowboy Picture Library* 273, by Giorgio de Gaspari.

Sep E. Scott's original cover painting for *Cowboy Picture Library* 291.

Giorgio De Gaspari's original cover painting for *Cowboy Picture Library* 298.

Jordi Penalva's original cover painting for *Cowboy Picture Library* 305.

Jordi Penalva's original cover painting for *Cowboy Picture Library* 317.

Jordi Penalva's original cover painting for *Cowboy Picture Library* 333.

Jordi Penalva's original cover painting for *Cowboy Picture Library* 359.

Jordi Penalva's original cover painting for *Cowboy Picture Library* 379.

Jordi Penalva's original cover painting for *Cowboy Picture Library* 411.

Jordi Penalva's original cover painting for *Cowboy Picture Library* 432.

Jordi Penalva's original cover painting for *Cowboy Picture Library* 434.

Nino Caroselli's original cover painting for *Cowboy Picture Library* 440.

Jordi Penalva's original cover painting for *Cowboy Picture Library* 454.

An unused *Cowboy Picture Library* cover by Nino Caroselli.

 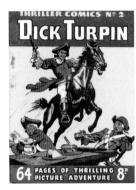  

01 (01/11/51)
The Three Musketeers
The Adventure of the Iron Mask
Title: **The Three Musketeers &**
the Man in the Iron Mask
Cover: W. Bryce-Hamilton
Art: W. Bryce-Hamilton; reprints (with a new ending
replacing the old) from *Knockout* 536–557
(04/06–29/10/49)
Script: Edward Holmes; based on the film *The Iron Mask*
(1929) starring Douglas Fairbanks, using characters from
the novel *Le Vicomte de Bragelonne ou Dix ans plus tard*
(Paris, Michel Lévy frères, 1848–1850) by Alexandre Dumas

02 (01/11/51)
Dick Turpin
Cover: Geoff Campion
(a) Dick Turpin's Ride to York
Art: D. C. Eyles; reprints from *Knockout* 490–498
(17/07–11/09/48)
Script: Leonard Matthews; loosely based on an incident
in the novel *Rookwood* (London, Richard Bentley, 1834)
by W Harrison Ainsworth
(b) Dick Turpin & the Goldsmith's Daughter
Art: Stephen Chapman
(c) Dick Turpin to the Rescue
Art: Colin Merrett

03 (06/12/51)
Treasure Island
Cover: Philip Mendoza
Art: Mike Hubbard; reprints from *Knockout* 330–349
(23/06–03/11/45)
Script: Percy Clarke; based on the 1934 MGM movie
starring Wallace Beery and Jackie Coogan, itself based on
the novel (London, Cassell & Co., 1883) by Robert Louis
Stevenson

04 (06/12/51)
Robin Hood
Cover: Geoff Campion
(a) Robin Hood & the Sheriff's Ransom
Art: Philip Mendoza
(b) Robin Hood & the Phantom Knight
Art: Philip Mendoza
(c) Robin Hood & the Tyrant Earl
Art: D. C. Eyles; reprints 'Hereward the Wake' from
Knockout Fun Book 1950
Script: Leonard Matthews

05 (03/01/52)
Gulliver's Travels
Cover: Philip Mendoza
Art: Divided into two untitled chapters;
(a); **Art:** Selby Donnison; (b); **Art:** Graham Coton
Script: Peter O'Donnell; based on the novel, originally
published as *Travels Into Several Remote Nations of the
World. In four parts by Lemuel Gulliver* (London, Benj.
Motte, 1726), by Jonathan Swift

06 (03/01/52)
Swords of the Musketeers
Cover: Geoff Campion
**(a) The Three Musketeers & the Chateau of
a Thousand Pillars**
Art: Philip Mendoza
(b) The Three Musketeers & the Wolves of Zarkoff
Art: Cyril Holloway
**(c) The Three Musketeers & the Siege of Castle
Varonne**
Art: Philip Mendoza

07 (07/02/52)
Ali Baba and the Forty Thieves
Cover: Philip Mendoza
Art: Philip Mendoza
Script: Peter O'Donnell; based on the story from the
Middle Eastern texts originally translated into French as *Les
mille et une nuits* by Antoine Galland (12 vols., 1704/17),
subsequently translated into English as *The Book of One
Thousand and One Nights or Arabian Nights
Entertainments*

  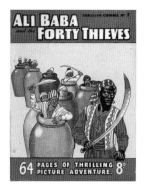 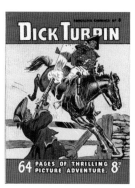

08 (07/02/52)
Dick Turpin
Cover: Geoff Campion
(a) The Fake Dick Turpin
Art: Colin Merrett
(b) Dick Turpin & the Turk of Calzedo
Art: Stephen Chapman
(c) Dick Turpin & the Rogue's Roundup
Art: Graham Coton

09 (06/03/52)
Hunted on the Highway (Dick Turpin)
Cover: D. C. Eyles
Art: H. M. Brock; reprints 'Breed of the Brudenels' from
Knockout 564–584 (17/12/49–06/05/50)
Script: Leonard Matthews

10 (06/03/52)
Robin Hood
Cover: D. C. Eyles
(a) Robin Hood's Jest
Art: Geoff Campion
(b) Robin Hood & the Rescue of Little John
Art: Stephen Chapman
(c) Robin Hood & the Battle of Sherwood Forest
Art: Peter Sutherland

11 (03/04/52)
The Black Arrow
Cover: D. C. Eyles
Art: Selby Donnison
Script: Unknown; based on the novel *The Black Arrow.*
A tale of the two roses (London, Cassell & Co., 1888) by
Robert Louis Stevenson

12 (03/04/52)
Musketeers of the King
Cover: Patrick Nicolle & D. C. Eyles
**(a) The Three Musketeers Ride For the Glory
of France**
Art: Patrick Nicolle
(b) Musketeers to the Rescue
Art: Graham Coton

13 (01/05/52)
Captain Flame
Cover: Sep. E. Scott
Art: Sep. E. Scott, with some minor additions by Stephen
Chapman; reprints from *Knockout* 506–524
(06/11/48–12/03/49)
Script: Leonard Matthews

14 (01/05/52)
The Secret of Monte Cristo
Cover: Jack Grandfield and Eric R. Parker
Art: Eric R. Parker; reprints 'Sexton Blake and Tinker in
The Secret of Monte Cristo' from *Knockout* 515–528
(08/01–09/04/49), heavily reworked by Reg Bunn and with
Sexton Blake=Rod Stewart
Script: Edward Holmes

15 (05/06/52)
The Last of the Mohicans
Cover: Geoff Campion
Art: Geoff Campion
Script: Joan Whitford; based on the novel *The Last of the
Mohicans. A narrative of 1775* (Philadelphia, H. C. Carey &
I. Lea, 2 vols, 1826) by J. Fenimore Cooper

16 (05/06/52)
The Green Archer
Cover: D. C. Eyles
Art: Philip Mendoza
Script: Unknown; based on the novel (London, Hodder &
Stoughton, 1923) by Edgar Wallace

17 (03/07/52)
The Outlaw Orphan
Cover: James E. McConnell
Art: Colin Merrett
Script: Unknown; based on the novel *The Orphan*
(New York, The Outing Publishing Co., 1908) by
Clarence E Mulford

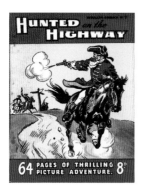   

18 (03/07/52)
Again the Ringer
Cover: Heade (Reginald C. Webb)
(a) The Man With the Red Beard
Art: Reg Bunn
Script: J. H. Higgins; based on the story (*Again the Ringer*, London, Hodder & Stoughton, 1929) by Edgar Wallace
(b) Mr Bash the Brutal
Art: Eric R. Parker
Script: J. H. Higgins; based on the story 'The End of Mr Bash – the Brutal' (*Again the Ringer*, London, Hodder & Stoughton, 1929) by Edgar Wallace
(c) The Servant of Women
Art: Reg Bunn
Script: J. H. Higgins; based on the story 'A Servant of Women' (*Again the Ringer*, London, Hodder & Stoughton, 1929) by Edgar Wallace
(d) The Murderer with Many Names
Art: Unknown
Script: J. H. Higgins; based on the story 'The Murderer of Many Names' (*Again the Ringer*, London, Hodder & Stoughton, 1929) by Edgar Wallace

19 (07/08/52)
Quo Vadis
Cover: Colour still from movie
Art: Geoff Campion
Script: Joan Whitford; adaptation of the Metro-Goldwyn-Meyer movie (1951) starring Robert Taylor and Deborah Kerr, based on the novel *Quo vadis. Powiese z czas w Nerona* (Warszawa, Poland, 3 vols., 1896) by Henryk Sienkiewicz, translated by Jeremiah Curtin as *Quo Vadis . A narrative of the time of Nero* (London, J. M. Dent & Co., 1896; Boston, Little, Brown & Co., 1896)

20 (07/08/52)
"Phantom Footsteps"
Cover: Philip Mendoza
Art: Philip Mendoza
Script: Unknown; based on the novella (*The Thriller* 292, 09/09/34) by John Hunter

21 (04/09/52)
Black Hood
Cover: Patrick Nicolle
Art: Reg Bunn
Script: Unknown; based on the serial 'Stand & Deliver' (*Chums*, 1926) by John Worthing (John Hunter)

22 (04/09/52)
King of the Road (Dick Turpin)
Cover: James E. McConnell
(a) King of the Road
Art: H. M. Brock
(b) Dick Turpin & the Buried Treasure
Art: Stephen Chapman
(c) Dick Turpin & the Masked Marvel
Art: Stephen Chapman

23 (02/10/52)
The Saint in California
Cover: John Spranger (based on frame from strip)
Art: John Spranger; reprints US newspaper strip syndicated by New York Herald Tribune
Script: Leslie Charteris (possibly ghosted)

24 (02/10/52)
Kevin the Bold
Cover: Kreigh Collins (based on frame from strip)
(a) Kevin the Bold
Art: Kreigh Collins; reprints US newspaper strip syndicated by (Newspaper Enterprise Association?)
Script: Jay Heavlin
(b) Robin Hood to the Rescue of Maid Marian
Art: Patrick Nicolle; reprints 'Robin Hood to the Rescue' from *Knockout* 600 (26/08/50)

25 (06/11/52)
The Loring Mystery
Cover: H. M. Brock
Art: H. M. Brock
Script: Joan Whitford; based on the novel (London, Sampson Low & Co., 1925) by Jeffrey Farnol

  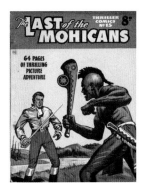 

26 (06/11/52)
The Musketeers Ride Again
Cover: George Cattermole
(a) The Three Musketeers & the Reign of Terror
Art: W. Bryce-Hamilton
(b) Aramis Rejoins the Musketeers
Art: Graham Coton
**(c) The Three Musketeers & the Swordsman
of Provence**
Art: Reg Bunn

27 (04/12/52)
Robin Hood's Peril
Cover: D. C. Eyles
(a) Robin Hood's Peril
Art: Patrick Nicolle
(b) Robin Hood & the Giants Fist
Art: Stephen Chapman
(c) Robin Hood's Ruse
Art: Selby Donnison

28 (04/12/52)
The Return of Captain Flame
Cover: Sep. E. Scott
Art: Sep. E. Scott; reprints 'The Return of Captain Flame'
and 'Captain Flame Sails Again' from *Knockout* 525–535,
585–591 (19/03–28/05/49 and 13/05–24/06/50) with
some panels touched up by Reg Bunn
Script: Leonard Matthews

29 (01/01/53)
Ivanhoe
Cover: D. C. Eyles
Art: Peter Jackson, with some additonal frames reprinted
from the movie adaptation from *Sun* (1952) by Patrick
Nicolle
Script: Unknown; based on the novel (Edinburgh, Archibald
Constable, 3 vols., 1819) by Sir Walter Scott

30 (01/01/53)
The Strange Affair of the Lyons Mail
Cover: Sep. E. Scott
Art: Robert Forrest
Script: Leonard Matthews

31 (05/02/53)
Jane Eyre
Cover: Sep. E. Scott
Art: Sep. E. Scott
Script: Joan Whitford; based on the novel *Jane Eyre.
An autobiography edited by Currer Bell* (London, Smith,
Elder & Co., 3 vols., 1847) by Charlotte Brontë

32 (05/02/53)
The Border Trumpet
Cover: D. C. Eyles
Art: Reg Bunn
Script: Joan Whitford; based on the novel (Boston, Little,
Brown & Co., 1939) by Ernest Haycox

33 (05/03/53)
Tom Brown's Schooldays
Cover: Sep. E. Scott
Art: Stephen Chapman
Script: Peter O'Donnell; based on the novel *Tom Brown's
School Days by An Old Boy* (Cambridge, Macmillan & Co.,
1857) by Thomas Hughes

34 (05/03/53)
The Sword of Fortune
Cover: Sep. E. Scott
Art: Philip Mendoza
Script: Joan Whitford; based on the novel by (London
& Melbourne, Ward, Lock & Co., 1927) by Ben Bolt
(Otwell Binns)

35 (02/04/53)
Bardelys the Magnificent
Cover: Sep. E. Scott
Art: Robert Forrest
Script: Unknown; based on the novel (London, Eveleigh
Nash, 1906) by Rafael Sabatini

36 (02/04/53)
Castle Dangerous
Cover: Sep. E. Scott
Art: Tom Peddie
Script: Unknown; based on the novel (Edinburgh, Robert
Cadell, 1832) by Sir Walter Scott

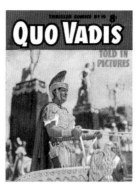
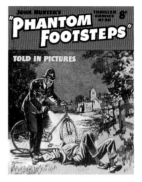

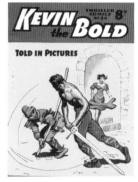

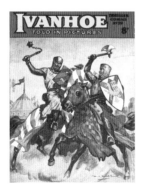

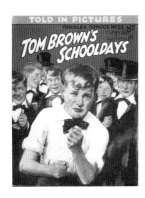

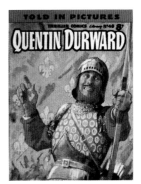

   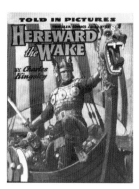

37 (07/05/53)
Windsor Castle
Cover: Sep. E. Scott
Art: C. L. Doughty
Script: Leonard Matthews; based on the novel *Windsor Castle. An historical romance* (London, Henry Colburn, 3 vols., 1843) by W Harrison Ainsworth

38 (07/05/53)
The Children of the New Forest
Cover: Sep. E. Scott
Art: Eric R. Parker; reprints from *Knockout* 309–329 (27/01–16/06/45) with many additional new panels by Parker
Script: Percy Clarke; based on the novel (London, H. Hurst, 2 vols., 1847) by Capt Frederick Marryat

39 (04/06/53)
The Gay Corinthian
Cover: Sep. E. Scott
Art: Philip Mendoza
Script: Unknown; based on the novel (London, Herbert Jenkins, 1924) by Ben Bolt (Otwell Binns)

40 (04/06/53)
Westward Ho!
Cover: Sep. E. Scott
Art: John McNamara
Script: Unknown; based on the novel *Westward Ho! or, The Voyages and Adventures of Sir Amyas Leigh, knight, of Burrough, in the county of Devon, in the reign of Her Most Glorious Majesty, Queen Elizabeth* (Cambridge, Macmillan, 3 vols., 1855) by Charles Kingsley

41 (02/07/53)
The Man Who Stole the Crown Jewels
Cover: Sep. E. Scott
Art: Sep. E. Scott

42 (02/07/53)
The Hunchback of Notre Dame
Cover: Sep. E. Scott
Art: Unknown
Script: Unknown; based on the novel *Notre-Dame de Paris* (Paris, Charles Gosselin, 2 vols., 1831) by Victor Hugo

43 (06/08/53)
The Snare
Cover: Sep. E. Scott
Art: Eric R. Parker
Script: Unknown; based on the novel (London, M. Secker, 1917) by Rafael Sabatini

44 (06/08/53)
King of Sherwood (Robin Hood)
Cover: D. C. Eyles
(a) King of Sherwood
Art: John McNamara
(b) Robin Hood & the Outlaw Traitor
Art: Selby Donnison
(c) Robin Hood's Prank
Art: C. L. Doughty

45 (03/09/53)
The Count of Monte Cristo
Cover: Sep. E. Scott
Art: T. Heath Robinson, with many faces by Patrick Nicolle
Script: Peter O'Donnell; based on the novel *Le Comte de Monte-Cristo* (Paris, Michel Lévy frères, 2 vols., 1846) by Alexander Dumas

46 (03/09/53)
Paul Clifford
Cover: D. C. Eyles
Art: Robert Forrest
Script: Unknown; based on the novel (London, Colburn, 3 vols., 1830) by Lord Lytton

47 (01/10/53)
Lorna Doone
Cover: Sep. E. Scott
Art: H. M. Brock, with many faces by Patrick Nicolle
Script: Unknown; based on the novel *Lorna Doone. A romance of Exmoor* (London, Sampson Low & Co, 3 vols., 1869) by R. D. Blackmore

48 (01/10/53)
Quentin Durward
Cover: Sep. E. Scott
Art: Tom Peddie
Script: Unknown; based on the novel (Edinburgh, Archibald Constable, 1823) by Sir Walter Scott

49 (05/11/53)
Guy Fawkes
Cover: Sep. E. Scott
Art: Philip Mendoza
Script: Joan Whitford

50 (05/11/53)
Captain Blood
Cover: Sep. E. Scott
Art: C. E. Drury
Script: Joan Whitford; based on the novel *Captain Blood. His Odyssey* (London, Hutchinson & Co., 1922) by Rafael Sabatini

51 (03/12/53)
Kenilworth
Cover: Sep. E. Scott
Art: Stephen Chapman
Script: Unknown; based on the novel (Edinburgh, Archibald Constable, 1821) by Sir Walter Scott

52 (03/12/53)
Hereward the Wake
Cover: Sep. E. Scott
Art: Tom Peddie
Script: Unknown; based on the novel *Hereward the Wake: "Last of the English"* (London, Macmillan, 2 vols., 1866) by Charles Kingsley

53 (07/01/54)
Pride of the Ring
Cover: Sep. E. Scott
Art: Sep. E. Scott
Script: Unknown; based on the novel (London, G. H. Robinson & J. Birch, 1921) by Ben Bolt (Otwell Binns)

54 (07/01/54)
The Red Badge of Courage
Cover: Sep. E. Scott
Title Page: Patrick Nicolle
Art: John McNamara
Script: Leonard Matthews; based on the novel *The Red Badge of Courage. An episode of the American civil war* (New York, D. Appleton & Co., 1895) by Stephen Crane

55 (04/02/54)
Hopalong Cassidy Rides In
Cover: James E. McConnell
Art: Harry Winslade
Script: Peter O'Donnell?; based on the novel *The Coming of Cassidy – and the others* (Chicago, A. C. McClurg & Co., 1913) by Clarence E Mulford

56 (04/02/54)
To Sweep the Spanish Main
Cover: Sep. E. Scott
Art: Stephen Chapman
Script: Unknown; based on the novel (London, George G. Harrap & Co., 1930) by Rear-Admiral E. R. G. R. Evans (later Admiral Lord Mountevans); the story was actually ghosted for him by Draycott M. Dell

57 (04/03/54)
In the Reign of Terror
Cover: Sep. E. Scott
Art: T. Heath Robinson
Script: Unknown; based on the novel *In the Reign of Terror. The adventures of a Westminster boy* (New York, C. Scribner's Sons, 1887) by G. A. Henty

58 (04/03/54)
The Scottish Chiefs
Cover: Sep. E. Scott
Art: Reg Bunn
Script: Unknown; based on the novel (London, Longman & Co., 5 vols., 1810) by Jane Porter

59 (01/04/54)
The Talisman
Cover: Sep. E. Scott
Art: Tom Peddie
Script: Unknown; based on the novel (Edinburgh, Archibald Constable, 1825) by Sir Walter Scott

60 (01/04/54)
The Prairie
Cover: Sep. E. Scott
Art: John McNamara
Script: Unknown; based on the novel (Philadelphia, Carey, Lea & Carey, 2 vols., 1827) by J. Fenimore Cooper

61 (06/05/54)
The Black Swan
Cover: Heade (Reginald C. Webb)
Art: Robert Forrest
Script: Unknown; based on the novel (London, Hutchinson & Co., 1932) by Rafael Sabatini

62 (06/05/54)
Mr Midshipman Easy
Cover: Sep. E. Scott
Art: Unknown
Script: Unknown; based on the novel (London, Saunders & Otley, 1836) by Capt. Frederick Marryat

63 (03/06/54)
St George For England
Cover: Sep. E. Scott
Art: Stephen Chapman
Script: Peter O'Donnell; based on the novel *St. George for England. A tale of Cressy and Poitiers* (London, Blackie & Son, 1885 [1884]) by G. A. Henty

64 (03/06/54)
The Prisoner of Zenda
Cover: Sep. E. Scott
Art: Patrick Nicolle; reprints from *Sun* 205–214 (10/01–14/03/53)
Script: Unknown; based on the MGM film (1952) starring Stewart Granger from the novel *The Prisoner of Zenda. Being the history of three months in the life of an English Gentleman* (Bristol, Arrowsmith, 1894) by Anthony Hope

65 (01/07/54)
Bugles in the Afternoon
Cover: Sep. E. Scott
Art: C. E. Drury
Script: Joan Whitford; based on the novel (Boston, Little, Brown & Co., 1944) by Ernest Haycox

66 (01/07/54)
The Rogue's Moon
Cover: Sep. E. Scott
Art: Philip Mendoza
Script: Uknown; based on the novel (New York, D. Appleton & Co., 1929) by Robert W. Chambers

67 (01/07/54)
The Four Feathers
Cover: Sep. E. Scott
Art: Eric R. Parker
Script: Unknown; based on the novel (London, Smith, Elder & Co., 1902) by A. E. W. Mason

68 (05/08/54)
Hopalong Cassidy
Cover: Sep. E. Scott
Art: John McNamara
Script: Peter O'Donnell; based on the character created by Clarence E. Mulford

69 (05/08/54)
The Last of the Barons
Cover: Sep. E. Scott
Art: Tom Peddie
Script: Unknown; based on the novel (London, Saunders & Otley, 3 vols., 1843) by Lord Lytton

70 (05/08/54)
The Three Musketeers
Cover: George Cattermole, based on a film still of Douglas Fairbanks
Art: Robert Forrest
Script: Peter O'Donnell?; derived from the 1946 adaptation by Leonard Matthews from *Knockout*, based on the novel *Les Trois Mousquetaires* (Paris, Baudry, 1844) by Alexandre Dumas

 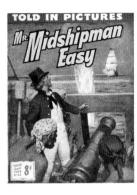  

71 (02/09/54)
No Dust on My Saddle
Cover: D. C. Eyles
Art: C. E. Drury
Script: Unknown; based on the novel by (Kingswood, World's Work, 1951) by Charles H. Lee

72 (02/09/54)
To Arms, Musketeers!
Cover: Geoff Squire
Art: Selby Donnison

73 (07/10/54)
Secret Operator
Cover: Sep. E. Scott
Art: Sep. E. Scott
Script: Unknown; based on the novel *Secret Service Operator 13* (New York, D. Appleton-Century Co., 1934) by Robert W. Chambers

74 (07/10/54)
Bold Robin Hood
Cover: Sep. E. Scott
Art: Patrick Nicolle; reprints 'Lord of Sherwood' from *Sun* 198–210 (22/11/52–14/02/53)
Script: Michael Butterworth

75 (04/11/54)
The King's Captain
Cover: George Cattermole, based on a film still of Douglas Fairbanks from *The Iron Mask* (1929)
Art: Unknown

76 (04/11/54)
The Covered Wagon
Cover: Sep. E. Scott
Art: Bill Lacey
Script: Joan Whitford; based on the novel (New York & London, D. Appleton & Co., 1922) by Emerson Hough

77 (02/12/54)
Greenwood Outlaw (Robin Hood)
Cover: Sep. E. Scott
Art: John McNamara
Script: Unknown; based on the serial 'Gilbert the Outlaw' (*Little Folks*) by Morton Pike (D. H. Parry)

78 (02/12/54)
The Red Rapiers (Richard Trevor)
Cover: Sep. E. Scott
Art: Robert Forrest
Script: Unknown; based on the serial 'The Red Rapiers; or, The Days of King James' (*The Boys Friend*, 14/06–11/10/02) by Morton Pike (D. H. Parry)

79 (06/01/55)
Trumpeter, Sound!
Cover: D. C Eyles (after R. Caton Woodville)
Art: Eric R. Parker
Script: Michael Butterworth; based on the novel (London, Hodder & Stoughton, 1933) by D. L. Murray

80 (06/01/55)
Robin Hood Rides Again
Cover: Sep. E. Scott
Art: Patrick Nicolle; reprints 'Robin Hood's Quest' from *Sun* 211–225 (21/02–30/05/53)
Script: Joan Whitford

81 (03/02/55)
The New Adventures of the Three Musketeers
Cover: Sep. E. Scott
(a) The Three Musketeers in The Outlaw's Lair
Art: Stephen Chapman
(b) The Three Musketeers & the Battle of Spanish Pass
Art: H. M. Brock; reprints 'The Kings Musketeers', *Sun* 197–204 (22/11/52–03/01/53)

82 (03/02/55)
The Swordsman
Cover: Eric R. Parker
Art: John McNamara
Script: Unknown; based on a story by John Hunter

 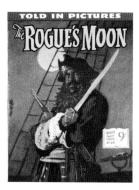  

83 (03/03/55)
The Apache Curse
Cover: D. C. Eyles
Art: C. E. Drury
Script: Joan Whitford; based on the novel *The Apache* (Greenwich, CT, Fawcett Publications, 1951) by James Warner Bellah

84 (03/03/55)
The Chronicles of Captain Blood
Cover: George Cattermole
Art: Robert Forrest
Script: Unknown; based on the novel (London, Hutchinson & Co., 1931) by Rafael Sabatini

85 (07/04/55)
Dick Turpin – For Justice and the Right
Cover: Eric R. Parker
Art: C. L. Doughty
Script: Leonard Matthews

86 (07/04/55)
The Adventures of Rob Roy
Cover: D. C. Eyles
Art: Fred Holmes
Script: Michael Butterworth; based on the novel (Edinburgh, Archibald Constable, 1818) by Sir Walter Scott

87 (05/05/55)
D'Artagnan and the Three Musketeers
Cover: George Cattermole, based on a film still of Douglas Fairbanks from *The Iron Mask* (1929)
Art: Stephen Chapman

88 (05/05/55)
The White Invader
Cover: D. C. Eyles
Art: Reg Bunn
Script: Joan Whitford; based on the serial (*Saturday Evening Post*, 21 January–4 February 1950; reissued in book form as *Rear Guard*, New York, Popular Library, 1951) by James Warner Bellah

89 (02/06/55)
Ho For the Highway! The Days of Dick Turpin
Cover: Sep. E. Scott
(a) Dick Turpin & the Young Recruit
Art: Patrick Nicolle
(b) Dick Turpin & the Mill of Peril
Art: Stephen Chapman
(c) Dick Turpin & the Kidnapped Nobleman
Art: Eric R. Parker; reprints *Sun* 168–169 (26/04–03/05/52)

90 (02/06/55)
The Black Dragoons (Richard Trevor)
Cover: Sep. E. Scott
Art: Robert Forrest
Script: Unknown; based on the serial 'The Black Dragoons; or, The Further Adventures of Richard Trevor, Gentleman, in the Wars of King William' (*The Boys Friend*, 18/10/02–24/01/03) by Morton Pike (D. H. Parry)

91 (07/07/55)
Robin Hood of Sherwood
Cover: Sep. E. Scott
(a) Robin Hood of Sherwood
Art: Fred Holmes; reprints from *Sun* 234–237 (01/08–22/08/53)
(b) Robin Hood's Justice
Art: George Roussos; reprints 'For Sherwood and Liberty' from *Sun* 228–233 (20/06–25/07/53)
(c) Robin Hood's Merry Jest
Art: Patrick Nicolle; reprints from *Sun* 226–227 (06/06–13/06/53)

92 (07/07/55)
Dick Turpin and the Lost Heir
Cover: D. C. Eyles
Art: C. L. Doughty
Script: Joan Whitford

93 (07/07/55)
Forward, the Musketeers!
Cover: James E. McConnell
Art: Stephen Chapman
Script: Michael Butterworth & C. F. Thomas

94 (04/08/55)
The Highway Blade
Cover: D. C. Eyles
Art: C. L. Doughty

95 (04/08/55)
Sabre and Tomahawk
Cover: D. C. Eyles
(a) The Big Hunt
Art: Reg Bunn
Script: Barry Ford (Joan Whitford); based on the short story (*Saturday Evening Post*, 6 December 1947) by James Warner Bellah
(b) Ambush At White River
Art: Reg Bunn
Script: Barry Ford (Joan Whitford); based on the short story 'Massacre' (*Saturday Evening Post*, 22 February 1947) by James Warner Bellah
(c) The Last Fight
Art: Reg Bunn
Script: Barry Ford (Joan Whitford); based on the short story (*Saturday Evening Post*, 16 October 1948) by James Warner Bellah
(d) Stagecoach From Elkhorn
Art: Reg Bunn
Script: Barry Ford (Joan Whitford); based on the story 'Stage for Elkhorn' (*Saturday Evening Post*, 20 November 1948) by James Warner Bellah

96 (04/08/55)
Captain Kidd, Buccaneer
Cover: Heade (Reginald C. Webb)
Art: Lucien Nortier; reprints 'Le Cormoran' from *Vaillant* (France, 1948).
Script: Jean Ollivier, translated and revised

97 (01/09/55)
Ambush at Ghost Creek
Cover: D. C. Eyles
Art: Unknown
Script: Barry Ford (Joan Whitford); based on the serial (*Saturday Evening Post*, 13 June–1 August 1953) by James O'Mara

98 (01/09/55)
The Sword of Robin Hood
Cover: Sep. E. Scott
(a) Robin Hood's Lone Fight
Art: Reg Bunn
(b) Robin Hood & the Tyrant's Gold
Art: Angel Pardo
(c) Robin Hood & the Irish Chieftans
Art: Angel Pardo

99 (01/09/55)
Claude Duval, the Laughing Cavalier
Cover: Sep. E. Scott
Art: Fred Holmes; reprints from *Comet* 270–291 (19/09/53–13/02/54)
Script: Michael Butterworth

100 (06/10/55)
Buffalo Bill and the Battle of Sun Valley
Cover: D. C. Eyles
Title Page: D. C. Eyles
Art: Robert Forrest
Script: Barry Ford (Joan Whitford)

101 (06/10/55)
Dick Turpin and the Secrets of Wolf Castle
Cover: D. C. Eyles
Art: C. L. Doughty

102 (06/10/55)
To Victory With the Iron Duke
Cover: Sep. E. Scott
Art: H. M. Brock
Script: Unknown; based on the serial 'Sabre and Spurs! A tale of the Light Dragoons' (*The Boy's Own Paper*, 1920) by D. H. Parry

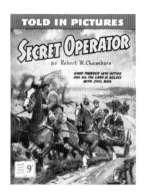

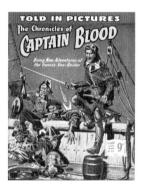
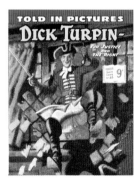
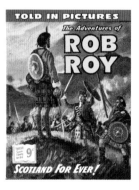

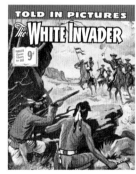

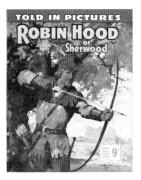

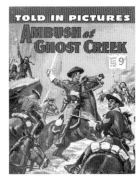

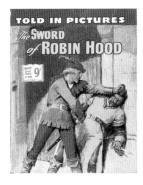

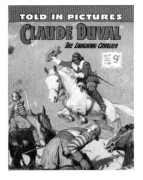

103 (03/11/55)
War Party
Cover: Sep. E. Scott
(a) A Lesson in Command
Art: C. E. Drury
Script: Barry Ford (Joan Whitford); based on the short story 'Command" (*Saturday Evening Post*, 8 June 1946) by James Warner Bellah
(b) Captain Brittle's Final Battle
Art: C. E. Drury
Script: Barry Ford (Joan Whitford); based on the short story 'War Party" (*Saturday Evening Post*, 19 June 1948) by James Warner Bellah
(c) The Colonel's Son
Art: C. E. Drury
Script: Barry Ford (Joan Whitford); based on the short story 'Mission With No Record' (*Saturday Evening Post*, 27 September 1947) by James Warner Bellah
(d) Spanish Man's Grave
Art: C. E. Drury
Script: Barry Ford (Joan Whitford); based on the short story (*Saturday Evening Post*, 3 May 1947) by James Warner Bellah

104 (03/11/55)
Musketeers At Bay
Cover: James E. McConnell
Art: Stephen Chapman
Script: Michael Butterworth & C. F. Thomas

105 (03/11/55)
Captain Kidd of the Spanish Main
Cover: Heade (Reginald C. Webb)
Art: Reg Bunn

106 (03/11/55)
Robin Hood The Forest Lord
Cover: Sep. E. Scott
(a) Robin Hood & Roderick the Hammer
Art: D. C. Eyles
(b) Robin Hood To the Rescue
Art: Reg Bunn
(c) Robin Hood Lone Avenger
Art: Angel Pardo
(d) (untitled end-paper strip)
Art: H. M. Brock

107 (01/12/55)
Billy the Kid Lone Avenger
Cover: Geoff Squire
(a) Billy the Kid & the Showboat Bandits
Art: Geoff Campion; reprints from *Sun* 210 (14/02/53)
Script: Michael Butterworth?
(b) Billy the Kid & the Dandy Desperado
Art: Geoff Campion; reprints from *Sun* 195 (01/11/52)
Script: Michael Butterworth?
(c) Billy the Kid & the Dynamite Gang
Art: Geoff Campion; reprints from *Sun* 192 (11/10/52)
Script: Michael Butterworth?
(d) Billy the Kid The Fighting Fury
Art: Geoff Campion; reprints from *Sun*
Script: Michael Butterworth?
(e) Billy the Kid & Goliath the Rustler
Art: Geoff Campion; reprints from *Sun* 194 (25/10/52)
Script: Michael Butterworth?

108 (01/12/55)
The Sea Hawk
Cover: Sep. E. Scott
Art: Robert Forrest
Script: Barry Ford (Joan Whitford); based on the novel *The Sea-Hawk* (London, M. Secker, 1915) by Rafael Sabatini

109 (01/12/55)
A Christmas Carol
Cover: D. C. Eyles
Art: H. M. Brock
Script: Unknown; based on the novel (London, Chapman & Hall, 1843) by Charles Dickens

110 (01/12/55)
Robin Hood the Triumphant
Cover: Sep. E. Scott
Title Page: D. C. Eyles
(a) Robin Hood & the Vanishing Venison
Art: Reg Bunn
(b) Robin Hood & the Secret of the Old Dark Inn
Art: D. C. Eyles
(c) Robin Hood & the Viking Raiders
Art: Reg Bunn

  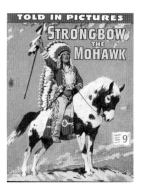 

111 (05/01/56)
Strongbow the Mohawk
Cover: Sep. E. Scott
Title Page: Geoff Campion
Art: Philip Mendoza
Script: Michael Butterworth & C. F. Thomas

112 (05/01/56)
Draw Near to Battle
Cover: D. C. Eyles (after Meissonier)
Art: John McNamara
Script: Unknown; based on the novel (New York, Charles Scribner's Sons, 1953) by Jere Wheelwright

113 (05/01/56)
Rob Roy Forever
Cover: Sep. E. Scott
(a) Rob Roy & the Giant of Glenfarg
Art: Fred Holmes
Script: Michael Butterworth
(b) Rob Roy & the Last of the Lochabers
Art: Fred Holmes
Script: Michael Butterworth

114 (05/01/56)
Robin Hood Fighter For Freedom
Cover: Sep. E. Scott
Title Page: D. C. Eylcs
Art: Arthur Horowicz and Reg Bunn (faces for Robin Hood, Sheriff and other major characters)

115 (02/02/56)
Guns At Broken Bow
Cover: Sep. E. Scott
Art: Unknown
Script: Barry Ford (Joan Whitford); based on the novel (Greenwich, CT, Fawcett Publications, 1950) by William Heuman

116 (02/02/56)
The Cavalier and the Crown
Cover: D. C. Eyles
Art: Sep. E. Scott; reprints 'The King's Captain' from *Comet* 172–183 (03/11/51–19/01/52)
Script: Leonard Matthews

117 (02/02/56)
Dick Turpin and the Phantom of the Highway
Cover: H. M. Brock, originally drawn for *The High Toby* by H. B. Marriott Watson (London, Newnes' Sixpenny Novels, 1906), repainted by D. C. Eyles with an additional insert of Dick Turpin by Eyles
Title Page: D. C. Eyles
Art: Hugh McNeill; reprints 'Dick Turpin and the Phantom Highwayman' from *Sun* 205–215 (10/01–21/03/53)
Script: Michael Butterworth

118 (02/02/56)
Robin Hood Against Norman Foes
Cover: Sep. E. Scott
Title Page: D. C. Eyles
(a) Robin Hood Strikes Back
Art: Patrick Nicolle
(b) Robin Hood & the Condemned Merchant of York
Art: Vitor Peon
(c) Robin Hood & the Hounds of Doom
Art: Sep. E. Scott

119 (01/03/56)
Buffalo Bill and the Spectre of the Plains
Cover: D. C. Eyles
Art: Vitor Peon
Script: Barry Ford (Joan Whitford)

120 (01/03/56)
Frontier Fury
Cover: James E. McConnell
Art: Robert Forrest
Script: Barry Ford (Joan Whitford); based on the novel *The Sun Hawk* (New York, D. Appleton & Co., 1928) by Robert W. Chambers

121 (01/03/56)
Dick Turpin and the Seven Stars
Cover: D. C. Eyles
Art: C. L. Doughty

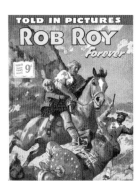 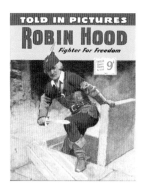 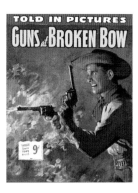 

122 (01/03/56)
Robin Hood
Cover: Sep. E. Scott
Title Page: D. C. Eyles
(a) Robin Hood & the Treasure of Richard the Lionheart
Art: Reg Bunn
(b) Robin Hood & the Sheriff's Feast
Art: Patrick Nicolle

123 (01/03/56)
Crazy Horse, Warlord of the Sioux
Cover: D. C. Eyles
Title Page: Geoff Campion
Art: Sergio Tarquinio

124 (29/03/56)
The Three Bravos
Cover: H. M. Brock, reprint, probably from *The Sphere*
Art: Guido Buzzelli
Script: Michael Butterworth

125 (29/03/56)
Rob Roy and the Highland Feud
Cover: Sep. E. Scott
Art: C. E. Drury
Script: Michael Butterworth

126 (29/03/56)
Robin Hood
Cover: Sep. E. Scott
Title Page: D. C. Eyles
(a) Robin Hood & the King in the Iron Mask
Art: Angel Pardo
(b) Robin Hood & the Stongest Man In the World
Art: Vitor Peon

127 (01/05/56)
Wild Bill Hickok
Cover: D. C. Eyles
Title Page: D. C. Eyles
(a) The Revenge of Flaming Arrow
Art: Colin Merrett
Script: Barry Ford (Joan Whitford)

(b) Silver Mine Pete
Art: Ruggero Giovannini
Script: Barry Ford (Joan Whitford)
(c) The Thumbless Bandit
Art: D. C. Eyles
Script: Barry Ford (Joan Whitford)

128 (01/05/56)
Dick Turpin and the Vultures of the Road
Cover: D. C. Eyles
Art: Fred Holmes
Script: Barry Ford (Joan Whitford)

129 (01/05/56)
The Jaws of Terror
Cover: James E. McConnell
Art: Stephen Chapman

130 (01/05/56)
Robin Hood the Magnificent
Cover: Sep. E. Scott
Title Page: D. C. Eyles
(a) The Saxon Traitor
Art: Nadir Quinto
(b) Robin Hood & the Witch of Withfield
Art: Dino Battaglia
(c) Robin Hood – Knight At Arms
Art: Patrick Nicolle

131 (05/07/56)
Ambush at Rincon
Cover: D. C. Eyles
Art: Mario Cubbino
Script: Unknown; based on the novel (Greenwich, CT, Fawcett Publications, 1953) by Dudley Dean (Dudley Dean McGaughy)

132 (05/07/56)
Under the Golden Dragon
Cover: W. R. Calvert
Art: Patrick Nicolle; reprints from *Comet* 285–306
(03/01–29 05/54)
Script: Michael Butterworth

133 (05/07/56)
Tales of the Highway
Cover: Sep. E. Scott
(a) The Knight Errant
Art: Robert Forrest
Script: Barry Ford (Joan Whitford); based on a story by Rafael Sabatini
(b) The Wager
Art: Robert Forrest
Script: Barry Ford (Joan Whitford); based on a story by Rafael Sabatini
(c) The Recruits
Art: Robert Forrest
Script: Barry Ford (Joan Whitford); based on a story by Rafael Sabatini

134 (05/07/56)
Robin Hood
Cover: Geoff Squire
(a) Robin Hood & the Spectre of Doomsday Keep
Art: Eduardo Coelho
(b) Robin Hood & the Man of Peace
Art: Angel Pardo
(c) Robin Hood & the Riddle of Three
Art: Sep. E. Scott
(d) Robin Hood & the River of Peril
Art: Reg Bunn

135 (02/08/56)
Apache War Trail
Cover: D. C. Eyles
Art: Leone Cimpellin
Script: Barry Ford (Joan Whitford); based on a story by Clifton Adams

136 (02/08/56)
The Dashing Musketeer
Cover: James E. McConnell
Art: Stephen Chapman
Script: Michael Butterworth & C. F. Thomas

137 (02/08/56)
Dick Turpin, King of the Highway
Cover: D. C. Eyles
(a) Dick Turpin & the Fighting Irishman
Art: C. L. Doughty
Script: Leonard Matthews
(b) On the Trail of Justice
Art: Fred Holmes

138 (02/08/56)
Robin Hood
Cover: D. C. Eyles
Title Page: D. C. Eyles
(a) Robin Hood & the Sheriff's Captain
Art: Reg Bunn
(b) Robin Hood's Birthday
Art: Angel Pardo
(c) The Sword of Valour
Art: Reg Bunn

139 (04/09/56)
Wild Bill (Wild Bill Hickok)
Cover: D. C. Eyles
(a) Wild Bill Hickok & the Rancher's Secret
Art: D. C. Eyles
(b) Wild Bill Hickok & the Outlaw Round-Up
Art: Colin Merrett
(c) Wild Bill Hickok & Water-Hole Scotty
Art: D. C. Eyles

140 (04/09/56)
Fighting Days
Cover: Sep. E. Scott
Art: Unknown [possibly Sergio Tarquinio pencils]

141 (04/09/56)
The Daring of Dick Turpin
Cover: D. C. Eyles
(a) Dick Turpin & the Five Aces
Art: C. L. Doughty
(b) Dick Turpin & the Kidnapped Duke
Art: Lino Jeva

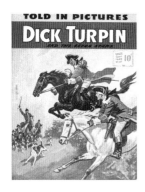   

142 (04/09/56)
Robin Hood
Cover: Sep. E. Scott
Title Page: D. C. Eyles
(a) Robin Hood & the Red Raven
Art: Angel Pardo
(b) Robin Hood & the Treasure of Sherwood Forest
Art: Angel Pardo
(c) Robin Hood & the Sheriff's Forester
Art: Patrick Nicolle
(d) Robin Hood & the Stranger of Sherwood
Art: Angel Pardo

143 (02/10/56)
Close Range
Cover: Enrico De Seta; based on a film still featuring
George Montgomery
Art: Jesus Blasco
Script: Unknown; based on the novel *War Bonnet Pass*
(Greenwich, CT, Fawcett Publications, 1950) by Logan
Stewart (Leslie H. Savage, Jr.)

144 (02/10/56)
Claude Duval – Swordsman of the King
Cover: Sep. E. Scott
Art: Fred Holmes; reprints from *Comet* 292–305
(20/02–22/05/54), with some additional redrawing by
Unknown
Script: Michael Butterworth

145 (02/10/56)
The Fortunes of Captain Blood
Cover: John Millar Watt
Art: John Millar Watt
Script: Barry Ford (Joan Whitford); based on the novel
(London, Hutchinson & Co., 1936) by Rafael Sabatini
(see also 168)

146 (02/10/56)
Robin Hood
Cover: Sep. E. Scott
(a) Robin Hood & the Sheriff's Prisoner
Art: Guido Buzzelli
(b) Little John's Happy Day
Art: Guido Buzzelli

147 (06/11/56)
Stonewall Jackson Wins His Spurs
Cover: Sep. E. Scott
Art: Geoff Campion
Script: Leonard Matthews

148 (06/11/56)
The Picture of Dorian Gray
Cover: Sep. E. Scott
Art: Robert Forrest
Script: Leonard Matthews; based on the novel (*Lippincott's
Magazine*, July 1890) by Oscar Wilde

149 (06/11/56)
Dick Turpin and the Double Faced Foe
Cover: D. C. Eyles
Title Page: C. L. Doughty
Art: Ruggero Giovannini

150 (06/11/56)
Robin Hood
Cover: Sep. E. Scott
(a) Robin Hood & the Black Dragon
Art: Patrick Nicolle
(b) The Haunted Priory
Art: Vitor Peon
(c) Robin Hood & Little John, Knight Errant
Art: Reg Bunn and Vitor Peon

151 (04/12/56)
Jesse James
Cover: Enrico De Seta, based on a film still featuring
George Montgomery
Art: Harry Bishop

152 (04/12/56)
**The Three Musketeers and the Cardinal's
Secret**
Cover: Patrick Nicolle (after Molino)
Art: Stephen Chapman
Script: Michael Butterworth & C. F. Thomas

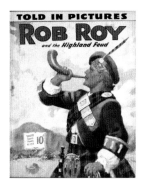 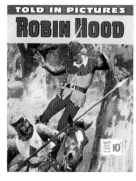  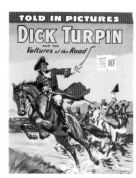

153 (04/12/56)
Dick Turpin
Cover: D. C. Eyles
(a) Dick Turpin & the Riot at the Red Robin Inn
Art: C. L. Doughty
(b) Dick Turpin & the Fatal Shot
Art: C. L. Doughty

154 (04/12/56)
Robin Hood
Cover: D. C. Eyles
Title Page: D. C. Eyles
(a) Robin Hood & the Saxon Pretender
Art: Guido Buzzelli
Script: R. Perrins
(b) Robin Hood & the Outlaw's Wager
Art: Reg Bunn
Script: Michael Butterworth
(c) Robin Hood & the Plague
Art: Angel Pardo

155 (01/01/57)
Billy the Kid
Cover: Sep. E. Scott
Title Page: Sep. E. Scott
(a) Billy the Kid & the Man From the Past
Art: Geoff Campion; reprints from *Sun*
Script: Michael Butterworth?
(b) Billy the Kid & the Bank Busters
Art: Geoff Campion; reprints from *Sun*
Script: Michael Butterworth?
(c) Billy the Kid on the Trail of Vengeance
Art: Geoff Campion; reprints from *Sun*
Script: Michael Butterworth?
(d) Billy the Kid & the Gun Runners
Art: Geoff Campion; reprints from *Sun*
Script: Michael Butterworth?
(e) The Courage of Billy the Kid
Art: Geoff Campion; reprints from *Sun*
Script: Michael Butterworth?
(f) Billy the Kid & the Hooded Raiders
Art: Geoff Campion; reprints from *Sun*
Script: Michael Butterworth?

(g) Billy the Kid & the Bailey Bros
Art: Geoff Campion; reprints from *Sun*
Script: Michael Butterworth?
(h) Billy the Kid's Double
Art: Geoff Campion; reprints from *Sun*
Script: Michael Butterworth?
(i) Billy the Kid & the Bullet-Proof Gunman
Art: Geoff Campion; reprints from *Sun*
Script: Michael Butterworth?

156 (01/01/57)
The Dark Shadows Of London
Cover: Sep. E. Scott
Art: Sep. E. Scott
Script: Leonard Matthews.

157 (01/01/57)
Moby Dick
Cover: James E. McConnell
Art: Robert Bunkin
Script: Unknown; based on the novel *The Whale* (London, Richard Bentley, 3 vols., 1851) by Herman Melville, published in America as *Moby-Dick; or, The Whale* (New York, Harper, 1851)

158 (01/01/57)
Robin Hood
Cover: Sep. E. Scott
Title Page: D. C. Eyles
(a) Robin Hood & the Sheriff's Ruby Ring
Art: Eduardo Coelho
Script: Michael Butterworth
(b) Robin Hood & the Devil's Horseman
Art: Reg Bunn
Script: V. A. L. Holding
(c) Robin Hood & the Downfall of Saul o'the Sword
Art: Angel Pardo

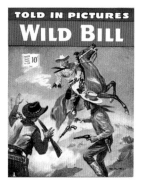

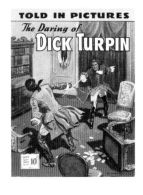

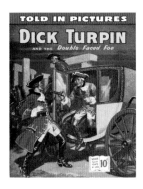

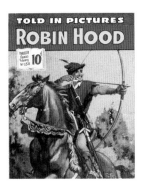

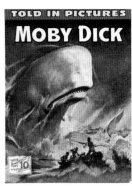

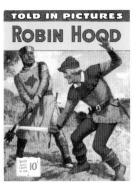

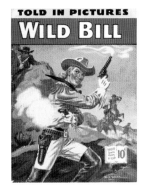

159 (05/02/57)
Wild Bill (Wild Bill Hickok)
Cover: D. C. Eyles
Title Page: Geoff Campion
(a) Wild Bill Hickok & the Siege of Arrowhead
Art: D. C. Eyles
(b) Wild Bill Hickok & the Limping Gunman
Art: Peter Gallant
Script: Michael Butterworth
(c) Wild Bill Hickok & the Noon Avenger
Art: Gianluigi Coppola
Script: R. Perrins

160 (05/02/57)
Battler Britton – War Ace
Cover: Bruce Windo?
Art: Colin Merrett
Note: published in two parts:
Pt. 1 *Malta Convoy*; Pt. 2 *The Eagles of Malta*

161 (05/02/57)
Dick Turpin in The Smugglers' Grip
Cover: D. C. Eyles
Art: Leone Cimpellin
Script: Barry Ford (Joan Whitford)

162 (05/02/57)
Robin Hood
Cover: Sep. E. Scott
Title Page: D. C. Eyles
(a) Robin Hood & Will Scarlet's Revenge
Art: Eduardo Coelho
(b) Robin Hood & the Wonder Sword
Art: Vitor Peon

163 (05/03/57)
The Strong Room
Cover: Sep. E. Scott
Art: Patrick Nicolle
Script: Unknown; Based on the novel (New York, Charles Scribner's Sons, 1948) by Jere Wheelwright

164 (05/03/57)
Claude Duval and the Roundhead's Revenge
Cover: H. M. Brock, reprint, probably from *The Sphere*
Art: Stephen Chapman
Script: Michael Butterworth

165 (05/03/57)
Rob Roy and the Castle of Doom
Cover: Sep. E. Scott
Art: Robert Forrest
Script: Michael Butterworth

166 (05/03/57)
Robin Hood
Cover: Sep. E. Scott
Title Page: D. C. Eyles
(a) Robin Hood & the Lionheart's Return
Art: Reg Bunn
Script: R. Perrins
(b) Robin Hood & the Phantom Army
Art: Vitor Peon
Script: Alf Wallace
(c) Robin Hood & the Mysterious Monks
Art: Vitor Peon
Script: V. A. L. Holding

167 (02/04/57)
He Came From Arizona
Cover: D. C. Eyles
Title Page: Geoff Campion
Art: Mario Cubbino
Script: Barry Ford (Joan Whitford); based on the novel *Winchester Cut* (Greenwich, CT, Fawcett Publications, 1951) by Mark Sabin

168 (02/04/57)
Captain Blood Sails Again
Cover: James E. McConnell
Art: Guido Buzzelli
Script: Barry Ford (Joan Whitford); based on the novel *The Fortunes of Captain Blood* (London, Hutchinson & Co., 1936) by Rafael Sabatini (see also 145)

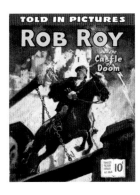   

169 (02/04/57)
Dick Turpin of the King's Highway
Cover: Sep. E. Scott
Art: Mario Uggeri and Virgilio Muzzi
Script: Barry Ford (Joan Whitford)

170 (02/04/57)
Robin Hood
Cover: Sep. E. Scott
Title Page: D. C. Eyles
(a) Robin Hood's Merry Venture
Art: Reg Bunn
Script: Michael Butterworth
(b) Robin Hood & the Slave Pirates
Art: Angel Pardo
(c) Robin Hood & the Man Who Made One Mistake
Art: Angel Pardo
Script: R. Perrins

171 (07/05/57)
The Mystery of the Red Barn
Cover: Unknown
Art: Robert Forrest
Script: Leonard Matthews/R. Perrins

172 (07/05/57)
Knight of the Red Eagle
Cover: James E. McConnell
Art: Eduardo Coelho
Script: R. Perrins

173 (07/05/57)
Battling With the Three Musketeers
Cover: Geoff Squire
Art: Stephen Chapman
Script: G. Allman

174 (07/05/57)
Robin Hood
Cover: D. C. Eyles
Title Page: D. C. Eyles
(a) Robin Hood & the Crusader's Crescent
Art: Arthur Horowicz
Script: R. Perrins

(b) Robin Hood & the Pride of Gilbrain
Art: Arthur Horowicz
Script: J. Hunt
(c) Robin Hood & Roderic the Faint-Heart
Art: Guido Buzzelli
Script: V. A. L. Holding

175 (04/06/57)
Crazy Horse on the War-Path
Cover: Sep. E. Scott
Art: D. C. Eyles
Script: R. Perrins

176 (04/06/57)
Rob Roy
Cover: Sep. E. Scott
Title Page: Reg Bunn
(a) Rob Roy & the Cunning of Lord Kilross
Art: Reg Bunn
Script: J. A. Storrie
(b) Rob Roy & Treason in the Highlands
Art: Reg Bunn
Script: J. A. Storrie
(c) Rob Roy & the Revenge of McAlpine
Art: Reg Bunn
Script: G. Allman

177 (04/06/57)
Dick Turpin and the Man in the Blue Mask
Cover: Sep. E. Scott
Art: C. L. Doughty
Script: Barry Ford (Joan Whitford)

178 (04/06/57)
Robin Hood
Title: **Robin Hood & the Runaway Princess**
Cover: Sep. E. Scott
Title Page: D. C. Eyles
Art: C. L. Doughty; reprints from *Sun* 241–256
(19/09/53–02/01/54), with some additional redrawing
by Unknown

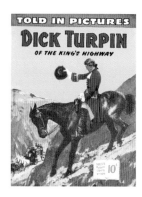   

179 (02/07/57)
Battler Britton Flies Again
Cover: Unknown
Title Page: Arthur Horowicz
(a) Battler Britton Flies Again
Art: Geoff Campion
(b) Battler Britton's Dangerous Mission
Art: Geoff Campion
(c) Battler Britton & the Surface Raider
Art: Geoff Campion
(d) Battler Britton & the Enemy Agent
Art: Guido Buzzelli and Eric Bradbury

180 (02/07/57)
Around the World in Eighty Days
Cover: J. Spurling
Art: Eric R. Parker
Script: Unknown; based on the novel *Le Tour du monde en quatre-vingts jours* (Paris, Hetzel, 1893) by Jules Verne, translated by G. M. Towle as *A Tour of the World in Eighty Days* (Boston: J. R. Osgood, 1873)

181 (02/07/57)
Claude Duval and the Traitor Cavalier
Cover: Enrico De Seta
Art: Fred Holmes
Script: Michael Butterworth

182 (02/07/57)
Robin Hood
Cover: Sep. E. Scott
Title Page: Reg Bunn
(a) Robin Hood & the Kidnapped Countess
Art: Guido Buzzelli
Script: R. Perrins
(b) Robin Hood & the Jester of Lenby
Art: Vitor Peon
Script: Alan Fennell
(c) Robin Hood & the Sherwood Assassin
Art: Angel Pardo
Script: M. Edwards

183 (06/08/57)
The Three Musketeers and the Prince of Peril
Cover: Enrico De Seta; based on film still
Art: John Millar Watt
Script: Leonard Matthews/G. Allman

184 (06/08/57)
Scotland the Brave (Rob Roy)
Cover: Sep. E. Scott
(a) Rob Roy & the Black Sheep of Inveraray
Art: Robert Forrest
Script: David Motton
(b) Rob Roy & the Golden Trap
Art: Robert Forrest
(c) Rob Roy & the Cannons of Macfie
Art: Robert Forrest
Script: Alan Fennell

185 (06/08/57)
Dick Turpin
Cover: Sep. E. Scott
(a) Dick Turpin & the Secret of the Oxford Student
Art: C. L. Doughty
Script: V. A. L. Holding
(b) Dick Turpin & the Well of Darkness
Art: Arthur Horowicz
Script: V. A. L. Holding

186 (06/08/57)
Robin Hood
Cover: Sep. E. Scott
Title Page: Geoff Campion
(a) Robin Hood & the Magic Medicine
Art: Guido Buzzelli
(b) Robin Hood & the Sheriff's New Suit
Art: Vitor Peon
(c) Robin Hood & Friar Tuck's Wonderful Day
Art: Angel Pardo
Script: R. Perrins

187 (03/09/57)
Whiplash
Cover: D. C. Eyles
Art: Ruggero Giovannini
Script: Unknown; based on the novel *Medicine Whip* (New York, William Morrow, 1953) by John & Margaret Harris

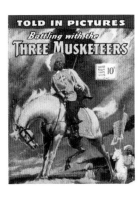   

188 (03/09/57)
Max Bravo, War-Eagle of France
Cover: Eric R. Parker
Art: Eric R. Parker; reprints episodes from *Sun*
Script: Michael Butterworth

189 (03/09/57)
Dick Turpin and the Followers of the Fang
Cover: D. C. Eyles
Art: H. M. Brock, tidied up and with a concluding frame by Patrick Nicolle

190 (03/09/57)
Robin Hood
Cover: Sep. E. Scott
Title Page: Reg Bunn
(a) Robin Hood & the Vengeance of Edric
Art: Angel Pardo
Script: V. A. L. Holding
(b) Robin Hood & the Sorcerer of Sherwood
Art: Armando Monasterolo?
(c) Robin Hood & the New Lute
Art: Unknown
Script: Alan Fennell

191 (01/10/57)
The Three Musketeers in New Adventures
Cover: Lalauze
Title Page: Stephen Chapman
(a) The Three Musketeers & the Spy From the Past
Art: Leone Cimpellin (and Lina Buffolente inking?)
Script: David Motton
(b) The Three Musketeers & the Mask of Treason
Art: Stephen Chapman
Script: David Motton
(c) The Three Musketeers & the Duel At Dawn
Art: Stephen Chapman
Script: David Motton

192 (01/10/57)
Robin Hood
Cover: Sep. E. Scott
Title Page: Geoff Campion
(a) Robin Hood & the Tournament of Doom
Art: C. L. Doughty
Script: V. A. L. Holding
(b) Robin Hood & the Hand of Kazan
Art: Nadir Quinto
Script: V. A. L. Holding
(c) Robin Hood & the Sea Raiders
Art: Angel Pardo
Script: R. Perrins

193 (01/10/57)
Battler Britton, Sky Commando
Cover: Patrick Nicolle, from a layout by Geoff Campion
Title Page: Geoff Campion
(a) Battler Britton & the Secret Raid
Art: Silvano Marinelli?
(b) Battler Britton – Lone Attacker
Art: Renzo Calegari
(c) Battler Britton & the Island Fortress
Art: Ferdinando Tacconi

194 (01/10/57)
Run of the Arrow
Cover: D. C. Eyles
Title Page: Geoff Campion
Art: Unknown
Script: David Motton; based on the RKO Radio Pictures movie starring Rod Steiger (1957)

195 (05/11/57)
Thunder in the South
Cover: Patrick Nicolle, from a layout by Geoff Campion
Art: Franco Bignotti/Mario Uggeri
Script: Barry Ford (Joan Whitford); based on the novel *The Valiant Virginians* (New York, Ballantine Books, 1953) by James Warner Bellah (see also 215)

196 (05/11/57)
By the Sword
Cover: Stephen Chapman
(a) The Three Musketeers & the Divided Village
Art: Stephen Chapman
Script: David Motton
(b) Dick Turpin & the Debt of Honour
Art: Arthur Horowicz
Script: V. A. L. Holding
(c) Rob Roy & the Black Feather
Art: Reg Bunn
Script: J. A. Storrie

197 (05/11/57)
Jack Thurtell Gentleman Thief
Cover: R. M. Sax
Art: Robert Forrest, with additional art by Patrick Nicolle
Script: Leonard Matthews/V. A. L. Holding

198 (05/11/57)
Robin Hood
Cover: Sep. E. Scott
Title Page: Geoff Campion
(a) Robin Hood & the Fortunes of Simon
Art: Angel Pardo
Script: J. A. Storrie
(b) Robin Hood & the Kidnapping Sheriff
Art: Vitor Peon
Script: R. Perrins
(c) Robin Hood & the Scroll of Fate
Art: Angel Pardo
Script: V. A. L. Holding

199 (03/12/57)
Dick Turpin
Title: Dick Turpin & Leather Face, the Wrecker Chief
Cover: Unknown
Art: C. L. Doughty
Script: Barry Ford (Joan Whitford)

200 (03/12/57)
Battler Britton & the Burma Buccaneers
Cover: James E. McConnell
Art: Nevio Zeccara
Script: V. A. L. Holding

201 (03/12/57)
Strongbow the Mohawk Avenger
Cover: D. C. Eyles
Art: Peter Gallant
Script: C. F. Thomas

202 (03/12/57)
Robin Hood
Title: Robin Hood & the Outlaw Recruit
Cover: Sep. E. Scott
Title Page: Geoff Campion
Art: Reg Bunn
Script: V. A. L. Holding

203 (07/01/58)
War Bonnet
Cover: D. C. Eyles
Art: Franco Bignotti
Script: Barry Ford (Joan Whitford); based on the novel (Boston, Houghton Mifflin Co.-New York, Ballantine Books, 1952) by Clay Fisher (Henry Wilson Allen)

204 (07/01/58)
Battler Britton, Flying Fury
Cover: Patrick Nicolle, from a layout by Geoff Campion
(a) Target Berlin
Art: Gino D'Antonio
Script: Graeme Thomas
(b) Battler Britton & the Rocket Raiders
Art: Ferdinando Tacconi
Script: C. F. Thomas

205 (07/01/58)
The Black Musketeer
Cover: Stephen Chapman
Title Page: Patrick Nicolle
Art: European (French?) reprint, with some frames by Patrick Nicolle
Script: Unknown, rescripted by David Roberts

206 (07/01/58)
Robin Hood
Cover: Geoff Squire
Title Page: Geoff Campion
Art: Edgar Spenceley; reprints 'Robin Hood & the Peril of the Black Bat' from *Sun* 281–292 (26/06–11/ 09/54), with some additional art by Reg Bunn

207 (04/02/58)
The Fighting Tornado
Cover: D. C. Eyles
Art: Franco Bignotti/Mario Uggeri
Script: Barry Ford (Joan Whitford); based on the novel *Son of the Flying "Y"* (Greenwich, CT, Fawcett Publications, 1951) by Will F. Jenkins

208 (04/02/58)
The Man They Called the Bloodhound
Cover: Eric R. Parker
Art: Eric R. Parker
Script: Michael Butterworth; based on the novel *Les Misérables* (Brussels: Lacroix, Verboeckhoven et Cie., 12 vols., 1862) by Victor Hugo, translated by Charles E. Wilbour (New York, Carleton Publishing Co., 1862) and by Lascelles Wraxall (London, Hurst & Blackett, 1862)

209 (04/02/58)
Battler Britton, The Fighting Ace of the Skies
Cover: J. Francis
(a) Battler Britton & Operation Destruction
Art: Eric Bradbury, reprints from *Sun*
(b) Battler Britton & the Secret Weapon
Art: Eric Bradbury, reprints from *Sun*
(c) Battler Britton & the Plot Against Suez
Art: Geoff Campion, reprints from *Sun*

210 (04/02/58)
Robin Hood
Cover: Sep. E. Scott
Title Page: Geoff Campion
(a) Robin Hood & the Road To Freedom
Art: Reg Bunn
(b) Robin Hood & the Fate of Much
Art: Angel Pardo
Script: J. Lockhead

(c) Robin Hood & the Doors of Doom
Art: Angel Pardo
Script: J. A. Storrie

211 (04/03/58)
Gunman
Cover: Enrico De Seta?; based on film still
Art: Robert Forrest
Script: Barry Ford (Joan Whitford); Based on the novel *To Tame A Land* (Greenwich, CT, Fawcett Publications, 1955) by Louis Lamour

212 (04/03/58)
Swords of the Musketeers
Cover: Ruggero Giovannini?
Title Page: Stephen Chapman
(a) The Three Musketeers & the Swords of Freedom
Art: Stephen Chapman
Script: David Motton
(b) The Three Musketeers & Swords Across the Sea
Art: Stephen Chapman
Script: David Motton

213 (04/03/58)
Battler Britton
Cover: Patrick Nicolle, from a layout by Geoff Campion
(a) Battler Britton & the Q Boat
Art: Renzo Calegari/Carlo Porciani
Script: V. A. L. Holding
(b) Battler Britton – Tank Buster
Art: Carlo Porciani/Renzo Calegari
Script: C. F. Thomas

214 (04/03/58)
Robin Hood
Title: **Robin Hood & the Wolf Boy**
Cover: Sep. E. Scott
Title Page: Geoff Campion
Art: C. L. Doughty; reprints *Sun* 257–266 (09/01–13/03/54)
Script: Unknown, rescripted by J. A. Storrie

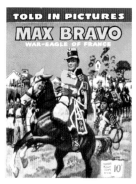

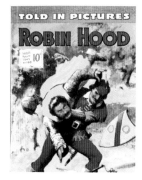

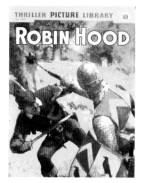

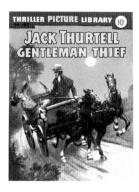

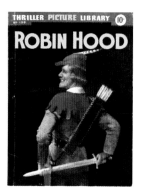

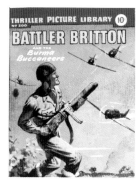

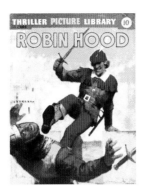

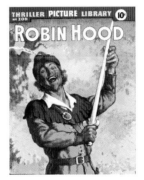

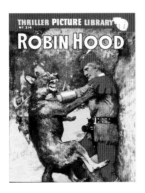

215 (01/04/58)
Under the Stars and Bars
Cover: Patrick Nicolle, from a layout by Geoff Campion
Art: Franco Bignotti/Mario Uggeri
Script: Barry Ford (Joan Whitford); based on the novel *The Valiant Virginians* (New York, Ballantine Books, 1953) by James Warner Bellah (see also 195)

216 (01/04/58)
Battler Britton
Cover: Patrick Nicolle, from a layout by Geoff Campion
(a) Battler Britton & the Lone Wolf
Art: Luigi Sorgini
Script: David Motton
(b) Battler Britton & the Flight of Fear
Art: Sergio Tarquinio
Script: C. F. Thomas
(c) Battler Britton & the Ace Saboteur
Art: Renzo Calegari/D'Ami Studio
Script: Alan Fennell

217 (01/04/58)
Daring of the Mounties
Title: **Dick Daring & the Standard of the 17th Canadian Hussars**
Cover: Gallieno Ferri
Art: Sergio Tarquinio

218 (01/04/58)
Robin Hood
Cover: Unknown (Rogers)
(a) Robin Hood & the Happy Hermit
Art: Vitor Peon
Script: J. A. Storrie
(b) Robin Hood & the Exiled Knight
Art: Reg Bunn
Script: V. A. L. Holding
(c) Robin Hood & Sir Rusty Sword
Art: Jose Ortiz
Script: J. A. Storrie

219 (21/04/58)
Vengeance Trail
Cover: Jordi Penalva?; based on a film still
Art: Robert Forrest

Script: Joan Whitford/Alf Wallace; based on the novel *The Range Buster* (Greenwich, CT, Fawcett Publications, 1954) by William Heuman

220 (21/04/58)
Dick Daring of the Mounties
Cover: Sep. E. Scott
Title Page: Geoff Campion
(a) Dick Daring & the Pony Soldiers Justice
Art: Franco Bignotti
Script: Joan Whitford
(b) Dick Daring & the Queen's Peace
Art: Franco Bignotti/Mario Uggeri
(c) Dick Daring & the Ghost Town Battle
Art: Sergio Tarquinio and Franco Bignotti
Script: M. Edwards

221 (21/04/58)
Battler Britton
Cover: George Stokes
Title Page: George Stokes
(a) Battler Britton & the Destroyer of Doom
Art: D'Ami Studio/Sergio Tuis
Script: C. F. Thomas
(b) Battler Britton & the Bomb Sight
Art: D'Ami Studio/Sergio Tuis
Script: C. F. Thomas
(c) Battler Britton & the Masked Allies
Art: George Stokes
Script: V. A. L. Holding

222 (21/04/58)
Robin Hood
Cover: Sep. E. Scott
Title Page: Geoff Campion
(a) Robin Hood & the Greedy Baron
Art: Raffaele Paparella
Script: David Motton
(b) Robin Hood & the Village Traitor
Art: Angel Pardo
Script: J. H. Higgins
(c) Robin Hood & the Sheriff's Treasure
Art: Reg Bunn
Script: D. Thompson

 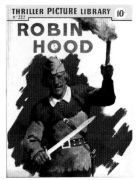  

223 (19/05/58)
Dick Turpin
Title: **Dick Turpin & the Miser Highwayman**
Cover: Stephen Chapman
Art: C. L. Doughty
Script: Barry Ford (Joan Whitford)

224 (19/05/58)
Battler Britton
Cover: Unknown
Title Page: Geoff Campion
(a) Battler Britton & the Arctic Convoy
Art: Unknown
Script: C. F. Thomas
(b) Battler Britton & the Maquis
Art: Studio D'Ami
(c) Battler Britton & the Burning Oil
Art: Antonio Canale/D'Ami Studio

225 (19/05/58)
Daring of the Mounties
Cover: Jordi Penalva?
(a) Dick Daring & the Timber Wolf
Art: Franco Bignotti
Script: James Stagg
(b) Dick Daring & the Border Bandit
Art: Franco Bignotti/Mario Uggeri
Script: Joan Whitford
(c) Dick Daring & the Blood Brothers
Art: Sergio Tarquinio
Script: Joan Whitford

226 (19/05/58)
Robin Hood
Cover: Sep. E. Scott
Title Page: Geoff Campion
(a) Robin Hood & the Lincoln Robbers
Art: Angel Pardo
Script: Alan Fennell
(b) Robin Hood & Kaf, the Giant
Art: Reg Bunn
Script: V. A. L. Holding?
(c) Robin Hood & the Seal of Doom
Art: Raffaele Paparella

227 (16/06/58)
Guns on the Prairie
Cover: Gaetano Albanese
Art: Jesus Blasco
Script: Barry Ford (Joan Whitford); based on the novel
Tough Hombre (Greenwich, CT, Fawcett Publications,
1956) by Dudley Dean (Dudley Dean McGaughy)

228 (16/06/58)
Daring of the Mounties
Title: **Dick Daring & the Untamed Land**
Cover: Gallieno Ferri?
Art: Stephen Chapman and Patrick Nicolle, partly adapted
from 'Macdonald of the Canadian Mounties' (by Nicolle)
from *Sun* 228–237 (20/06–22/08/53) with McDonald =
Dick Daring
Script: Michael Butterworth; based on the 20th Century
Fox movie starring Tyrone Power, rescripted by James
Stagg

229 (16/06/58)
Battler Britton
Cover: George Stokes
(a) Battler Britton & the Pick-a-Back Plane
Art: George Stokes
Script: V. A. L. Holding?
(b) Battler Britton & the Fighting Guardsmen
Art: D'Ami Studio
Script: D. Thompson?

230 (16/06/58)
Robin Hood
Cover: John Millar Watt
Title Page: Geoff Campion
(a) Robin Hood & the Emerald Battle Axe
Art: Renato Polese
Script: C. F. Thomas
(b) Robin Hood & the Peaceful Man
Art: Raffaele Paparella
Script: C. F. Thomas
(c) Robin Hood & the Wraith of Sherwood
Art: Reg Bunn
Script: James Stagg

 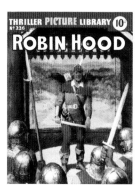  

231 (21/07/58)
Dick Turpin
Title: **Dick Turpin & the Outlaw Prince**
Cover: John Millar Watt
Art: Unknown
Script: Barry Ford (Joan Whitford)

232 (21/07/58)
Daring of the Mounties
Cover: Unknown
(a) Dick Daring & the Bogus Mountie
Art: Sergio Tarquinio
Script: Joan Whitford
(b) Dick Daring & the Secret Gold
Art: Gianluigi Coppola
Script: Joan Whitford
(c) Dick Daring & the Blacksmith Badman
Art: Sergio Tarquinio
Script: Joan Whitford

233 (21/07/58)
Battler Britton
Cover: Unknown
(a) Battler Britton & the Flying Dutchman
Art: Nevio Zeccara
Script: C. F. Thomas
(b) Battler Britton & the Sinews of War
Art: Renzo Calegari/D'Ami Studio
Script: D. Thompson?
(c) Battler Britton & the Great Rescue
Art: Eric Bradbury; reprint from *Sun* with alterations by Studio D'Ami

234 (21/07/58)
The Silver Lion
Cover: Sep. E. Scott
Title Page: Stephen Chapman
Art: Patrick Nicolle; reprints 'The Banner of the Silver Lion' from *Comet* 330–341 (13/11/54–29/01/55)
Script: Michael Butterworth

235 (18/08/58)
The Sea Lord
Cover: R. M. Sax
Art: Eric R. Parker; reprints 'Nelson' from *Comet* 359–379 (04/06–22/10/55)
Script: Michael Butterworth, rescripted by James Stagg

236 (18/08/58)
Robin Hood
Cover: Sep. E. Scott
(a) Robin Hood & Kazar the Turk
Art: Raffaele Paparella
Script: Alan Fennell
(b) Robin Hood & the Frightened Village
Art: Reg Bunn
Script: James Stagg
(c) Robin Hood & the Crusader's Gold
Art: Angel Pardo
Script: David Motton

237 (18/08/58)
Battler Britton
Cover: George Stokes
(a) Battler Britton & the Bleep
Art: George Stokes
Script: David Motton
(b) Battler Britton & the Tank Break-Through!
Art: Nevio Zeccara, reprints from *Sun*
Script: Unknown, rescripted by J. A. Storrie
(c) Battler Britton & the Missing Major
Art: Geoff Campion

238 (18/08/58)
Dick Daring of the Mounties
Cover: Giorgio De Gaspari
(a) Dick Daring & the Robber's Revenge
Art: Gianluigi Coppola
Script: Alan Fennell
(b) Dick Daring & the Ambush at Eagle River
Art: Sergio Tarquinio and Franco Bignotti
Script: Joan Whitford
(c) Dick Daring & the Indian Horse-Thief
Art: Franco Bignotti
Script: Joan Whitford

 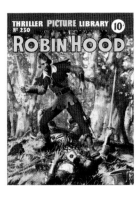  

239 (15/09/58)
Dick Turpin
Title: Dick Turpin & Creepy Crawley
Cover: John Millar Watt
Art: Hugh McNeill; reprints 'Dick Turpin & the Mystery of Creepy Crawley' from *Sun* 252–264 (05/12/53–27 03/54)
Script: Michael Butterworth, rescripted by James Stagg

240 (15/09/58)
Daring of the Mounties
Title: Dick Daring & the Fur Thieves
Cover: Giorgio De Gaspari
Art: Renato Polese
Script: Ralph Coveney

241 (15/09/58)
Battler Britton
Cover: Patrick Nicolle, from a layout by Geoff Campion
(a) Battler Britton & the VIP
Art: George Stokes
Script: James Stagg
(b) Battler Britton & the Guns of Jura
Art: Nevio Zeccara
Script: George Allen/C. F. Thomas

242 (15/09/58)
Spy 13
Cover: Giorgio De Gaspari
(a) Spy 13 & the Secret Enemy
Art: Sergio Tuis
Script: James Stagg
(b) Spy 13 & the Gestapo Trap
Art: Ferdinando Tacconi
Script: James Stagg

243 (20/10/58)
Robin Hood
Cover: James E. McConnell
(a) Robin Hood & the Border Feud
Art: Renato Polese
Script: Alan Fennell
(b) Robin Hood & the Norman Adventurers
Art: Robert Forrest
Script: V. A. L. Holding

(c) Robin Hood & the Ruined Castle
Art: Angel Pardo
Script: Alan Fennell

244 (20/10/58)
Dick Daring of the Mounties
Cover: Giorgio De Gaspari
(a) Dick Daring & the Lying Chieftain
Art: Mario Uggeri
Script: James Stagg?
(b) Dick Daring & the Kidnapped Boy
Art: Sergio Tarquinio
(c) Dick Daring & the Border Invaders
Art: Enrique Badia Romero
Script: Joan Whitford

245 (20/10/58)
Battler Britton
Cover: Nino Caroselli?
(a) Battler Britton & the Malta Convoy
Art: Ian Kennedy, reprint from *Sun*, with some additional artwork by Eric Bradbury
Script: Unknown, rescripted by J. A. Storrie
(b) Battler Britton & the Desert Cavalry
Art: Geoff Campion, reprint from *Sun*, with some additional artwork by Eric Bradbury
Script: Unknown, rescripted by J. A. Storrie
(c) Battler Britton & the Atlantic Peril
Art: Geoff Campion
Script: Unknown, rescripted by J. A. Storrie

246 (20/10/58)
Gunplay
Cover: Giorgio De Gaspari
Art: Robert Forrest
Script: Barry Ford (Joan Whitford); based on the novel *The Broken Spur* (Greenwich, CT, Fawcett Publications, 1955) by Dudley Dean (Dudley Dean McGaughy)

247 (17/11/58)
Dick Turpin
Cover: John Millar Watt
Art: Hugh McNeill; reprints 'Dick Turpin in Terror Keep' from *Sun* 243–251 (03/10–28/11/53), with some additional artwork by W. Ward
Script: Michael Butterworth

  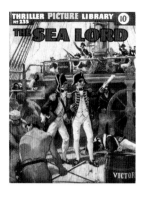 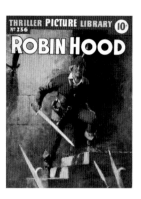

248 (17/11/58)
Daring of the Mounties
Cover: Sep. E. Scott
(a) Dick Daring & the Saloon Robber
Art: Sergio Tarquinio
Script: Joan Whitford
(b) Dick Daring & the Tell-tale Fur
Art: Virgilio Muzzi/Mario Uggeri
Script: James Stagg/Ralph Coveney
(c) Dick Daring & the Bogus Doctor
Art: Stephen Chapman
Script: Ralph Coveney

249 (17/11/58)
Battler Britton
Cover: Giorgio De Gaspari
(a) Battler Britton & the Dash For Freedom
Art: Eric Bradbury, with some additional art by George
Stokes
Script: J. A. Storrie
(b) Battler Britton & the Convoy of Peril
Art: Nevio Zeccara
Script: D. M. Garbutt

250 (17/11/58)
Spy 13
Title: Spy 13 & the Mission to Norway
Cover: Giorgio De Gaspari
Art: Graham Coton; reprints 'Captain Phantom' from
Knockout 716–728 (16/11/52–07/02/53), partly redrawn
by Reg Bunn
Script: Ron Clark, rescripted by Alf Wallace

251 (15/12/58)
Robin Hood
Cover: Sep. E. Scott
(a) Robin Hood & the Forest Trap
Art: Angel Pardo
Script: J. H. Higgins
(b) Robin Hood & the Greedy Sheriff
Art: Nadir Quinto
Script: J. H. Higgins
(c) Robin Hood & the Sheriff's Ghost
Art: Martin Salvador
Script: Alan Fennell

252 (15/12/58)
Dick Daring of the Mounties
Cover: Sep. E. Scott
(a) Dick Daring & the Sun Lizard
Art: Reg Bunn
Script: Ralph Coveney
(b) Dick Daring & the Renegades
Art: Unknown
Script: James Stagg

253 (15/12/58)
Battler Britton
Cover: Patrick Nicolle, from a layout by Geoff Campion
Title Page: George Stokes
(a) Battler Britton & Treachery Afloat
Art: Vettor Cassinari
Script: E. J. Bensberg
(b) Battler Britton & the Decoy Plane
Art: Renzo Calegari
Script: R. Clegg

254 (15/12/58)
Redman's Vengeance
Cover: Unknown
Art: Franco Bignotti?/Mario Uggeri
Script: Barry Ford (Joan Whitford); based on *Cheyenne
Saturday* (Greenwich, CT, Fawcett Publications, 1957)
by Richard Jessup

255 (19/01/59)
Robin Hood
Cover: Sep. E. Scott
(a) All Hallows Eve
Art: Martin Salvador
(b) Robin Hood & the Sherwood Spy
Art: Angel Pardo
Script: Angus Allan
(c) Robin Hood & the Giant Catapult
Art: John Millar Watt
Script: J. H. Higgins
(d) Robin Hood & the Rival Lord
Art: Fred Holmes; reprint from *Sun* (24/11–08/12/56),
with some redrawing by T. Barling
Script: Unknown, rescripted by Alf Wallace

 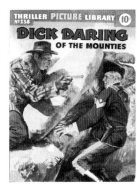 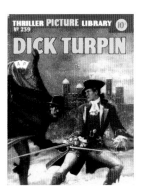 

256 (19/01/59)
Dick Daring of the Mounties
Cover: Giorgio De Gaspari
(a) Dick Daring & the Cookstown Hold-Up
Art: Sergio Tarquinio
Script: Alan Fennell
(b) Dick Daring & the Forest Fire
Art: Vittorio Cossio
Script: Alan Fennell
(c) Dick Daring & the Gunmans Brother
Art: Sergio Tarquinio
Script: Angus Allan

257 (19/01/59)
Battler Britton
Cover: Giorgio De Gaspari
Title Page: Gino D'Antonio
(a) Battler Britton & the Runaway Gun
Art: George Stokes
Script: E. J. Bensberg
(b) Battler Britton & the Tunnel Stronghold
Art: Carlos Friexas, reprint from *Sun*
Script: Unknown, rescripted by Alf Wallace
(c) Battler Britton – Fighting Tornado
Art: Ferdinando Tacconi
Script: Gordon Sowman

258 (19/01/59)
Spy 13
Title: Spy 13 & the Sand Spiders
Cover: Giorgio De Gaspari
Title Page: Reg Bunn
Art: Graham Coton; reprints 'Captain Phantom' from *Knockout* 729–737 (14/02–11/04/53), with some additional drawing by Reg Bunn
Script: Ron Clark, rescripted by James Stagg & Alf Wallace

259 (16/02/59)
Robin Hood
Cover: Sep. E. Scott
(a) Robin Hood & the Singing Soothsayer
Art: Mario Uggeri
Script: Angus Allan

(b) Robin Hood & the Saxon Footman
Art: Reg Bunn
Script: Alf Wallace
(c) Robin Hood & the Dungeons of DeMowbray
Art: Angel Pardo
Script: Angus Allan

260 (16/02/59)
Dick Daring of the Mounties
Cover: Giorgio De Gaspari
(a) Dick Daring & Wild Jack
Art: Reg Bunn
Script: W. Prout
(b) Dick Daring & the Trail of Justice
Art: Sergio Tarquinio
Script: R. Clegg
(c) Dick Daring & the Battle of Cougar River
Art: Jose Grau
Script: D. M. Garbutt

261 (16/02/59)
Battler Britton
Cover: Giorgio De Gaspari
Title Page: George Stokes
(a) Battler Britton & the Surface Raider
Art: John Gillatt
(b) Battler Britton & the General's Vengeance
Art: Eric Bradbury, reprint from *Sun,* with some additional artwork by George Stokes
Script: Unknown, rescripted by Alf Wallace
(c) Battler Britton & the Frogmen
Art: Unknown
Script: R. Clegg

262 (16/02/59)
Ambush
Cover: Sep. E. Scott
Art: Jesus Blasco
Script: Barry Ford (Joan Whitford); based on *Bugles on the Prairie* (Greenwich, CT, Fawcett Publications, 1957) by Gordon D. Shirreffs

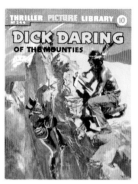

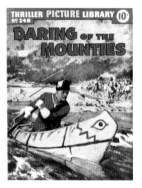

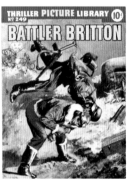

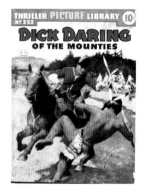

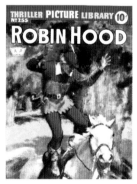

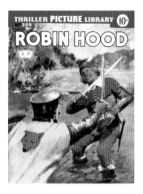
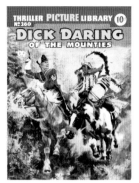

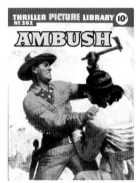
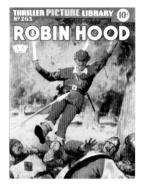

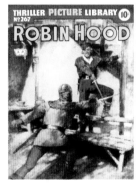
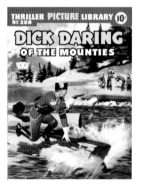

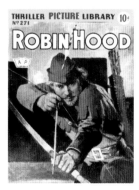
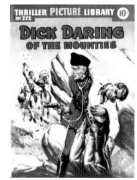

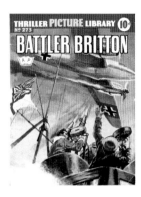   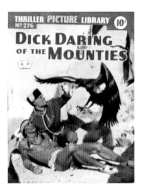

263 (16/03/59)
Robin Hood
Cover: Sep. E. Scott
(a) Robin Hood & the Press Gang Army
Art: Martin Salvador
Script: W. Prout
(b) Robin Hood & Black Mask
Art: Reg Bunn
Script: W. Prout
(c) Robin Hood & the Toll-Chain
Art: Mario Uggeri
Script: Ralph Coveney

264 (16/03/59)
Dick Daring of the Mounties
Cover: Giorgio De Gaspari
(a) Dick Daring & the Feud at Wolf Creek
Art: Sergio Tarquinio
(b) Dick Daring – Lone-Handed Lawman
Art: Vittorio Cossio
Script: Angus Allan
(c) Dick Daring & the Bogus Banker
Art: Unknown
Script: W. Ward

265 (16/03/59)
Battler Britton
Cover: Giorgio De Gaspari
Title Page: Gino D'Antonio
(a) Battler Britton & the Victory Weapon
Art: Ferdinando Tacconi
Script: E. Evans
(b) Battler Britton & the Pusser's Spitfire
Art: Ian Kennedy, reprint from *Sun*, with some additional art by Unknown (Strathmore Studios)
(c) Battler Britton & the Prisoner of the Gestapo
Art: Guy Mouminoux
Script: Gordon Sowman

266 (16/03/59)
Spy 13
Title: **Spy 13 & the Man of Power**
Cover: Giorgio De Gaspari
Art: Graham Coton; reprints 'Captain Phantom' from *Knockout* 759–771 (12/09–05/12/53), with some

additional redrawing by Reg Bunn
Script: Ron Clark, rescripted by Alf Wallace & G. P. Mann

267 (20/04/59)
Robin Hood
Cover: Sep. E. Scott
(a) Robin Hood & the Secret of the Inn
Art: Martin Salvador
Script: Alf Wallace
(b) Robin Hood & the Magic Bow
Art: Angel Pardo
Script: Ralph Coveney
(c) Robin Hood & the Greenwood Tower
Art: Ruggero Giovannini
Script: Ralph Coveney

268 (20/04/59)
Dick Daring of the Mounties
Cover: Jordi Penalva
(a) Dick Daring & the Long Lost Mine
Art: Renato Polese
Script: W. Prout
(b) Dick Daring Gets His Man
Art: Gianluigi Coppola
Script: W. Prout
(c) Dick Daring & the Great Bullion Robbery
Art: Vittorio Cossio
Script: W. Prout

269 (20/04/59)
Battler Britton
Title: **Battler Britton & Goliath**
Cover: Giorgio De Gaspari
Art: Carlo Porciani/Renzo Calegari/D'Ami Studio
Script: Rinaldo D'Ami, rescripted by Alf Wallace

270 (20/04/59)
Stampede
Cover: Giorgio De Gaspari
Art: Ruggero Giovannini
Script: Barry Ford (Joan Whitford); based on the novel *The Longhorn Legion* (New York, Dell Publishing Co., 1951) by Norman Fox

 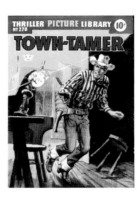  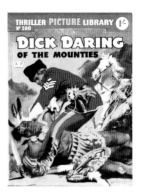

271 (18/05/59)
Robin Hood
Title: **The Seal of King Richard**
Cover: Sep. E. Scott
Title Page: Geoff Campion
Art: Martin Salvador
Script: Alf Wallace

272 (18/05/59)
Dick Daring of the Mounties
Cover: P. Carey?
(a) Dick Daring & the Strange Recruit
Art: Jose Bielsa
Script: W. Prout
(b) Dick Daring & the Methodical Outlaw
Art: P. Green
Script: G. P. Mann
(c) Dick Daring & the Redskin Millionaire
Art: Renato Polese
Script: W. Prout

273 (18/05/59)
Battler Britton
Cover: Giorgio De Gaspari
Title Page: Gino D'Antonio (2pgs)
(a) Battler Britton & the Raid That Must Not Fail
Art: George Stokes
Script: E. Evans
(b) Battler Britton & the German Invasion
Art: Eric Bradbury, reprint from *Sun*, with additional artwork by Sergio Tuis
Script: Unknown, rescripted by Alf Wallace & G. Coombs
(c) Battler Britton & the Big Gun
Art: Unknown
Script: R. Clegg

274 (18/05/59)
Spy 13
Cover: Giorgio De Gaspari
(a) Spy 13 & the Phoney Invasion
Art: Reg Bunn
Script: R. Clegg

(b) Behind Enemy Lines
Art: Graham Coton; reprints 'Captain Phantom' from *Knockout* 702–706 (09/08 – 08/09/52), with some additional art by Reg Bunn
Script: Unknown, rescripted by Alf Wallace

275 (15/06/59)
Robin Hood
Cover: Sep. E. Scott
(a) Robin Hood & the Man From the Dungeons
Art: Guido Buzzelli
Script: J. H. Higgins
(b) Robin Hood & Zoltan the Terrible
Art: Nadir Quinto
Script: Ralph Coveney
(c) Robin Hood & the Nottingham Stocks
Art: Nadir Quinto
Script: Ralph Coveney

276 (15/06/59)
Dick Daring of the Mounties
Cover: Jordi Penalva
(a) Dick Daring & the Bells of Danger
Art: Renato Polese
Script: W. Prout
(b) Dick Daring & the Secret Bank Robber
Art: Sergio Tarquinio
Script: W. Prout
(c) Champion of the North West
Art: Franco Bignotti
Script: W. Prout

277 (15/06/59)
Battler Britton
Cover: Nino Caroselli
Title Page: Gino D'Antonio
(a) Battler Britton & the Beach of Peril
Art: Ortega
Script: Alan Fennell
(b) Battler Britton & the Master Swordsman
Art: Reg Bunn & Eric Bradbury
Script: Alf Wallace

278 (15/06/59)
Town Tamer
Cover: Renato Fratini
Art: Virgilio Muzzi/Mario Uggeri
Script: J. H. Higgins; based on the novel *A Town To Tame* (Greenwich, CT, Fawcett Publications, 1958) by Joseph Chadwick

279 (20/07/59)
The Worst Boy in School
Cover: Patrick Nicolle, from a layout by Geoff Campion
Art: Fred Holmes
Script: V. A. L. Holding

280 (20/07/59)
Dick Daring of the Mounties
Cover: Giorgio De Gaspari
(a) Dick Daring & the River Pirates
Art: Virgilio Muzzi/Mario Uggeri
Script: Unknown [possibly Rinaldo D'Ami], rescripted by V. A. L. Holding
(b) Dick Daring & the Man Trap
Art: Vittorio Cossio
Script: W. Prout

281 (20/07/59)
Battler Britton
Cover: Giorgio De Gaspari
Title Page: Gino D'Antonio (2pgs)
(a) Battler Britton & Operation Crusoe
Art: Ortega
Script: G. Coombs
(b) Battler Britton & the Island of Doom
Art: Eric Bradbury, reprint from *Sun*, with additional artwork by Sergio Tuis
Script: Unknown, rescripted by Alf Wallace & G. Coombs
(c) Battler Britton & the High Escape
Art: Ferdinando Tacconi
Script: E. Evans

282 (20/07/59)
Spy 13
Title: **Spy 13 & the Nazi Fire Raisers**
Cover: Nino Caroselli
Art: Reg Bunn
Script: R. Clegg

283 (09/59)
Robin Hood
Cover: John Millar Watt
(a) Robin Hood & the Saxon Inheritance
Art: Martin Salvador
Script: Ralph Coveney
(b) Robin Hood & the Hounds of Andromas
Art: Angel Pardo
Script: Alf Wallace

284 (09/59)
Dick Daring of the Mounties
Cover: Giorgio De Gaspari
(a) Dick Daring & the Crooked Foreman
Art: Jose Grau
Script: Ralph Coveney
(b) Dick Daring & the Doomed City
Art: Vittorio Cossio
Script: W. Prout
(c) Dick Daring & the White King of the Mountains
Art: Franco Bignotti
Script: W. Prout

285 (09/59)
Battler Britton
Cover: Giorgio De Gaspari
Title Page: Gino D'Antonio
(a) Battler Britton & the Sea Wolves Lair
Art: Giorgio Bellavitis
Script: V. A. L. Holding
(b) Battler Britton & the German Prototype
Art: Aldo Di Gennaro/Sergio Tuis
Script: D. M. Garbutt

286 (09/59)
The Bounty Hunters
Cover: Jordi Penalva
Art: Ruggero Giovannini
Script: Barry Ford (Joan Whitford); based on the novel *Massacre at San Pablo* (Greenwich, CT, Fawcett Publications, 1957) by Lewis B. Patton

   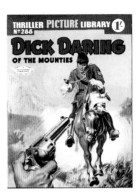

287 (10/59)
Robin Hood
Cover: John Millar Watt
(a) Robin Hood & the Greenwood Pits
Art: Nadir Quinto
Script: Ralph Coveney
(b) Robin Hood & the Lake of Doom
Art: Martin Salvador
Script: Ralph Coveney

288 (10/59)
Dick Daring of the Mounties
Cover: Giorgio De Gaspari
(a) Dick Daring & the Mistaken Redskin
Art: Vittorio Cossio
Script: J. H. Higgins
(b) Dick Daring & the Rival Kidnappers
Art: Vittorio Cossio
Script: W. Prout
(c) Dick Daring & the Lust For Gold
Art: Franco Bignotti
Script: W. Prout

289 (10/59)
Battler Britton
Cover: Giorgio De Gaspari
Title Page: Gino D'Antonio
(a) Battler Britton & the Radar Raid
Art: Renzo Calegari (4pp)/Giorgio Bellavitis
Script: G. Coombs
(b) Battler Britton & the Target in Poland
Art: Vettor Cassinari
Script: E. Evans

290 (10/59)
Spy 13 of World War II
Cover: Giorgio De Gaspari
(a) Spy 13 & Code ZX913
Art: Franco Paludetti
Script: Gordon Sowman
(b) Spy 13 & the Peril of the Panzers
Art: Leone Cimpellin
Script: E. J. Bensberg

291 (11/59)
Robin Hood
Cover: John Millar Watt
Art: Jesus Blasco; reprints 'Robin Hood the Magnificent' from *Sun* 397–406 (15/09–17/11/56), with some additional art by Reg Bunn
Script: Michael Butterworth, rescripted by Alf Wallace

292 (11/59)
Dick Daring of the Mounties
Cover: Jordi Penalva
(a) Dick Daring & the Silenced Witness
Art: Carlos V Roume
Script: Ralph Coveney
(b) Dick Daring & the King of Caribou Pass
Art: Sergio Tarquinio
Script: J. H. Higgins

293 (11/59)
Battler Britton
Cover: Giorgio De Gaspari
Title Page: Gino D'Antonio
(a) Battler Britton & the Flying Monstrosity
Art: Sergio Tuis/Aldo Di Gennaro (8pp)/Vettor Cassinari/D'Ami Studio
Script: R. Clegg
(b) Battler Britton & the Challenge
Art: Vettor Cassinari
Script: G. Coombs

294 (11/59)
Lone Justice
Cover: Giorgio De Gaspari
Art: Mario Uggeri
Script: Barry Ford (Joan Whitford); based on the novel *Wyoming Jones* (Greenwich, CT, Fawcett Publications, 1958) by Richard Telfair

  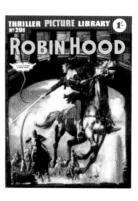 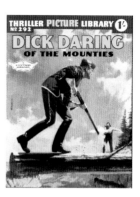

295 (12/59)
Robin Hood
Cover: Sep. E. Scott
(a) Robin Hood & the Grey Riders of the Fens
Art: Martin Salvador
Script: David Satherley
(b) Robin Hood & the Race For Life
Art: Raffaele Paparella
Script: Ralph Coveney

296 (12/59)
Dick Daring of the Mounties
Cover: Jordi Penalva
(a) Dick Daring & the Frightened Lumber-Boss
Art: Renato Polese
Script: Ralph Coveney
(b) Dick Daring & the Braggart Lawman
Art: Vittorio Cossio
Script: Ralph Coveney
(c) Dick Daring & the Trappers of Rainbow Creek
Art: Franco Bignotti
Script: J. Mather

297 (12/59)
Battler Britton
Cover: Giorgio De Gaspari
(a) Battler Britton & Operation Atom
Art: Sergio Tuis (some panels inked by Renzo Calegari)
Script: Danny Kelleher
(b) Battler Britton & the Wagons of Gold
Art: Hugo Pratt
Script: V. A. L. Holding

298 (12/59)
Spy 13 of World War II
Cover: Nino Caroselli
(a) Spy 13 & the Rocket Expert
Art: Franco Paludetti
Script: E. J. Bensberg
(b) Spy 13 & the Secret of the Lakes
Art: Ruggero Giovannini
Script: E. J. Bensberg

299 (01/60)
Robin Hood
Cover: Enrico De Seta?
(a) Robin Hood & the Saxon Rising
Art: Jesus Blasco; reprints 'Robin Hood Lord of Sherwood'
from *Sun* 410–416 (15/12/56–26/01/57), with some
additional art by Reg Bunn
Script: Michael Butterworth, rescripted by Alf Wallace
(b) Robin Hood & the Sheriff's Plot
Art: Martin Salvador
Script: Ralph Coveney

300 (01/60)
Dick Daring of the Mounties
Cover: Jordi Penalva
(a) Dick Daring & the Sioux Invasion
Art: Renato Polese
Script: W. Howard Baker
(b) Dick Daring & the Devil's Playground
Art: Martin Salvador
Script: W. Ward

301 (01/60)
Battler Britton
Cover: Giorgio De Gaspari
Title Page: Gino D'Antonio
(a) Battler Britton & the Malta Ferry
Art: Antonio Canale
Script: D. M. Garbutt
(b) Battler Britton & the Fighting Merchant Men
Art: Syd Jordan, with some additional panels by unknown
Italian artist
Script: R. Clegg
(c) Battler Britton & the Secret of F.E. 934
Art: Franco Paludetti
Script: E. Evans

302 (01/60)
Branded
Cover: Nino Caroselli
Art: Robert Forrest
Script: Michael Butterworth/Harold Lamb

  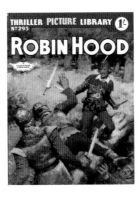 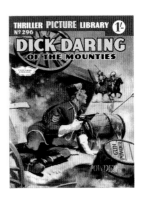

303 (02/60)
Robin Hood
Cover: Enrico De Seta?
(a) Robin Hood & the Fateful Ruby
Art: Martin Salvador
Script: Ralph Coveney
(b) Robin Hood & the Make Believe Army
Art: Nadir Quinto
Script: W. Prout

304 (02/60)
Dick Daring of the Mounties
Cover: Mario Uggeri
(a) Dick Daring & the Swamp Gang
Art: Renato Polese
Script: W. Howard Baker
(b) Dick Daring & the Railroad Troublemaker
Art: Carlos V Roume
Script: J. Mather
(c) Dick Daring & the Robber Brothers
Art: Vittorio Cossio
Script: D. M. Garbutt

305 (02/60)
Battler Britton
Title: **Battler Britton & the Castaway Squadron**
Cover: Giorgio De Gaspari
Art: James Bleach?
Script: R. Clegg

306 (02/60)
Spy 13 of World War II
Cover: Giorgio De Gaspari
Title Page: Graham Coton
(a) Spy 13 & the Nazi Invasion Code
Art: Reg Bunn
Script: E. J. Bensberg
(b) Spy 13 & the Dummy Gun Battery
Art: Reg Bunn
Script: E. J. Bensberg
(c) Spy 13 & the Lake of Eagles
Art: Reg Bunn
Script: E. J. Bensberg

307 (03/60)
Dogfight Dixon RFC
Title: **Thunder In the Blue!**
Cover: Giorgio De Gaspari
Art: Aldo Di Gennaro?
Script: Ralph Coveney

308 (03/60)
Dick Daring of the Mounties
Cover: Unknown
(a) Dick Daring & the Cossack Horsemen
Art: Sergio Tarquinio
Script: W. Howard Baker
(b) Dick Daring & the Great Bank Plot
Art: Mario Uggeri
Script: Ralph Coveney

309 (03/60)
Battler Britton
Cover: Giorgio De Gaspari
Title Page: Gino D'Antonio
(a) Battler Britton & the Danger Signal
Art: John Gillatt
Script: E. Evans
(b) Battler Britton & the Minelayers
Art: Guy Mouminoux
Script: R. Clegg
(c) Operation Pipeline
Art: Unknown
Script: G. Coombs

310 (03/60)
Spy 13 of World War II
Title: **Spy 13 & the Night Sky Menace**
Cover: Nino Caroselli
Art: Reg Bunn
Script: R. Clegg

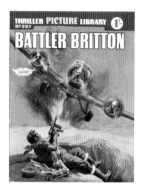

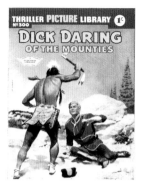

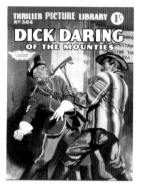

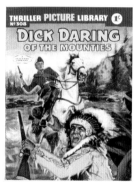

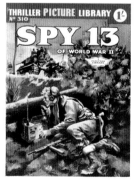

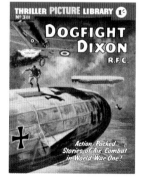

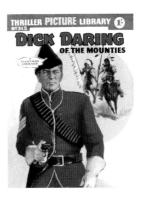

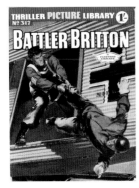

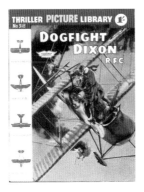

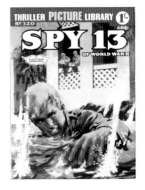

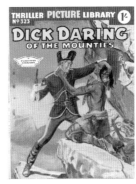

 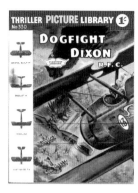 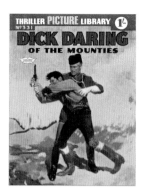 

311 (04/60)
Dogfight Dixon, RFC
Cover: Nino Caroselli
(a) Dogfight Dixon & the Giant of the Skies
Art: Harry Farrugia
Script: Michael Moorcock
(b) Dogfight Dixon & the Hill of Peril
Art: Antonio Canale, with faces redrawn by Unknown
Script: Ken Mennell

312 (04/60)
Dick Daring of the Mounties
Cover: Stefan Barany
(a) Dick Daring & the Hooded Riders!
Art: Carlos V Roume
Script: J. Mather
(b) Dick Daring & the Target For Treachery!
Art: Martin Salvador
Script: J. Roswell
(c) Dick Daring & the Mystery Marksman!
Art: Martin Salvador

313 (04/60)
Battler Britton
Cover: Giorgio De Gaspari
(a) Battler Britton & the The Money Blitz
Art: Sergio Tuis
Script: G. Coombs
(b) Battler Britton's Army
Art: Sergio Tuis
Script: G. Coombs

314 (04/60)
Spy 13 of World War II
Title: **Spy 13 & the Nazi Boffin**
Cover: Giorgio De Gaspari
Art: Unknown
Script: Gordon Sowman

315 (05/60)
Dick Daring of the Mounties
Cover: Nino Caroselli?
(a) Dick Daring & the Haunted Silver Mine
Art: Sergio Tarquinio
Script: W. Howard Baker

(b) Dick Daring & the Plotters of Pine Creek
Art: Sergio Tarquinio
Script: D. M. Garbutt
(c) Dick Daring & the Vanishing Jail-Breakers
Art: Vittorio Cossio
Script: J. Mather

316 (05/60)
Spy 13 of World War II
Cover: Mike Western
(a) Spy 13 & the Guns of Mount Eagle
Art: Bert Van Der Put
Script: Harold Lamb
(b) Spy 13 & the Turkish Diplomat
Art: Franco Paludetti
Script: E. J. Bensberg

317 (05/60)
Battler Britton
Cover: Nino Caroselli
Title Page: Gino D'Antonio
(a) Battler Britton's Quiet Leave
Art: Aldo Di Gennaro
Script: G. Coombs
(b) Battler Britton & the Nazi Trap
Art: Carlo Porciani
Script: G. Coombs

318 (05/60)
Dogfight Dixon, RFC
Cover: Giorgio De Gaspari
(a) Dogfight Dixon's Perilous Mission
Art: Jorge Moliterni
Script: Michael Moorcock
(b) Dogfight Dixon & the Hun's Vengeance
Art: George Heath
Script: Ralph Coveney
(c) Dogfight Dixon & the Flight of Fear
Art: Kurt Caesar
Script: Michael Moorcock

319 (06/60)
Dick Daring of the Mounties
Title: **Dick Daring & the Trail of Iron Face**
Cover: Nino Caroselli
Art: Martin Salvador

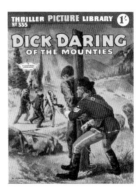

320 (06/60)
Spy 13 of World War II
Cover: Nino Caroselli
Title Page: Mike Western
(a) Spy 13 & the Hidden Enemy
Art: Aurelio Bevia
Script: Douglas Leach
(b) Spy 13 & the Nuisance Raiders
Art: George Heath
Script: Roy McAdorey

321 (06/60)
Battler Britton
Cover: Nino Caroselli
(a) The Chests of Gold
Art: Geoff Campion; reprints from *Sun*?
Script: Unknown, rescripted by Alf Wallace
(b) Battler Britton & the Desert Patrol
Art: Ian Kennedy; reprints from *Sun*?
Script: Unknown, rescripted by Alf Wallace
(c) Battler Britton & the Secret of the U-Boat Lair
Art: Luis
Script: D. M. Garbutt

322 (06/60)
Dogfight Dixon, RFC
Cover: Stefan Barany
(a) Dogfight Dixon Takes a Leave
Art: Alan Pollack
Script: Ken Mennell
(b) Dogfight Dixon & the Mission of Mercy
Art: Nevio Zeccara
Script: Ralph Coveney

323 (07/60)
Dick Daring of the Mounties
Title: **Dick Daring & the Hired Gunman**
Cover: Gallieno Ferri?
Art: Carlos V Roume
Script: Michael Moorcock

324 (07/60)
Spy 13 of World War II
Title: Spy 13 & the Missile Menace
Cover: Nino Caroselli
Art: D'Ami Studio/Franco Paludetti
Script: T. E. Moore

325 (07/60)
Battler Britton
Cover: Nino Caroselli
(a) Battler Britton & the Treasure of Lake Margo
Art: Chic Jack
Script: T. E. Moore
(b) Battler Britton & the German Jet
Art: Unknown
Script: R. Clegg
(c) Battler Britton & the Pavlow Affair
Art: Geoff Campion, reprints from *Sun*, with additional art by Eric Bradbury
Script: Unknown, rescripted by Alf Wallace

326 (07/60)
Dogfight Dixon, RFC
Cover: Stefan Barany
(a) Dogfight Dixon & the Honourable Foe!
Art: Aldoma Puig
Script: Ralph Coveney
(b) Dogfight Dixon & the Top Secret
Art: Kurt Caesar
Script: Ralph Coveney

327 (08/60)
Gun Fury!
Cover: Jordi Penalva
Art: Ruggero Giovannini
Script: Barry Ford (Joan Whitford); based on the novel *The Long Ride West* (Greenwich, CT, Fawcett Publications, 1957) by Richard Jessup

328 (08/60)
Spy 13 of World War II
Cover: Nino Caroselli
(a) Spy 13 & the Secret Weapon
Art: Aldo Di Gennaro
Script: Gordon Sowman
(b) Spy 13 & the Cargo of Doom
Art: Bert Van Der Put
Script: Douglas Leach
(c) To Die At Dawn!
Art: Leone Cimpellin
Script: Gordon Sowman

329 (08/60)
Battler Britton
Cover: Nino Caroselli
(a) Battler Britton & the Nazi Air Mystery
Art: Armando Bonato
Script: R. Clegg
(b) Battler Britton & the Greek Guerillas
Art: Nevio Zeccara, reprints from *Sun*
Script: Unknown, rescripted by Alf Wallace
(c) Battler Britton's African Adventure
Title Page: Ian Kennedy
Art: Colin Merrett, reprinted from *Sun*
Script: Unknown, rescripted by Alf Wallace

330 (08/60)
Dogfight Dixon, RFC
Cover: Stefan Barany
(a) Dogfight Dixon & the Rescue Raid
Art: Kurt Caesar
Script: Ralph Coveney
(b) Dogfight Dixon – Lone Eagle
Art: Unknown
Script: Michael Moorcock

331 (09/60)
Dick Daring of the Mounties
Title: **Dick Daring & the Debt of Danger!**
Cover: Jordi Penalva
Art: Carlos V Roume

332 (09/60)
Spy 13 of World War II
Cover: Giorgio De Gaspari
(a) Spy 13 & the Swimming Pig
Art: Leone Cimpellin
Script: Frank S. Pepper
(b) Spy 13 & the Secret Patriot
Art: Pat Williams
Script: T. E. Moore

333 (09/60)
Battler Britton
Cover: Giorgio De Gaspari
(a) Battler Britton & the Temple of the Sun
Art: Frank Pashley
Script: T. E. Moore
(b) Sabotage in Turkey
Art: Silvano Marinelli?
Script: Unknown, rescripted by Alf Wallace
(c) Formula 17
Art: Unknown
Script: Gordon Sowman

334 (09/60)
Dogfight Dixon, RFC
Title: **Dogfight Dixon & the Reluctant Recruit!**
Cover: Unknown
Art: Aldoma Puig
Script: Ken Mennell

335 (10/60)
Dick Daring of the Mounties
Title: **Dick Daring & the Woodville Mystery**
Cover: Stefan Barany
Art: Martin Salvador
Script: J. Roswell

336 (10/60)
Spy 13 of World War II
Cover: Nino Caroselli
(a) Spy 13 & the Secret Fleet
Art: Peter Sutherland
(b) Spy 13 & the Mountains of Terror
Art: Alberto Breccia
Script: Douglas Leach

337 (10/60)
Battler Britton
Cover: Nino Caroselli
Title Page: Gino D'Antonio
(a) Battler Britton's Double Trouble
Art: Sergio Tuis
Script: G. Coombs
(b) Battler Britton & the War Trophy!
Art: Sergio Tuis
Script: G. Coombs
(c) Battler Britton's Desert Blitz
Art: Peter Sutherland
Script: J. H. Higgins

338 (10/60)
Dogfight Dixon, RFC
Title: **Dogfight Dixon & the Traitors of the Air**
Cover: Stefan Barany
Art: Kurt Caesar
Script: Ralph Coveney

339 (11/60)
Dick Daring of the Mounties
Title: **Dick Daring & the Klondike Mission**
Cover: Mario Uggeri?
Art: Stephen Chapman
Script: Bob Kesten

340 (11/60)
Spy 13 of World War II
Title: **Spy 13 & the Sign of the Zodiac**
Cover: Nino Caroselli
Art: Leone Cimpellin
Script: R. P. Yunnil(??)

341 (11/60)
Battler Britton
Cover: Nino Caroselli
(a) Battler Britton & the Secret Agent
Art: Unknown
(b) Battler Britton & the Gold Ship
Art: Syd Jordan
Script: R. Clegg
(c) Battler Britton & the Wizard Pilot
Art: Gary Keane
Script: E. J. Bensberg

342 (11/60)
Dogfight Dixon, RFC
Title: **Dogfight Dixon & the Squadron of Doom**
Cover: Unknown
Art: Aldoma Puig
Script: J. Roswell

343 (12/60)
John Steel Special Agent World War II
Title: **Mission to Maru**
Cover: P. Carey?
Art: Victor Hugo Arias

344 (12/60)
Spy 13 of World War II
Title: **Spy 13 & the Double Trap**
Cover: Unknown
Art: Aurelio Bevia
Script: J. A. Stockbridge

345 (12/60)
Battler Britton
Cover: Pino Dell'orco
(a) Battler Britton & the Prison Ship
Art: Aldo Di Gennaro
(b) Battler Britton & Operation Schmidt
Art: Colin Page
Script: A. G. B. Parlett

346 (12/60)
Dogfight Dixon, RFC
Title: **Dogfight Dixon & the Hawks of the Desert!**
Cover: Nino Caroselli?
Art: Aldoma Puig
Script: Donne Avenell

347 (01/61)
John Steel Special Agent World War II
Title: **John Steel & Operation Freedom**
Cover: P. Carey?
Art: Bill Lacey

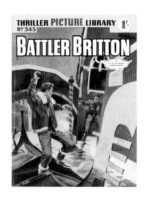  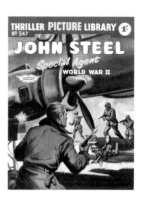 

348 (01/61)
Spy 13 of World War II
Title: **Gamble With Danger**
Cover: Pino Dell'orco
Art: Alberto Breccia

349 (01/61)
Battler Britton
Cover: Stefan Barany?
(a) Battler Britton & the Bomb Sight Boffin
Art: Giorgio Trevisan at start, then Unknown
Script: G. Coombs
(b) Battler Britton & the Tunnel Menace
Art: D'Ami Studio/Leone Cimpellin

350 (01/61)
Dogfight Dixon, RFC
Title: **Dogfight Dixon & the Traitor Pilot**
Cover: Nino Caroselli
Art: Amador Garcia

351 (02/61)
John Steel Special Agent World War II
Title: **John Steel & the Debt of Honour**
Cover: Agustin Navarro?
Art: Unknown

352 (02/61)
Spy 13 of World War II
Title: **Operation South Pacific**
Cover: Nino Caroselli?
Art: F Alan Philpott?

353 (02/61)
Battler Britton
Title: **Battler Britton – Pathfinder**
Cover: Nino Caroselli
Art: Aurelio Bevia

354 (02/61)
Dogfight Dixon, RFC
Title: **Dogfight Dixon & the Savage Sky**
Cover: Pino Dell'orco
Art: Alan Pollack

355 (03/61)
Meet Me In Lisbon (John Steel)
Cover: Allessandro Biffignandi
Art: Lopez Espi

356 (03/61)
Spy 13 of World War II
Title: **Danger Before D-Day**
Cover: Pino Dell'orco
Art: Luigi Sorgini, Santo D'Amico & others

357 (03/61)
Battler Britton
Title: **Battler Britton & the Wolf Pack**
Cover: Pino Dell'orco
Art: Giorgio Trevisan

358 (03/61)
Dogfight Dixon, RFC
Title: **Dogfight Dixon & the Balkan Battle**
Cover: P. Carey?
Art: Amador Garcia

359 (05/61)
Downbeat (John Steel)
Cover: Allessandro Biffignandi
Art: Graham Coton; reprints 'The Door With the Seven Locks' from *Super Detective Library* 6 (06/53) with Dick Martin=John Steel
Script: Peter O'Donnell; based on the novel *The Door with the Seven Locks* (London, Hodder & Stoughton, 1926) by Edgar Wallace

360 (05/61)
Spy 13 of World War II
Title: **Spy 13 & the Atom Bomb Peril**
Cover: Nino Caroselli
Art: Victor Hugo Arias

361 (05/61)
Battler Britton
Title: **Battler Britton & the Captured Secret**
Cover: Nino Caroselli
Art: Sergio Tuis

  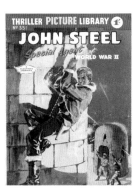 

362 (05/61)
Dick Daring of the Mounties
Title: **Dick Daring & the Blue Star Revolt**
Cover: Jordi Penalva
Art: Virgilio Muzzi/Mario Uggeri
Script: Unknown [possibly Rinaldo D'Ami], rescripted by Alf Wallace

363 (06/61)
Blues For Danger (John Steel)
Cover: Enrico De Seta?
Art: Luis Bermejo

364 (06/61)
Spy 13 of World War II
Title: **Spy 13 & the Phantom Afrika Korps**
Cover: Pino Dell'orco
Art: Antonio Canale

365 (06/61)
Battler Britton
Title: **Battler Britton & the Piece of Cake**
Cover: Nino Caroselli
Art: Renato Polese/Sergio Tuis?

366 (06/61)
Dogfight Dixon, RFC
Title: **Dogfight Dixon & the Trojan War Horse**
Cover: Nino Caroselli?
Art: Alan Pollack
Script: I. B. Kellie

367 (07/61)
Violent Tempo (John Steel)
Cover: Enrico De Seta?
Art: Reg Bunn

368 (07/61)
Spy 13 of World War II
Title: **Crisis in Casablanca**
Cover: Pino Dell'orco
Art: Leone Cimpellin

369 (07/61)
Battler Britton
Title: **Battler Britton & the Fighting Scientist**
Cover: Pino Dell'orco
Art: Aldo Di Gennaro

370 (07/61)
Dogfight Dixon, RFC
Title: **Courage – Sky-High**
Cover: Pino Dell'orco
Art: Aldo Marcuzzi?
Script: I. B. Kellie

371 (08/61)
Bullets in the Sun (John Steel)
Cover: P. Carey?
Art: Luis Bermejo

372 (08/61)
Spy 13 of World War II
Title: **Spy 13 & the Invasion of Ireland**
Cover: Pino Dell'orco
Art: Peter Sutherland

373 (08/61)
Battler Britton
Title: **Battler Britton & the Vanishing Patrol**
Cover: Pino Dell'orco
Art: Giorgio Trevisan

374 (08/61)
Dogfight Dixon, RFC
Title: **Dogfight Dixon & the Phantom Camel**
Cover: Pino Dell'orco
Art: Amador Garcia
Script: I. B. Kellie

375 (09/61)
A Picture of Guilt (John Steel)
Cover: Pino Dell'orco
Art: Robert Forrest

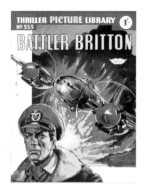

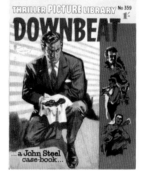

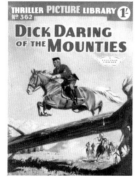

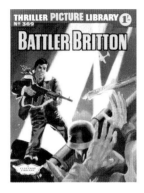

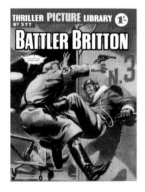

   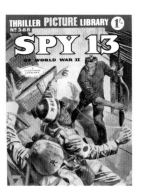

376 (09/61)
Spy 13 of World War II
Title: **Spy 13 & the Sea Scourge**
Cover: Nino Caroselli
Art: Alberto Breccia

377 (09/61)
Battler Britton
Title: **Battler Britton & the Unseen Enemy**
Cover: Nino Caroselli
Art: Sergio Tuis

378 (09/61)
Dogfight Dixon, RFC
Title: **Dogfight Dixon & the Zeppelin Menace**
Cover: Nino Caroselli?
Art: Alan Pollack
Script: Michael Moorcock?

379 (10/61)
Play It Cool (John Steel)
Cover: P. Carey?
Art: Luis Bermejo

380 (10/61)
Spy 13 of World War II
Title: **Spy 13 & the Reign of Terror**
Cover: Stefan Barany?
Art: Antonio Canale

381 (10/61)
Battler Britton
Title: **Battler Britton & the Commando Legion**
Cover: Unknown (possibly Patrick Nicolle & Geoff Campion?)
Art: Peter Sutherland

382 (10/61)
Dogfight Dixon, RFC
Title: **Dogfight Dixon & the Mark of Doom**
Cover: Allessandro Biffignandi
Art: Aldo Marcuzzi?

383 (11/61)
Jet Ace Logan Dare-Devil Ace of the RAF Space Command
Title: **Jet Ace Logan & the Piebald Men**
Cover: Allessandro Biffignandi
Art: Kurt Caesar

384 (11/61)
Spy 13 of World War II
Title: **The Jungle Menace**
Cover: Pino Dell'orco
Art: Amador Garcia

385 (11/61)
Battler Britton
Title: **Battler Britton & the Viking Vengeance**
Cover: Pino Dell'orco
Art: Aldo Di Gennaro

386 (11/61)
Dogfight Dixon, RFC
Title: **Dogfight Dixon & the Clash of Arms**
Cover: Allessandro Biffignandi?
Art: Alan Pollack

387 (12/61)
Dead Heat (John Steel)
Cover: Enrico De Seta?
Art: Raffaele Paparella

388 (12/61)
Spy 13 of World War II
Title: **Paper Enemy**
Cover: Allessandro Biffignandi
Art: Leone Cimpellin

389 (12/61)
Battler Britton
Title: **Warrior's Wings**
Cover: Pino Dell'orco?
Art: Mike Western

390 (12/61)
Dogfight Dixon, RFC
Title: **Dogfight Dixon & the Chain of Command**
Cover: Pino Dell'orco
Art: Aldo Marcuzzi?

391 (01/62)
Time Slip! (Jet Ace Logan)
Cover: Allessandro Biffignandi
Art: Kurt Caesar

392 (01/62)
Spy 13 of World War II
Title: **Rendezvous in Berlin**
Cover: Allessandro Biffignandi?
Art: Antonio Canale

393 (01/62)
Battler Britton
Title: **Battler Britton & the Day of Vengeance**
Cover: Nino Caroselli
Art: Colin Page

394 (01/62)
Dogfight Dixon, RFC
Title: **Freedom in the Clouds**
Cover: Pino Dell'orco
Art: Amador Garcia

395 (02/62)
City of Shadows (John Steel)
Cover: Unknown
Art: Luis Bermejo

396 (02/62)
Spy 13 of World War II
Title: **Spy 13 & the Sons of Nippon**
Cover: Leone Cimpellin
Art: Leone Cimpellin

397 (02/62)
Battler Britton
Title: **Battler Britton & the Arctic Furies**
Cover: Nino Caroselli
Art: Sergio Tuis

398 (02/62)
Dogfight Dixon, RFC
Title: **Dogfight Dixon & the Flying Joker**
Cover: Allessandro Biffignandi
Art: Aldo Marcuzzi?
Script: I. B. Kellie

399 (03/62)
Motif For Murder (John Steel)
Cover: Nino Caroselli
Art: Raffaele Paparella

400 (03/62)
Spy 13 of World War II
Title: **Spy 13 & the Man From Lisbon**
Cover: Allessandro Biffignandi
Art: Erio Nicolo

401 (03/62)
Battler Britton
Title: **Battler Britton & the Killer Plane**
Cover: Allessandro Biffignandi
Art: Daniel Haupt

402 (03/62)
Seven Went to Sirius (Jet Ace Logan)
Cover: Allessandro Biffignandi
Art: Alan Pollack
Script: David Motton

403 (04/62)
The Rising Tide (John Steel)
Cover: Nino Caroselli
Art: Luis Bermejo

404 (04/62)
Spy 13 of World War II
Title: **Spy 13 & the Danger From the Depths**
Cover: Allessandro Biffignandi
Art: Amador Garcia?

405 (04/62)
Battler Britton
Title: **Battler Britton & the Jinx Squadron**
Cover: Nino Caroselli?
Art: F. Solano Lopez

406 (04/62)
Space Trap (Jet Ace Logan)
Cover: Allessandro Biffignandi
Art: Kurt Caesar

407 (05/62)
The Town That Died (John Steel)
Cover: Allessandro Biffignandi
Art: Erio Nicolo

408 (05/62)
Spy 13 of World War II
Title: **Spy 13 & the Phantom Legion**
Cover: Allessandro Biffignandi
Art: Antonio Canale

409 (05/62)
Battler Britton
Title: **Battler Britton & the Floating Fortress**
Cover: Unknown
Art: Sergio Tuis

410 (05/62)
Evil in Orbit (Jet Ace Logan)
Cover: Allessandro Biffignandi
Art: Unknown

411 (06/62)
The Devil's Lair (John Steel)
Cover: Unknown
Art: Ferran Sostres

412 (06/62)
Spy 13 of World War II
Title: **Spy 13 & the Sands of Doom**
Cover: Allessandro Biffignandi
Art: Ernesto Moraga

413 (06/62)
Battler Britton
Title: **Fighting Fury**
Cover: Pino Dell'orco
Art: Daniel Haupt

414 (06/62)
Sun Smash! (Jet Ace Logan)
Cover: Allessandro Biffignandi
Art: Alan Pollack

415 (07/62)
The Demon Drums (John Steel)
Cover: Allessandro Biffignandi
Art: Gerry Wood

416 (07/62)
Spy 13 of World War II
Title: **Spy 13 & the Pawn of Fate**
Cover: Allessandro Biffignandi
Art: Leone Cimpellin

417 (07/62)
Battler Britton
Title: **Battler Britton & the Hornet's Nest**
Cover: Allessandro Biffignandi
Art: Mike Western

418 (07/62)
Times 5 (Jet Ace Logan)
Cover: Allessandro Biffignandi
Art: Ron Turner
Script: David Motton

419 (08/62)
One False Step (John Steel)
Cover: Allessandro Biffignandi
Art: Luis Bermejo

420 (08/62)
Spy 13 of World War II
Title: **Deadly Delusion**
Cover: Allessandro Biffignandi
Art: Sebastià Boada

421 (08/62)
Battler Britton
Title: **Battler Britton & the Serpents of the Skies**
Cover: Allessandro Biffignandi
Art: Aldo Marcuzzi?

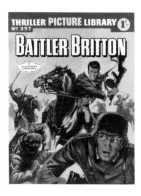   

422 (08/62)
The Nameless Ones (Jet Ace Logan)
Cover: Allessandro Biffignandi
Art: Kurt Caesar

423 (09/62)
The Big Take (John Steel)
Cover: Unknown
Art: Erio Nicolo

424 (09/62)
Spy 13 of World War II
Title: Spy 13 & the Jaws of Death
Cover: Allessandro Biffignandi
Art: Sebastià Boada

425 (09/62)
Battler Britton
Title: Between Two Fires
Cover: Allessandro Biffignandi
Art: Daniel Haupt

426 (09/62)
10 Days To Doom (Jet Ace Logan)
Cover: Allessandro Biffignandi
Art: Kurt Caesar

427 (10/62)
The Eye Of the Hunter (John Steel)
Cover: Jordi Penalva
Art: Victor Hugo Arias

428 (10/62)
Spy 13 of World War II
Title: Spy 13 & the Grotto of Death
Cover: Allessandro Biffignandi
Art: Amador Garcia?

429 (10/62)
Battler Britton
Title: Desert Fury
Cover: Allessandro Biffignandi
Art: Aldo Marcuzzi?

430 (10/62)
Planet of Fear (Jet Ace Logan)
Cover: Allessandro Biffignandi
Art: Juan Gonzalez Alacreu

431 (11/62)
Shakedown! (John Steel)
Cover: Unknown
Art: Luis Bermejo

432 (11/62)
Spy 13 of World War II
Title: Spy 13 & the Atlantic Raiders
Cover: Jordi Penalva
Art: Armando Bonato

433 (11/62)
Battler Britton
Title: Battler Britton & the Valley of Death
Cover: Pino Dell'orco
Art: Sergio Tuis

434 (11/62)
The Day the Earth Stood Still (Jet Ace Logan)
Cover: Allessandro Biffignandi
Art: Alan Pollack

435 (12/62)
The Silent Enemy (John Steel)
Cover: Pino Dell'orco
Art: Erio Nicolo

436 (12/62)
Spy 13 of World War II
Title: Chateau of Vengeance
Cover: Jordi Penalva
Art: Amador Garcia?

437 (12/62)
Battler Britton
Title: Battler Britton & the Rebel Squadron
Cover: Jordi Penalva
Art: Aldo Marcuzzi?

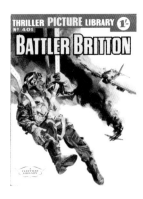

438 (12/62)
Sea Of Satan (Jet Ace Logan)
Cover: Allessandro Biffignandi
Art: Kurt Caesar

439 (01/63)
The Fatal Blow (John Steel)
Cover: Unknown
Art: Unknown

440 (01/63)
Spy 13 of World War II
Title: Spy 13 & the Deadly Decision
Cover: Nino Caroselli
Art: Sebastià Boada

441 (01/63)
Battler Britton
Title: The Baited Trap
Cover: Allessandro Biffignandi?
Art: Aldo Marcuzzi?

442 (01/63)
Power From Beyond (Jet Ace Logan)
Cover: Unknown
Art: Ron Turner

443 (02/63)
Gunpoint (John Steel)
Cover: Unknown
Art: Manuel Zatarin

444 (02/63)
Penalty of Fear (Barford)
Cover: Allessandro Biffignandi
Art: Unknown
Script: E C Tubb
Note: originally sold to *Tiger Sports Library* and featured
Carford F.C.

445 (02/63)
Return of the Renegade
Cover: Jordi Penalva?
Art: Alberto Salinas

446 (02/63)
Death Lay Deep (Jet Ace Logan)
Cover: Rutzu?
Art: Kurt Caesar

447 (03/63)
Six-Gun Fury
Cover: Nino Caroselli
Art: Joao Mottini

448 (03/63)
Spy 13 of World War II
Title: Spy 13 & the Peril From Asia
Cover: Nino Caroselli
Art: Erio Nicolo

449 (03/63)
Battler Britton
Title: Battler Britton & the Danger Zone
Cover: Nino Caroselli
Art: Colin Page?

450 (03/63)
Flight From the Sun (Jet Ace Logan)
Cover: Allessandro Biffignandi?
Art: Alan Pollack

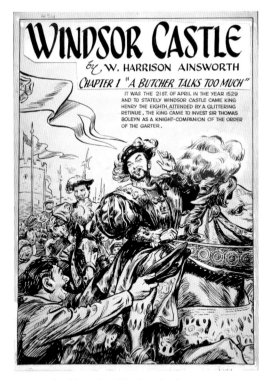

Above: Cecil Doughty, *Windsor Castle*

Above: Tom Peddie, *The Talisman*

Below: Robert Forrest, *Dorian Gray*

Below: John Millar Watt, *The Three Musketeers*

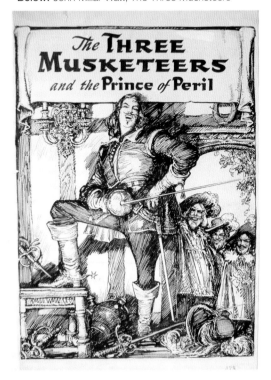

Sep E. Scott's original cover painting for *Windsor Castle* (*Thriller Comics* 37).

Sep E. Scott's original cover painting for *Westward Ho!* (*Thriller Comics* 40).

Sep E. Scott's original cover painting for *The Count of Monte Cristo* (*Thriller Comics* 45).

Sep E. Scott's original cover painting for *Lorna Doone* (*Thriller Comics* 47).

Sep E. Scott's cover for *Greenwood Outlaw* (*Thriller Comics* 77).

Sep E. Scott's cover for *Rogue's Moon* (*Thriller Comics* 66).

D. C. Eyles' original cover for *The White Invader* (*Thriller Comics* 88).

Sep E. Scott's original cover for *To Victory with the Iron Duke* (*Thriller Comics* 102).

Sep E. Scott's original cover for *Rob Roy Forever* (*Thriller Comics* 113).

Sep E. Scott's original cover for *Guns at Broken Bow* (*Thriller Comics* 115).

James E. McConnell's original cover for *Frontier Fury* (*Thriller Comics* 120).

W. R. Calvert's original cover for *Under the Golden Dragon* (*Thriller Comics* 132).

D. C. Eyles' original cover for *Dick Turpin, King of the Highway* (*Thriller Comics* 137).

Sep E. Scott's original cover painting for *The Dark Shadows of London* (*Thriller Comics* 156).

H. M. Brock's original cover painting for *Claude Duval and the Roundhead's Revenge* (*Thriller Picture Library* 164).

D. C. Eyles' original cover painting for *He Came From Arizona* (*Thriller Picture Library* 167).

Stephen Chapman's original cover painting for *The Black Musketeer* (*Thriller Picture Library* 205).

George Stokes' original cover painting for *Thriller Picture Library* 221.

Giorgio De Gaspari's original cover painting for *Thriller Picture Library* 261.

John Millar Watt's original cover painting for *Thriller Picture Library* 283.

SUPER DETECTIVE LIBRARY

01 (02/04/53)
Meet the Saint in the Case of the Contraband People (The Saint)
Cover: John Spranger (based on frame from strip)
Art: John Spranger; reprints US newspaper strip syndicated by New York Herald-Tribune (28/06-27/09/52)
Script: Leslie Charteris

02 (02/04/53)
Ernest Dudley, the Armchair Detective, in the Riddle of the Frensham Will
Cover: Unknown
Art: Reg Bunn
Script: Unknown; based on the BBC Radio series written and starring Ernest Dudley

03 (05/05/53)
Bulldog Drummond
Cover: Unknown
Art: Bill Lacey
Script: Edward Holmes; based on the novel (London, Hodder & Stoughton, 1920) by 'Sapper' (H. C. McNeile)

04 (05/05/53)
The Return of the Third Man
Cover: Unknown
(a) The Secret of the Circus
Art: Peter Sutherland
Script: Unknown; based on the character Harry Lime created by Graham Greene in the movie *The Third Man* (1949)
(b) Too Many Crooks
Art: Unknown
Script: Unknown; based on the character Harry Lime created by Graham Greene in the movie The Third Man (1949)

05 (04/06/53)
The Great Flying Saucer Mystery (The Saint)
Cover: Unknown
Art: John Spranger; reprints US newspaper strip syndicated by New York Herald-Tribune (29/09/52-02/01/53)
Script: Leslie Charteris

06 (04/06/53)
The Door With the 7 Locks
Cover: Heade (Reginald C. Webb)
Art: Graham Coton
Script: Peter O'Donnell; based on the novel (London, Hodder & Stoughton, 1926) by Edgar Wallace.

07 (02/07/53)
The Treasure House of Martin Hews
Cover: Arnold Beauvais
Art: Selby Donnison
Script: Unknown; based on the novel (London, Hodder & Stoughton, 1929) by E. Phillips Oppenheim

08 (02/07/53)
The Case of the Sinister Castle (Ernest Dudley, the Armchair Detective)
Cover: Arnold Beauvais
Art: W. Bryce-Hamilton
Script: Unknown; based on the BBC Radio series written and starring Ernest Dudley

09 (06/08/53)
The Island of Fu Manchu
Cover: Arnold Beauvais
Art: Philip Mendoza
Script: Rex Hardinge; based on the novel (London, Cassell & Co., 1941) by Sax Rohmer (A. Sarsfield Ward)

10 (06/08/53)
The Black Abbot
Cover: Arnold Beauvais
Art: Colin Merrett
Script: Unknown; based on the novel (London, Hodder & Stoughton, 1926) by Edgar Wallace

11 (03/09/53)
The Menace of the Poison Pen! (The Saint)
Cover: Arnold Beauvais
Art: John Spranger; reprints US newspaper strip syndicated by New York Herald-Tribune (04/04-18/07/53)
Script: Leslie Charteris

12 (03/09/53)
Dick Barton Finds the City Under the Sea
Cover: Arnold Beauvais
Art: Selby Donnison
Script: A. W. Henderson; based on the BBC Radio series created by Geoffrey Webb and Edward J. Mason

13 (01/10/53)
Bulldog Drummond Again – The Final Count
Cover: Selby Donnison
Art: Reg Bunn
Script: John Newton Chance; based on the novel *The Final Count* (London, Hodder & Stoughton, 1926) by 'Sapper' (H. C. McNeile)

14 (01/10/53)
The Men From the Stars (Rod Collins)
Cover: Arnold Beauvais
Art: Bill Lacey
Script: Edward Holmes

15 (05/11/53)
The Saint and the Case of the Vanishing Policemen
Cover: Arnold Beauvais
Art: Graham Coton/Reg Bunn (first 3 pages)/Anon
Script: Ernest Player; based on the story 'The House on the Moors' (*The Thriller 29*, 24 Aug 1929; also published as 'The Policeman With Wings') by Leslie Charteris

16 (05/11/53)
The Riddle of the Race Gang (Lesley Shane)
Cover: Arnold Beauvais
Art: Oliver Passingham
Script: Conrad Frost

17 (03/12/53)
The Phantom of the Fun-Fair
Cover: Arnold Beauvais
Art: Selby Donnison
Script: Unknown; based on the novel *The Dead Ringer* (New York, Dutton, 1949) by Fredric Brown

18 (03/12/53)
The Mystery of the Hooded Man
(Ernest Dudley, the Armchair Detective)
Cover: Arnold Beauvais
Art: Reg Bunn
Script: Unknown; based on the BBC Radio series written and starring Ernest Dudley

19 (07/01/54)
The Last Jest of Angelo Yates (Lesley Shane)
Cover: Arnold Beauvais
Art: Oliver Passingham
Script: Conrad Frost

20 (07/01/54)
Menace From the Moon (Rod Collins)
Cover: Arnold Beauvais
Art: Selby Donnison & Bill Lacey
Script: Edward Holmes

21 (04/02/54)
The Rocket Racketeers
(Blackshadow/Colin Benson)
Cover: Arnold Beauvais
(a) The Rocket Racketeers
Art: Bill Lacey
(b) Blackshadow's Spy Trap
Art: Philip Mendoza

22 (04/02/54)
The Secret of Lessinger's Loot
(Ernest Dudley, the Armchair Detective)
Cover: Arnold Beauvais
Art: Reg Bunn
Script: Unknown; based on the BBC Radio series written and starring Ernest Dudley

23 (04/03/54)
Kidnapped By Martians
Cover: Arnold Beauvais
Art: Selby Donnison

24 (04/03/54)
The Phantom of Dracos Island (Lesley Shane)
Cover: Arnold Beauvais
Art: Oliver Passingham
Script: Conrad Frost

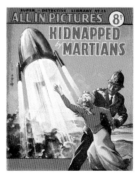

 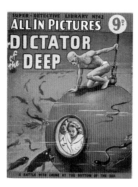  

25 (01/04/54)
Diamonds to Burn (Colin Benson)
Cover: Arnold Beauvais
Art: Bill Lacey

26 (01/04/54)
The Phantom of the Flying Fort (Lesley Shane)
Cover: Arnold Beauvais
Art: Oliver Passingham
Script: Conrad Frost

27 (06/05/54)
Jungle Manhunt (Lesley Shane)
Cover: Arnold Beauvais
Art: Oliver Passingham
Script: Conrad Frost

28 (06/05/54)
You Can't Stop the Saint
Cover: Arnold Beauvais, after Ernest Hubbard
Art: Selby Donnison
Script: Unknown; based on a story 'The Man Who Knew'
(*The Thriller* 280, 16 Jun 1934; also published as 'The High
Fence' and 'The Saint and Mr. Teal') by Leslie Charteris

29 (03/06/54)
The Planet of Peril
Cover: Arnold Beauvais
Art: Bill Lacey

30 (03/06/54)
**Edgar Wallace's The Fatal Feather
(The Three Just Men)**
Cover: Arnold Beauvais
(a) The Fatal Feather
Art: Selby Donnison
Script: Unknown; based on the story by Edgar Wallace
(b) The Gambler's Doom!
Art: Reg Bunn
Script: Unknown; based on the story by Edgar Wallace

31 (01/07/54)
The Riddle of the City in Space
Cover: Arnold Beauvais
Art: Reg Bunn

32 (01/07/54)
The Case of the Secret Archer (Lesley Shane)
Cover: Arnold Beauvais
Art: Oliver Passingham
Script: Conrad Frost

33 (01/07/54)
Danger – The Saint at Work! (The Saint)
Cover: Arnold Beauvais
Art: John Spranger; reprints US newspaper strip
syndicated by New York Herald-Tribune (03/01-04/03/53)
Script: Leslie Charteris

34 (05/08/54)
Jet Scott and the Sword of Fire
Cover: Arnold Beauvais
Art: Jerry Robinson; reprints US newspaper strip
syndicated by New York Herald-Tribune with linking art by
Selby Donnison
Script: Sheldon Stark

35 (05/08/54)
Revolt on Venus
Cover: Arnold Beauvais
Art: Oliver Passingham
Script: Conrad Frost

36 (05/08/54)
Crime Under the Ocean
Cover: Arnold Beauvais
Art: Graham Coton

37 (02/09/54)
Crime Rides the Spaceways (Rick Random)
Cover: Arnold Beauvais
Art: Bill Lacey
Script: Edward Holmes

38 (02/09/54)
The Saint Plays the Joker (The Saint)
Cover: Arnold Beauvais
Art: Peter Sutherland
Script: Unknown; based on a story 'The Five Kings' (*The
Thriller* 13, 5 May 1929; also published as 'The Man Who
Was Clever') by Leslie Charteris

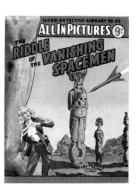

39 (07/10/54)
**Lesley Shane and the Stolen Crown
(Lesley Shane)**
Cover: Arnold Beauvais
Art: Oliver Passingham
Script: Conrad Frost

40 (07/10/54)
The Case of the Hunted Man
Cover: Arnold Beauvais
Art: Oliver Passingham

41 (04/11/54)
Enter the Mastermind (Lesley Shane)
Cover: Arnold Beauvais
Art: Oliver Passingham
Script: Conrad Frost

42 (04/11/54)
Dictator of the Deep (Paul Darrow)
Cover: Arnold Beauvais
Art: Raymond Poïvet; reprints 'Les Pionniers de
l'Espérance' ('Aquatide, la Cité des Ondes', 1951) from
Pif Gadget (France) with linking art by Selby Donnison
Script: Roger Lécureaux

43 (02/12/54)
Meet Captain Dack (Captain Dack)
Cover: Arnold Beauvais
Art: James Holdaway
Script: Unknown; based on the character created
by John Hunter

44 (02/12/54)
Kidnappers From Space (Rick Random)
Cover: Arnold Beauvais
Art: Ron Turner
Script: Unknown (Edward Holmes?)

45 (06/01/55)
Crime From the Sky (Lesley Shane)
Cover: Arnold Beauvais
Art: Oliver Passingham
Script: Conrad Frost

46 (06/01/55)
**The Man Who Made Gold (Ernest Dudley,
The Armchair Detective, & Capt Dack)**
Cover: Arnold Beauvais
Art: W. Bryce-Hamilton
Script: Unknown; based on the BBC Radio series written
and starring Ernest Dudley and the character created by
John Hunter

47 (03/02/55)
Baghdad Manhunt (Inspector Chafik)
Cover: Arnold Beauvais
Art: James Holdaway
Script: Unknown; based on the character created by
Charles B. Child (C. Vernon Frost)

48 (03/02/55)
**The Riddle of the Vanishing Spacemen
(Rick Random)**
Cover: Arnold Beauvais
Art: Bill Lacey
Script: Richard Wise?/Conrad Frost

49 (03/03/55)
**The Case of the Man Who Owned the Moon
(Rick Random)**
Cover: Arnold Beauvais
Art: Ron Turner

50 (03/03/55)
Lost in the Underworld (Paul Darrow)
Cover: Raymond Poïvet
Art: Raymond Poïvet; reprints 'Les Pionniers de
l'Espérance' from *Pif Gadget* (France) with linking art
by Bill Lacey
Script: Roger Lécureaux

51 (07/04/55)
The Mystery of Table 13 (Lesley Shane)
Cover: Ron Turner
Art: Oliver Passingham
Script: Conrad Frost

52 (07/04/55)
Who Killed the Ghost? (Inspector Chafik)
Cover: Oliver Passingham
Art: Oliver Passingham
Script: Unknown; based on the character created by
Charles B. Child (C. Vernon Frost)

53 (02/05/55)
The Case of the Space Bubble (Rick Random)
Cover: Ron Turner
Art: Oliver Passingham
Script: Conrad Frost

54 (02/05/55)
The Riddle of the Blue Men (Paul Darrow)
Cover: Arnold Beauvais
Art: Raymond Poïvet; reprints 'Les Pionniers de
l'Espérance' from *Pif Gadget* (France) with linking art
by Bill Lacey
Script: Roger Lécureaux

55 (02/06/55)
**Captain Dack and the Mystery of Peril Island
(Captain Dack)**
Cover: James McConnell
Title page: Guy Mouminoux
Art: Ron Turner
Script: Unknown; based on the character created by
John Hunter

56 (02/06/55)
**Lesley Shane and the Circus Riddle
(Lesley Shane)**
Cover: James McConnell
Art: Oliver Passingham
Script: Conrad Frost

57 (07/07/55)
Despot of the Underworld (Paul Darrow)
Cover: Arnold Beauvais
Art: Raymond Poïvet; reprints 'Les Pionniers de
l'Espérance' from *Pif Gadget* (France) with some linking
material by Guy Mouminoux
Script: Roger Lécureaux

58 (07/07/55)
Panthers' Moon
Cover: Arnold Beauvais
Art: Ron Embleton
Script: Unknown; based on the novel (London, Hodder &
Stoughton, 1949) by Victor Canning

59 (07/07/55)
The Saint's Sunken Gold! (The Saint)
Cover: Arnold Beauvais
Art: John Spranger; reprints US newspaper strip
syndicated by New York Herald-Tribune (25/01-21/03/54)
Script: Leslie Charteris

60 (04/08/55)
The House of the Seven Flies
Cover: Bill Lacey
Art: Bill Lacey
Script: Unknown; based on the novel (London, Hodder &
Stoughton, 1952) by Victor Canning

61 (04/08/55)
The Toff At Butlins (The Toff)
Cover: Arnold Beauvais
Art: Oliver Passingham
Script: Unknown; based on the novel (London, Hodder &
Stoughton, 1954) by John Creasey

62 (04/08/55)
The Hush Money Riddle (Lesley Shane)
Cover: Arnold Beauvais
Art: Oliver Passingham
Script: Conrad Frost

63 (01/09/55)
**The Riddle of the Paintings That Came to Life
(Lesley Shane)**
Cover: Arnold Beauvais
Art: Oliver Passingham
Script: Conrad Frost

64 (01/09/55)
The Five Lives of Mr Quex (Rick Random)
Cover: Arnold Beauvais
Art: Ron Turner, with faces by Fred Holmes

65 (06/10/55)
Sherlock Holmes Solves the Mystery of The Red-Headed League and The Case of the Greek Interpreter (Sherlock Holmes)
Cover: Arnold Beauvais
(a) The Mystery of The Red-Headed League
Art: Mike Sekowsky/Frank Giacoia; reprints US newspaper strip (28 Feb 1955–?) syndicated by New York Herald-Tribune
Script: Edith Meiser; based on the story ('The Red-Headed League', *The Strand*, August 1891) by Sir Arthur Conan Doyle
(b) The Case of the Greek Interpreter
Art: Frank Giacoia; reprints US newspaper strip syndicated by New York Herald-Tribune
Script: Edith Meiser; based on the story ('The Adventure of the Greek Interpreter', *The Strand*, 1893) by Sir Arthur Conan Doyle

66 (06/10/55)
Rick Random and the Gold-Rush Planet (Rick Random)
Cover: Arnold Beauvais
Art: Ron Turner

67 (03/11/55)
Paul Darrow and the Crime King (Paul Darrow)
Cover: Arnold Beauvais
Art: Raymond Poïvet; reprints 'Les Pionniers de l'Espérance' from *Pif Gadget* (France)
Script: Roger Lécureaux

68 (03/11/55)
Sexton Blake's Diamond Hunt (Sexton Blake)
Cover: Arnold Beauvais
Art: Oliver Passingham
Script: Unknown; based on the character created by Harry Blyth

69 (01/12/55)
Lesley Shane and the Riddle of the Bull-Ring (Lesley Shane)
Cover: Arnold Beauvais
Art: Oliver Passingham
Script: Conrad Frost

70 (01/12/55)
Rick Random and the Mystery of the Moving Planet (Rick Random)
Cover: Arnold Beauvais
Art: Ron Turner
Script: Conrad Frost

71 (05/01/56)
Mystery in Baghdad (Inspector Chafik).
Cover: Arnold Beauvais
(a) The Little Shadow
Art: Bill Lacey
Script: Unknown; based on the story 'He Had a Little Shadow' (*Colliers*, 14 Jan 1950) by Charles B. Child (C. Vernon Frost)
(b) A Ghost Walks in Baghdad
Art: Selby Donnison
Script: Unknown; based on a story by Charles B. Child (C. Vernon Frost)

72 (05/01/56)
The Golden Salamander
Cover: Arnold Beauvais
Art: Ron Embleton
Script: Unknown; based on the novel (London, Hodder & Stoughton, 1949) by Victor Canning

73 (02/02/56)
Paul Darrow in Peril Beneath the Earth (Paul Darrow)
Cover: Unknown
Art: Raymond Poïvet; reprints 'Les Pionniers de l'Espérance' from *Pif Gadget* (France) with some filler material by Guy Mouminoux
Script: Roger Lécureaux

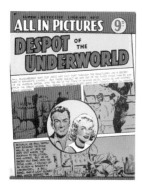

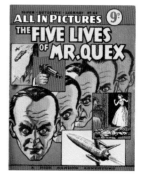

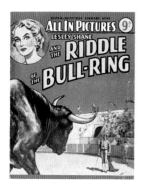

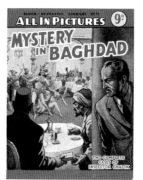

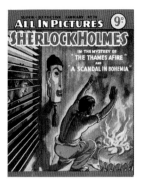

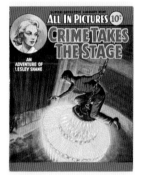

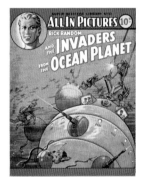

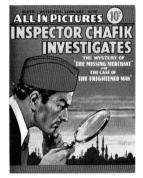

74 (02/02/56)
Sherlock Holmes in The Mystery of the Thames Afire and A Scandal in Bohemia (Sherlock Holmes)
Cover: Arnold Beauvais
(a) The Mystery of the Thames Afire
Art: Frank Giacoia; reprints US newspaper strip (1954) syndicated by New York Herald-Tribune
Script: Edith Meiser; based on the characters created by Sir Arthur Conan Doyle
(b) A Scandal in Bohemia
Art: Mike Sekowsky/Frank Giacoia; reprints US newspaper strip (13 Dec 1954-8 Jan 1955) syndicated by New York Herald-Tribune
Script: Edith Meiser; based on the story (*The Strand*, July 1891) by Sir Arthur Conan Doyle

75 (01/03/56)
Rick Random and the Secret of the Ocean Planet
Cover: Arnold Beauvais
Art: Bill Lacey
Script: Richard Wise/Conrad Frost

76 (01/03/56)
Lesley Shane and the Mystery of the Chinaman's Island
Cover: Arnold Beauvais
Art: Oliver Passingham
Script: Conrad Frost with additional material by Edward Holmes

77 (05/04/56)
Vic Terry and the Phantom Racehorse
Cover: Unknown
Art: Frank Lazenby; reprints newspaper strip with additional drawing by James Bleach
Script: Unknown, rescripted and with additional material by Edward Holmes

78 (05/04/56)
Sherlock Holmes Meets The Hound of the Baskervilles and The Missing Heiress (Sherlock Holmes)
Cover: Arnold Beauvais
(a) The Hound of the Baskervilles
Art: Frank Giacoia; reprints US newspaper strip (1955-27 October 1955) syndicated by New York Herald-Tribune
Script: Edith Meiser, rescripted and with additional material by Edward Holmes; based on the novel (*The Strand*, August 1901-April 1902) by Sir Arthur Conan Doyle
(b) The Missing Heiress
Art: Frank Giacoia; reprints US newspaper strip (1954) syndicated by New York Herald-Tribune
Script: Edith Meiser, rescripted and with additional material by Edward Holmes; based on the character created by Sir Arthur Conan Doyle

79 (07/06/56)
The Planet of Lost Men (Rick Random)
Cover: Arnold Beauvais
Art: Ron Turner
Script: Conrad Frost

80 (07/06/56)
Crime Takes the Stage (Lesley Shane)
Cover: Arnold Beauvais
Art: Oliver Passingham
Script: Conrad Frost, rescripted and with additional material by Edward Holmes

81 (05/07/56)
Blackshirt and the Golden Horse (Blackshirt)
Cover: Selby Donnison
Art: Selby Donnison
Script: Unknown; based on the novel *Blackshirt Passes By* (London, Hutchinson, 1953) by Roderic Graeme

82 (05/07/56)
Vic Terry and The Man Who Broke the Bookies (Vic Terry)
Cover: Arnold Beauvais
Art: Frank Lazenby; reprints newspaper strip
Script: Unknown, rescripted and with additional material by Edward Holmes

  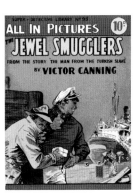 

83 (05/07/56)
Rick Random and The Invaders From the Ocean Planet (Rick Random)
Cover: Arnold Beauvais
Art: Ron Turner
Script: Richard Wise/Conrad Frost

84 (02/08/56)
A Forest of Eyes
Cover: Arnold Beauvais
Art: Manuel Salo
Script: Unknown; based on the novel (London, Hodder & Stoughton, 1950) by Victor Canning

85 (02/08/56)
Dirk Rogers in The Java Wreckmen (Dirk Rogers)
Cover: Arnold Beauvais
Art: Bill Lacey
Script: Danny Kelleher; based on the novel (London, Hodder & Stoughton, 1955) by Frank Crisp

86 (02/08/56)
Lesley Shane and the Girl Who Never Was (Lesley Shane)
Cover: Arnold Beauvais
Art: Oliver Passingham
Script: Conrad Frost, rescripted and with additional material by Edward Holmes

87 (06/09/56)
Inspector Chafik Investigates the Mystery of the Missing Merchant and The Case of the Frightened Man (Inspector Chafik)
Cover: Arnold Beauvais
(a) The Mystery of the Missing Merchant
Art: Bill Lacey
Script: Adrian Vincent; based on the story 'Blessed are the Merciful' by Charles B. Child (C. Vernon Frost)
(b) The Case of the Frightened Man
Art: James Holdaway
Script: Unknown; based on the character created by Charles B. Child (C. Vernon Frost)

88 (06/09/56)
Blackshirt's Treasure Hunt (Blackshirt)
Cover: Arnold Beauvais
Art: Peter Sutherland
Script: Unknown; based on the novel *Salute To Blackshirt* (London, Hutchinson, 1954) by Roderic Graeme

89 (10/56)
Vic Terry and the Horse With the Cloven Hoof (Vic Terry)
Cover: Arnold Beauvais
Art: Frank Lazenby; reprints newspaper strip with additional drawing by James Bleach
Script: Unknown, rescripted and with additional material by Edward Holmes

90 (10/56)
Rick Random's Manhunt Through Space (Rick Random)
Cover: Arnold Beauvais
Art: Ron Turner
Script: Bob Kesten

91 (06/11/56)
Rick Random and Mystery in the Milky Way (Rick Random)
Cover: Arnold Beauvais
Art: Ron Turner (opening page and some panels on pages 2-3) and Terry Patrick
Script: Bob Kesten

92 (06/11/56)
The Mystery of the Fatal Photographs (Lesley Shane)
Cover: Bruce Windo
Art: Oliver Passingham
Script: Conrad Frost, rescripted and with additional material by Edward Holmes

93 (04/12/56)
The Riddle of the Haunted Reef (Dirk Rogers)
Cover: Arnold Beauvais
Art: Bill Lacey
Script: J. H. Higgins; based on a novel *The Haunted Reef* (London, John Lane, 1950) by Frank Crisp

94 (04/12/56)
**Temple Fortune and the Mona Lisa Mystery
(Temple Fortune)**
Cover: Arnold Beauvais
Art: Arthur Horowicz
Script: Barry Coker; based on the story 'Mona Lisa'
by T.C.H. Jacobs

95 (01/01/57)
The Jewel Smugglers
Cover: C. E. Drury
Art: C. E. Drury
Script: Bob Kesten?; based on *The Man From the Turkish
Slave* (London, Hodder & Stoughton, 1954) by Victor
Canning

96 (01/01/57)
The Riddles of the Ring (Vic Terry)
Cover: Arnold Beauvais
**(a) Vic Terry and the First Riddle – The Boxer from
Bond Street**
Art: Mollie Higgins; adapts stories into Vic Terry adventures
Script: Unknown, rescripted and with additional material by
Miss H. Martin
(b) The Mystery of the Missing Muscles
Art: Mollie Higgins; adapts stories into Vic Terry adventures
Script: Unknown, rescripted and with additional material by
Miss H. Martin

97 (05/02/57)
**Rick Random and the Mystery of the
Time Travellers**
Cover: Arnold Beauvais
Art: Ron Turner
Script: Bob Kesten

98 (05/02/57)
**Lesley Shane and the Mystery of the
Dream Crimes**
Cover: Arnold Beauvais
Art: Oliver Passingham
Script: Conrad Frost, rescripted and with additional
material by Miss H. Martin

99 (05/03/57)
**Dirk Rogers and the Battleship Mystery
(Dirk Rogers)**
Cover: Arnold Beauvais
Art: Bill Lacey
Script: Ernest Player; based on the novel *The Manila
Menfish* (London, John Long, 1957) by Frank Crisp

100 (05/03/57)
**Temple Fortune and the Monte Cristo Riddle
(Temple Fortune)**
Cover: Arnold Beauvais
Art: Arthur Horowicz
Script: Barry Coker; based on a story 'Good Night Sailor'
by T.C.H. Jacobs

101 (02/04/57)
The Riddle of the Vanishing People (Rick Random)
Cover: Arnold Beauvais
Art: Ron Turner
Script: Bob Kesten

102 (02/04/57)
Lesley Shane and the House of Mystery
Cover: James McConnell?
Art: Oliver Passingham with additional art by Giorgio
Giogetti
Script: Conrad Frost, rescripted and with additional
material by Miss H. Martin

103 (07/05/57)
Wanted – Blackshirt!
Cover: Arnold Beauvais
Art: Bill Lacey
Script: Richard Wise; based on the novel *The Amazing Mr
Blackshirt* (London, Hutchinson, 1955) by Roderic Graeme

104 (07/05/57)
**Tod Claymore and the Mystery at
the Mardi-Gras**
Cover: Arnold Beauvais
Art: Luis Bermejo
Script: Unknown; based on the novel *Appointment in New
Orleans* (London, Cassell & Co., 1950) by Tod Claymore
(T. C. H. Jacobs)

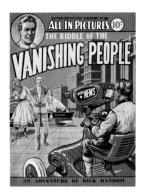   

105 (04/06/57)
Rick Random and the Mystery of the Man Who Put Out the Sun
Cover: Arnold Beauvais
Art: Unknown, with additional art by Terry Patrick
Script: Richard Wise/Conrad Frost

106 (04/06/57)
The Three Riddles
Cover: Arnold Beauvais
(a) The Smugglers Secret
Art: Bruce Windo
Script: Angus Allan; based on the story 'A Matter of Time' (*Evening Standard*, 15 Aug 1950) by Victor Canning
(b) The Mystery of the Lighthouse
Art: Bob Webster
Script: Adrian Vincent; based on the story 'Message to the Mainland' (*John Bull*, 3 November 1956) by Victor Canning
(c) The Riddle of the Coral Tree
Art: Ernest Ratcliff
Script: Richard Wise; based on the story 'The Coral Tree' (*John Creasey Mystery Magazine*, January 1957) by Victor Canning

107 (02/07/57)
Blackshirt and the Bloodstone
Cover: Arnold Beauvais
Art: Bill Lacey
Script: Robert Sommerville/Richard Wise; based on the story 'Blackshirt and the Moonstone' by Roderic Graeme

108 (02/07/57)
The Mystery of the Blazing Cottage (Tod Claymore)
Cover: Arnold Beauvais
Art: Bruce Windo, with additional art by Bob Webster
Script: Danny Kelleher; based on the novel *Reunion in Florida* (London, Cassell & Co., 1952) by Tod Claymore (T. C. H. Jacobs)

109 (06/08/57)
The Oasis of Mystery
Cover: James McConnell
Art: Ron Turner
Script: Ernest Player; based on the novella 'Oasis Nine' (*Everybody's*, 3 March-17 March 1956, by Victor Canning

110 (06/08/57)
The Missing Millionaire (The Toff)
Cover: James McConnell
Art: James Bleach
Script: Ernest Player; based on the novel *A Six for the Toff* (London, Hodder & Stoughton, 1955) by John Creasy

111 (03/09/57)
Rick Random in Sabotage From Space
Cover: James McConnell
Art: Ron Turner
Script: Bob Kesten, rescripted by Adrian Vincent

112 (03/09/57)
Vic Terry and the Secret of the Stables
Cover: Arnold Beauvais
Art: Douglas Perry; adapts story into Vic Terry adventure by Tom Laidler
Script: Unknown, rescripted with additional material by Miss H. Martin

113 (01/10/57)
Blackshirt and the Secret of Corey's Castle
Cover: James McConnell
Art: Bill Lacey
Script: Robert Sommerville/Richard Wise; based on the character created by Roderic Graeme

114 (01/10/57)
Lesley Shane and the Jungle Treasure
Cover: James McConnell
Art: Oliver Passingham
Script: Conrad Frost, rescripted and with additional material by Miss H. Martin

115 (05/11/57)
Rick Random and the S.O.S. From Space
Cover: James McConnell
Art: Ron Turner
Script: Bob Kesten

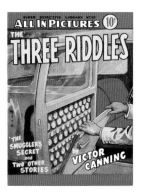

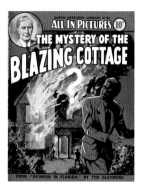

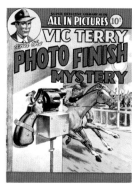

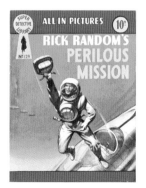

116 (05/11/57)
Vic Terry and the Photo Finish Mystery
Cover: James McConnell
Art: Douglas Perry; adapts newspaper strip to feature Vic Terry, with additional art by Miss H. Martin
Script: Unknown, rescripted and with additional material by Miss H. Martin

117 (03/12/57)
Blackshirt and the Circus Mystery
Cover: James McConnell
Art: Bill Lacey
Script: Robert Sommerville/Richard Wise; based on the character created by Roderic Graeme

118 (03/12/57)
Lesley Shane and the Mystery of the Masks of Manton
Cover: James McConnell
Art: Oliver Passingham
Script: Conrad Frost, rescripted and with additional material by Miss H. Martin

119 (07/01/58)
Blackshirt and the King's Treasure
Cover: James McConnell
Art: Bill Lacey
Script: Robert Sommerville/Richard Wise; based on the character created by Roderic Graeme

120 (07/01/58)
Rip Kirby and the Man Who Stole a Million Dollars
Cover: James McConnell?
Art: Alex Raymond; reprints US newspaper strip (25/12/50-28/04/51) syndicated by King Features
Script: Fred Dickenson, rescripted and with additional material by Miss H. Martin

121 (04/02/58)
Blackshirt and the Island of Fear
Cover: James McConnell
Art: Bill Lacey
Script: Robert Sommerville/Richard Wise; based on the character created by Roderic Graeme

122 (04/02/58)
Rip Kirby in Duel With Danger
Cover: James McConnell
Art: Alex Raymond; reprints US newspaper strip (12/06-23/09/50) syndicated by King Features
Script: Fred Dickenson, rescripted and with additional material by Miss H. Martin

123 (04/03/58)
Rick Random and the Planet of Terror
Cover: James McConnell
Art: Ron Turner, with some additional art by Bob Webster
Script: Bob Kesten

124 (04/03/58)
Rip Kirby in Desert Fury
Cover: James McConnell and Mollie Higgins
Art: Alex Raymond; reprints US newspaper strip (24/09/51-24/05/52) syndicated by King Features
Script: Fred Dickenson, rescripted and with additional material by Miss H. Martin

125 (07/04/58)
Blackshirt's Jungle Adventure
Cover: James McConnell
Art: Bill Lacey
Script: Richard Wise; based on a story by Roderic Graeme

126 (07/04/58)
Rip Kirby and the Runaway Lady
Cover: James McConnell
Art: Alex Raymond; reprints US newspaper strip (28/01-24/05/52) syndicated by King Features
Script: Fred Dickenson, rescripted and with additional material by Miss H. Martin

127 (05/05/58)
Rick Random and the Space Pirates
Cover: James McConnell
Art: Ron Turner
Script: Harry Harrison

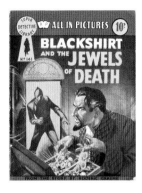   

128 (05/05/58)
Rip Kirby and the Fatal Target
Cover: James McConnell
Art: Alex Raymond; reprints US newspaper strip (30/04-22/09/51) syndicated by King Features
Script: Fred Dickenson, rescripted and with additional material by Miss H. Martin

129 (02/06/58)
Rick Random's Perilous Mission
Cover: James McConnell
Art: Ron Turner
Script: Harry Harrison

130 (02/06/58)
Rip Kirby and the Race of Death
Cover: James McConnell
Art: Alex Raymond; reprints US newspaper strip (11/05-05/09/53) syndicated by King Features
Script: Fred Dickenson, rescripted and with additional material by Miss H. Martin

131 (07/07/58)
Blackshirt and the Secret of the Devil's Ravine
Cover: James McConnell
Art: Bill Lacey
Script: Barry Coker; based on a story by Roderic Graeme

132 (07/07/58)
Rip Kirby on Terror Island
Cover: James McConnell
Art: Alex Raymond; reprints US newspaper strip (02/02-09/05/53) syndicated by King Features
Script: Fred Dickenson, rescripted and with additional material by Miss H. Martin

133 (04/08/58)
Rick Random and the Mystery of the Frozen World
Cover: Unknown
Art: Ron Turner
Script: Bob Kesten

134 (04/08/58)
Rip Kirby and the Clue of the Vanishing Gun
Cover: Unknown
Art: Alex Raymond; reprints US newspaper strip (08/09-21/11/53) syndicated by King Features
Script: Fred Dickenson, rescripted and with additional material by Miss H. Martin

135 (01/09/58)
Blackshirt and the Secret of the Sahara
Cover: James McConnell
Art: Bill Lacey
Script: Barry Coker; based on a story by Roderic Graeme

136 (01/09/58)
Rip Kirby's Dangerous Manhunt
Cover: James McConnell.
Art: Alex Raymond; reprints US newspaper strip (26/05-27/09/52) syndicated by King Features
Script: Fred Dickenson, rescripted and with additional material by Miss H. Martin

137 (06/10/58)
Rick Random and the Mystery of the Robot World
Cover: Unknown
Art: Ron Turner
Script: Conrad Frost/Barry Coker

138 (06/10/58)
Rip Kirby and the Trail of Terror
Cover: James McConnell
Art: Alex Raymond; reprints US newspaper strip (11/04-09/07/55) syndicated by King Features
Script: Fred Dickenson, rescripted and with additional material by Miss H. Martin

139 (03/11/58)
Rick Random and the Mystery of the Knights of Space
Cover: James McConnell?
Art: Ernest Ratcliff
Script: Harry Harrison

140 (03/11/58)
Rip Kirby and the Mystery of the Prisoner of Doom Castle
Cover: James McConnell
Art: Alex Raymond; reprints US newspaper strip (12/07-25/12/54) syndicated by King Features
Script: Fred Dickenson, rescripted and with additional material by Miss H. Martin

141 (01/12/58)
Blackshirt and the Jewels of Death
Cover: James McConnell
Art: Bill Lacey
Script: Barry Coker; based on a story by Roderic Graeme

142 (01/12/58)
Rip Kirby and the Case of the Man From Nowhere
Cover: James McConnell
Art: Alex Raymond; reprints US newspaper strip (23/11/53-17/04/54) syndicated by King Features
Script: Fred Dickenson, rescripted and with additional material by Miss H. Martin

143 (05/01/59)
Rick Random and the Terror From Space
Cover: Unknown
Art: Ron Turner
Script: Harry Harrison

144 (05/01/59)
Rip Kirby's Invitation To Danger
Cover: James McConnell
Art: Alex Raymond; reprints US newspaper strip (11/07-24/09/55) syndicated by King Features
Script: Fred Dickenson, rescripted and with additional material by Miss H. Martin

145 (02/02/59)
Blackshirt and the Case of the Murdered Matadors
Cover: Unknown
Art: Bill Lacey
Script: J. Heale; based on a story by Roderic Graeme

146 (02/02/59)
Rip Kirby in Design For Murder
Cover: James McConnell
Art: Alex Raymond; reprints US newspaper strip (27/12/54-09/04/55) syndicated by King Features
Script: Fred Dickenson, rescripted and with additional material by Miss H. Martin

147 (02/03/59)
Dangerous Waters
Cover: M. Tompkins
Art: Luis Bermejo, with additional art by Veronica Fryer and Giorgio Giorgetti
Script: J. H. Higgins; based on the novel (London, Lutterworth Press, 1955) by Jack Cox

148 (02/03/59)
Rip Kirby and the Devil's Henchman
Cover: James McConnell
Art: Alex Raymond; reprints US newspaper strip (20/02-19/05/56) syndicated by King Features
Script: Fred Dickenson, rescripted and with additional material by Miss H. Martin

149 (06/04/59)
Vic Terry and the Case of the Haunted Racehorse
Cover: Derek C. Eyles?
Art: Frank Lazenby
Script: Conrad Frost

150 (06/04/59)
Rip Kirby and The Case of the Crooked Mile
Cover: James McConnell
Art: Alex Raymond; reprints US newspaper strip (21/05-28/08/56) syndicated by King Features
Script: Fred Dickenson, rescripted and with additional material by Miss H. Martin

151 (04/05/59)
Blackshirt and the Case of the Faceless Man
Cover: M. Tompkins
Art: Bill Lacey
Script: J. Heale; based on a story by Roderic Graeme

 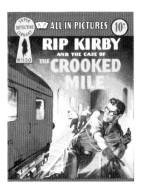  

152 (04/05/59)
Rip Kirby and the Playground of Fear
Cover: James McConnell
Art: Alex Raymond; reprints US newspaper strip syndicated by King Features
Script: Fred Dickenson, rescripted and with additional material by Miss H. Martin

153 (01/06/59)
Rick Random and the Threat From Space
Cover: M. Tompkins
Art: Ron Turner
Script: Bob Kesten

154 (01/06/59)
Rip Kirby and the Case of the Phantom Film Star
Cover: James McConnell
Art: Alex Raymond; reprints US newspaper strip syndicated by King Features
Script: Fred Dickenson, rescripted and with additional material by Miss H. Martin

155 (06/07/59)
Blackshirt in Marked For Murder
Cover: M. Tompkins
Art: Bill Lacey
Script: Roderic Graeme

156 (06/07/59)
Buck Ryan in Appointment With Danger
Cover: James McConnell
Art: Jack Monk; reprints newspaper strip from the Daily Mirror
Script: Unknown, rescripted and with additional material by Miss H. Martin

157 (21/09/59)
John Steel, Special Agent World War II
Cover: Giorgio De Gaspari
Art: Bill Lacey & another (Letteri?)
Script: Colin Thomas

158 (21/09/59)
Buck Ryan and the Funfair of Evil
Cover: M. Tompkins
Art: Jack Monk; reprints newspaper strip ('Funfair Fence', 11/52-05/53) from the Daily Mirror
Script: Unknown, rescripted and with additional material by Miss H. Martin

159 (16/10/59)
Buck Ryan and the Phantom Prowler
Cover: M. Tompkins
Art: Jack Monk; reprints newspaper strip ('The Fight Game', 01-04/52) from the Daily Mirror
Script: Unknown, rescripted and with additional material by Miss H. Martin

160 (16/10/59)
John Steel Special Agent World War II
Title: John Steel & the Riddle of the Sands
Cover: Giorgio De Gaspari
Art: Bill Lacey
Script: Colin Thomas

161 (08/11/59)
John Steel Special Agent World War II
Title: John Steel & The Unknown Traitor
Cover: Giorgio De Gaspari
Art: Unknown
Script: Colin Thomas

162 (08/11/59)
Buck Ryan in Gamble With Death
Cover: Nino Caroselli?
Art: Jack Monk; reprints newspaper strip ('The Nocturnal Fox', 09-12/53) from the Daily Mirror
Script: Unknown, rescripted and with additional material by Miss H. Martin

163 (11/12/59)
Rick Random and the Kidnapped Planet
Cover: Unknown
Art: Ron Turner
Script: Bob Kesten

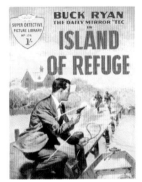

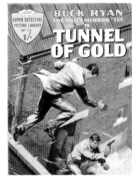

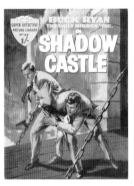

 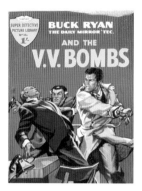 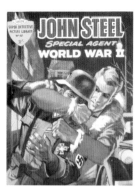 

164 (11/12/59)
Buck Ryan in Thieves' Highway
Cover: James McConnell?
Art: Jack Monk; reprints newspaper strip from the *Daily Mirror*
Script: Unknown, rescripted and with additional material by Miss H. Martin

165 (21/01/60)
John Steel Special Agent World War II
Title: Operation Treachery
Cover: Allessandro Biffignandi?
Art: Bill Lacey
Script: Colin Thomas

166 (21/01/60)
Buck Ryan in The House of Fear
Cover: James McConnell
Art: Jack Monk; reprints newspaper strip ('Chocolates, Cigarettes', 07-12/55) from the *Daily Mirror*
Script: Unknown, rescripted and with additional material by Miss H. Martin

167 (02/60)
John Steel Special Agent World War II
Title: War in the Jungle
Cover: Giorgio De Gaspari
Art: Unknown
Script: Colin Thomas

168 (02/60)
Buck Ryan and the Secret Enemy
Cover: James McConnell
Art: Jack Monk; reprints newspaper strip ('The Strato Midget', 01-04/54) from the *Daily Mirror*
Script: Unknown, rescripted and with additional material by Miss H. Martin

169 (22/03/60)
John Steel Special Agent World War II
Title: Gateway To Glory
Cover: Giorgio De Gaspari
Art: Ron Turner
Script: James Stagg

170 (22/03/60)
Buck Ryan and the Four Faced Bandit
Cover: James McConnell
Art: Jack Monk; reprints newspaper strip ('The Four-Faced Bandit-, 1956) from the *Daily Mirror*
Script: Unknown, rescripted and with additional material by Miss H. Martin

171 (04/60)
John Steel Special Agent World War II
Title: One Way Journey
Cover: Giorgio De Gaspari
Art: Bill Lacey
Script: David Motton

172 (04/60)
Passport to Peril
Cover: Giorgio De Gaspari
Art: Alberto Breccia
Script: Joan Whitford; based on the novel *Assignment Helené* (Greenwich, CT, Fawcett Publications, 1959) by Edward S. Aarons

173 (02/05/60)
John Steel Special Agent World War II
Title: The Fuhrer Plot
Cover: Nino Caroselli?
Art: Alan Philpott
Script: James Stagg

174 (02/05/60)
Buck Ryan in Island of Refuge
Cover: James McConnell
Art: Jack Monk; reprints newspaper strip ('The Island of Refuge', 08-12/54) from the *Daily Mirror*, with some additional artwork by Unknown (Creazioni D'Ami)
Script: Unknown, rescripted and with additional material by Miss H. Martin

175 (01/06/60)
John Steel Special Agent World War II
Title: Desert Spy
Cover: Nino Caroselli
Art: Adolpho Buylla?
Script: James Stagg

176 (01/06/60)
Buck Ryan in Tunnel of Gold
Cover: James McConnell
Art: Jack Monk; reprints newspaper strip ('Twilight Goes to Town', 05-11/52) from the *Daily Mirror*
Script: Unknown, rescripted and with additional material by Miss H. Martin

177 (05/07/60)
John Steel Special Agent World War II
Title: Operation 'Tina'
Cover: Nino Caroselli
Art: Ron Turner
Script: Bob Kesten

178 (05/07/60)
Buck Ryan in Murder By Mail
Cover: Nino Caroselli
Art: Jack Monk; reprints newspaper strip ('The Surprise Bag', 06-09/53) from the *Daily Mirror*

179 (08/60)
John Steel Special Agent World War II
Title: Cargo X
Cover: Nino Caroselli
Art: Roland Davies
Script: Douglas Leach

180 (08/60)
Buck Ryan in Shadow Castle
Cover: Nino Caroselli
Art: Jack Monk; reprints newspaper strip from the *Daily Mirror*

181 (09/60)
John Steel Special Agent World War II
Title: Wings of Escape
Cover: Nino Caroselli
Art: Victor Hugo Arias
Script: James Stagg.

182 (09/60)
Buck Ryan — The Enemy Within
Cover: Nino Caroselli
Art: Jack Monk; reprints newspaper strip ('The Enemy Within', 10/51-01/52) from the *Daily Mirror*

183 (03/10/60)
John Steel Special Agent World War II
Title: The Hidden War
Cover: Nino Caroselli?
Art: Ron Turner

184 (03/10/60)
Buck Ryan and the Bank Bandits
Cover: Allessandro Biffignandi?
Art: Jack Monk; reprints newspaper strip ('The Bank Bandits', 01-04/55) from the *Daily Mirror*

185 (11/60)
John Steel Special Agent World War II
Title: House of Bamboo
Cover: Nino Caroselli?
Art: Luis Bermejo

186 (11/60)
Buck Ryan and the V.V. Bombs
Cover: Nino Caroselli
Art: Jack Monk; reprints newspaper strip from the *Daily Mirror*

187 (05/12/60)
John Steel Special Agent World War II
Title: The Reign of Terror
Cover: Giorgio De Gaspari?
Art: Unknown

188 (05/12/60)
The Shadow Mystery Man of World War II
Title: School For Spies
Cover: Pino Dell'orco?
Art: Ron Turner

John Millar Watt's original cover painting for *Thriller Picture Library* 231.

BUCK JONES
ANNUAL 1958

RELATED PUBLICATIONS
& CONTRIBUTORS

A superb spin-off from their highly successful *Cowboy Comics Library*, *Kit Carson's Cowboy Annual*, which appeared in the shops on September 1, 1953, was the Amalgamated Press' first all-adventure comic annual. It was also the first of its annuals since the War to contain pages printed in full colour. The new annual boasted not only full colour title pages and three long full colour picture strips but also four resplendent colour plates by the great Derek Charles Eyles. It is difficult to overestimate the impact this colourful, new-style annual had on young readers of the time.

It was Eyles who stamped his style on *Kit Carson's Cowboy Annual* and the very first issue was practically all his work, reminding readers of Boardman's *Buffalo Bill Annuals*, which were all designed, drawn and painted by one artist, Denis McLoughlin. Unlike the latter annuals, of course, there was far less interest taken in the authenticity of its western tales, although Barry Ford's 'Western Scrapbook', which appeared in each of the annuals (reprinted from *Sun*), guaranteed that readers were made aware of the real, historical American West. Barry Ford (the pen name of Joan Whitford) was also almost certainly responsible for the majority of the text stories featured in the annual.

The annuals are also somewhat reminiscent of the old Aldine Western annuals of the 1920s, edited by Wingrove Willson. They also contained text stories featuring those 'Scouts of the Prairie', Buffalo Bill, Wild Bill Hickok and Texas Jack, as well as, on occasion, Kit Carson. Each issue of the Aldine annuals also contained four colour plates (mostly painted by Robert Prowse). There, however, the comparison ends, for *Kit Carson's Cowboy Annual* was mostly made up of picture strips and, it must be said, the artwork was mostly infinitely superior to anything in the Aldine books.

Four years after *Kit Carson's Cowboy Annual* first appeared, the other major star of the *Cowboy Comics Library*, Buck Jones, was given his own annual. They were not of the same quality as the Kit Carson annuals and the *Buck Jones Annual* did not catch on with readers and lasted for only two issues.

"Welcome to the Greenwood!" In September 1956, the first spin-off from the *Thriller Comics Library* appeared on the scene. Designed and printed in the same style as the cowboy annuals, it was a delightful and highly enjoyable glimpse into the medieval world of Robin Hood and knightly chivalry. As with the Kit Carson annual, there were a fair number of reprints but, as they were by the likes of Patrick Nicolle, Reginald Heade and Mike Hubbard, they were most welcome – especially as some were reprinted in full colour! Nicolle, who was steeped in medieval history (he was a founder member of the world-wide Arms and Armour Society), also contributed factual features to the annual. In addition, the last two annuals featured magnificent, jewel-like colour plates (and covers) by John Millar Watt. As with the Kit Carson annuals, one cannot help thinking of these volumes as updated – and far superior – versions of the Aldine annuals of the 1920s.

It is always interesting to contemplate what might have been and, in my correspondences with two major artists of the Amalgamated Press, I have come across tantalising glimpses into further annuals seemingly planned as spin-offs from the *Thriller Comics Library*. Shortly before he died, Hugh McNeill wrote to me that at some stage he had drawn a Jack o'Justice strip for a 'Dick Turpin Book'. A letter from Fred Holmes' agent dated 3 May 1955, now in my possession, states clearly that the editor would 'like to see the Duval Annual pages fairly soon'. Yet another such letter, dated 23 November 1956, is even more precise and intriguing: 'In addition to the pages you have in hand for the Rob Roy Annual, I would like you to take on 2 more to be used as frontispieces and will be printed in full colour'. The letter goes on to describe in detail exactly what the editor had in mind for the pictures. So, it seems obvious that, during the mid 1950s, some people at the Amalgamated Press were seriously contemplating bringing out no less than three more annuals to feature stars of the *Thriller Comics Library*!

Key to abbreviations

In the following section, a few abbreviations have been used to identify the various features listed as follows:

cs = comic strip
ss = short story
ar = article
ia = illustrated article (not an article that is
     illustrated but a primarily illustrated feature
     with some explanatory text)
il = illustration (colour plates and full page
     illustrations unrelated to stories)
ms = miscellaneous
qz = quiz

KIT CARSON'S COWBOY ANNUAL

Kit Carson's Cowboy Annual 1954 (1953; 112pp; 7/6; front & rear cover illus.
D. C. Eyles (rear cover circular insert illus. Peter Sutherland))
    [Misc. Material] (untitled plate) il; illus. D.C.Eyles
1   [Misc. Material] (colour title page) il; illus. D.C.Eyles
2   [Misc. Material] (colour) A Few Words from Kit Carson ed; illus. D.C.Eyles
3   [Comic Strip] Kit Carson Drives 'em West! cs (col);
    illus. D.C.Eyles; scr. Mike Butterworth
17 Anon. A Trap for Kit Carson ss; illus. D.C.Eyles
22 [Comic Strip] Rescued from the Redskins cs; illus. Stephen Chapman (same storyline
    used for *Knockout*, 10/07/48 illus. C.L. Doughty)
24 [Misc. Material] Weapons of the Redman il; illus. Patrick Nicolle
23 Anon. Pals of the Saddle ss; illus. D. C. Eyles
32 [Misc. Material] Western Scrapbook il; illus. Patrick Nicolle
    [Misc. Material] In Bruin's Domain (plate) il;illus. Sep. E. Scott
33 [Colour Comic Strip] Kit Carson and the Army Deserters cs; illus. D. C. Eyles
    (reprints 'Kit Carson – King of the West' from *Kit Carson* 1 (Australia))
49 Anon. [Whitford, Joan] Wild Bill and the Arizona Bandits ss; illus. D. C. Eyles
61 [Misc. Material] Western Scrapbook ill; illus. Patrick Nicolle
62 [Comic Strip] Buffalo Bill's Close Call cs; illus. D. C. Eyles (reprinted from *Knockout*,
    15/01/49)
64 [Misc. Material] Western Scrapbook ill; illus. Patrick Nicolle
    [Misc. Material] A Leap for Life! (plate) il; illus. D. C. Eyles
65 [Colour Comic Strip] Kit Carson and the Rodeo Raiders cs; illus. Geoff Campion
    (reprinted from *Cowboy Comics* 8)
75 [Comic Strip] Kit Carson and the Iron Horse cs (col); illus. D. C. Eyles (top panel of
    title page); illus. Geoff Campion (reprinted from single page strip in *Comet* no. 144,
    21/04/51)
81 Anon. [Baker, W. Howard] Texas Jack's Enemy ss; illus. D. C. Eyles
    [Misc. Material] Outwitting the Outlaws (plate) il;illus. D. C. Eyles
97 Anon. [Whitford, Joan] Buffalo Bill and the Phantom Chieftain ss;
    illus. D. C. Eyles (p. 100 illus. Geoff Campion)
107 [Misc. Material] The Pathfinder il; illus. D. C. Eyles
108 [Comic Strip] Kit Carson Fights the Grizzly cs; illus. Geoff Campion (reprint from
    Comet 128, 30/12/50, an episode of serial, 'Kit Carson and the Golden Arrow')
    [Misc. Material] Western Scrapbook il; illus. Patrick Nicolle
    [Misc. Material] Indian Superstitions il; illus. Patrick Nicolle
    [Misc. Material] Two Fighting men of the West il; illus. D. C. Eyles

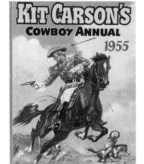

Kit Carson's Cowboy Annual 1955 (1954; 112pp; 7/6; front cover illus. D. C. Eyles)
    [Misc. Material] (untitled plate) il; illus. D.C.Eyles
1   [Misc. Material] (colour title page) il; illus. D.C.Eyles
2   [Misc. Material] (colour) Howdy, Pards ed; illus. D.C.Eyles
3   [Colour Comic Strip] Kit Carson's Duel with Danger cs; illus. Patrick Nicolle; scr. Joan
    Whitford (reprinted from *Cowboy Comics Library* 38)
17 Anon. Kit Carson and the Pay Wagon Robbery ss; illus. D.C.Eyles
24 [Comic Strip] Billy the Kid cs; illus. Geoff Campion (reprinted from *Sun* 184, 16/8/52)
29 [Comic Strip] Wild Bill Hickok's Justice cs; illus. Stephen Chapman
24 [Misc. Material] Western Scrapbook il; illus. Stephen Chapman; scr. Joan Whitford
    [Misc. Material] In Perilous Territory (plate) il; illus. D. C. Eyles
33 [Colour Comic Strip] Kit Carson's Buffalo Ride cs; illus. Colin Merrett
49 Anon. Wild Bill Hickok and the Redskin Revolt ss; illus. D. C. Eyles
61 [Misc. Material] Western Scrapbook ill; illus. Stephen Chapman; scr. Joan Whitford
62 [Comic Strip] Billy the Kid and the Bad Boy of Little Fallscs; illus. Geoff Campion
    (reprinted from *Comet* 199, 29/11/52)
62 [Misc. Material] Western Scrapbook il; illus. Stephen Chapman; scr. Joan Whitford
64 [Misc. Material] Western Scrapbook ill; illus. Patrick Nicolle; scr. Joan Whitford
    [Misc. Material] Trapping the Bandits (plate) il; illus. D. C. Eyles
65 [Colour Comic Strip] Kit Carson and the Red Rock Mountain Bandits cs;

illus. Colin Merrett; scr. Joan Whitford

[Misc. Material] Kit Carson's Duel (plate) il; illus. D. C. Eyles

81   Anon. Kit Carson and the Outlaw Trail ss; illus. Stephen Chapman

94   [Comic Strip] Billy the Kid and the Runaway Crook cs; illus. Geoff Campion
(reprinted from *Sun* 198, 22/11/52)

100 Anon. [Whitford, Joan] Buffalo Bill and the Menace of the Modocs ss;
illus. Stephen Chapman

106 [Comic Strip] Billy the Kid's Christmas Adventure cs; illus. Geoff Campion
(reprinted from *Sun* 202, 20/12/52)

[Misc. Material] Advert. for *Cowboy Comics* il; illus. D. C. Eyles

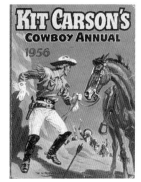

Kit Carson's Cowboy Annual 1956 (1955; 112pp; 7/6; front and rear cover illus.
D. C. Eyles)

[Misc. Material] (endpapers, red/black) il; illus. Patrick Nicolle

[Misc. Material] (untitled plate) il; illus. D.C.Eyles

1   [Misc. Material] (colour title page) il; illus. D.C.Eyles

2   [Misc. Material] (colour) Howdy, Pards ed; illus. D.C.Eyles

3   [Colour Comic Strip] Kit Carson and the Wonder-Guns cs; illus. Colin Merrett

17   Anon. [Higgins, J. H.] Kit Carson's Danger Patrol ss; illus. Stephen Chapman

24   [Comic Strip] Yip! Yip! Hi-Yo! Here Comes Billy the Kid cs; illus. Geoff Campion
(reprinted from *Sun*)

[Misc. Material] Indian Ambush (plate) il; illus. D. C. Eyles

33   [Colour Comic Strip] Kit Carson and the Kiowa Fury cs; illus. Colin Merrett;
scr. David Roberts

49   [Misc. Material] Western Scrapbook il; illus. Patrick Nicolle; scr. Joan Whitford

50   Anon. [Whitford, Joan] Wild Bill Hickok and the Runaway Redskin ss; illus. D. C. Eyles

56   [Comic Strip] Billy the Kid and the Mystery of Injun Joe cs; illus. Geoff Campion
(reprint from *Sun*)

61   [Misc. Material] Western Scrapbook ill; illus. Stephen Chapman; scr. Joan Whitford

62   [Comic Strip] Buffalo Bill and the Golden Lance of the Pawnees cs; illus. Stephen
Chapman; scr. Len Wenn

64   [Misc. Material] Western Scrapbook il; illus. Patrick Nicolle; scr. Joan Whitford

[Misc. Material] Trapped (plate) il; illus. D. C. Eyles

65   [Colour Comic Strip] Kit Carson Battles Through cs; illus. Geoff Campion;
scr. David Roberts (reprints 'Kit Carson and the Redskin Rising!' from *Cowboy
Comics* 14; new first panel and some redrawing in places by Campion)

[Misc. Material] A Race with Death (plate) il; illus. D. C. Eyles

81   Anon. [Roberts, David] Buffalo Bill and the Forbidden Peaks ss;
illus. Stephen Chapman

94   [Comic Strip] Buck Jones and the Red Bandit cs; illus. Geoff Campion (reprint from
Sun 132-138, 18/8–29/9/51 with the last three panels by Patrick Nicolle)

112 [Misc. Material] Western Scrapbook il; illus, Patrick Nicolle; scr. Joan Whitford

Advert. for *Cowboy Comics*, *Sun* and *Comet* il; illus. Colin Merrett

[Misc. Material] (endpapers red/black) il; illus. Patrick Nicolle

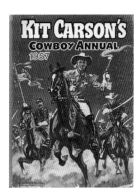

Kit Carson's Cowboy Annual 1957 (1956; 112pp; 7/6; front and rear cover illus.
D. C. Eyles

[Misc. Material] (endpapers, red/black) il; illus. Colin Merrett

[Misc. Material] (untitled plate) il; illus. D.C.Eyles

1   [Misc. Material] (colour title page) il; illus. D.C.Eyles

2   [Colour Comic Strip] Kit Carson and the Apach Ambush cs; illus. Colin Merrett;
scr. Joan Whitford

16   [Misc. Material] Savage Splendour il; illus. Colin Merrett

17   Anon. [Whitford, Joan] Cavaliers of the West ss; illus. Colin Merrett

24   [Comic Strip] Billy the Kid and the Great Gold-Trick cs; illus. Jesus Blasco
(reprint from *Sun*)

30   [Misc. Material] The Wild West Rodeo il; illus. Geoff Campion (partial reprint from
Comet 96, 20/5/50)

32   [Misc. Material] Barry Ford's Western Scrapbook: Kit Carson, the Great Frontiersman

ill; illus. Patrick Nicolle; scr. Joan Whitford (reprinted from *Sun*)
    [Misc. Material] Shooting the Rapids (plate) il; illus. D. C. Eyles
33 [Colour Comic Strip] Kit Carson Races Through Fire and Fury cs; illus. Colin Merrett; scr. Joan Whitford
    [Misc. Material] Winged Attacker (plate) il; illus. D. C. Eyles
49 Anon. [Payne, E. M.] Buffalo Bill Rounds 'em Up! ss; illus. Stephen Chapman
53 [Comic Strip] Billy the Kid and the Heap Big Medicine cs; illus. Eugenio Giner
59 Anon. The Courage of Kit Carson ss; illus. Stephen Chapman
65 [Colour Comic Strip] Kit Carson and the Unknown Spy cs; illus. Colin Merrett; scr. Joan Whitford
    [Misc. Material] Between Two Perils (plate) il; illus. D. C. Eyles
81 [Comic Strip] Buffalo Bill and the Terror of Tombstone Valley cs; illus. Francisco Hidalgo; scr. Mike Butterworth
88 Anon. [Wenn, Len] The True Story of Custer's last Stand ss; illus. Patrick Nicolle (illustrations reprinted from 'A Deed of Daring' series in *Comet* 276, 31/10/53)
90 [Comic Strip] Wild Bill Hickok and the Renegade Rustler cs; illus. Colin Merrett
112 [Misc. Material] Western Scrapbook il; illus, Patrick Nicolle; scr. Joan Whitford
    Advert. for *Cowboy Comics* il; illus. Colin Merrett
    [Misc. Material] (endpapers red/black) il; illus. Colin Merrett

Kit Carson's Cowboy Annual 1958 (1957; 112pp; 7/6; front and rear cover illus. James McConnell
    [Misc. Material] (endpapers, red/black) il; illus. Selby Donnison
    [Misc. Material] (colour title page) il; illus. James McConnell
2   [Colour Comic Strip] Kit Carson's Desert Battle-Wagons cs; illus. Bill Lacey; scr. J. H. Higgins
17 Anon. [Giggal, Kenneth] Davy Crockett's Duel with Danger ss; illus. Terry Aspin
    [Misc. Material] Western Round-Up (plate) il; illus. D. C. Eyles
33 [Colour Comic Strip] Kit Carson Wins Through cs; illus. Bob Webster; scr. A. Vincent
    [Misc. Material] A Race with Redskins (plate) il; illus. D. C. Eyles
49 [Comic Strip] Kit Carson – Outlaw cs; illus. Giorgio Giorgetti
65 [Colour Comic Strip] Kit Carson and the Wild Stallion cs; illus. Bill Lacey; scr. R. Garner
    [Misc. Material] Kit Fools the Redskins (plate) il; illus. D. C. Eyles
81 [Comic Strip] Davy Crockett and the Prairie Gypsies cs; illus. Selby Donnison; scr. A. Vincent
112 [Misc. Material] Advert. for *Cowboy Picture Library* il; illus. Peter Sutherland
    [Misc. Material] (endpapers red/black) il; illus. Selby Donnison

Kit Carson's Cowboy Annual 1959 (1958; 112pp; 7/6; front cover illus. D. C. Eyles; rear cover illus. James McConnell
    [Misc. Material] (endpapers, red/black) il; illus. D. C. Eyles
    [Misc. Material] Ready for Anything (plate) il; illus. Sep E. Scott
    [Misc. Material] (colour title page) il; illus. Geoff Campion
    [Misc. Material] (colour) Howdy, Pards! ed; illus. Geoff Campion
3   [Colour Comic Strip] Kit Carson and the Golden Coach! cs; illus. D. C. Eyles
17 Anon. Buffalo Bill and Eagle Claw's Challenge ss; illus. Philip Mendoza
27 [Comic Strip] Strongbow the Mohawk cs; illus. (Creazioni D'Ami)
33 [Colour Comic Strip] Davy Crockett and the Silver Stallion cs; illus. Bill Lacey
    [Misc. Material] The Challenge (plate) il; illus. Giorgio Di Gaspari
49 Anon. Kit Carson and the Outcast Chief ss; illus. Geoff Campion
60 [Comic Strip] Buck Jones and the Blind Cowboy cs; illus. Rafaelle Paparella
    [Misc. Material] The Feud! (plate) il; illus.Rialdo Guizzardi
65 [Comic Strip] The Kansas Kid and the Wonder Horse cs; illus. (Creazioni D'Ami)
72 Anon. Davy Crockett and the Powder Boat ss; illus. Unknown
81 [Colour Comic Strip] Kit Carson and the Gold Snatch cs; illus. D. C. Eyles
    [Misc. Material] The Grizzly Reared Up! (plate) illus. Sep E. Scott
97 Anon. Texas Jack and the Lost River ss; illus. Geoff Campion
103 [Comic Strip] Buffalo Bill and the Little Guy cs; illus. D. C. Eyles

108 [Misc. Material] Western Scrapbook il; illus. Patrick Nicolle
[Misc. Material] Advert. for Cowboy Picture Library il; illus. Charles Roylance
(Buck Jones)/Selby Donnison (Kansas Kid)
[Misc. Material] (endpapers red/black) il; illus. D. C. Eyles

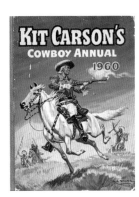

Kit Carson's Cowboy Annual 1960 (1959; 112pp; 7/6; front and rear cover illus. D. C. Eyles

[Misc. Material] (endpapers, red/black) il; illus. D. C. Eyles
[Misc. Material] Kit Carson – King of the West! (plate) il; illus. Jordi Penalva
[Misc. Material] (colour title page) il; illus. Geoff Campion
[Misc. Material] (colour) Howdy, Pards! ed; illus. Geoff Campion
3 [Colour Comic Strip] Kit Carson and the Redskin's Vow cs; illus. Sergio Tarquinio
17 [Comic Strip] Buffalo Bill and the Traitor of Fort Bellew cs; illus. Guido Buzzelli
27 [Comic Strip] Texas Jack and The Rag Doll! cs; illus. D. C. Eyles
33 [Colour Comic Strip] Buck Jones and Old Dan's Diamond cs; illus. Rafaelle Paparella
[Misc. Material] The Rawhide Rescue (plate) il; illus. Jordi Penalva
49 [Comic Strip] Strongbow the Mohawk cs; illus. Angelo Platania
59 [Comic Strip] The Emperor's Mistake cs; illus. Antonio Canale
49 Anon. Davy Crockett and the Timber Trail ss; illus. Dino Battaglia
[Misc. Material] The Treacherous Blow! (plate) il; illus.Jordi Penalva
72 [Comic Strip] The Kansas Kid and the Mystery of Copper Creek cs; illus. Selby Donnison
81 [Colour Comic Strip] Kit Carson and the Runaway Coach cs; illus. Franco Bignotti
97 Anon. Kit Carson and the Bandit's Secret ss; illus. Robert Forrest
103 [Comic Strip] Buffalo Bill and the Pawnee Spy cs; illus. D. C. Eyles
108 [Misc. Material] Western Scrapbook il; illus. Stephen Chapman
[Misc. Material] (endpapers red/black) il; illus. D. C. Eyles

BUCK JONES ANNUAL

Buck Jones Annual 1957 (1956; 112pp; 7/6; front & rear cover illus. Sep E. Scott)

[Misc. Material] A Wild West Gunfight (endpapers, red/black) il; illus. D. C. Eyles

[Misc. Material] (untitled plate) il; illus. Sep. E. Scott

1 [Misc. Material] (colour title page) il; illus. Geoff Campion (face by Eric Bradbury)

2 [Misc. Material] (colour) A Message from Buck Jones ed; illus. Geoff Campion (face by Eric Bradbury)

3 [Comic Strip] Buck Jones and the Indian Traitors cs (col); illus. Unknown.

17 Anon. Buck Jones and the Rustler's Revenge ss; illus. Eric Bradbury

23 Anon. Wagons Westward ss; illus. D. C. Eyles

33 [Comic Strip] Buck Jones and the War on the Range! cs (col); illus. Geoff Campion (reprint from *Cowboy Comics Library* 41)

[Misc. Material] Claw Against Steel (plate) il; illus. Sep. E. Scott

49 [Comic Strip] Davy Crockett and the Sharp-Shooting Badman cs; illus. Ian Kennedy

[Misc. Material] Strongbow the Mohawk (plate) il; illus. Sep. E. Scott

65 (comic strip) Strongbow the Mohawk cs; illus. Geoff Campion (reprint from *Comet* 264, 8/8/53, with new title page)

78 Anon. The True Life-Story of Davy Crockett ss; illus. D. C. Eyles

80 [Misc. Material] Advert. for Cowboy Comics ia; illus. Peter Sutherland

81 [Comic Strip] Buck Jones and the Rock Valley Raiders cs (col); illus. Geoff Campion (reprint from *Comet* 126-131, 15/12/50–20/1/51)

[Misc. Material] Desperate Journey (plate) il; illus. Sep. E. Scott

97 Anon. The Vengeance of Texas Jack ss; illus. D. C. Eyles

105 Anon. Dodge City The Wildest Town in the West ss; illus. D. C. Eyles

107 [Comic Strip] Strongbow's Christmas Adventure cs; illus. Robert Forrest (reprint from *Comet* 284, 26/12/53)

[Misc. Material] Scouts at Bay (endpapers, red/black) il; illus. D. C. Eyles

Buck Jones Annual 1958 (1957; 112pp; 7/6; front & rear cover illus. James E. McConnell)

[Misc. Material] Alkali City (endpapers, red/black) il; illus. Unknown

[Misc. Material] (colour title page plate) il; illus. James E. McConnell

[Misc. Material] (b/w plate) This Book Belongs To ed; illus. Unknown.

1 [Comic Strip] Little Buffalo Rides the Iron Horse cs (col); illus. Bill Lacey

17 Anon. Buck Jones and the Bandit-Proof Bank ss; illus. R. Charles Roylance

33 [Comic Strip] Buck Jones and the Stage Coach Hold-Up! cs (col); illus. Unknown

[Misc. Material] Dance of the War Drum (plate) il; illus. James E. McConnell

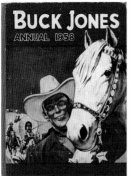

49 [Comic Strip] Buck Jones and Dia Volo the Bandit cs; illus. Reg Bunn and Don Lawrence

[Misc. Material] The Pole Fight (plate) il; illus. James E. McConnell

65 Anon. The Kansas Kid's Treasure Hunt ss; Illus. Bill Lacey (title illus. R. Charles Roylance)

81 [Comic Strip] Buck Jones and the Buffalo Robe cs (col); illus. Unknown

[Misc. Material] The Prisoner's Turkey! (plate) il; illus. James E. McConnell

97 Anon. The Kansas Kid and Jackson's Gold Mine ss; illus. Unknown

112 [Misc. Material] Advert. for *Cowboy Picture Library* ia; illus. R. Charles Roylance

[Misc. Material] The Double-D Ranch (endpapers, red/black) il; illus. Unknown

  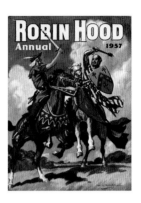

ROBIN HOOD ANNUAL

Robin Hood Annual 1957 (1956; 112pp; 7/6; front & rear cover illus. D. C. Eyles)

[Misc. Material] (untitled endpapers) il; illus. E. T. Coehlo

[Misc. Material] (untitled plate) il; illus. Sep. E. Scott

1   [Misc. Material] (title page) il; illus. D. C. Eyles

2   [Misc. Material] Come to the Greenwood! ed; illus. D. C. Eyles

3   [Comic Strip] Robin Hood and the Saxon Feud cs (col); illus. E. T. Coehlo

16 [Misc. Material] Relics of Robin Hood and His Merry Men ia; illus. Pat Nicolle

17 Anon. [Wallace, Alf] Robin Hood's Merry Party ss; illus. Guido Buzzelli

29 [Comic Strip] Robin Hood and The Road of No Return cs; illus. Stephen Chapman; scr. Alf Wallace

    [Misc. Material] Two Forest Kings (plate) il; illus. Sep. E. Scott

33 [Comic Strip] Robin Hood and the Double-Dyed Traitor cs (col); illus. Pat Nicolle

49 [Comic Strip] The Story of Wat o' the Whip cs; illus. E. T. Coelho

59 Anon. [Wallace, Alf] Hereward the Wake ss; illus. E. T. Coehlo

    [Misc Material] A Daring Rescue (plate) il; illus. Sep. E. Scott

65 [Misc. Material] Sports and Pastimes of Robin Hood's Day ia; illus. Pat Nicolle; scr. R. Perrins

66 [Comic Strip] Robin Hood and the Red Fox cs (col); illus. E. T. Coehlo; scr. R. Perrins

78 [Misc. Material] The Splendour of Heraldry ia; illus. Pat Nicolle

79 [Misc. Material] A Knight in His Full Glory ia; illus. Pat Nicolle

80 [Misc. Material] Saxons and Normans of Robin Hood's Day ia; illus. Pat Nicolle

    [Misc. Material] A Norman Ambush (plate) il; illus. Sep. E. Scott

81 [Comic Strip] The Story of Richard the Lionheart cs; illus. Reg Bunn; scr. R. Perrins

91 Anon. [Wenn, Len] Robin Hood—the Invincible ss; illus. Stephen Chapman

100 [Comic Strip] The Strange Capture of Robin Hood cs; illus. Roberto Diso/Santo D'Amico with faces by Reg Bunn; scr. E. J. Bensberg

112 [Misc. Material] Robin Hood The Lord of Sherwood il; advert for Thriller Comics Library; illus. D. C. Eyles

    [Misc. Material] (untitled endpapers) il; illus. E. T. Coehlo

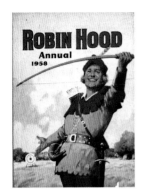

Robin Hood Annual 1958 (1957; 112pp; 7/6; front & rear cover illus. Sep E. Scott)
    [Misc. Material] (untitled endpapers) il; colour still from 'Ivanhoe' film
    [Misc. Material] (untitled plate) il; illus. Sep. E. Scott
1   [Misc. Material] (title page) il; illus. D. C. Eyles
2   [Misc. Material] A Call to Adventure ed; illus. D. C. Eyles
3   [Comic Strip] Robin Hood and the Mystery of the Mill cs (col); illus. Reg Bunn;
    scr. R. Perrins
17   Anon. [Whitford, Joan] The Norman Fury ss; illus. C. L. Doughty
26   [Comic Strip] Ginger Tom's Schooldays cs; illus. Pat Nicolle; scr. Ron Clark
    [Misc. Material] The Norman Bullies (plate) ia; illus. Sep E. Scott
33   [Comic Strip] Robin Hood and the Crusader's Castle cs (col); illus. Heade (reprint from
    Sun 293–300, 18/9 – 6/11/54); scr. revisions by E. J. Bensberg
49   [Comic Strip] The Saga of Eric the Red cs; illus. Heade (reprinted from *Knockout*
    524–531, 12/3 – 30/4/49); scr. revisions by R. Perrins
    [Misc. Material] The Daring Descent (plate) il; illus. Sep. E. Scott
65   [Comic Strip] Robin Hood and the Brothers-in-Arms cs (col); illus. Reg Bunn
    (Pat Nicolle title page); scr. R. Perrins
    [Misc. Material] A Perilous Leap (plate) il; illus. Sep. E. Scott
81   Anon. [Wallace, Alf] Robin Hood and the Sheriff's Champion ss; illus. Arthur Horowicz
91   [Comic Strip] Ginger Tom and the Rebels cs; illus. Pat Nicolle; scr. Ron Clark
98   [Misc. Material] Arms of Offence ia; illus. Pat Nicolle
99   [Misc. Material] Arms of Defence ia; illus. Pat Nicolle
100 [Comic Strip] Will Scarlet the Brave cs; illus. Arthur Horowicz; scr. G. Allman
107 [Comic Strip] Robin Hood and the Three Plotters cs; illus. Alfredo Marculeta;
    scr. R. Perrins
    [Misc. Material] Robin Hood The Lord of Sherwood il; advert for *Thriller Comics
    Library*; illus. D. C. Eyles
    [Misc. Material] (untitled endpapers) il; colour film still from 'Ivanhoe' film

Robin Hood Annual 1959 (1958; 112pp; 7/6; front & rear cover illus. John Millar Watt)
[Misc. Material] (untitled endpapers, colour) il; illus. Unknown
[Misc. Material] (untitled plate) il; illus. John Millar Watt
1   [Misc. Material] (title page) il; illus. John Millar Watt
2   [Misc. Material] Come Adventuring! ed; illus. John Millar Watt
3   [Comic Strip] Robin Hood's Jest cs (col); illus. Geoff Campion (reprint from *Thriller Comics Library* 52 with new title page), partly redrawn by Pat Nicolle
17   Anon. [Stagg, James] The Phantom Knight ss; illus. F. Allan Philpott
29   [Misc. Material] Warriors of the Past ia; illus. Pat Nicolle
[Misc. Material] (untitled plate) il; illus. John Millar Watt
33   [Comic Strip] Robin Hood's Winter Adventure cs (col); illus. Mario Uggeri; scr. V. A. L. Holding
49   [Comic Strip] The King of Treachery cs; illus. E. T. Coelho; scr. R. Perrins
60   [Comic Strip] The Legend of Roland cs; illus. John Millar Watt; scr. V. A. L. Holding
[Misc. Material] (untitled plate) il; illus. John Millar Watt
65   [Comic Strip] Robin Hood and the Prince's Assassin cs (col); illus. Mario Uggeri; scr. V. A. L. Holding
[Misc. Material] Robin Hood's Reward (plate) il; illus. John Millar Watt
81   Anon. [Stagg, James] The Fighting Lord of the Fens ss; illus. F. Allan Philpott
90   [Comic Strip] The Last of the Saxon Chiefs cs; illus. Philip Mendoza; scr. James Stagg
92   [Comic Strip] Robin Hood and the Traitor Prince cs; illus. Mike Hubbard (reprint from 'The Adventures of Robin Hood', *Knockout* 434–447, 21/6 – 20/9/47, adapted from the Errol Flynn movie); scr. revised by James Stagg
[Misc. Material] Robin Hood The Lord of Sherwood il; advert for *Thriller Comics Library*; illus. D. C. Eyles
[Misc. Material] (untitled endpapers, colour) il; illus. Unknown

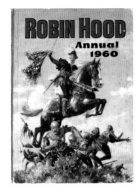   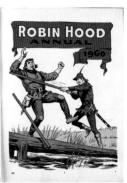

Robin Hood Annual 1960 (1959; 112pp; 7/6; front & rear cover illus.John Millar Watt)

[Misc. Material] (untitled endpapers) il; illus. colour still from 'Ivanhoe' film

[Misc. Material] (untitled plate) il; illus. John Millar Watt

[Misc. Material] (title page) il; illus. D. C. Eyles

2   [Misc. Material] The Greenwood Beckons… ed; illus. D. C. Eyles

3   [Comic Strip] Robin Hood and the Bargaincs (col); illus. D. C. Eyles; scr. Alan Fennell

17   [Comic Strip] The Glory of Glenurchy cs; illus. C. L. Doughty; scr. Michael Moorcock

22   Anon. [Moorcock, Michael] Hereward the Wake and the Saxon Traitor ss; illus. C. L. Doughty

32   [Misc. Material] In the Days of Robin Hood ia; illus. Pat Nicolle

[Misc. Material] A Toast to Freedom (plate) il; illus. John Millar Watt

33   [Comic Strip] Robin Hood and the Sword of Freedom cs (col); illus. Angel Pardo; scr. J. H. Higgins

49   [Misc. Material] In the Days of Robin Hood ia; illus. Pat Nicolle

51   Anon. [Giggal, Kenneth.] Robin Hood and the Fearless Fletcher ss; illus. C. L. Doughty

64   [Misc. Material] In the Days of Robin Hood ia; illus. Pat Nicolle

[Misc. Material] Saving the Standard (plate) il; illus. John Millar Watt

65   [Comic Strip] Robin Hood and the Tree of Happiness cs (col); illus. Nadir Quinto; scr. Alan Fennell

[Misc. Material] The Human Tower (plate) il; illus. John Millar Watt

81   [Misc. Material] In the Days of Robin Hood ia; illus. Pat Nicolle

83   [Comic Strip] Young Lochinvar cs; illus. Unknown (Greystock & Marsh); scr. R. Perrins

100   [Misc. Material] In the Days of Robin Hood ia; illus. Pat Nicolle

102   [Comic Strip] Robin Hood and the Vikings cs; illus. Reg Bunn (reprinted from *Thriller Comics Library* 110); scr. revised by Alan Fennell

112   [Misc. Material] (advert. for *Thriller Picture Library*) il; illus. D. C. Eyles

[Misc. Material] (untitled endpapers) il; colour still from 'Ivanhoe' film

BATTLER BRITTON

In 1960, the Amalgamated Press released the first of two hardback anthologies featuring the adventures of their number one air ace, Robert Hereward 'Battler' Britton. Originally created by Mike Butterworth for the pages of *Sun*, the weekly comic then edited by Leonard Matthews, Battler was to become one of British comics' most enduring characters.

Debuting in issue 361 of *Sun* (January 7, 1956), Battler's adventures were related by a variety of writers and artists over the next few years. His popularity was such that he soon graduated to star in further adventures in the pages of *Thriller Comics Library* in February 1957. As time went by, Battler would appear in *Knockout*, *Valiant*, *Tiger*, *Lion*, *Champion* and in many full-length adventures in *Air Ace Picture Library* and *Battle Picture Library*. New stories appeared until 1975, but even then Battler continued to fly in the (reprinted) pages of *Battler Britton Picture Library Holiday Special* until 1984.

Fifty years after his first appearance, Battler was revived for an American-published mini-series penned by Garth Ennis. Although limited to only four issues, the series was generally considered to be the most faithful and entertaining of the 'Albion Universe' titles to appear from WildStorm in 2005-06.

The Battler Britton hardcovers were a new direction for the Amalgamated Press and it is a shame that the experiment did not continue further. It is surprising that they were not more of a success with the buying public. The two volumes that appeared in 1960 and 1961 were an interesting mixture of fact, fiction, illustration and comic strip and, at six shillings, they were no more expensive than similarly sized hardbacks. Released in time for Christmas, perhaps the single character anthology format worked against the books, parents feeling that the traditional annuals, with their wider range of subject matter, would be more appealing to young boys.

Battler Britton (1960; 256pp; 6/-; d/j)
illus. Giorgio Di Gaspari (front)/Nino Caroselli (back))
6 [Misc. Material] Contents ms
8 Anon. (untitled introduction) ed
9 [Misc. Material] (untitled illustration) il; illuc. Gooff Campion
10 [Comic Strip] Battler Britton and the Flying Freak cs; illus. Joe Colquhoun
31 [Misc. Material] The JU 87 "Stuka" il; illus. Batchelor?
32 Anon. Destructive "Dora" ar; illus. Batchelor?
34 Anon. The Gun That Wasn't There! ss; illus. Peter Sutherland
45 [Misc. Material] de Havilland Mosquito il; illus. Batchelor?
46 [Comic Strip] Battler Britton: Operation Pluto cs; illus. Gary Keane
62 [Misc. Material] Lockheed Lightning il; illus. Batchelor?
63 Anon. Perilous Rendezvous ss; illus. Peter Sutherland
78 Anon. Atom-Age Battle-Wagon ar; illus. Batchelor?
80 [Comic Strip] Battler Britton and the Dangerous Decoy! cs; illus. Aldo di
   Gennaro/Sergio Tuis
144 Anon. Submarine Super-Fort (1975 Model) ar; illus. Batchelor?
146 [Misc. Material] Bader and the "Spitfire" ia; illus. Juan Abellan
149 Anon. Island of No Return ss; illus. Geoff Campion
158 [Comic Strip] Battler Britton: The Runaway Bomber cs; illus. Sergio Tuis?;
   scr. R. Clegg
174 Anon. Weirdies of World War I ar; illus. Batchelor?
176 Anon. Into Action! ss
180 [Comic Strip] Battler Britton and the Phantom U-Boat cs; illus. Boixcar /D'Ami Studio
   with BB faces by Geoff Campion; scr. G. Coombs
200 Anon. Battler Takes Over ss; illus. Reg Bunn
205 [Misc. Material] What Do You Know? qz
206 [Misc. Material] Jet-Age Pioneers ia; illus. Juan Abellan
209 Anon. Jungle Death Trap ss; illus. Joe Colquhoun
217 Anon. Fire Below! ar
221 [Comic Strip] Battler Britton and the Escape from North Africa cs;
   illus. Gary Keane; scr. E. Evans
242 [Misc. Material] Marseille and the ME-109 ia; illus. Juan Abellan
245 Anon. In Enemy Skies ss; illus. Reg Bunn
252 [Misc. Material] Battler Calling! ms; illus. Geoff Campion

Battler Britton (November 1961; 256pp; 6/-; d/j illus. Nino Caroselli)

Canadian reprints

The Canadian reprints of *Thriller Picture Library* are almost unknown, even to the most devout *Thriller* collectors.

We know of only one existing copy of the first issue, although the rear cover lists 20 titles.

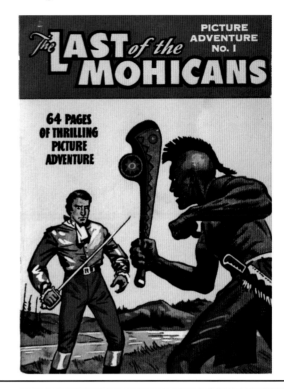

Launch advertising

Fleetway announced the launch of the fourth monthly *Thriller Picture Library* title, featuring Robin Hood, with advertisements in *Knockout* (below) and on the back of *Super-Detective Library* (right).

Contributing Artists

Please note that, due to the lack of surviving records, some ascriptions are unconfirmed and others speculative. Any uncertainty is indicated by a question mark in the main listings, but not indicated in this index. Similarly, the roles of penciller (p) and inker (i) indicated in the index are not absolutely clear, certainly in the case of artwork supplied by the D'Ami studio, where some some stories were a team effort involving numerous artists (some, but possibly not all, are listed under the heading D'Ami Studio below). There are still quite a few artists' names unknown to us, but three examples, whose work has been linked stylistically, are listed below as Unknown Artist [A], [B], and [D]. Bracketed numbers are used where an artists' contribution is a title page, redrawing or providing linking art.

Juan Abellan
Battler Britton: 1960-1961.

Jose Gonzalez Alacreu
Thriller: 430.

Gaetano Albanese
Thriller: *Cover:* 227.

Vic Anderson
Buck Jones (Australia): 32b, 36b; **Cowboy:** 57b, 61a.

Victor Hugo Arias
SDL: 181; **Thriller:** 343, 360, 427.

Terry Aspin
Cowboy: 183a-b, 191, 199, 207, 211, 223, 227, 235, 239, 251, 255, 267, 279c, 287a; **Kit Carson Annual:** 1958.

Stefan Barany
Thriller: *Covers:* 312, 322, 326, 329, 335, 338, 349, 380.

T. Barling
Thriller: (255d).

John Batchelor
Battler Britton: 1960-1961.

Dino Battaglia
Thriller: 130b; **Kit Carson Annual:** 1960.

Arnold Beauvais
SDL: *Covers:* 7-12, 14-49, 54, 57-59, 61-72, 74-76, 78-80, 82-91, 93-94, 96-101, 103-108, 112.

Giorgio Bellavitis
Thriller: 285a, 289a.

Luis Bermejo
SDL: 104, 147, 185; **Thriller:** 363, 371, 379, 395, 403, 419, 431.

Aurelio Bevia
Thriller: 320a, 344, 353; **Battler Britton:** 1961.

Jose Bielsa
Cowboy: 281b, 293a, 309a, 333, 336a, 377, 409a, 430, 454; **Thriller:** 272a.

Alessandro Biffignandi
Cowboy: *Covers:* 395, 438, 447, 462; **SDL:** *Covers:* 165, 184; **Thriller:** *Covers:* 355, 359, 382-383, 386, 388, 391-392, 398, 400-402, 404, 406-408, 410, 412, 414-422, 424-426, 428-430, 434, 438, 441, 444, 450.

Franco Bignotti
Cowboy: 190b, 202c, 276a, 282b, 294a, 301b, 308a, 316a, 322a, 338a, 370; **Thriller:** 195(p), 203, 207(p), 215(p), 220a-c, 225a-b, 238b-c, 254, 276c, 284c, 288c, 296c; **Kit Carson Annual:** 1960.

Harry Bishop
Cowboy: 99c; **Thriller:** 151.

Basil Blackaller
SDL: 114, 118.

Jesus Blasco
Cowboy: 265a, 276b, 300a, 305a, 316b, 318b, 329b, 341, 353, 357b, 386, 389, 401, 413, 429, 446, 457; **Thriller:** 143, 227, 262, 291, 299a; **Kit Carson Annual:** 1957.

James Bleach
SDL: (77), (89), 110; **Thriller:** 305.

Sebastià Boada
Thriller: 420, 424, 440.

Juan Boixcar
Battler Britton: 1960.

Frank Bolle
Buck Jones (Australia): 9a, 10c; **Tim Holt** (Australia): 1, 2, 3, 4; **Cowboy:** 9, 12, 15, 20, 23.

Armando Bonato
Cowboy: 169a, 177a, 181a, 189b, 209b, 237b, 329a, 432

Eric Bradbury
Cowboy: 302b, 347d, 369b; **Thriller:** 179d, 209a-b, 233c, (244a-b), 249a, 261b, 273b, 277b, 281b, (325c); **Buck Jones Annual:** 1957.

Alberto Breccia
Cowboy: 361, 395a, 402, 410, 439, 447, 450; **SDL:** 172; **Thriller:** 336b, 348, 376.

H. M. Brock
Thriller: 9, 22a, 25, 47, 81b, 102, 106d, 109, 189, *Covers:* 25, 117, 124, 164.

W. Bryce-Hamilton
Captain Flame (Australia) *Cover*: 1; **Kit Carson** (Australia): 2a; **Cowboy**: 2c; **SDL**: 8, 46; **SDL**: (64); **Thriller**: 1, 26a; Cover: 1.

Robert Bunkin
Thriller: 157.

Reg Bunn
Buck Jones (Australia): 6b, 7b-c, 10a, 11c, 13b, 20a, 23b, 24a, 25b, 26a,c, 27c, 29b, 30b-c, 31c, 33d, 34c, 36c; **Kit Carson** (Australia): 5b, 6d, 15a,c, 23c, 24c; **Cowboy**: 3b, 5d, 6d, 7a, 11c, 19b, 28d, 29c, 33a, 36a, 37c, 39a, 39c, 41b, 43b,d, 45b, 51c, 53c, 61b, 71b, 79c, 101a, 103c, 106a, 110b, 111c, 112b, 113a,c, 117b, 119b, (122b), (125c), 128b, 139b, 177b, 189a, (257b), 260, (262d), 266a, (273a), (275), 277a, 279a, 283a, 288b, (291a), 292b, 295a, 311c, 312a, (314b), 323b, (326), 328b, (329a), 334b, 340a, 344b, 356a, 382; **SDL**: 2, 13, (15), 18, 22, 30b, 31; **Thriller**: (14), 18a,c, 21, 26c, (28), 32, 58, 88, 95a-d, 98a, 105, 106b, 110a,c, (114), 122a, 134d, 138a,c, 150c, 154b, 158b, 166a, 170a, 176a-c, (182), (190), 196c, 202, (206), 210a, 218b, 222c, 226b, 230c, 236b, (250), 252a, (258), 259b, 260a, 263b, (266), 274a-(b), 277b, 282, (291), (299a), 306a-c, 310, 367; **Buck Jones Annual**: 1958; **Robin Hood Annual**: 1958, 1960; **Battler Britton**: 1960.

J. W. Butler
Cowboy: 100c.

A. Buylla
SDL: 175.

Guido Buzzelli
Thriller: 124, 146a-b, 154a, 168, 174c, 179d, 182a, 186a, 275a; **Kit Carson Annual**: 1960; **Robin Hood Annual**: 1957.

Kurt Caesar
Thriller: 318c, 326b, 330a, 339, 383, 391, 406, 422, 426, 438, 446.

Renzo Calegari
Cowboy: 324b; **Thriller**: 193b, 213a-b, 216c, 233b, 253b, 269, 289a, (297a).

W. R. Calvert
Thriller: *Cover*: 132.

Geoff Campion
Battling Samson (Australia): 1a-b, *Covers*: 1; **Billy the Kid** (Australia): 38, *Covers*: 38; **Buck Jones** (Australia): 1a-b, 2a-c, 3a,c, 4a,c, 5a,c, 6a,c, 7a, (9a), 11a, 12a, 15a, 21a, 25a, 28c, (36b), *Covers*: 2-29, 31-32, 41; **Kit Carson** (Australia): 9a, 11a, *Covers*: 8-19, 21-26, 28-32; **Thunderbolt Jaxon** (Australia): 6a, *Covers*: 4-6; **Tim Holt** (Australia) *Covers*: 1-4; **Cowboy**: 1, 3a,d, 5a-c, 7b-c, 8a, 11a, (13b), 14a, 17a-b,d, 19a, 21d, 31c, 41a, 43c, (61a), 252b-e, 256b, 261c-f, (264d), 268b, 277b, (290c), 308b, 317, 318c, 320b, (324), 324c, 325a, 330c, (336), 337c,

338b, 366b, (367), (369), (371), (375), 383b, (391), (438), 453, (461), *Covers*: 1, 18, 30-35, 37-47, 49-53, 56, 61, 81, 90, 94; **Thriller**: 10a, 15, 19, 107a-e, (111), (123), 147, 155a-i, (159), (167), 170a c, (186), (192 194), (198), (202), (206), 209c, (210), (214), (220), (222), (224), (226), (230), 237c, 244b-c, (271), 321a, 325c, *Covers*: 2, 4, 6, 8, 15; **Kit Carson Annual**: 1954-1957, 1959-1960; **Buck Jones Annual**: 1957; **Robin Hood Annual**: 1959; **Battler Britton**: 1960-1961.

Antonio Canale
SDL: 161, 406b, 409b; **Thriller**: 224c, 301a, 311b, 364, 380, 392, 408; **Kit Carson Annual**: 1960.

P. Carey
Thriller: *Covers*: 272, 343, 347, 358, 371, 379.

Nino Caroselli
Cowboy: *Covers*: 353-354, 362, 372, 382, 394, 408, 420, 440, 453, 464; **SDL**: *Covers*: 162, 173, 175, 177-183, 185-186; **Thriller**: *Covers*: 245, 277, 282, 298, 302, 310-311, 315, 317, 319-321, 324-325, 328-329, 336-337, 340-341, 346, 350, 352-353, 360-361, 365-366, 376-378, 393, 397, 399, 403, 405, 440, 447-449.

Annibale Casabianca
Cowboy: 313.

Vettor Cassinari
Thriller: 253a, 289b, 293a-b.

George Cattermole
Cowboy: *Covers*: 2-6, 11-12, 14, 17, 19-29; **Thriller**: *Covers*: 26, 70, 74, 84, 87.

Stephen Chapman
Buck Jones (Australia): 32c; **Cowboy**: 40c, 49d, 79d, 263, 281a,c, (283), 287b, 291b, 299a, 309c, 315b, (319), 319b, 321c, 342a, 343c, 351, 365b, 374b; **Thriller**: 2b, 8b, 10b, (13), 22b-c, 27b, 33, 51, 56, 63, 81a, 87, 89b, 93, 104, 129, 136, 152, 164, 173, (191), 191b-c, 196a, 212a-b, 228, (234), 248c, 339, *Covers*: 196, 205, 223; **Kit Carson Annual**: 1954-1957, 1960; **Robin Hood Annual**: 1957.

Leone Cimpellin
Cowboy: Cover: 360; **Thriller**: 135, 161, 191a, 290b, 328c, 332a, 340, 349b, 368, 388, 396, 416, *Cover*: 396.

Eduardo Coelho
Thriller: 134a, 158a, 162a, 172; **Robin Hood Annual**: 1957.

Joe Colquhoun
Kit Carson (Australia): 32a; **Cowboy**: 52c, 64c; **Battler Britton**: 1960.

Kreigh Collins
Thriller: 24a, *Cover*: 24.

John Compari
Kit Carson (Australia): (34c), (36c); **Cowboy:** (58c), (59c), (61b), (62c).

Gianluigi Coppola
Thriller: 159c, 232b, 238a, 268b.

Antonio Correa
Cowboy: 305b

Vittorio Cossio
Thriller: 256b, 264b, 268c, 280b, 284b, 288a-b, 296b, 304c, 315c.

Graham Coton
Buck Jones (Australia): 14b, *Covers:* 36, 39; **Kit Carson** (Australia): 12b, 13a-b, 14a, 16a,(c), 17b, 18a, 19c, 20c, 22b, 29b, 32b, 37b, 40b, 44b, *Covers:* 37, 40, 44; **Cowboy:** 24a, 24c, 28b, 30a, 48d, 50b, 52a, 56b, 58a, 62a, 68c, 72b, 114b, *Covers:* 63-68; **SDL:** 6, 15, 36, 14c, 16c, 18c, 19c, 22b, 36b; **Thriller:** 5b, 8c, 12b, 26b, 250, 258, 266, 274b, (306), 359.

Mario Cubbino
Thriller: 131, 167.

D'Ami Studio
Thriller: 216c, 221a-b, 224b-c, 229b, 233b, 269, 293a, 324, 349b; **Battler Britton:** 1961.

Santo D'Amico
Thriller: 356; **Robin Hood Annual:** 1957(i).

Gino D'Antonio
Cowboy: 269a, (301-302), (305), (309), (318), (321-322), (329-331), (337), (339-340), (342-345), (347), (349-350), (357), (365-366), (388), 453; **Thriller:** 204a, (257), (265), (273), (277), (281), (285), (289), (293), (301), (309), (317), (337); **Battler Britton:** 1961.

Roland Davies
Kit Carson (Australia): 10a; **Cowboy:** 10a; **SDL:** 179.

Arturo del Castillo
Cowboy: 463.

Pino Dell'orco
SDL: *Cover:* 188; **Thriller:** *Covers:* 345, 348, 354, 356-357, 364, 368-370, 372-375, 384-385, 389-390, 394, 413, 433, 435.

Enrico De Seta
Thriller: *Covers:* 143, 151, 181, 183, 211, 299, 303, 363, 367, 387.

Roberto Diso
Robin Hood Annual: 1957(p).

Luis Dominguez
Cowboy: 425.

Selby Donnison
Buck Jones (Australia): 41b; **Cowboy:** 65b, 76b, 120a, 124, (131), 132a-b, (137), 140c, 141b, 147b, 153a, 175, 208c, 236a, 238b, 252a, 254b; **SDL:** 7, 12, 17, 20, 23, 28, 30a, (42), 71b, 81, Cover: 13, 81; **Thriller:** 5a, 11, 27c, 44b, 72; **Kit Carson Annual:** 1958-1960.

C. L. Doughty
Thriller: 37, 44c, 85, 92, 94, 101, 121, 137a, 141a, (149), 153a-b, 177, 178, 185a, 192a, 199, 214, 223; **Robin Hood Annual:** 1958, 1960.

G. Douglas
Cowboy: 290b.

C. E. Drury
Kit Carson (Australia): 27a; **Cowboy:** 42c, 200b, 215; **SDL:** 95, *Cover:* 95; **Thriller:** 50, 65, 71, 83, 103a-d, 125.

Leo Duranona
Cowboy: 468.

Gerry Embleton
Cowboy: 311a, 315a, 319c, 323a,c, 339a, 349b, 396, 456.

Ron Embleton
Cowboy: 104b, 106b, (107), 109b, 115, 121, 127, 137, 143b, 245b, (408); **SDL:** 58, 72.

A. W. Ende
Cowboy: 71a,c.

Lopez Espi
Thriller: 355.

D. C. Eyles
Buck Jones (Australia) *Cover:* 43; **Kit Carson** (Australia): 1a-c, 2b, 5a, 6a, 36a, 42a, *Covers:* 2-7, 20; **Cowboy:** 2a,d, 4a, 6a, 66a, (155), 155c, (249), (264b-c), 264d, 268b, (281), 283b, 289b, (290-292), (298-299), 299b, (300), (304), 306a, (311-312), (315-316), (318c), 337b, 343a, 363, *Covers:* 48, 54, 70, 77, 259, 2; **SDL:** Cover: 149; **Thriller:** 2a, 4c, (100), 106a, (110), 110b, (114), (117-118), (122), (126-127), 127c, (130), (138), 139a, 139c, (142), (154), (158), 159a, (162), (166), (170), (174), 175, (178), *Covers:* 9-12, 16, 27, 29, 32, 44, 46, 71, 79, 83, 86, 88, 92, 94-95, 97, 100-101, 109, 112, 116, 119, 121, 123, 127-128, 131, 135, 137-139, 141, 149, 153-154, 159, 161, 167, 174, 187, 189, 194, 201, 203, 207; **Kit Carson Annual:** 1954-1960; **Buck Jones Annual:** 1957; **Robin Hood Annual:** 1957-1960.

Harry Farrugia
Thriller: 311a.

Gallieno Ferri
Thriller: *Covers:* 217, 228, 323.

Robert Forrest
Buck Jones (Australia) *Cover:* 30; **Kit Carson** (Australia): 19a, 20a, 22a, 24a, 25a, 26b, 27b, 28a, 20b, 33b, 34a, 35a, 42b, Cover: 27; **Cowboy:** 26a, 30b, 32a, 40a, 42b, 44a, 46c, 48b, 52b, 54c, 56a, 58b, 62b, 68b, 78b, 80c, 264b-c, 273b-c, 321a, 334a, 354b, 362, 427, 448, *Cover:* 36, 69, 76; **Thriller:** 30, 35, 46, 61, 70, 78, 84, 90, 100, 108, 120, 133a-c, 148, 165, 171, 184a-c, 197, 211, 219, 243b, 246, 302, 375; **Kit Carson Annual:** 1960; **Buck Jones Annual:** 1957.

Henry Fox
Cowboy: *Cover:* 366.

J. Francis
Thriller: *Cover:* 209.

Renato Fratini
Thriller: *Cover:* 278.

J. R. Freeman
Cowboy: 82c.

Emilio Frejo
Cowboy: 288a, 324a, 345b, 347a, 352, 381.

Carlos Friexas
Thriller: 257b.

Veronica Fryer
SDL: (147).

D. Gale
Cowboy: 66b, 70b, 74a, 75b, 81a, 85b, 89a, 90c, 91b, 95b, 101b, 120b, 133a, 136a, 140b, 145b, 148b, 149c, 152b, 163a, 172b, 182a, 194a, 203, 208b, 210c, 219, 231, 247, 259, 271, 279b, 291a, 303a, 325b, 327a, 339b, 374a.

Peter Gallant
Cowboy: 249a, 257a, 285a, (342b), 372; **Thriller:** 159b, 201.

Amador Garcia
Thriller: 350, 358, 374, 384, 394, 404, 428, 436.

Giorgio De Gaspari
Cowboy: *Covers:* 265, 270, 273, 277, 283-284, 292, 295-300, 309-310, 315, 320-321, 323-327, 330, 341, 344, 347-348, 351, 355; **SDL:** *Covers:* 169, 171-172, 187; **Thriller:** *Covers:* 238, 240, 242, 244, 246, 249-250, 256-258, 260-261, 264-266, 269-270, 273-274, 280-281, 284-285, 288-290, 293-294, 297, 301, 305-307, 309, 313-314, 318, 332-333; **Kit Carson Annual:** 1959; **Battler Britton:** 1960.

Aldo di Gennaro
Thriller: 285b(p), 293a, 307, 317a, 328a, 345a, 369, 385; **Battler Britton:** 1960(p).

Frank Giacoia
SDL: 65, 74, 78.

John Gillatt
Thriller: 261a, 309b; **Battler Britton:** 1961.

Eugenio Giner
Kit Carson Annual: 1957.

Giorgio Giorgetti
SDL: (102), (147); **Kit Carson Annual:** 1958.

Ruggero Giovannini
Cowboy: 403; **Thriller:** 1267b, 149, 187, 267c, 270, 286, 298b, 327, *Cover:* 212.

Jack Grandfield
Thriller: Cover: 14.

Jose Grau
Thriller: 260c, 284a.

P. Green
Thriller: 272b.

Rialdo Guizzardi
Cowboy: *Cover:* 260, 263; **Kit Carson Annual:** 1959.

Daniel Haupt
Thriller: 401, 413, 425.

Heade (Reginald C. Webb)
SDL: *Covers:* 6; **Thriller:** *Covers:* 18, 61, 96, 105; **Robin Hood Annual:** 1958.

George Heath
Thriller: 318b, 320b.

Francisco Hidalgo
Kit Carson Annual: 1957.

Mollie Higgins
SDL: 96; *Cover:* 124.

James Holdaway
SDL: 43, 47, 87b.

Cyril Holloway
Buck Jones (Australia): 15b, 29c; **Kit Carson** (Australia): 6c, 7b, 8b, 9b, 11c, 18c, 20b, 22c, 31b, 35b, 42c; **Cowboy:** 4b, 6c, 16b, 28a,c, 30c, 34b, 44b, 45c, 54a, 60b, 72c; **Thriller:** 6b.

Fred Holmes
Cowboy: 289c, 297c, 304b, 310c, 330b, 348a,d; **SDL:** (64); **Thriller:** 86, 91a, 99, 113a-b, 128, 137b, 144, 181, 255d, 279.

Adam Horne
Buck Jones (Australia): 8b, 10b, 11b, 13a,d, 14a, 16b, 22c, 23c; Kit Carson (Australia): 3c, 4c, 7c, 9c, 10b-c, 11b, 12c, 16b, 17c, 19b, 21b, 23b, 25b, 26c, 27c, 30c, 31c, 34b, 36b, 37c; Cowboy: 7d, 8b-d, 10c, 13b,d, 14b,d, 17c, 18d, 21c, 26c, (29d), 32c, 35c, 36c, 37a, 38c, (40c), 46b, 48c, 49b, 54b, 61b, 64b, 74c, 76c, 78c, 93b, 94b, 102c, 110c, 142c, Covers: 7-8, 10, 79.

Arthur Horowicz
SDL: 94, 100; Thriller: 114, 174a-b, (179), 185b, 196b; Robin Hood Annual: 1958.

Mike Hubbard
Thriller: 3; Robin Hood Annual: 1959.

Chic Jack
Thriller: 325a.

Peter Jackson
Thriller: 29.

Lino Jeva
Thriller: 141b.

Syd Jordan
Thriller: 301b, 341b.

E. C. Julian
Kit Carson (Australia): (2b), 2c, 3a-b, 4a-b, 7a, 8c; Cowboy: 4d, 10b, 18b, 64d.

Gary Keane
Thriller: 341c; Battler Britton: 1960-1961.

Ian Kennedy
Cowboy: 150b, 261b, 274b, 278b, 332b; Thriller: 244a, 265b, 321b, (329c); Buck Jones Annual: 1957.

Bill Lacey
Buck Jones (Australia): 41a, 43a; Cowboy: 65a,c, 75a, 87b, (165), 168b, 184a, 216a, 234c, 264a; SDL: 3, 14, 20, 21a, 25, 29, 37, 48, (50), (54), 60, 71a, 75, 85, 87a, 93, 99, 103, 107, 113, 117, 119, 121, 125, 131, 135, 141, 145, 151, 155, 157, 160, 165, 171, Covers: 60, 155, 157; Thriller: 76, 347; Kit Carson Annual: 1958-1959; Buck Jones Annual: 1958.

Tom Laidler
Buck Jones (Australia): 15c, 16c, 18b, 20b, 24b, 26b, 27b, 31a, 34b, 35c; Cowboy: 25c, 27d, 33c, 39b, 47b, 59b, 63c, 77b, 83c, 95c, 159b, 164b, 170b.

Lalauze
Thriller: Cover: 191.

Don Lawrence
Cowboy: (102), 375a; Buck Jones Annual: 1958.

Frank Lazenby
SDL: 77, 82, 89, 149.

F. Solano Lopez
Thriller: 405.

Luis
Thriller: 321c.

Jorge Macabich
Cowboy: 204a, 208a, 212a, 220a, 232a, 240a, 248a, 256a, 272, 280b, 284, 304a, 320a, 328a, 332a, 373, 387.

James E. McConnell
Cowboy: Covers: 132, 137, 141, 144, 147, 150, 156, 159, 162, 164, 167-168, 170-172, 174, 178, 180-182, 185-186, 188-190, 192-195, 197-203, 205, 207-226, 228-235, 237, 239, 241-243, 245-247, 251-252, 256, 258, 264, 266, 269, 280; SDL: Covers: 55-56, 102, 109-111, 113-132, 135-136, 138-142, 144, 146, 148, 150, 152, 154, 156, 164, 166, 168, 170, 174, 176; Thriller: Covers: 17, 22, 55, 93, 104, 120, 129, 136, 157, 168, 172, 199, 243; Kit Carson Annual: 1958-1959; Buck Jones Annual: 1958.

McEvoy
Cowboy: Cover: 456

Robert Macgillivray
Buck Jones (Australia): 8a, 12b, 16a, 17a,c, 19b, 20c, 22b, 33c; Kit Carson (Australia): 14b; Cowboy: 11b, 13c, 18a, 25a, 27b-c, 29a, 33b, 35b, 37b.

John McNamara
Thriller: 40, 44a, 54, 60, 68, 77, 82, 112.

Hugh McNeill
Buck Jones (Australia): 1c, 4b; Thunderbolt Jaxon (Australia): 1a-c, 2a-c, 3a-c, 4b-c, 5a, 6c, Covers: 1-3; Cowboy: 3c; Thriller: 117, 239, 247.

Alfredo Marculeta
Cowboy: 169b, 312b; Robin Hood Annual: 1958

Aldo Marcuzzi
Thriller: 370, 382, 390, 398, 421, 429, 437, 441.

Silvano Marinelli
Thriller: 193a, 333b.

Fred Meagher
Cowboy: 107.

Philip Mendoza
Kit Carson (Australia): 32c; Cowboy: 50c, 70c, 90a, 109a, Covers: 91, 97; SDL: 9, 22b; Thriller: 4a-b, 6a,c, 7, 16, 20, 34, 39, 49, 66, 111, Covers: 3, 5, 7, 20; Kit Carson Annual: 1959; Robin Hood Annual: 1959.

Colin Merrett
Buck Jones (Australia): 19a, 22a, 23a, 27a, 28a, 30a, 33b, 43b; Cowboy: 26a, 31a, 35a, 43a, 45a, 47c, 49a, 67a, 73a, 81c, 98c, 105h, 314h, 322b, 326, 336b, 342b, 348b, 350c, 368a,c, 418b; SDL: 10; Thriller: 2c, 8a, 17, 127a, 139b, 160, 329c; Kit Carson Annual: 1955-1958.

H. C. Milburn
Buck Jones (Australia): 18a,c, 19c, 31b, 32a, 33a, 35a, 36a, 39b, Covers: 33-35; Kit Carson (Australia) Covers: 33-35; Cowboy: 21b, 25d, 47d, 49c, 51a, 53a, 57a, 63a, 67b, 70a, 77a, 79a, 80b, 83a, 87a, 91a, 97a, 99b, 103a, 111b, 116c, 117a, 129b, 136b, 173a, 202a, 214b, 275, 285b, 297a, 309b, 329a, 393a, Covers: 57-60, 62.

Jorge Moliterni
Cowboy: 375b, 384, 395b; Thriller: 318a.

Armando Monasterolo
Thriller: 190b.

Jack Monk
SDL: 156, 158, 159, 162, 164, 166, 168, 170, 174, 176, 178, 180, 182, 184, 186.

C. E. Montford
Buck Jones (Australia): 3b, 8c, 14c, 18d, 21c, 25c, 28b, 34a, 35b, 39a, 41c; Kit Carson (Australia): 8a; Cowboy: 10d, 25b, 29b, 31b, 41c-d, 51b, 53b, 57c, 59a, 63b, 67c, 69a, 81b, 102b, 106c, 112c, 116a, 156c, 201b, 246b, 268a, 278a, 280a, 302a, 306b, 330a, 350a-b, 368b, 393b.

Ernesto Moraga
Thriller: 412.

Joao Mottini
Cowboy: 354a, 379, 390, 408, 411b, 422, 460; Thriller: 447.

Guy Mouminoux
SDL: (55), (57), (73); Thriller: 265c, 309b.

Virgilio Muzzi
Cowboy: 277c, 289a, 294b, 385, 416(p), 436(p); Thriller: 169, 248b(p), 278(p), 280a(p), 362(p).

Agustin Navarro
Thriller: Cover: 351.

Patrick Nicolle
Kit Carson (Australia): 24b, 28b; Cowboy: 34a, 38b, 50a, 88c, (330b), 347b; Thriller: 12a, 24b, 27a, (29), (45), (47), (54), 64, 74, 80, 89a, 91c, 118a, 122b, 130c, 132, 142c, 150a, 163, (189), (205), 228, 234, Covers: 12, 21, 152, 193, 195, 204, 213, 215-216, 241, 253, 279; Kit Carson Annual: 1954-1959; Robin Hood Annual: 1957-1960; Battler Britton: 1961.

Erio Nicolo
Thriller: 400, 407, 423, 435, 448.

Lucien Nortier
Thriller: 96.

Ortega
Thriller: 277a, 281a.

Jose Ortiz
Thriller: 218c.

Colin Page
Cowboy: (66a), (69a), 84c, 86b; Thriller: 345b, 393, 449; Battler Britton: 1961.

Franco Paludetti
Cowboy: 423(p), 445(p), 462(p); Thriller: 290a, 298a, 301c, 316b, 324.

Raffaele Paparella
Cowboy: 265b, 331b, 345a, 357a, 461; Thriller: 222a, 226c, 230b, 236a, 295b, 387, 399; Kit Carson Annual: 1959-1960.

Angel Pardo
Thriller: 98b-c, 106c, 126a, 134b, 138b, 142a-b,d, 154c, 158c, 170b-c, 182c, 186c, 190a, 192c, 198a,c, 210b-c, 222b, 226a, 236c, 243c, 251a, 255b, 259c, 267b, 283b; Robin Hood Annual: 1960.

Eric R. Parker
Buck Jones (Australia): 9b; Captain Flame (Australia): 1a-c; Kit Carson (Australia): 25c, 31a, Cover: 36; Cowboy: 2b, 44c, 59c, 60c, 69b, 74b, 79b, 286a-b, 290a, 298a-c, 302c, 306c, 310a-b, 314a, 318a, 322c, 388b, 397a, 418a,c; Thriller: 14, 18b, 38, 43, 67, 79, 89c, 180, 188, 208, 235, Covers: 14, 82, 85, 188, 208.

George Parlett
Cowboy: 87c, 101c, 338b.

Frank Pashley
Thriller: 333a.

Oliver Passingham
SDL: 16, 19, 24, 26, 27, 32, 35, 39, 40, 41, 45, 51, 52, 53, 56, 61, 62, 63, 68, 69, 76, 80, 86, 92, 98, 102, Covers: 52.

Terry Patrick
Kit Carson (Australia) Cover: 42; Cowboy: 176c, 185b, 188b-c, 189c, 190a, 192b, 196b, 197b, 204b, 210b, 216b; SDL: 91, (105).

Ivo Pavone
Cowboy: 307c, 327b.

Tom Peddie
Thriller: 36, 48, 52, 59, 69.

Jordi Penalva
Cowboy: *Covers:* 254, 261, 268, 274-275, 278-279, 281-282, 285-290, 293-294, 301-308, 311-314, 316-319, 328-329, 331-337, 339-340, 342-343, 345-346, 349-350, 352, 356-359, 361, 364-365, 367-371, 373-381, 383-393, 396-407, 409-419, 421-437, 439, 441-446, 448-452, 454-455, 457-460, 463, 465-468; **Thriller:** *Covers:* 219, 225, 268, 276, 286, 292, 296, 300, 327, 331, 362, 427, 432, 436-437, 445; **Kit Carson Annual:** 1960.

Vitor Peon
Thriller: 118b, 119, 126b, 150b-c, 162b, 166b-c, 182b, 186b, 198b, 218a.

Douglas Perry
SDL: 112, 116.

F. Alan Philpott
Buck Jones (Australia): 29a; **Kit Carson** (Australia): 21a,c, 28c; **Cowboy:** 32b, 34c, 40b, 47a, 66c, 123c, 126b, 216c, 224b, 360; **SDL:** 173; **Thriller:** 352; **Robin Hood Annual:** 1959.

Angelo Platania
Kit Carson Annual: 1960.

Raymond Poïvet
SDL: 42, 50, 54, 57, 67, 73, *Cover:* 50.

Renato Polese
Cowboy: 253, 295b, 364, 414, 440; **Thriller:** 230a, 240, 243a, 268a, 272c, 276a, 296a, 300a, 304a, 365.

Alan Pollack
Thriller: 322a, 354, 366, 378, 386, 402, 414, 434, 450.

Carlo Porciani
Thriller: 213a-b, 269, 317b.

Hugo Pratt
Thriller: 297b; **Battler Britton:** 1961.

Aldoma Puig
Thriller: 326a, 334, 342, 346.

Bert Van Der Put
Thriller: 316a, 328b.

Nadir Quinto
Thriller: 130a, 192b, 251b, 275b-c, 287a, 303b; **Robin Hood Annual:** 1960.

Ernest Ratcliff
SDL: 106c, 139.

Alex Raymond
SDL: 120, 122, 124, 126, 128, 130, 132, 134, 136, 138, 140, 142, 144, 146, 148, 150, 152, 154.

Jerry Robinson
SDL: 34.

T. Heath Robinson
Thriller: 45, 57.

Robert Rodger
Thunderbolt Jaxon (Australia) *Cover:* 5; **Cowboy:** 26c.

Enrique Badia Romero
Thriller: 244c.

Carlos V. Roume
Cowboy: 358, 378, 388a, 391b, 398, 404, 405, 412, 424, 432, 434, 451, 459, 466; **Thriller:** 292a, 304b, 312a, 323, 331.

George Roussos
Thriller: 91b.

R. Charles Roylance
Cowboy: 69c, 73b, 78a, 80a, 82a, 84a, 86a, 89b, 93a, 94a, 95a, 97b, 103b, 105a, 109a, 111a, 123a, 126a, 135, 138a,c, 141a, 144a, 147a, 150a, 156a, 159a, 162a, 164a, 167a, 170a, 174a, 176a, 180a, 186a, 188a, 192a, 196a, 197a, 198a, 200a, 206a, 210a, 214a, 222a-b, 226a, 230a-b, 234a, 238a, 242a, 246a, 250a-b, 254a, 258a, 262a, (266), 270a, 274a,c, 282a, 296, 301c, 343b, 344a, 356b, 371a-b, 376, 399a, 400a, 415, 419, 426, 435, 443, 465; **Kit Carson Annual:** 1959; **Buck Jones Annual:** 1958.

Rutzu
Thriller: *Cover:* 446.

Alberto Salinas
Cowboy: 428, 433, 449, 445.

Jose Luis Salinas
Cowboy: 55, *Cover:* 55.

Salo
SDL: 84.

Martin Salvador
Cowboy: 394; **Thriller:** 251c, 255a, 263a, 267a, 271, 283a, 287b, 295a, 299b, 300b, 303a, 312b-c, 319, 335.

Alf Saporito
Buck Jones (Australia): (9a), (10c).

R. M. Sax
Thriller: *Covers:* 197, 235.

Mike Sekowsky
SDL: 65a, 74b.

Septimus E. Scott
Cowboy: *Covers:* 253, 255, 262, 291; **Thriller:** 13, 28, 31, 41, 53, 73, 116, 118c, 134c, 156, *Covers:* 13, 28, 30-31, 33-43, 45, 47-54, 56-60, 62-69, 73-74, 76-78, 80-81, 89-

91, 98-99, 102-103, 106, 108, 110-111, 113-115, 118, 122, 125-126, 130, 133, 140, 142, 144, 146-148, 150, (155), 156, 158, 162-163, 165-166, 169-170, 175-178, 182, 184-186, 190, 192, 197, 202, 210, 214, 220, 222, 226, 234, 236, 248, 251-252, 255, 259, 262-263, 267, 271, 275, 295; **Kit Carson Annual:** 1954, 1959; **Buck Jones Annual:** 1957; **Robin Hood Annual:** 1957-1958.

Leandro Sesarego
Cowboy: 369a, 380, 431, 444, 464.

Ron Smith
Buck Jones (Australia): 17b.

Luigi Sorgini
Thriller: 216a, 356.

Ferran Sostres
Thriller: 411.

Edgar Spenceley
Kit Carson (Australia): 12a; Cowboy: 16a; Thriller: 206.

John Spranger
SDL: 1, 5, 11, 33, 59, *Cover:* 1; Thriller: 23, *Cover:* 23.

J. Spurling
Thriller: *Cover:* 180.

Geoff Squire
Cowboy: *Covers:* 165, 175, 179, 183, 187; **Thriller:** *Covers:* 72, 107, 134, 173, 206.

George Stokes
Thriller: (221), 221c, 229a, 237a, 241a, (249a), (253), 257a, (261), (261b), 272a, *Covers:* 221, 229, 237.

J. Stokes
Cowboy: 97c.

Studio SGS
Cowboy: 303b.

Peter Sutherland
Kit Carson (Australia): 17a, 23a, 26a, 29a, 30a, 33a, 37a, 40a, 44a; **Cowboy:** 22a, 38a, 42a, 46a, 48a, 60a, 64a, 68a, 72a, 76a, 82b, 84b, 85a, 88a, 90b, 92a, 96a, 98b, 100a, 100b, 102a, 104a, 108a, 110a, 112a, 114a, 116b, 118, 119a, 122a, 125a, 128a, 130, 131a-b, 133b, 134a, 139a, 140a, 142a, 145a, 146a, 148a, 151a, 152a, 154a, 155a, 158a, 160b, 161b-c, 163b, 166a, 171, 172a, 179, 185a, 187, 193a, 195, 201a, 205a, 209a, 213a-b, 217a, 221a, 222b, 225a, 229a, 233, 237a, 241a, 245a, 249b, 257b, *Covers:* 131, 149; **SDL:** 4a, 38, 88; **Thriller:** 10c, 336a, 337c, 372, 381; **Kit Carson Annual:** 1954, 1958; **Buck Jones Annual:** 1957; **Battler Britton:** 1960.

Ferdinando Tacconi
Thriller: 193c, 204b, 242b, 257c, 265a, 281c.

Sergio Tarquinio
Cowboy: 292a, 300b, 307a, 312c, 319a, 331a, 335, 339c, 346, 359, 367a-b, 383a, 391a, 392, 399b, 400b, 407, 411a, 417, 438a-b, 458; **Thriller:** 123, 140(p), 216b, 217, 220c, 225c, 232a,c, 238b, 244b, 248a, 256a,c, 260b, 264a, 276b, 292b, 308a, 315a-b; **Kit Carson Annual:** 1960.

Alfred Taylor
Kit Carson (Australia): 16c.

Tom Thursby
Buck Jones (Australia): 12c, 21b; **Kit Carson** (Australia): 13c; **Cowboy:** 13a, 21a.

Toldo
Cowboy: *Cover:* 461.

M. Tomkins
SDL: *Covers:* 147, 151, 153, 155, 158-159.

Giorgio Trevisan
Thriller: 349a, 357, 373.

Sergio Tuis
Thriller: 221a-b(i), 242a, (272b), (281b), 285b(i), 293a, 297a, 313a-b, 337a-b, 361, 365, 377, 397, 409, 433; **Battler Britton:** 1960(i).

Ron Turner
Cowboy: 174b; **SDL:** 44, 49, 55, 64, 66, 70, 79, 83, 90, (91), 97, 101, 109, 111, 115, 123, 127, 129, 133, 137, 143, 153, 163, 169, 177, 183, 188, *Covers:* 51, 53; **Thriller:** 418, 442.

Mario Uggeri
Cowboy: 269b, 347c, 416(i), 423(i), 436(i), 445(i), 462(i), *Covers:* 267, 271-272, 276, 322p; **Thriller:** 169, 195(i), 207(i), 215(i), 220b(i), 225b(i), 244a, 248b(i), 254, 259a, 263c, 278(i), 280a(i), 294, 308b, 362(i), *Covers:* 304, 339; **Robin Hood Annual:** 1959.

Unknown Artist [A] British, worked via Temple Art
Kit Carson (Australia): 14c, 15b, 18b, 29c, 34c, 36c; **Cowboy:** 22c, 24b, 58c, 62c.

Unknown Artist [B] Del Castillo-esque, possibly Argentinean
Cowboy: 455, 467.

Unknown Artist [D]
Cowboy: 142b, 143a, 146b, 149a-b, 151b, 152c, 155b, 156b, 157b, 158b, 159c, 160c, 163c, 166b, 167b, 173b, 176b, 177c, 178a,c, 180b, 182b, 186b, 190c, 194b, 198b, 200c, 202b, 220b, 221b, 224a, 228a, 236b, 242c, 244a, *Covers:* 111, 173.

Julio Vivas
Cowboy: 441.

W. Ward
Thriller: (247).

John Millar Watt
Thriller: 145, 183, 255c, *Covers:* 145, 230-231, 239,
247,283, 287, 291; **Robin Hood Annual:** 1959-1960.

Tony Weare
Cowboy: 83b, 129a, 144b.

Bob Webster
SDL: (108), (123); **Kit Carson Annual:** 1958.

Mike Western
Cowboy: 258b-c, 262b-c, 266b-c, 270b-c, 278c-d, 290c;
Thriller: (320), 389, 417, *Cover:* 316.

Pat Williams
Thriller: 332b.

Bruce Windo
SDL: 106a, 108, *Cover:* 92; **Thriller:** *Cover:* 160.

Harry Winslade
Thriller: 55.

Gerry Wood
Thriller: 415.

John Woods
Kit Carson (Australia): 5c; **Cowboy:** 4c.

David Wright
Cowboy: 56c.

Manuel Zatarin
Thriller: 443.

Nevio Zeccara
Thriller: 200, 233a, 237b, 241b, 249b, 322b, 329b.

Dino Zuffi
Cowboy: 262d, 437.

Contributing Authors

The following authors are known to have contributed original scripts to the various titles included in this index. Unfortunately, few contemporary records have survived and, unlike artwork, where an artists' style may make identification reasonably certain, to similarly i.d. a story author is almost impossible. This listing below is, therefore, patchy even where some inroads have been made.

Some issues involved two authors, one to write a story outline (s), the second to write the script (sc); these contributions are indicated where known. Bracketed numbers are used where an authors' contribution is rescripting a story, which usually occurred when an old story was being reprinted.

Angus Allan
Cowboy: 92b, 103c, 104b, 126b; **SDL:** 106a; **Thriller:** 255b, 256c, 259a,c, 264b

George Allen
Thriller: 241b(s)

G. Allman
Thriller: 173, 176c, 183(sc); **Robin Hood Annual:** 1958

Donne Avenell
Thriller: 346

W. Howard Baker
Thriller: 300a, 304a, 308a, 315a; **Kit Carson Annual:** 1954

E. J. Bensberg
Thriller: 253a, 257a, 290b, 298a-b, 306a-c, 316b, 341c; **Robin Hood Annual:** 1957, (1958).

Michael Butterworth
Thriller: 74, 79, 86, 93(s), 99, 107a-e, 111(s), 113a-b, 117, 124, 125, 132, 136(s), 144, 152(s), 154b, 155a-l, 158a, 159b, 164, 165, 170a, 181, 188, 208, 228, 235, 239, 247, 291, 299a, 302(s); **Kit Carson Annual:** 1954, 1957

John Newton Chance
SDL: 13

Leslie Charteris (possibly ghosted)
SDL: 1, 5, 11, 33, 59; **Thriller:** 23

Ron Clark
Kit Carson (Australia): 1; **Thriller:** 250, 258, 266; **Robin Hood Annual:** 1958

Percy Clarke
Buck Jones (Australia): 3a,c, 4a, 5a; **Captain Flame** (Australia): 1b-c; **Cowboy:** 1b, 3d, 6b, 21d, 91b; **Thriller:** 3, 38

R. Clegg
Thriller: 253b, 260b, 261c, 273c, 274a, 282, 293a, 301b, 305, 309b, 310, 325b, 329a, 330a, 341b; **Battler Britton:** 1960.

Barry Coker
SDL: 94, 100, 131, 135, 137(sc), 141

G. Coombs
Thriller: (273b), 281a,(b), 289a, 293b, 309c, 313a-b, 317a-b, 337a-b, 349a; **Battler Britton:** 1960.

Ralph Coveney
Thriller: 240, 248b(sc), 248c, 252a, 263c, 267b-c, 275b-c, 283a, 284a, 287a-b, 292a, 295b, 296a-b, 299b, 303a, 307, 308b, 318b, 322b, 326a-b, 338

Maurice Creswick
Kit Carson (Australia): 15c; **Cowboy:** 36a, 74(s)

Rinaldo D'Ami
Thriller: 269, 280a, 362

Fred Dickenson
SDL: 120, 122, 124, 126, 128, 130, 132, 134, 136, 138, 140, 142, 144, 146, 148, 150, 152, 154

M. Edwards
Thriller: 182c, 220c

E. Evans
Thriller: 265a, 273a, 281c, 289b, 301c, 309a; **Battler Britton:** 1960.

Alan Fennell
Cowboy: (contributions unknown); **Thriller:** 182b, 184c, 189c, 216c, 226a, 236a, 238a, 243a,c, 251c; **256a-b, 277a; **Robin Hood Annual:** 1960.

Barry Ford (see Joan Whitford)

Conrad Frost
Cowboy: 235, 239, 241b; **SDL:** 16, 19, 26, 27, 32, 35, 39, 41, 45, 48(sc?), 51, 53, 56, 62, 63, 70, 75(sc), 76, 79, 80, 83(sc), 86, 92, 98, 102, 105(sc), 114, 118, 137(s), 149

D. M. Garbutt
Thriller: 249b, 260c, 285b, 301a, 304c, 315b, 321c

R. Garner
Kit Carson Annual: 1958.

H. H. C. Gibbons
Cowboy: 60a, 94b

Kenneth Giggal
Cowboy: 260(s); **Kit Carson Annual:** 1958; **Robin Hood Annual:** 1960.

Roderic Graeme
SDL: 155

E. H. Hamil
Kit Carson (Australia): 8d; Thunderbolt Jaxon (Australia): 5c(s); Cowboy: 10b

Rex Hardinge
SDL: 9

Harry Harrison
SDL: 127, 129, 139, 143

J. Heale
SDL: 145, 151

Jay Heavlin
Thriller: 24a

Alex W. Henderson
Buck Jones (Australia): 13b, 15c, 16c, 17a,c, 19c, 22c, 26a, 27c, 28a-b, 29c, 30b, 31a-b, 32a-b, 34a-c, 35a-c, 36b, 39b, 41a,c, 43a; Kit Carson (Australia): 11a, 12c, 13a, 16c, 17a-c, 20a, 24c, 25a-c, 26c, 27c, 28b-c, 30a, 32c, 33b, 34a,c, 35a, 36c, 37a-b, 40b, 42b-c; Cowboy: 11b, 14a, 16c, 19b, 21b, 22a-b, 24c, 25a-d, 26b, 27b, 30b-c, 32b, 33a-c, 34b, 35a, 37a, 38b-c, 39a, 40b-c, 41b-c, 42a-b, 43a,d, 44c, 45a-c, 47b,d, 48a,c, 49b-c, 50a,c, 51a-b, 52a-b, 53b-c, 54a-c, 56a,c, 57a-c, 58a-c, 59b, 60b, 61a, 62b-c, 63a-c, 64a, 65a,c, 66b-c, 67a, 68a, 69b-c, 70a,c, 71a,c, 72c, 73a-b, 74a, 75a, 76c, 77c, 78a,c, 79a,c, 80a, 81a, 82c, 83b, 84a, 85b, 86a-c, 87a,c, 88a,c, 89a-b, 91a, 94a, 95b, 98c, 100b, 101b-c, 103b, 105a; SDL: 12

James H. Higgins
Buck Jones (Australia): 5c, 8a, 11b-c, 15b, 31c, 32c, 39a, 41b; Kit Carson (Australia): 6d, 7b, 8a-b, 12b, 13b, 15a-b, 22b; Thunderbolt Jaxon (Australia): 5a, 5c(sc), 6c; Cowboy: 5c, 6c, 10d, 11c, 13c, 14c, 18d, 22c, 24a-b, 26a, 28d, 29c, 35c. 36c, 37c, 38a, 39c, 48d, 49d, 51c, 59a, 61b, 65b, 67b, 74(sc), 75b, 76a-b, 77b, 80b, 83a, 92a, 93a, 96b, 99b-c, 104a, 260(sc); SDL: 93, 147; Thriller: 18a-d, 222b, 251a-b 255c, 275a, 278, 288a, 292b, 337c; Kit Carson Annual: 1956, 1958; Robin Hood Annual: 1960.

V. A. L. Holding
Thriller: 158b, 166c, 174c, 185a-b, 189a, 192a-b, 196b, 197(sc), 198c, 200, 202, 213a, 218b, 221c, 226b, 229a, 243b, 279, 285a, 297b; Robin Hood Annual: 1959.

Edward Holmes
Kit Carson (Australia): 2a, 6a,c, 9a,c; Thunderbolt Jaxon (Australia): 5b, 6a-b; Cowboy: 5a-b, 8a,c; SDL: 3, 14, 20, 37, 44, (77), (78a-b), (80), (82), (86), (89), (92); Thriller: 1, 14

Mrs. J. Hopkinson
Cowboy: 82a

Jack Hunt
Buck Jones (Australia): 7b, 24c, 30a, 33d; Kit Carson (Australia): 10b, 14a, 21c, 26b, 27b, 28a, 29b, 30b, 21a, 37c, 42a; Cowboy: 3b, 10c, 13a, 18c, 21a, 27d, 28a, 32c, 34c, 37b,c, 40a, 42c, 43b-c, 44a, 46c, 47c, 48b, 49a, 50b, 60c, 64b, 66a, 67c, 68b-c, 71b, 77a, 79b, 84c, 85a, 87b, 102c; Thriller: 174b

John Hunter
Cowboy: 115, 121, 124, 127, 130

T. C. H. Jacobs
Battling Samson (Australia): 1a-b; Thunderbolt Jaxon (Australia): 1a-c(s)

Danny Kelleher
SDL: 85, 108; Thriller: 297a

Ian B. Kellie
Thriller: 366, 370, 374, 398

Bob Keston
Cowboy: 231; SDL: 90, 91, 95, 97, 101, 111, 115, 123, 133, 153, 163, 177; Thriller: 339

Albert King
Cowboy: 236a

Harold Lamb
Thriller: 302(sc), 316a

Douglas Leach
SDL: 179; Thriller: 320a, 328b, 336b

Roger Lécureaux
SDL: 42, 50, 54, 67, 73

C. A. Lewins
Cowboy: 69a, 74c, 78b, 80c

Eric Leyland
Cowboy: 99a, 136b

J. Lockhead
Thriller: 210b

Roy McAdorey
Thriller: 320b

George P. Mann
Thriller: (266), 272b

Miss H. Martin
SDL: (96a-b), (98), (102), (112), (114), (116), (118), (120), (122), (124), (126), (128), (130), (132), (134), (136), (138), (140), (142), (144), (146), (148), (150), (152), (154), (156), (158), (159), (162), (164), (166), (168), (170), (174), (176).

J. Mather
Thriller: 296c, 304b, 312a, 315c

Leonard Matthews
Captain Flame (Australia): 1a; Kit Carson (Australia): 1; Thunderbolt Jaxon (Australia): 1a-c(sc); Thriller: 2a, 4c, 9, 13, 28, 30, 37, 54, 85, 116, 137a, 147, 148, 156, 171(s), 183(s), 197(s)

C. Mattin
Cowboy: 70b, 72b, 88b

Edith Meiser
SDL: 65a-b, 74a-b, 78a-b

Ken Mennell
Thriller: 311b, 322a, 334

Michael Moorcock
Cowboy: 321b, 337a, 349b; Thriller: 311a, 318a,c, 323, 330b, 378; Robin Hood Annual: 1960.

T. E. Moore
Thriller: 324, 325a, 332b, 333a

David Motton
SDL: 171; Thriller: 184a, 191a-c, 194, 196a, 212a-b, 216a, 222a, 236c, 237a, 402, 418

Peter O'Donnell
SDL: 6; Thriller: 5, 7, 33, 45, 55, 63, 68, 70, 359

Jean Ollivier
Thriller: 96

A. G. B. Parlett
Thriller: 345b

F. R. Passmore
Cowboy: 90a

E. M. Payne
Kit Carson Annual: 1957.

Frank S. Pepper
Thriller: 332a

R. Perrins
Thriller: 154a, 159c, 166a, 170c, 171(sc), 172, 174a, 175, 182a, 186c, 192c, 198b; Robin Hood Annual: 1957-1960.

R. Phillips
Cowboy: 109b

Ernest Player
SDL: 15, 99, 109, 110

Raymond V. Pothecary
Buck Jones (Australia): 7c, 9c, 10b, 11a, 12a, 13d, 15a, 17b, 33a; Kit Carson (Australia): 11b, 30c; Cowboy: 5d, 11a, 13b,d, 14b, 17a,c, 19a, 21c, 26c, 27c, 31a,c, 32a, 39b, 46b, 47a, 52a, 59c

W. Prout
Thriller: 260a, 263a-b, 268a-c, 272a,c, 276a-c, 280b, 284b-c, 288b-c, 303b

Ron Reed
Cowboy: 55

David Roberts
Cowboy: 36b; Thriller: (205); Kit Carson Annual: 1956

J. Roswell
Thriller: 312b, 335, 342

B. Rowland
Cowboy: 84b, 90c, 102c

David Satherley
Thriller: 295a

Robert Sommerville
SDL: 107(s), 113(s), 117(s), 119(s), 121(s)

Gordon Sowman
Thriller: 257c, 265c, 290a, 314, 328a,c, 333c

James Stagg
SDL: 169, 173, 175, 181; Thriller: 225a, (228), 230c, 236b, (239), 241a, 242a-b, 244a, 248b(s), 252b, (258); Robin Hood Annual: 1959.

Sheldon Stark
SDL: 34

J. A. Stockbridge
Cowboy: 408; Thriller: 344

James A. Storrie
Thriller: 176a-b, 196c, 198a, 210c, (214), 218a,c, (237b), (245a-c), 249a; Battler Britton: (1961).

Colin F. Thomas
SDL: 157, 160, 161, 165, 167; Thriller: 93(sc), 111(sc), 136(sc), 152(sc), 201, 204b, 213b, 216b, 221a-b, 224a, 230a-b, 233a, 241b(sc)

Graeme Thomas
Cowboy: 102a, 103a, 112c; Thriller: 204a

D. Thompson
Thriller: 222c, 229b, 233b

E. C. Tubb
Thriller: 444

Adrian Vincent
Cowboy: 90b, 95a,c, 97a,c, 100a, 101a, 134b; **SDL:** 87a, 106b, (111); **Kit Carson Annual:** 1958

Alf Wallace
Thriller: 166b, 219(sc), (250), (255d), (257b), (258), 259b, (261b), (266), 267a, (269), 271, (273b), (274b), 277b, (281b), 283b, (291), (299a), (321a-b), (325c), (329b-c), (333b), (362); **Robin Hood Annual:** 1957-1958.

W. Ward
Thriller: 264c, 300b

Len Wenn
Kit Carson Annual: 1956-1957; **Robin Hood Annual:** 1957

Joan Whitford
Cowboy: 227, 255, 377, 420, 448; **SDL:** 172; **Thriller:** 15, 19, 25, 31, 32, 34, 49, 50, 65, 76, 80, 83, 88, 92, 95a-d, 97, 100, 103a-d, 108, 115, 119-120, 127a-c, 128, 133a-c, 135, 161, 167-169, 177, 195, 199, 203, 207, 211, 215, 219(s), 220a, 223, 225b-c, 227, 231, 232a-c, 238b-c, 244c, 246, 248a, 254, 262, 270, 286, 294, 327; **Kit Carson Annual:** 1954-1957; **Robin Hood Annual:** 1958.

Richard Wise
SDL: (48s?), 75(s), 83(s), 103, 105(s), 106c, 107(sc), 113(sc), 117(sc), 119(sc), 121(sc), 125

R. P. Yunnil
Thriller: 340

THE FLEETWAY PICTURE LIBRARY INDEX VOLUME 1

THE WAR LIBRARIES

compiled by
Steve Holland and **David Roach**

www.illustrationartgallery.com

Over 3,000 original art boards from comics, books and magazines for sale online.

New art added every week.

THE BEST OF BRITISH

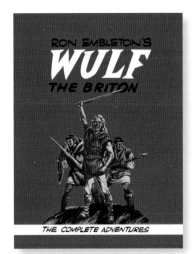

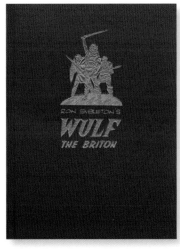

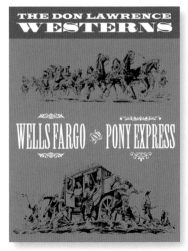

Ron Embleton's Wulf the Briton
At last… all of Ron Embleton's Wulf the Briton stories – from *Express Weekly* and the Annuals – reproduced in high quality colour at the same size as the original comic.

Deluxe hardcover edition limited to 400 copies

Also available as a **deluxe leatherbound slipcased edition limited to 100 copies** with an extra 24 pages showing original Wulf art.

Plus **26 lettered leatherbound slipcased editions** with the extra 24 pages plus an exclusive print.

The Don Lawrence Westerns
Don Lawrence's Wells Fargo and Pony Express stories reprinted for the first time in their entirety.

Limited edition Hardcover

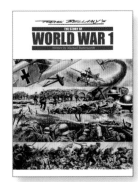

www.bookpalacebooks.com